REVIEWS OF BOOKS ABOUT HAUNTED ILLINOIS BY TROY TAYLOR

How does Troy Taylor continue to produce one quality book after another? Perhaps only the spirits know for sure! HAUNTED ILLINOIS is truly another top-notch, in-depth look at the Land of Lincoln. I highly recommend this book to anyone interested in Illinois ghost stories, as it goes to show that ghosts can be found anywhere throughout the state!
DALE KACZMAREK, author of WINDY CITY GHOSTS

Troy Taylor has done it yet again. In HAUNTED ILLINOIS, the author has hit that rare (and delightful) middle ground between fascinating paranormal research and compelling storytelling. His stories will put you on the edge of your seat and his insights into the supernatural will keep you there. A rare and delightful find and a must-read from one of the best ghost authors writing today.
MARK MARIMEN, author of HAUNTED INDIANA and SCHOOL SPIRITS

HAUNTED ILLINOIS is a generous introduction to the resident wraiths of one of the nation's most haunted states, from its most prolific ghost writer. This book is a must for natives, ghost hunters and aficionados of Americana and holds captive anyone with an interest in the wonderful experiences so often omitted from the "proper" historical record.
URSULA BIELSKI, author of CHICAGO HAUNTS

Troy Taylor works hard to unearth new hauntings and to keep the old lore alive. In spite of this, many of the stories which shaded our cemeteries and lingered over our abandoned buildings are lost. So while some of us wonder about the light burning in the old warehouse, or quicken our step in the dusky graveyard, or pause to make sure those are our own footsteps echoing off the attic wall, most of us won't. Yesterday's stories, like yesterday's spirits, draw their power from being remembered. In the absence of memory, legends die, and like forgotten ghosts are left to fade away.
JOE RICHARDSON in ILLINOIS COUNTRY LIVING Magazine

GHOST BOOKS BY TROY TAYLOR

Haunted Illinois (1999 / 2001)
Spirits of the Civil War (1999)
Ghost Hunter's Guidebook (1999 / 2001)
Season of the Witch (1999 / 2002)
Haunted Alton (2000)
Haunted New Orleans (2000)
Beyond the Grave (2001)
No Rest for the Wicked (2001)
Haunted St. Louis (2002)
Confessions of a Ghost Hunter (2002)
Haunted Chicago (2003)

The History & Hauntings Series
I. The Haunting of America (2001)
II. Into the Shadows (2002)

Haunted Decatur (Illinois) Series
Haunted Decatur (1995)
More Haunted Decatur (1996)
Ghosts of Millikin (1996 / 2001)
Where the Dead Walk (1997 / 2002)
Dark Harvest (1997)
Haunted Decatur Revisited (2000)
Flickering Images (2001)
Vaudeville, Moving Pictures & Ghosts (2002)

Ghosts of Springfield (1997)
Ghost Hunter's Handbook (1997 / 1998)
Ghosts of Little Egypt (1998)

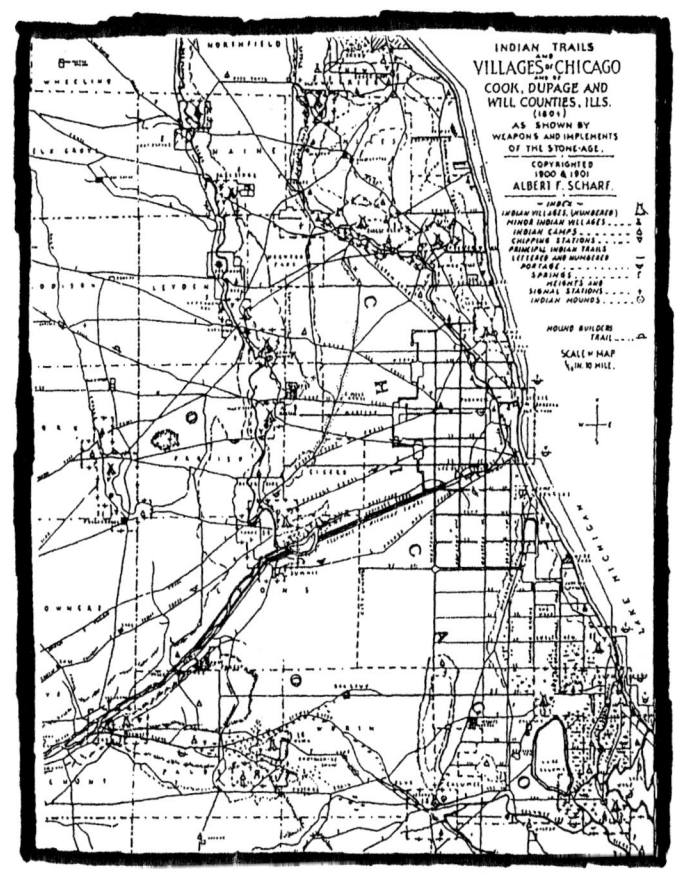

HAUNTED CHICAGO
HISTORY & HAUNTINGS OF THE WINDY CITY

~ A Whitechapel Productions Press Publication ~

This book was truly a labor of love and is the end result of a lifetime of fascination with the city of Chicago, its rich history and legacy of ghosts and hauntings. I dedicate the book to my Chicago friends, many of whom blazed the trail long before me, and who have penned their own books on the subject. To Ursula and to Dale, I can only say "thanks" and that I never hope to write one better - only different! And to Tom, Michelle and Rob, I can only say "thanks" for all the good times and laughter!

And as with each book, I dedicate this one to Amy. Without her, I never would have discovered the city in the way that I did and for that (and for many other things), I can't thank you enough. I love you!

Copyright © 2002 by Troy Taylor
All Rights Reserved, including the right to copy or reproduce this book, or portions thereof, in any form, without express permission of the author and publisher

Original Cover Artwork Designed by
Michael Schwab, M & S Graphics & Troy Taylor
Visit M & S Graphics at www.msgrfx.com

This Book is Published by
~ Whitechapel Productions Press ~
A Division of the History & Hauntings Book Co.
515 East Third Street ~ Alton, Illinois ~62002
(618) 465~1086 / 1~888~GHOSTLY
Visit us on the Internet at www.prairieghosts.com

First Edition ~ October January 2003
ISBN: 1~892523~29~9

Printed in the United States of America

- THE HAUNTED ILLINOIS SERIES -

I was born and raised in the state of Illinois and have my entire life within the confines of this odd and unusual place. Over the years, I have tried to make myself very familiar with the ghosts, haunted places, mysterious, and sometimes bloody, history of Illinois. In fact, I have traveled extensively in search of strange tales and dark places and have yet to be disappointed with what I have discovered here in the Prairie State. With that in mind, my work has spawned what will become a series of books about the mysterious side of Illinois, including the first in the series, HAUNTED ILLINOIS.

The series has become a labor of love for me and I hope to share with others my fascination with stories and tales that do not fit into the "proper" historical record. In previous books (and books to come), the series will travel all over the state from the Windy City to Southern Illinois to the regions along the Great River Road to the windswept plains of Illinois' haunted heart.

I hope that this series will contain more about Illinois history, and hauntings, than you will find anywhere else but it may never collect every story to "haunt" this state. However, I do believe that it will collect stories that are both familiar and strange. Some of them may be old favorites, but regardless, every single one of them comes from the landscape of Illinois. They are tales of haunted houses, old cemeteries, terrifying locations, unusual people, bizarre legends and more.

Hopefully, this series will serve as your travel guide to Haunted Illinois and will manage to take you not only to the most shadowed corners of our state's history - but to the farthest reaches of your imagination as well!

-TROY TAYLOR-

TABLE OF CONTENTS

INTRODUCTION - PAGE 8
Welcome to Haunted Chicago

I. GHOSTS BY GASLIGHT - PAGE 13
The History & Hauntings of Old Chicago

Born in Blood - The Settlers & Pioneers - The Fort Dearborn Massacre - Chicago Legends & Lore - The Curse of Streeterville - Pride & Progress - Chicago in the Civil War - Eighty Acres of Hell - The Great Chicago Fire - Chicago Riot & Unrest - Haymarket Square Riot - The Pullman Era - Chicago Stockyards - The Sausage Vat Murder - Ghosts of Fort Sheridan - Crooks & Corruption: Lore of Chicago Politics - Columbian Exposition of 1893 - The Black Sox Scandal - Tragedy & Death - Our Lady of Angels - Iroquois Theater Fire - The Hand of Death - Eastland Disaster - Trolley of Death - Spirits of Flight 191

II. GHOSTLY GREETINGS FROM THE GRAVEYARD
Mysteries of Chicago's Haunted Burial Grounds

Mystery of Death - America's Garden Cemeteries - Graveyards in Chicago - Bachelor's Grove Cemetery - Ghosts of Graceland - Phantoms of Rosehill - The Italian Bride - Miracle Child of Chicago - Spectral Figures of Chicago Graveyards - Spring Valley Vampire - Specter of St. Casimir's - The Aviator of Calvary Cemetery - Hauntings on Cuba Road - Mysteries of Robinson Woods - Haunts Along Archer Avenue - Chicago's Phantom Hitchers Prophesying Passengers - The Flapper Ghost - Kennedy Road Phantom - The History & Haunts of Resurrection Mary

III. SCHOOL SPIRITS
Hauntings of Chicago Schools & Colleges

Enigma of School Spirits - Ghosts of Barat College - Hauntings of Lake Forest College - Lost Spirit of Morton College - Haunted Bendictine University - Beneath Channing Memorial Elementary

IV. DINNER & SPIRITS
Ghosts of Chicago's Haunted Pubs, Restaurants & Taverns

Chicago's Historic Taverns - The Curse on the Cubs - Chicago's "Mickey Finn" - The Whitechapel Club - Hauntings at the Red Lion Pub - The Drunken Ghost of the Old St. Andrew's Inn - Lingering Spirit of Bucktown Pub - Ghosts of Excalibur - Historic Spirits of Al Capone's Hideway & Steak House - Chicago's Most Haunted Restaurant: That Steak Joynt - Ghosts of the Country House Restaurant

V. HOLY SPIRITS
Haunted Churches, Miraculous Visions & Blessed Apparitions

The Virgin Mary Comes to Chicago - The Queen of Heaven Apparitions - Mysteries & Miralces: Religious Visions and Visitations in Chicago - Church Mysteries & Hauntings - Legends of Holy Family - The Apparitions at St. Rita's - The Ghost of St. Turibius - The Irish Castle

VI. NO REST FOR THE WICKED
History & Hauntings of Chicago Crime

Crime comes to the Windy City - Chicago Cops & Robbers - Bloody Maxwell & the Haunts of the old Maxwell Street Police Station - Chicago's Famous Crime & Vice Districts - The Black Hole - The Bad Lands & Little Cheyenne - Hell's Half Acre - Custom House Place - The Murder Castle: The Monster of 63rd Street - The "Wizard" of Chicago - Chicago's Thrill Killers: Leopold & Loeb - Farewell to the Grimes Sisters - Richard Speck: Born to Raise Hell - John Wayne Gacy: The Clown that Killed - A Voice from the Grave

Gangland Ghosts - The Mob Comes to Chicago - The Black Hand - Curse of the "Green Chair" - Big Jim Colosimo - Johnny Torrio - Al Capone - Dion O' Bannion - George "Bugs" Moran - The St. Valentine's Day Massacre and its Lingering Ghosts - Haunting of Al Capone - Frank Nitti: The Last Walk of Al Capone's Enforcer - Depression Era Desperadoes - The History & Haunts of John Dillinger - The Biograph Theater - Dillinger: Dead or Alive?

VII. HAUNTED HISTORY
Some of Chicago's Most Famous & Little Known Haunted Houses

Chicago's Historic Haunted Houses - The Fanning House Ruins - The Schuttler Mansion - The Roberts Mansion - Hauntings of Hull House - The House with No Square Corners - Ghost of the Glessner House - Mysteries of the Schweppe Mansion - The Maple Lake Ghost Light: The True Story - Tom & Mo's House

INTRODUCTION

WELCOME TO HAUNTED CHICAGO

The only thing that keeps Chicago from being the greatest city in America is the weather. There seems to be something about blizzards and below zero wind chills that tends to put the damper on people's enthusiasms. But whatever Chicago might lack in this regard, it more than makes up for it with its history, legends and lore - and especially with its ghosts!

There are a number of American cities that make the claim of being "most haunted", but in my opinion, Chicago leads the pack. There is simply no other city that can boast the sheer number of haunts that Chicago can. The spirits here are simply a part of the city's culture and can be connected to Chicago's long, and often bloody, history. The history and the hauntings of the city go hand in hand and as it has often been said, the events of the past create the hauntings of today. In no place is such a statement as true as it is in Chicago, Illinois.

You see, ghost stories have always been a part of the history of Chicago. Tales of haunted graveyards, phantom figures and beautiful spirits who wander the area highways have always held great appeal for those with a taste for the unusual and the unknown.

Growing up in Illinois, I have always been fascinated with Chicago and the history and hauntings that surround the city. When I later began to make my living as a writer of ghostly tales, I turned to the "Land of Lincoln" as a wonderful source of material and eventually, my attention turned to the Windy City. But this is not a book that is only about ghosts, it also encompasses my love of history as well. I have always believed that a good haunted tale cannot exist without a rich history behind it. However, this is no dry text about the history of Chicago, filled with dates and facts. I am fascinated with the darker side of the city's history, but I am no historical expert or collegiate scholar. I simply collected a history of the city and highlighted the stories, incidents and accounts that most intrigued me. This book is meant to be a journey into the past, a trip back into Chicago history that also includes the ghosts, spooks and specters of this haunted city.

So, ghosts are what may have brought you to this book but if you are looking for nothing more than breathless first-hand accounts of waking up in the middle of the night to see Aunt Gertrude standing at the end of the bed, this may not be the book for you! Those kinds of stories, lacking the already mentioned history, have never been of much interest to me. I have always had the need to "tell" the story and I like to let the documented accounts speak for themselves. You'll discover what I mean in the pages ahead...

And while this book does contain much of the history and the hauntings, it still falls short when it comes to collecting every single story to "haunt" this city. I don't think that you'll be disappointed though because I have managed to collect stories of hauntings and dark history that are both familiar and unknown, have been forgotten by time and most of all, are uniquely a part of the history of Chicago. Even with that said though, there are tales that have still managed to elude me. There are haunted places in this city that have remained unknown since the first pioneers came to the region and many of these spots remain hidden, or forgotten, today.

In addition, there have also been a number of books already written about Chicago and the city's history and hauntings (including some that have been penned by friends of mine) and this book was not written to compete with any of those. My book was not created in an attempt to be "better" than these earlier books, merely different. I wanted to collect not only Chicago's greatest ghost stories but the shadowy and often blood-soaked history too. This book was meant to be my own personal take on what is not only my favorite American city but also on some of my favorite ghostly tales and haunted legends as well. I'll allow you, the reader, to judge whether or not I was up to the task when you have finished the book you now hold in your hands.

But aside from simply growing up in Illinois, what would make a writer who lives far closer to St. Louis than the Windy City want to write a book about the hauntings of Chicago? To put it quite simply -- it was the ghosts! As I have already stated, no city is as haunted as Chicago and throughout my entire writing career (and before), the region has been home to some of my favorite ghost stories. I have been searching for hauntings for nearly fifteen years, as of this writing, but my interest goes back even further than that. I can't really remember when I first started to be fascinated with ghosts but I know that I must have been a very small child.

I have no idea what first caught my interest in the subject, but people often ask me that, usually just after I tell them what I do for a living. My reply is simply that "it's something that I have always been fascinated with" and this usually disappoints the person who asked me of my macabre curiosities. I have always suspected they want me to say that my mother died when I was 12 and came back to visit me from beyond the grave (but my mom is alive and well, thanks) or that I receive flashes of psychic insight from the spirit world (although I am about as psychic as a fence post).

Regardless, of how or why I got started collecting and investigating tales of ghosts and haunted places, I don't plan to stop doing gathering them any time soon. Over the past number of years, I have found there is just nothing like the thrill of finding a really good story, taking a trip to visit an alleged haunted house or even taking the first steps into a dark and forgotten graveyard. So, living in downstate Illinois, I have been delighted to find a treasure trove of not only strange and ghostly tales but many haunted places as well. My journey continued in Chicago and here, I have discovered a vast wealth of material, much of what you will be delving into in the pages ahead.

In many of the books I write though, I like to take the reader along on another short trip before beginning the journey into the heart of the book. That small trip always involves the "lore" of the ghosts themselves. What sort of hauntings can the reader expect to find in the eerie places ahead?

There are many theories and ideas out there as to what, or who, ghosts actually are and why they choose to haunt the places they do. I can't tell you that I know everything about ghosts because I don't believe there are any "experts" when it comes to the supernatural. I usually prefer the term "knowledgeable", because no one can say what ghosts really are, they can only describe their own experiences with these elusive creatures. As mentioned before, I have been tracking down ghosts for some time now and really don't know much more about them than I did when I started. Still, in that time, I have visited several hundred allegedly haunted locations.

People often ask me if I have ever seen a ghost? (That's the other question that people always ask when I tell them what I do for a living!). I would have to say that I have, on one occasion. In addition to this one lone sighting though, I have also experienced a lot of things that I have yet to find logical explanations for.

But what are ghosts? And what is a haunting? And how do these things relate to the ghostly locations in this book?

First of all, what exactly is a haunting?

It is defined as being the repeated manifestation of strange and inexplicable sensory phenomena at a certain location. There are no general patterns to hauntings, which is what makes them so hard to define. Some phenomena may manifest on occasion or even continually for periods that last from several days to centuries; others may only occur on certain anniversaries; and others may make no sense whatsoever.

The general public assumes that hauntings involve apparitions, or ghosts, of the dead, but in fact, apparitions are connected to only a minority of cases. Most hauntings involve noises like phantom footsteps; strange, unexplainable sounds; tapping; knocking sounds; strange smells; and sensations like the cold prickling of the skin, chilling breezes and even the feeling of being touched by an invisible hand. Other hauntings involve poltergeist-like activity such as furniture and solid objects being moved about; broken glass; doors which open and close by themselves; and the paranormal manipulation of lights and electrical devices.

While attempts have been made to try and categorize certain types of hauntings, as you'll soon see, many locations seem to defy this labeling and manifest a variety and a combination of different types. In fact, it has been my experience that some locations seem to act as catalyst for activity, causing visitors to manifest their own unconscious phenomena and giving rise to accounts which don't fit into any categories at all. The two different types of hauntings that seem to be most commonly reported are what we call the "intelligent haunting" and the "residual haunting", but they aren't alone.

The intelligent spirit is everyone's traditional idea of a ghost. It is a lost personality, or spirit, that for some reason did not pass over to the other side at the moment of death. It shows an intelligence and a consciousness and often interacts with people. It is the most widely accepted kind of paranormal activity because it is the easiest to understand. It "haunts" a place because of a connection to the site or to the people at the location. This ghost is the personality of a once living person who stayed behind in our world. This sometimes happens in the case of a murder, a traumatic event, or because of some unfinished business which was left undone in a person's life. At the time of death, this spirit refused to cross over to the other side because of these events. There is also a good chance that this spirit does not even realize that it has died, which could happen if the death was sudden or unexpected. Many of the greatest Chicago ghost stories involve these chilling and interactive spirits.

Another type of haunting that is often reported has nothing to do with intelligent, or conscious, spirits at all. It is more common than people think and you might be surprised as to how many ghost stories that you have heard over the years just may fit into this category. This haunting is both unexplainable and fascinating -- and can be downright spooky too!

This type of haunting is called a "residual haunting" and the easiest way to explain it is to compare it to an old film loop, meaning that it is a scene which is replayed over and over again through the years. These hauntings are really just a piece of time that is stuck in place. Many haunted places experience events that may imprint themselves on the atmosphere of a place in a way that we don't yet understand. This event suddenly discharges and plays itself at various times, thus resulting in a place being labeled as haunted. These "phantom" events are not necessarily just visual either. They are often replayed as sounds and noises that cannot be explained, like footsteps that go up and down the stairs when no one is there. They can also sometimes appear as smells or other sensory events.

Often the sounds and images "recorded" are related to traumatic events that took place at the location and caused what might be called a "psychic disturbance". In other situations, they have been events or actions repeated over and over again to cause the impression. The locations where these hauntings exist act like storage batteries, saving up the impressions of sights and sounds from the past. Eventually, many of these hauntings wear down and fade away, while others continue for eternity.

There is another type of haunting that you are bound to discover within the pages of this book as well. It's one that I have started to think deserves a category all its own and that's the "graveyard ghost". Let me first say that it is a common belief among students of the occult that cemeteries are not the best places to find ghosts. While most would fancy a misty, abandoned graveyard to be the perfect setting for a ghost story, such stories are not as common as you might believe. However, nearly every ghost enthusiast will concede that a place becomes haunted after a traumatic event occurs at that location, whether that event actually occurred to a person or to the place itself.

But what of a haunted cemetery? Do such places really exist? Most assuredly, they do, but ghosts who haunt cemeteries seem to be a different sort than those you might find lingering in a haunted house. Most of these ghosts seem to be connected to the cemetery in some way that excludes events that occurred during their lifetime. As most spirits reportedly remain in this world because of some sort of unfinished business in life, this seems to leave out a cemetery as a place where such business might remain undone.

Graveyard ghosts seem to have a few things in common. These spirits seems to be connected to the burial ground because of events that occurred after their deaths, rather than before. In other cases, the ghosts seem to be seeking eternal rest that eludes them at the spot where their physical bodies are currently found. Cemeteries gain a reputation for being haunted for reasons that include the desecration of the dead and grave robbery, unmarked or forgotten burials, natural disasters that disturb resting places, or sometimes even because the deceased was not properly buried at all!

Some of the best known, and the most frightening, ghost stories of Chicago center around its graveyards. In fact, the city has even become famous for the inordinate number of haunted cemeteries that can be found within its borders, as you will discover later on in this book.

So, what do you think? Do you find this all hard to believe?

Can I tell you that all of the stories that you will discover in the pages ahead are true? Can I vouch for their complete authenticity? No, I cannot do that. What I can tell you though is that each of them was told to me, or documented, as being the truth. The stories that are included in this book are presented as "real" stories that have been told by "real" people. The truth of each story is up to the reader to decide.

But what of ghosts themselves, are they real? And is Chicago really a haunted and mysterious place?

There are many readers who do believe that ghosts are real and who have had their own strange experiences over the years. Like many of us, they have tried to explain them away, but cannot. These folks are quick to accept the possibility that ghosts exist but not all readers are so open-minded.

Those who do not believe in ghosts say that spirits are merely the figments of our collective imagination. Ghost stories, these readers insist, are the creations of fools, drunkards and folklorists. Such a reader will most likely finish this book and will still be unable to consider the idea that ghosts might exist. In that case, I can only hope to entertain this person with the history and horrific tales from the eerie past of Chicago.

If you are such a person though, I hope that you will not be too quick to assume that you have all of the answers. Can you really say for sure that ghosts aren't real? Are you completely convinced that spirits do not wander throughout Chicagoland? Those are questions that you should ask yourself, but before you immediately reply from the comfort of your warm and brightly lit home, try answering them instead while standing in the mist-shrouded confines of one of Chicago's haunted graveyards at midnight.

Is that weeping sound you hear really just the wind whispering in your ear, or could it be the voice of a long dead woman, crying for eternal peace?

Is that merely a patch of fog that you see moving in and out of the trees, or could it be the ethereal form of a woman in white, still searching for her lost child?

Are those lights in the distance simply the reflections of passing headlights or are they the souls of the forgotten searching for their unmarked graves?

Is that rustling in the leaves really just the passing breeze, or is it the ominous sound of footsteps coming up behind you?

If you suddenly turn to look, then you might realize that, despite the fact that there is no living person around you, you just might not be alone! Perhaps you are not as sure as you thought you were about the existence of ghosts. Perhaps they are not simply a part of fanciful fiction after all. Perhaps no one person among us has all of the answers...

Remember that there are stranger things, to paraphrase the poet, than are dreamt of in our philosophies. Some of these strange things are lurking just around the corner, in dark shadows of Chicago!

Happy Hauntings!
Troy Taylor
Holidays 2002-03

- CHAPTER ONE -
GHOSTS BY GASLIGHT

THE HISTORY & HAUNTINGS OF OLD CHICAGO

I have struck a city - a real city - and they call it Chicago. The other places do not count... This is first real American city that I have encountered. Having seen it, I urgently desire to never see it again.
RUDYARD KIPLING

A façade of skyscrapers facing the lake and behind the façade, every bit of dubiousness!
E.M. FORSTER

You can get much further with a smile, a kind word and a gun than you can get with just a smile and a kind word.
AL CAPONE

Chicago is, and always has been, a lusty, brawling, violent city; a polyglot city, a rich city, a city powerful and unafraid. In a curious, oblique manner, Chicago is proud of her reputation.
SEWELL PEASLEE WRIGHT

It will likely come as no surprise to the reader to learn that Chicago was born in blood.

It will also come as no surprise to learn that no one really planned Chicago in the way that other great American cities were planned, with their sites carefully chosen and their streets laid out with care. The land on both sides of the Chicago River was low and wet, a brackish area of swamp and mud. The famous Loop district was only a few inches above Lake Michigan in those days and spent the greater part of the year under water. The mouth of the river itself was choked with sand, allowing passage by nothing larger than a canoe, while most of the stream was filled with wild rice and its banks covered by wild onion. This aromatic vegetation would give Chicago its first name.

Chicago began as nothing more than empty wilderness and open prairie, a desolate and isolated region on the shore of a great lake. The first explorers passed through this place in 1673 when Marquette and Jolliet crossed the area on their way back from exploring the Mississippi River. However, they left nothing of their presence behind. They were followed by LaSalle's soldier of fortune, Tonti, in 1681. He arrived at the Chicago River, also on a journey to the Mississippi, and claimed the entire area for France. LaSalle called it

"Louisiana". Three years later, the future city would appear as nothing more than a notation on a map as "Chekagou", a Potawatomi Indian name that meant "wild onion". But nearly one hundred years would pass before the first settlers came to this place.

A view of Chicago that was penned in 1842.

THE SETTLERS & THE PIONEERS

There were originally two settlements in early Chicago. One of them was at the junction of the north and south branches of the Chicago River, a place that was commonly known as Wolf Point. The other was at Hardscrabble, located about four miles to the south, where a man named Charles Lee cleared and cultivated a farm in 1803. A town later grew up around the Wolf Point, thanks to the natural advantages of the site and its proximity to Fort Dearborn, which would be constructed in 1803.

The first settler came in 1779 and opened a trading post at Wolf Point. His name was Jean Baptiste Point du Sable and he was a French trader and trapper who had been born on the Caribbean island of Santo Domingo. He was described as a "large man...was a trader, pretty wealthy and drank freely." He married a Cahokian woman named Catherine in 1788 and they had a daughter two years later. By 1796, after a failed bid to become the head of the Potawatomi Indians, du Sable sold out the inventory of his trading post and moved to Missouri. He died, allegedly in St. Charles, Missouri, in 1814.

Du Sable's inventory was purchased by a French trader named Le Mai and he was joined by three or four other traders at Wolf Point. The small settlement was little more than a collection of shanties, although one of the traders, Antoine Ouilmette, would later distinguish himself enough to lend his name to the north shore town of Wilmette. The trading post was later purchased by a man named Jean Lalime, who expanded the operation into a successful enterprise.

By 1803, America had expanded its borders to the west and an outpost called Fort Dearborn was established on the south bank of the Chicago River. The fort was commanded by Captain John Whistler and was held by a company of 66 soldiers. The fort had been named in honor of Secretary of War Henry Dearborn.

At the time, this corner of Illinois was one of the most remote regions of the frontier. It was a wilderness that was virtually cut off from all communication with the rest of the country. Access to the area was by means of river or Indian trail and the closest settlement was Fort Wayne. Today, this is a short journey, but in those days, it was a dangerous and difficult trek. The soldiers who came to man Fort Dearborn had no idea of the desolation they would face.

The fort was a simple stockade of logs. They were placed in the ground and then sharpened along the upper end. The outer stockade was a solid wall with an entrance in the southern section that was blocked with heavy gates. Another exit, this one underground, was located on the north side. Inside of the fort, there was room for a parade ground, officer's quarters, troop barracks, a guard house and a magazine for weapons and ammunition. Two block houses were also added along two corners of the fort, along with a raised walkway so that defenders could fire over the top of the wall. The fort offered substantial protection for the soldiers garrisoned there, but later they would find that it was not protection enough.

In 1804, a man named John Kinzie arrived in the region. He bought out the property of Jean Lalime and over the course of several years, became the self-appointed civilian leader of the settlement. He was known for his sharp dealings with the local Indians over trade goods and furs. He also established close ties with the Potawatomi Indians and even sold them liquor, which created tension among the other settlers. Kinzie managed to become very successful and this seemed to anger Jean Lalime, the man who had sold Kinzie his business. The two became bitter rivals.

John Kinzie was regarded for many years as the "father of Chicago", thanks to a book that was written about him by his devoted daughter-in-law, Juliette Magill Kinzie. Years later, Kinzie's real role in Chicago history would be called into question. Kinzie was born around 1763 and worked as a silversmith before setting out to trade among the Indians. His first wife, Margaret, had been kidnapped by Shawnee Indians at age 10 and after spending a decade in captivity, she escaped to Detroit, where she met and married Kinzie. The two of them had three children together but after a chance meeting with her birth father, Margaret abandoned her husband and returned to Virginia with the children. Kinzie never saw or heard from any of them again.

Kinzie later married Eleanor Little, the widow of Daniel McKillip, who supported the British during the American Revolution and who was killed at the Battle of Fallen Timbers. Eleanor's father was also a British loyalist and narrowly escaped being hanged in Pittsburgh in 1783. Kinzie had four children with Eleanor and in 1804; they arrived in Chicago, where Kinzie purchased the trading post from Lalime.

His business quickly prospered but it was not without problems. A partnership that the trader formed with Captain Whistler's son, John Whistler, Jr., deteriorated so badly that it caused a major conflict within the community. The disagreement became so heated that word of it reached officials in Detroit and Whistler, and all of the other officers at the fort, were recalled and assigned to various posts across the frontier.

In 1810, Captain Whistler was replaced at Fort Dearborn by Captain Nathan Heald. He brought with him Lieutenant Linus T. Helm, an officer, like Heald, who had much in the way of frontier experience. Not long after arriving, Helm met and married the stepdaughter of John Kinzie. In addition to she and Captain Heald's wife, there were a number of other women at the fort as well, all wives of the men stationed there. More families arrived and within two years, there were twelve women and twenty children at Fort Dearborn.

Throughout the changes at the fort, Kinzie and Lalime remained enemies and in constant conflict with one another. Finally, in April 1812, their animosity boiled over into violence. One day as the two men were leaving the fort, Lieutenant Helm warned Kinzie that the other man was looking for him. A brief struggle ensued, leading to Kinzie being shot in the shoulder and to Lalime being stabbed to death. Kinzie fled to Milwaukee and remained in hiding there until word came that the murder had been ruled as "justifiable homicide". Kinzie soon returned to Chicago, only to find that some of the officers at the fort who had been friends of Lalime had buried the dead man in Kinzie's own yard. Rather than be angry though, Kinzie erected a fence around the grave site and tended it until his own death. After he died, Lalime's bones were forgotten until they were accidentally disturbed during a construction project many years later. The remains were eventually given to the Chicago History Society, who placed them in a glass case, forever enshrining the bones of Chicago's first murder victim.

THE FORT DEARBORN MASSACRE

Fort Dearborn was constructed near the site of the present-day Michigan Avenue bridge in 1803. It was named for a man who would go on to be considered one of the most inept leaders in American history. During the War of 1812, Secretary of War General Henry Dearborn was placed in command of all of the

American troops between Lake Erie and the Atlantic. He then tried to capture Montreal but his troops were so disorganized that they never even made it across the Canadian border. Dearborn was finally relived of command by President James Madison in 1813 after he narrowly avoided being court-martialed. In spite of this, a number of later Chicago parks and developments were named in his honor leading author Norman Mark to refer to him as an "example of one of history's most successful failures."

The first commander at the fort was Captain John Whistler, who arrived in Chicago with a contingent of disgruntled troops in March 1803. They spent the next few years alternating between drinking and deserting and its no surprise that they were unhappy. The fort was far away from any semblance of civilization and was beset with problems from the beginning. During the first year, more than half of the men contracted debilitating diseases and when the first winter supply ship arrived, it brought 56 suits of clothing for the captain's 66 men.

Some would say that things grew even worse when Whistler was replaced by Captain Nathan Heald in 1810. Although experienced in frontier life, Heald was completely unprepared for the dangers that lay ahead for the men of the fort and the settlers of the small community. By August 1812, tensions were high in the wilderness. The conflict that had erupted between America and Great Britain had aroused unrest among the local Indian tribes, namely the Potawatomi and the Wynadot. The effects of the war brought many of the Indian tribes into alliance with the British for they saw the Americans as invaders into their lands. After the British captured the American garrison at Mackinac, Fort Dearborn was in great danger. Orders came stating that Captain Heald should abandon the fort and leave the contents to the local Indians.

Unfortunately, Heald delayed in carrying out the orders and soon, the American troops had nowhere to go. He refused to leave the fort in a hurry, hoping to avoid looking like a coward and in fact, delayed six days before making arrangements to evacuate. The unrest among the Indians brought a large contingent of them to the fort and they gathered in an almost siege-like state. The soldiers began to express concern over the growing numbers of Indians outside and matters grew even more serious after an Indian raid on Hardscrabble, a few miles from the fort. A party of soldiers discovered the bodies of a scalped French trapper and another man here. One of them had been shot and the other had been stabbed 11 times.

Heald realized that he was going to have to bargain with Indians if the occupants of Fort Dearborn were going to safely reach Fort Wayne. On August 12, Heald began several days of bargaining with the assembled tribes, which his junior officers refused to attend. The council eventually led to an agreement for the Indians to provide safe conduct for the soldiers and settlers to Fort Wayne in Indiana.

Part of the agreement was that Heald would leave the stores and ammunition in the fort for the Indians, but his officers disagreed. Alarmed, they questioned the wisdom of handing out guns and ammunition that could easily be turned against them. Heald reluctantly agreed with them and the extra weapons and ammunition were broken apart and dumped into an abandoned well. In addition, the stores of whiskey were dumped into the river. Needless to say, the Indians outside observed this and they too began making plans that differed from those agreed upon with Captain Heald.

On August 14, a visitor arrived at the fort in the person of Captain William Wells. He and 30 Miami warriors had managed to slip past the throng outside and they appeared at the front gates of the fort. Wells was a frontier legend among early soldiers and settlers in the Illinois territory. He was also the uncle of Captain Heald's wife, Rebekah, and after hearing of the evacuation of Fort Dearborn, and knowing the hostile fervor of the local tribes, headed straight to the fort to assist them in their escape. Unfortunately, he had arrived too late.

Throughout the night of August 14, wagons were loaded for travel and reserve ammunition was distributed, amounting to about 25 rounds per man. Early the next morning, the procession of soldiers, civilians, women and children left the fort. The infantry soldiers led the way, followed by a caravan of wagons and mounted men. A portion of the Miami who had accompanied Wells guarded the rear of the column.

The column of soldiers and settlers were escorted by nearly 500 Potawatomi Indians. As they marched southward and into a low range of sand hills that separated the beaches of Lake Michigan from the prairie, the Potawatomi moved silently to the right, placing an elevation of sand between them and the white men. The act was carried out with such subtlety that no one noticed it as the column trudged along the shoreline. A little further down the beach, the sand ridge ended and the two groups would come together again.

The column traveled to an area where 16th Street and Indiana Avenue are now located. There was a sudden milling about of the scouts at the front of the line and suddenly a shout came back from Captain Wells that the Indians were attacking! A line of Potawatomi appeared over the edge of the ridge and fired down at the column. Totally surprised, the officers nevertheless managed to rally the men into a battle line, but it was of little use. So many of them fell from immediate wounds that the line collapsed. The Indians overwhelmed them with sheer numbers, flanking the line and snatching the wagons and horses.

What followed was butchery. Officers were slain with tomahawks and the fort's surgeon was cut down by gunfire and then literally chopped into pieces. Rebekah Heald was wounded by gunfire but was spared when she was captured by a sympathetic chief, who spared her life. The wife of one soldier fought so bravely and savagely that she was hacked into pieces before she fell. In the end, cut down to less than half their original number, the garrison surrendered under the promise of safe conduct. In all, 148 members of the column were killed, 86 adults and 12 children were slaughtered in the initial attack. One of the dead was Captain Wells, who was captured and his heart cut out and eaten by his slayers. A Chicago street now bears the name of this brave frontiersman.

In the battle, Captain Heald was wounded twice, while his wife was wounded seven times. They were later released and a St. Joseph Indian named Chaudonaire took them to Mackinac, where they were turned over to the British commander there. He sent them to Detroit and they were exchanged with the American authorities.

The surrender that was arranged by Captain Heald did not apply to the wounded and it is said that the Indians tortured them throughout the night and then left their bodies on the sand next to those who had already fallen. Many of the other survivors later suffered terribly. One man was tomahawked when he could not keep pace with the rest of the group being marched away from the massacre site. One baby that cried too much during the march was tied to a tree and left to starve. Mrs. Isabella Cooper was pulled from a wagon containing women and children and was actually scalped before being rescued by an Indian woman. She had a small bald spot on her head for the rest of her life. Another man froze to death that winter, while Mrs. John Simmons and her daughter were forced to run a gauntlet, which both survived. In fact, the girl turned out to be the last survivor of the massacre, dying in 1900.

Perhaps the most tragic survivor was James Corbin, who was shot in the hip, the thigh and heel and who also had a tomahawk wound in his shoulder. He somehow made it through the winter with untreated wounds, literally crawling through the Indian camp eating scraps of food. He was eventually released and arrived in Quebec wearing nothing more than a breech cloth and a vest. He tried to make it home to Virginia but his discharge pay from the military only got him passage to Albany, New York, where he nearly starved to death. He tried to re-enlist but his wounds made him unfit for duty and so he applied for a pension, but was denied. No one believed that he had actually been involved in the massacre since he had been wounded but the Indians had not killed him. It took him six years to convince the government that he was actually owed a pension and when it came, it amounted to the grand sum of $4 per month!

John Kinzie and his family were spared in the slaughter. Appealing to the Potawatomi chiefs, they were taken away from the massacre site. He would return to Chicago one year later, but found that much had changed. He failed in re-starting his business and soon was working for his largest competitor, the American Fur Company. In time, the fur trade would end and Kinzie worked as a trader and Indian interpreter until his death in 1828. Thirty years later, his daughter-in-law would write a book that named Kinzie as the founding

A Monument to the Slain Settlers of the Fort Dearborn Massacre

settler of Chicago. The book would overlook Kinzie's questionable business practices and the murder of Jean Lalime and would be accepted as fact for many years. Later, it would be seen as evidence of Juliette Kinzie's affinity for social climbing and her need to be part of a Chicago dynasty. At that point, her historical "facts" were called into question.

After the carnage, the victorious Indians burned Fort Dearborn itself to the ground and the bodies of the massacre victims were left where they had fallen, scattered to decay on the sand dunes of Lake Michigan. When replacement troops arrived at the site of Fort Dearborn a year later, they were greeted with not only the burned-out shell of the fort, but also the grinning skeletons of their predecessors. The bodies were given proper burials and the fort was rebuilt in 1816, only to be abandoned again in 1836, when the city would be able to fend for itself.

Not surprisingly, the horrific massacre spawned its share of ghostly tales. For many years, the site of the fort itself was said to be haunted by those who were killed nearby.

The actual site of the massacre was quiet for many years, long after Chicago grew into a sizable city. According to author Dale Kaczmarek, in his book *Windy City Ghosts*, construction in the early 1980's unearthed a number of human bones. At first thought to be the victims of a cholera epidemic in the 1840's, the remains were later dated more closely to the early 1800's. Thanks to their location, they were believed to be the bones of victims from the massacre. They were reburied elsewhere but within a few weeks, people began to report the semi-transparent figures of people dressed in pioneer clothing and military uniforms. They were seen wandering in a lot just north of 16th and while many seemed to run about haphazardly, others appeared to move in slow motion. Many of them reportedly looked very frightened or were screaming in silence.

Perhaps these poor victims do not rest in peace after all...

CHICAGO PIONEERS - LEGENDS & LORE

In the years following these turbulent events, many things changed in Chicago. As time passed, more settlers came to the region and the small collection of crude buildings began to grow. It was not much to look at though. A visitor noted in 1823 that "the village presents no cheering prospect... It consists of a few huts, inhabited by a miserable race of men, scarcely equal to the Indians from whom they are descended. Their log or bark houses are low, filthy and disgusting, displaying not the least trace of comfort."

The center of the settlement remained at Wolf Point, which now hosted a rowdy district of saloons and taverns. One of the first of these to open was Miller's Tavern in 1829. It was located on the north branch of the river and operated until 1832. It was joined by the first hotel a short time later, operated by Archibald Caldwell and John Kinzie's son, James. Caldwell eventually sold out his interest to Kinzie and left for Wisconsin, never believing that Chicago would amount to anything.

The most famous of the early establishments were the Green Tavern and the Sauganash, both of which were near Wolf Point and fronted an ox-cart road and a footpath that become Lake Street. The Green Tree was opened in 1833 by James Kinzie but the bedrooms, as one traveler complained, were "altogether too dirty for the comfort of persons unaccustomed to such surroundings". The tavern remained in business under various names (including the Chicago, the Noyes, the Railroad House and others) until 1859, when it was converted into tenements. In 1880, the building was removed to Milwaukee Avenue, where it stood for many years.

The Sauganash Hotel, which was the first frame building erected in Chicago, was built in 1831 by "Jolly" Mark Beaubien. The owner was the father of 23 children and rarely had time for the place, spending most of his spare moments fiddling and shooting ducks from the establishment's front porch. The hotel was certainly no better than the Green Tree in its early days and was likely worse. Patrick Shirreff, a Scotch agriculturist who visited Chicago in 1833, wrote that Jolly Mark's tavern was "a vile two-story barrack" and was "dirty in the extreme." Somehow though, it became the most popular drinking spot in the city until it burned down in March 1851. On the site of the building, which became the southeast corner of Lake and Market Streets, was erected the Republican "wigwam" where Abraham Lincoln was nominated for president in 1860.

The popularity of the Sauganash began to decline in 1835 when a syndicate of businessmen built the imposing, three-story Lake House at the corner of Kinzie and Rush Streets. The Lake House was the first hotel in the city to have an actual chef and to use printed menus in the dining room. Two years after the Lake House came the Sherman House. It was built by Francis Sherman and the hotel remained the finest hotel in the Northwest until 1850, when Ira and James Couch, erected the famed Tremont House at Lake and Dearborn Streets. The hotel was over five stories high and beautifully furnished. The Tremont soon became known as "Couch's Folly" because few Chicagoans believed that the city would ever be large enough to support such a grand establishment. The hotel burned during the Great Fire in 1871.

Ironically, the tomb of Ira Couch holds a place of dubious honor in Chicago cemetery history and has been the source of an enduring mystery. In 1837, the old city cemetery in Chicago was disbanded by order of the city council (we'll explore that further in a later chapter) and all of the bodies interred there were to be moved to other sites. One set of remains buried in the cemetery were those of Ira Couch.

Couch had passed away in 1856 and he and his brother were hailed as two of the great, early businessmen of the city. As a monument to all that he had accomplished, his family had constructed a large mausoleum for him that had been made from imported stone. In 1863, when the city council ordered all of the remaining bodies moved from the old cemetery, the Couch family fought for the mausoleum to stay where it was. The family managed to endure the legal wrangling that followed and to this day, the mausoleum remains at its original site behind the Chicago Historical Society at the south end of Lincoln Park.

Ironically though, cemetery records claim that Ira Couch is actually buried in the family plot at Rosehill Cemetery. So where is he really? No one knows for sure because the opening of the tomb would take an order of the city council for the mystery to be investigated. Eventually, the tomb is likely to be opened but until that time, one has to wonder where the body of Ira Couch is actually located?

As Chicago continued to grow, it earned the first of its many nicknames. Most of the stores and dwellings that existed during this period were made from logs. Those that weren't were built in the "balloon fashion", a method of construction that was first used in Chicago. In order to build such a structure, posts were placed in the ground to make corners and blocks were laid down at proper distances between them. Foundations were laid on the blocks and to them were spiked, standing on end, wooden boards. Flat boards were then nailed to them and weatherboards were placed on the outside and then lathe and plaster were added to the inside to create a ceiling. Thanks to this unique method of building, Chicago became known as "Slab Town", by which it was generally known unless it was being referred to by its less affectionate nickname of "Mud Hole of the Prairies".

Unfortunately, the latter was likely the most accurate of the nicknames. There were few sidewalks and no paving of any kind at that time. Heavy traffic and frequent rains transformed the roads and footpaths into murky quagmires that were impossible and dangerous to pass through. A classic story of these days was often told about a citizen who spotted a man's head and shoulders sticking out of the mud. He asked the man if he could be of assistance. "No thanks," the man replied. "I have a horse under me."

In 1849, planks were laid on several of the downtown streets and an experiment was conducted that graded Lake Street down to the level of the lake and then covered it with wooden planks. It was thought that the sewage would settle into the gutters that had been created and be carried off but the opposite actually occurred. Soon, the stench in the streets made travel unbearable. Engineers advised the city council that the only way that Chicago could be drained was to raise the grade of the streets by 12 feet. This monumental task, which consisted of filling 1,200 acres and lifting almost every building in the city was started in 1855 and completed in the middle 1860's. While the work was in progress, pedestrian travel in the city was strange, and often dangerous, with sidewalks running at erratic levels and staircases that had to be used to travel just one block.

Chicago was officially incorporated as a city in August 1833, although no one has any idea just how many inhabitants actually resided here at that time. It is thought that the event of the city's incorporation was the first incident of "voter fraud" in Chicago and began a tradition that has besmirched the city's reputation ever since.

A preliminary election and vote on the city's incorporation was held on August 5 but only 13 voters showed up. Only one man voted against incorporating and since he lived outside of the proposed city limits, his vote didn't count anyway. The voters were invited to return to Jolly Mark's tavern on August 10 and this time, 28 showed up and 13 of those became candidates for office. The rule of thumb in those days was that each voter represented five other, non-voting persons, meaning that Chicago has about 140 residents at most. Unfortunately though, 150 inhabitants were needed to incorporate. In spite of this, the vote somehow went though and Chicago became a real city at last. It's no wonder that "vote early and vote often" became a phrase to ridicule Chicago voting habits in years to come.

In spite of these strides though, the city was still being seen by many as an "Indian town". Fur pelts, guns, blankets, knives and whiskey were still very much in evidence and the Indians were both the suppliers and consumers of these goods. No one wished to offend the Indians and the Potawatomi were so important to the early city that they contributed $200 of the $486 needed to construct the first bridge over the Chicago River. Even so, the Native Americans were becoming an embarrassment and could not be a part of the sort of city that Chicago wished to become.

Time ran out for the local Indian populace in 1833. During that summer, near 8,000 Chippewa, Ottawa and Potawatomi Indians assembled on the outskirts of the village and on September 28, their chiefs signed a treaty that relinquished their claim to all lands east of the Mississippi River, amounting to almost five million acres. In return, the government agreed to pay the tribes $1million dollars in cash and supplies over a 25 year period and to transport them, within two years, to an area equal in size to Kansas. A down payment of about $150,000 was made on that night but according to writers on the scene, no less that $20,000 worth of the goods were stolen the first night after the Indians had been plied with whiskey.

The Indians said their final farewell to Chicago in August 1835 and set out for the west. With the Indian presence removed, hordes of immigrants began swarming in from the east to claim the vast territory that had been opened for occupation by the treaty. Chicago became the gateway to the "promised land" and the city began to overflow with land hungry settlers.

One of the men to profit from the land speculation boom that came to Chicago was a man who many credit for making it possible for the city to survive to its prosperous days. His name was Gurdon S. Hubbard and in addition to being one of the early settlers of the city, he was famed for his trades with the Indians and for his uncanny ability to walk incredible distances. At one point, it was claimed that he had walked 75 miles in a single day!

Hubbard arrived in Chicago in 1818 as a 16 year-old fur trader for John Jacob Astor's American Fur Company. He did not remain in the settlement for long but he did return in 1829 with a herd of over 400 hogs. He started the first of Chicago's packing houses a short time later and by the 1830's, Chicago pork was in great demand in the east. By 1865, the Union Stock Yards were opened between Halsted and 39th Streets and the city's meat packing plants became famous all across the country. Hubbard also built the city's first brick building, became the city's first insurance underwriter, bought the first fire engine and was an early Republican and supporter of Abraham Lincoln.

In 1827 though, Hubbard became the focal point of an event that many would credit as "saving the city". As it turned out though, his dangerous excursion was unnecessary but did serve to create a reputation for the young man that would be remembered during his later years in business. In July of that year, word reached Chicago that the Winnebago Indians were going to attack the settlement. The residents were in a panic and Hubbard volunteered to ride 125 miles to Danville to get help. He left on horseback in torrents of rain and changed horses at Iroquois Creek, although he was unable to get his horse to swim the swollen river at night. Finally, he swam the creek himself and began walking. Hubbard, who had created a trail that later became State Street, was known to the local Indians as "Pa-ea-ma-at-be" or "Swift Walker", thanks to the fact that he could cover great distances at amazing speed. He arrived in Danville just 20 hours after his departure, covering 125 miles and most of that on foot.

A group of 100 men from Danville volunteered to save Chicago from attack. The group arrived at the flooded Vermillion River but couldn't cross it. Hubbard decided to try and swim his horse across, with the other mounts following behind. By the time the men arrived in Chicago though, the threat was over. A runner arrived to announce that the Winnebago had signed a treaty and were no longer threatening to attack. The volunteers from Danville remained at the settlement for the next several days, causing problems with the belligerent locals, before finally departing for home.

Tales of Hubbard's bravery served him well in later years and he was one of the first to capitalize on the real estate boom that followed the departure of the Native Americans from the region. In 1829, he had purchased two lots for $33.33 each and six years later, he sold the lots for an $80,000 profit! In 1835, he also bought 80 acres of the most undesirable land in Chicago for $5,000. He visited New York just 90 days later and sold the same land for $80,000.

THE CURSE OF STREETERVILLE

Captain George Wellington Streeter has been considered by many to have been the last Chicago pioneer. Whether he deserves this title or not is another question, but he was certainly a colorful character and one that is surrounded by lore that is uniquely a part of Chicago. During his years in the city, he defied the laws of Chicago and the state of Illinois, fought the courts and the police to a standstill and managed to keep the residents of the region in alternating states of anger and amusement for more than 30 years.

Streeter's greatest Chicago legacy was created by nature rather than man. The waves had been beating unchallenged against the shoreline of Lake Michigan for centuries before the settlers came to Chicago. Along the open area north of the river, the lake deposited generation after generation of silt and sand and as it did so, the shore crept ever eastward. The wealthy residents who

Cap Streeter's Boat in 1893
(Chicago Historical Society)

owned land to the west, across what was Sand Street in those days and now the streets of St. Clair and Pine, claimed rights to the water's edge, no matter where it might extend to. And there was never any dispute about this until one summer day in 1886 when a strange and eccentric creature laid claim to the vast Chicago shoreline.

George Wellington Streeter was the great-grandson of an American Revolution veteran and the grandson of a drum-major from the War of 1812. He was an avid showman and before he arrived in Chicago, he had roamed the west, had served in the Civil War (seeing action at Missionary Ridge and Lookout Mountain), had watched his first wife run off to become a vaudeville star, had worked as a freight hauler, a hotel owner and for a time, had been a business associate of two unsavory brothers from Missouri named Frank and Jesse James. After his service in the war, Streeter had brought together a menagerie composed of animals no more exciting than deer, otter, porcupines, and beavers but still managed to exhibit them at county fairs with some success. His prize exhibit was a white Normandy hog, which he insisted was 10 feet long and weighed over 1,500 pounds. Her usually billed the beast as a "white elephant", to the delight of the crowds who came to see him.

Streeter's dubious business prospered for awhile but when ticket sales slumped, he traded in his animals and became a ship navigator on the waters of Lake Michigan and the nearby rivers. He landed in Chicago in the 1870's and became part owner of the Wood's Museum, a famous showplace of the time. He soon sold out and became a salesman at county fairs, then left that business and served as a short-term owner of the Apollo Theater.

Not long after this, Streeter returned to the lake, lured by the hope of striking it rich in Honduras. His second wife, Maria, was a raging drunk and would often disappear for a week at a time on a bender. Cap Streeter, as he was often called, never worried about her when she went missing. "It don't matter where she is," he would often say. "She's having a good time and will come home when she's ready." During one of her disappearances, Maria made a friend, a Captain Bowen, who convinced her that there was money to be made in Honduras. There was a revolution taking place there at the time and all a seaman had to do was to arrive in the country with a boatload of guns and he would find himself with a steamship concession on the Honduras rivers.

Soon after, Streeter began to borrow money and to build his own steamship, which he called the *Reutan*. He wanted to test her for seaworthiness and decided the best place to do so was on Lake Michigan. Streeter, Maria, an engineer and four passengers set out on July 10, 1886. A sudden storm blew in off the lake and the steamboat was nearly lost. The boat managed to make it to a point near the Chicago harbor, missed the breakwater, drifted northward and finally washed up onto a sand bar along the beach. Streeter was the only person still on the boat by then and he was lashed to the wheel to prevent himself from being washed overboard in the storm. Despite the grounding of his boat, Streeter was not defeated. In fact, he took a look around and decided that the spot where the boat had washed ashore would make a fine place to live.

The boat remained on the site throughout the fall and into the winter. The sandbar began to grow up around it and Streeter offered local contractors the privilege of dumping sand, dirt, garbage or anything else they wanted near his new home. The lake continued to contribute sand as well and soon, the boat was no longer in the water but resting on dry land. In this way, Cap Streeter "created" 186 acres of his very own land. He had managed to find an older map of Chicago that indicated that the shoreline was actually west of his property and now claimed that he was beyond the shore of Chicago and Illinois. He dubbed this new property the "District of Lake Michigan" and while he recognized the laws of America, he declared that he was subject to no other rules or regulations.

The local property owners, the most noted of whom were Potter Palmer and N.K. Fairbanks, made it their common cause to get Streeter removed from the land along the lake. In their eyes, he was nothing more than a crude, obnoxious squatter and a blasphemous, drunken thief who had to be ousted. Streeter was throwing loud parties for other riff-raff in the region and worse, was selling liquor on Sunday. This was against the law in Chicago but Cap had decided that it was perfectly legal in his district. Palmer and Fairbanks soon learned that threats did not work with Streeter, so they began to pursue legal options. Had they gone to the civil courts at once, things might have turned out differently but they went to the police instead, which started a guerilla struggle that lasted for years. The battle involved the city police, the park police, special constables and dozens of lawyers. The courts were appealed to over and over again and Cap was arrested several times but always managed to go free.

Eventually, the Chicago gentry, with their now obstructed view of the lake, thanks to Cap's boat, outhouses and ramshackle buildings, chose less subtle methods of moving Streeter off his land. In the summer of 1894, five men from Chicago Title and Trust served Cap with orders to remove himself from the property. They received shotgun pellets in their backsides for their trouble. When three policemen came to arrest Cap for the shooting, Maria doused them with boiling water, forcing them to retreat. Cap was later arrested but no charges were pressed because there was still a dispute as to whether Streeter owned the property and whether or not the men were trespassing.

Later that fall, Cap's house was attacked by 25 police officers, working on an official payroll for Potter Palmer and his compatriots. Streeter opened fire on the men and Maria managed to nearly sever the arm of one of them. After they were arrested, all charges against them were dismissed after they claimed "self defense". Around this same time, Cap discovered the old Chicago map that indicated that his district was outside of the city limits. He named William H. Niles as his military governor and set about creating a separate state from Illinois. In 1899, he turned one of the outhouses on his property into a courthouse, raised an American flag and issued his own "declaration of independence". Streeter and a number of his friends were arrested on charges of illegal assembly but were later released.

On May 25, 1899 (just a few weeks after Streeter declared his district independent of Chicago and Illinois), more than 500 hand-picked police officers charged into Streeter's district because Cap allegedly shot at a police captain's carriage. Military governor Niles had already entrenched Cap's men around the property and he armed his men with a cannon that had been stolen from a nearby park. The city soon had Streeter's district surrounded with officers in the front and a tug boat that was armed with a gatling gun in the rear. The police charged but were repulsed by buckshot and rocks. Around nightfall, the police officers charged again and managed to overwhelm the small "army". Streeter was captured but was soon released and the police officers involved in the fiasco were reprimanded for their roles in the affair. In those days, it was not illegal to shoot at a police captain's carriage!

But no one was willing to let the matter go away quietly. One night while Streeter and his wife were out of the house, several officers broke into their house and confiscated a number of Cap's guns. Enraged, Streeter marched down to the Chicago Avenue police station and took all of the officers and staff members hostage. He demanded the return of his guns and when they were given back, he left the station peaceably. Cap was soon arrested and charges were filed against him. His defense turned out to be so eloquent though that he was acquitted.

Another bizarre incident occurred in the spring of 1900. A group of men, posing as land buyers (Cap had been selling off lots of real estate from an office in the Tremont Hotel) took over the District while Streeter was away and burned down his house. Cap quickly responded and after raising an army, marched into the District and took it back. Police officers were again raised in response. Three-inch guns were mounted onto two of the city's fire tugs, 16 patrol wagons were lined up outside of the District and over 400 officers were called in to serve as troops. The volatile standoff ended when a lone policeman convinced Streeter that he should surrender himself. He did so and was acquitted again of all charges against him.

In 1902, Streeter and several of his cronies were indicted for forging the name of President Grover Cleveland on a land grant that "proved" that his District was outside of the jurisdiction of Chicago. It was later reported that the document Streeter used was actually a paper signed by President Martin Van Buren that gave certain lands to John Kinzie and his heirs. The heirs then immediately sued to have the land returned to them, which meant that the wealthy citizens who were trying to get rid of Cap Streeter for being a squatter were now being accused of being squatters themselves! The case eventually went away and Palmer and the others were able to again focus their attentions on the Streeter problem.

And it was in this same year that things took another turn and for the first time, Streeter actually ended up in jail over the matter - only this time for something that he didn't do! The wealthy "behind the scenes" men hired a gunman from Missouri named John Kirk to go in and clear Cap out, no matter what it took. Days later, Kirk's body was discovered in a Chicago alleyway, riddled with bullet holes. Streeter was shortly arrested and railroaded through the courts with a guilty charge for murder. He was sent to Joliet prison and while he was there, Maria died from exposure and hunger. Streeter cursed Chicago for her death and when he was released after nine months, with a full and unconditional pardon from the governor, he was never the same again.

In 1906, he re-married though, this time to Alma Lockwood, who was 33 years his junior. Streeter had managed to hang on to his district, now dubbed Streeterville, for years but his days were numbered. By 1915, the land actually controlled by Cap had dwindled to nothing more than a fenced enclosure that surrounded the remains of his home. Streeter still held parties here though and sold liquor, even on Sundays, which was still illegal. The city informed him that he had to obtain a liquor license and sent several police officers to enforce the order. Streeter stabbed the sergeant who carried the papers in the behind with a bayonet as a reply. He was arrested but was quickly bailed out.

The following day, eight policemen charged into the District and attempted to arrest Cap again. Two of them grabbed Alma's ax but she managed to disarm six of the officers anyway. Another officer was wounded by bird shot from one of Cap's guns. Alma was arrested after the incident for "assault with intent to kill" but she was acquitted when it came out in court that none of the policemen ever identified themselves as officers.

After years of defending himself against attackers, the city of Chicago and the court system, Cap Streeter was finally defeated on December 11, 1918. On that day, the courts finally decided that Streeter had no real claim to the land that he called Streeterville. He was finally evicted and his home was burned to the ground, marking an end to one of the city's most unusual eras.

Streeter remained an eccentric Chicago character until the day that he died however. He began selling hot dogs and coffee at Navy Pier and lived comfortably in a new houseboat that he had purchased called the *Vamoose*. His final days came after he lost an eye one day while chopping wood. A sliver of kindling flew upward and put out his eye, which led to an infection. He contracted pneumonia in his weakened state and died on January 22, 1921 at the age of 84. The Mayor, and half of the city, attended his funeral.

The *Vamoose* became a menace to navigation and was destroyed by city order in 1928. Alma, who saved only Cap's musket as a memento of their life together, ended her days making and selling aprons and she died in 1936. She never gave up on her husband's claims to the ownership of Streeterville though and she and his heirs continued their lawsuits until 1940. In that year, a federal court finally dismissed the claims.

The original Streeterville District extended from the Chicago River to Oak Street Beach, east of Michigan Avenue. Cap's claims to this area were little more than a nuisance to the wealthy and privileged in his day but now, the land would be worth billions of dollars. Today, old Cap Streeter is barely remembered by most, except for the name Streeterville, which still persists in Chicago. For this reason, it would likely come as a surprise to many to learn that the presence of Streeter still lingers today -- in the form of a curse that allegedly "haunts" this part of the city.

Legend has it that Cap Streeter's final words were a curse on the politicians and on the city of Chicago for the real and imagined wrongs that had plagued the last several decades of his life. This story was often told but nothing much was thought of it until the 1970's. Just a few years before, Streeterville had been changed forever by the construction of the massive John Hancock building. Erected between 1965 and 1969, the giant structure loomed high over the city around it. Despite the stories though, no one died during the dangerous work that was done to create the building. According to a John Hancock spokesperson, not a single worker died during the millions of hours of labor needed to finish the building. That quickly changed though after the tenants began moving in. A series of strange deaths began to plague the building, including the murder of a man on the Sixth floor and a number of unusual fires.

The strangest and most widely reported death occurred during the early morning hours of August 12, 1971. The victim was one Lorraine Kowalski, the girlfriend of affluent Marshall Berlin, vice president of I.S. Berlin Press, a Chicago printing company. The two of them spent the evening of August 11 separately with

Berlin out for dinner with another woman and Kowalski visiting nightclubs on the near north side with her friend, Carol Thompson. Kowalski reportedly returned to the Hancock Building at about 3:30 am on the morning of August 12. She was incoherent, alone and exhausted from her night out. According to later reports from residents, Kowalski and Berlin became involved in a volatile argument but Berlin told investigators that Lorraine had simply been despondent over the direction their relationship had taken. Carol Thompson told police that her friend had been intoxicated well before midnight.

In the midst of the argument, and perhaps to cool things down, Berlin retreated into the bathroom. When he came back out a few minutes later, he stated that the bedroom window had been shattered and that Lorraine's clothing was scattered about the room. It was 4:10 am and Berlin placed a quick call to the Chicago Avenue police station.

Apparently, while he was in the bathroom, a naked Kowalski plunged out the window of the apartment and fell to the pavement many floors below. As she fell to the street, she took numerous shards of the window glass with her -- which remains one of the most puzzling parts to this mysterious incident. The double pane of glass in the apartment window was capable of withstanding 280 pounds of pressure per square foot and yet somehow, the slight 130-pound woman managed to break through it.

Berlin refused to take a polygraph test and only told the investigators that Kowalski had threatened to commit suicide just moments before he went into the bathroom. No charges were ever brought in the case and it remains unsolved to this day.

As the years passed, other deaths followed, including suicides at Water Tower Place next door. In December 1997, beloved comedian Chris Farley died in his Hancock building apartment from an overdose after a night of wild partying. My wife and I stayed at the Raphael Hotel next door just two weeks after Farley's death and flowers and messages that had been left in his memory still remained.

Another celebrity death that has been attributed to the Streeterville curse also links to another alleged curse, that of the curse on the *Poltergeist* series of films. Child actress Heather O'Rourke did not die in Chicago but she was a victim of what many have dubbed the *"Poltergeist* curse" and it has been mentioned by many that the illness that led to her death apparently flared up while she was in Chicago, filming on location at the John Hancock Building and at Water Tower Place for *Poltergeist III*.

Prior to O'Rourke's death, the series of films was plagued by the deaths of a number of the participants, including slain actress Dominique Dunne (Dana in the first film), Julian Beck (the creepy Reverend Kane in II) and Will Sampson (the Indian shaman Taylor). There had already been whispers of a "curse" when the third film went into production. The film set was hampered by a number of mishaps and fires and during production, Heather began to suffer from medical complications caused by obstruction of her bowels. She died in San Diego on February 1, 1988 and the film was released, dedicated to her memory, a short time later. It was universally panned by the critics and was a box office failure.

But was this part of the Streeterville Curse, the *Poltergeist* Curse or even a combination of both? Or was it simply a coincidence that marked the tragic end of a young girl's life?

Or could the strange events, deaths and tragedies that take place in this area be linked to something else? Could the area be strangely "affected" by other, even more mysterious forces than a mere curse? Could the legend of Cap Streeter's curse have been created to explain the anomalous atmosphere of Streeterville?

Perhaps it was -- for even nature behaves strangely here. A curious event occurs two times each year when thousands and thousands of spiders crawl up one side of the towering Hancock building and then ascend the other side. No one has been able to discover why this happens or why the creatures seem to be attracted to this point. And they are not the only creatures that seem be attached to this place either.

Staff members of a Chicago radio station that has its studios inside of the Hancock Building have reported some odd happenings at late hours of the night. It is not uncommon for overnight employees to tell of cold spots, strange whispers, knocking sounds and the presence of apparitions. On one occasion, a security officer noticed a person in the building after hours. Knowing that no one was supposed to be there, he called for the person to stop. The shadowy character began to run and the security guard gave chase. As the man began to outrun the officer, the guard called his partner in the video control room for help. His partner quickly looked up to the security monitors and saw the other officer running down an empty hallway! Even though the other man clearly saw the person he was chasing, there was no one on the video screen. The first guard pursued the figure around several corners and then he disappeared completely. A thorough search of the building discovered that no one else was present.

Could these continuing sightings be a part of Cap Streeter's "curse"? Or are stranger forces still at work in this enigmatic part of Chicago?

PRIDE AND PROGRESS

In March 1837, Chicago was still riding the wave of new arrivals and real estate booms that began in the late 1820's. On March 4, the Illinois Legislature passed an act that officially incorporated the city of Chicago to include a total area of about ten square miles. The first city election as held on May 2 and William B. Ogden was chosen as mayor, soundly defeating John H. Kinzie, the son of the early settler. A census was taken just two months later and at that time, Chicago boasted a population of 4,170 people and more than 500 buildings, including a court house, a jail, a fire engine house, almost 400 homes and dwellings, nearly 80 stores, 10 taverns and five churches.

In those days, most of the businesses and the homes of the city's most important families were on Lake and Water Streets between State and Franklin, as well as on a few streets running north and south from the river. The majority of the city though was still mostly a muddy mess, the result of having been built on such marshy ground. This did not deter the people of the city though, who stated that within the next two decades, Chicago would rank alongside other great American cities like New York and Philadelphia.

Unfortunately though, the banking panic and the Depression of 1837 brought Chicago's dreams to a temporary halt. By the middle of May, the building and development boom had ended and by June, the economy was in ruins. Lots that had been purchased at ridiculous prices just months before were now worthless and those with titles to huge tracts of land were too poor to pay their bills. The state of Illinois went bankrupt and only Mayor Ogden himself, on the verge of personal financial disaster, kept Chicago from doing the same. He declared that for Chicago to starts its career as a great city by repudiating its debts would be shameful. He suppressed the calls for a widespread moratorium on debts and with an appeal to civic pride, induced the city council to issue $5,000 in scrip, receivable for taxes and carrying an interest rate of one cent per month. The plan was backed by bankers and businessmen and more than served its purpose. Using this paper money, personal I.O.U.'s, certificates issued by banks and trade tickets that were given out by stores, Chicago was able to transact what little business there was and also kept the city's credit from being destroyed. In addition, almost every resident in the city planted a garden to raise at least a portion of the food that he was no longer able to buy. Within a year, Chicago had taken on the appearance of a huge vegetable patch with whole blocks being covered by potatoes, onions, peas and corn. Locally, the city was nicknamed the "Garden City" but to people who lived outside of the region, it was still the "Mud Hole of the Prairie".

For a number of years, Chicago was a wasteland and business and industry were stagnant during the entire period. Thousands of immigrants continued to pass through its muddy streets en route to the farmlands of the Northwest but there was nothing in the city to hold them here. The population simply refused to increase until the 1840's when Chicago began to stir once again. Real estate prices slowly began to rise and a few new stores and factories started up. Finally, by the middle 1840's, another boom got under way.

The event that really kicked things off was the first River and Harbor Convention, which was held by John Wentworth, the editor of the *Chicago Democrat* and a member of Congress. In 1847, he impressed about 3,000 delegates from 18 states with Chicago's natural advantages and its potential for greatness. Interest began to revive in the city and later that same year, Cyrus H. McCormick, with the financial support of William B. Ogden, erected the largest factory in Chicago and began manufacturing his famous grain reapers. These devices would not only change American farming methods forever, but would also serve to invigorate the Chicago economy.

In 1848, Ogden also saw an end to two projects with which he had been absorbed for years. One of them was the Lake Michigan-Illinois River Canal, which he had been raising money for almost since its inception. In April of that year, the first vessel was locked through the canal and by April 10, was floating on the lake. The canal was officially opened, to great celebration, on April 16.

On October 25, the first train locomotive, with a tender and two cars, began its first run along a five-mile stretch of the Galena & Chicago Union Railroad tracks. On November 20, the train ran ten miles out to the Des Plaines River and returned to Chicago with a load of grain. Two years after this, the Galena & Chicago had been completed as far as Elgin and in 1854; the first train actually chugged into Galena. Meanwhile, workmen were struggling to complete the Illinois Central line from the south and the Michigan Southern from the east. The first train on the Michigan line arrived in February 1852 to the cheers of the citizens, accompanied by the firing of cannons and the ringing of bells. Three months later, the Michigan Central arrived and by the end of the year, the tracks of the Chicago, Rock Island and Pacific had been laid as far as the Mississippi River.

By 1855, Chicago was the terminus of 10 railroad trunk lines and 11 branch lines. The city had also become the country's greatest meat-packing center and one of the world's greatest grain ports, shipping millions of bushels each year to New York and points beyond. The population had now grown to over 80,000 with hundreds of bustling factories, hundreds of new buildings being erected, gas lights and a land boom that was as spectacular as the one in 1836. The city was no longer sneered at for being the "Mud Hole of the Prairie". As historian Lloyd Lewis wrote, "Chicago had become Chicago."

CHICAGO IN THE CIVIL WAR

In 1860, Chicago was a city firmly entrenched in the ideals of the northern states. For all of its rowdy nightlife, gambling and crime, it was loyal to the Union and in the South was sneered at as "Abolitionist Chicago". Among its other drawbacks, a number of lines of the Underground Railroad, which moved many runaway slaves into Canada, terminated in Chicago. By the beginning of the 1860's, there were at least 1,500 free blacks in the city and at least 20 new escaped slaves arrived each day and were aided by Chicago abolitionists, who put them across the border. As one might imagine, this did nothing to endear the city to those in the south and in 1860, perhaps the most crushing blow was administered to the southern states with the nomination of Abraham Lincoln as the Republican candidate for president in the upcoming election.

But Lincoln's nomination almost did not come about and there are many who are still pondering the mystery as to how a minor contender in the presidential race managed to achieve a sweeping victory with the third nomination ballot. The convention was held at Chicago's "Wigwam" in May 1860 and Lincoln's supporters, who had fashioned the man with the image of the backwoods rail-splitter, were thrilled with the event was held in Chicago. The city was not far from being a frontier town itself and Lincoln had many friends and much newspaper support on the Illinois prairie.

The Republicans were holding what was only their second national convention and for the first time, had a chance to usher one of their candidates into power. The dominant Democratic Party was split over the issue of extending slavery into the territories and their divided vote gave the Republicans hope. Coming into Chicago, the favorite to win the nomination was New York senator William H. Seward and his supporters and delegates were so assured of his victory that they focused more on his choice of running mate than on his actual nomination.

The convention opened on the morning of Wednesday, May 16 and over 10,000 people packed into the Wigwam, while an additional 20,000 stood outside. Four years earlier, in Philadelphia, the Republicans had drawn no more than 4,000 people to their convention. The meeting was called to order and was followed by a stirring address from David Wilmot of Pennsylvania. After that, the remainder of the day was spent electing a chairman and constructing a platform. The platform was adopted and modified on Thursday, with the first ballot scheduled for later that evening. Many expected Seward to be chosen by a landslide, so a chorus of groans greeted Chairman George Ashmun when he announced that the printers had failed to deliver the tally sheets. Since no vote could be taken, a motion was adopted to adjourn until Friday.

Lincoln's campaign manager, David Davis, was thrilled. He and his compatriots, who included Lincoln's long-time friends Ward Hill Lamon, William H. Herndon and Stephen T. Logan, saw the delay as a sign from God. Led by Lamon, a number of Lincoln's friends began scrawling the names of convention officers on admission tickets while Norman B. Judd, a railroad attorney, arranged for special trains to bring more Lincoln supporters to the city.

While Lincoln's men worked behind the scenes, Seward's followers publicly declared their man the winner and even put a brass band into the streets on Friday morning. They marched from their hotel to discover that the Wigwam was so crowded that few people other than delegates were able to find seats. Bogus tickets that had been passed out by Lincoln's men had been used so well that the hall was now packed with supporters of Lincoln.

The first roll call of the states gave Seward 173.5 votes, but 236 were needed to win. Lincoln followed with 102 votes, with Simon Cameron of Pennsylvania, Salmon P. Chase of Ohio and Edward Bates of Missouri each receiving about 50 votes. Recognizing that Pennsylvania would be crucial in winning the nomination, David Davis arranged for delegates of the state to be seated between Illinois and Indiana, which both strongly backed Lincoln. He then convinced the delegates from Pennsylvania that if Seward won the nomination, the party would lose the election. As a result, Cameron withdrew.

When the second ballot was tallied, it offered a stunning surprise, especially to the supporters of Seward. Their candidate had only gained 11 votes but Lincoln's total had increased by 79. That left Chase of Ohio on third place with 42.5 votes.

Workers in the Lincoln campaign had been busy contacting delegates from every state, using a deceptively simple strategy. Instead of asking for votes on the first ballot, they persuaded as many men as possible to make Lincoln their second choice. They also stressed the contrast between Lincoln and Seward. Lincoln had been guarded in his campaign so far and had been careful not to offend anyone. Seward meanwhile, had made his position clear on most national issues. Seward was the only nationally known Republican who had allegedly praised John Brown's recent attack on Harper's Ferry and had hinted at a civil war by warning that an "irrepressible conflict" seemed to be coming because of slavery. Lincoln, on the other hand, was on record as opposing the extension of slavery into the territories but he also underscored the conviction that slavery where it existed was lawful and that it should not be challenged. He believed that the institution would die out on its own.

It was obvious that there was a sharp contrast between the familiar candidate with often controversial views and the little known rival who was not nearly as well known or so eager to enter into war, but the contrast was not enough to allow Lincoln to win on just those merits. Lincoln's managers seemed to be willing to promise almost anything to those who would back him. Legend has it that Lincoln sent a telegram to Davis from Springfield that instructed him to make no bargains. "Make no contracts that bind me," Lincoln allegedly wrote and it has been said that Davis used that message to show to those who hesitated in backing Lincoln that the candidate was not offering positions in his administration with a free hand. Legend tells otherwise though and stories have since been told that Davis managed to persuade delegates to abandon their favorite candidates with promises of positions in Lincoln's cabinet.

Whatever happened in Chicago's smoke-filled rooms remains a mystery though. What we do know is that when the third ballot was taken, Seward had lost 4.5 votes and now needed 56 to win. Lincoln however had gained 53.5 votes and was within 1.5 votes of the nomination. The interior of the Wigwam became nearly deafening with the mingled shouts, cries and laughter of the assembled party. And as soon as he could be heard above the commotion, David K. Carter of Ohio jumped up and shouted that five of the delegates from the Buckeye State wanted to switch their votes over to Lincoln! When the commotion subsided again, other states began to call for Lincoln as their new nomination. After all of the 466 votes had been cast, Lincoln had 364 of them -- 128 more than the number he needed to win!

But how did Lincoln manage to pull of such a sweeping victory? Did his campaign managers really trade positions for votes? No one knows and nothing was ever documented that said for sure either way. Journalist Charles H. Ray, a member of Lincoln's inner circle, later said that the managers promised Indiana and Pennsylvania anything and everything they asked for. Carter of Ohio, who started the dramatic third-ballot uprising, is said to have been promised a high level cabinet position and while other rumors abound, nothing has ever been proven.

One thing is clear though. Many who stepped aside for Lincoln, or who worked for him behind the scenes, were chosen for important posts. Seward was made secretary of state; Chase received the Treasury Department portfolio; Cameron became secretary of war and the fourth contender for the nomination, Edward Bates, became Lincoln's attorney general. David Davis had hoped to become a federal judge and was appointed to the U.S. Supreme Court in 1862. Ward Hill Lamon, who created all of the bogus tickets, became marshal of the District of Columbia. William P. Dole, who was credited with securing the Indiana and Pennsylvania votes, was named commissioner of Indian Affairs. And the list went on...

Not surprisingly, there have been those who went on to ponder that if any backroom dealing did occur with the nomination, then it was especially fitting that it took place in Chicago! For no city in America has gained as great a reputation for voting shenanigans than the Windy City has, as we'll be exploring later in the chapter.

Chicago responded immediately when war broke out between the north and the south in April 1861. War fever ran high in the city and businessmen quickly saw profits from the spending of soldier's pay, as did the criminal element, which operated the brothels, gambling parlors and saloons. Men and boys from all over the Chicago region quickly came to the defense of the Union. In the first ten weeks after the start of the war, 38 companies were formed and 35,000 men enlisted. All sorts of uniforms were designed and men from every class and culture joined up to fight the Confederacy. The local Jewish community raised their own company, as did the Germans, and prepared to fight side by side with both farmers and city dwellers.

In 1860, Lincoln had lost most of the Irish vote in the city to Stephen Douglas, as the little senator had spoken out against bigots who wanted to "protect their jobs" from immigrants. The Irish were discriminated against as a lower class of citizens. "Hit him again, he's Irish" was a popular Chicago saying and signs reading *No Irish Need Apply* were often found by those seeking work. But when President Lincoln's call came to preserve the Union, an Irish Brigade was quickly formed in Chicago. Congressman John A. Logan, who ancestors hailed from Ireland, was made the general.

By the time the fighting actually began, the state of Illinois had over 73,000 men in service and by the time it all ended, at least 231, 000 had answered the call to arms. Few men were ever drafted in Chicago, although many of the wealthier citizens hired substitutes. Chicago had a population of 100,000 at the start of the war and yet sent 15,000 men to war. Only 58 of these men were drafted. By war's end, every third man in the city had enlisted in the military.

The Civil War was a boom time for Chicago, gaining nearly 70,000 residents during the four years of conflict. The city saw much excitement during the war with the drinking, rioting, burning of saloons, shooting of gamblers and wrecking of whorehouses. But even these activities hardly compared with the wild speculation in land, the shipments of prairie grain and the deals negotiated for southern cotton that had been smuggled over enemy lines. The tavern owners, criminals and shysters all speculated and made enormous amounts of money. Even the bakers, meat packers and solid citizens made money as soldiers died on the distant battlefields. Men who had come to Chicago with nothing were soon driving splendid carriages and living in new homes. Jobs were plentiful and Canadians swarmed across the border to find higher wartime pay. By the end of the war, the population of the city had increased by huge percentages but real estate values had risen even more. By 1863, Chicago had grown to the point that another 24 square miles were added to the city limits. Over 6,000 new buildings were constructed during the war and the overworked railroads hauled hogs, steers and grain into the city with record numbers of box cars.

But the railroads brought other things as well, like drifters, vagrants, lawbreakers, hoodlums, whores and no-good types who were looking for a lucky break. These confidence men, counterfeiters, pickpockets and thieves joined the outlaws and killers who already roamed the Chicago streets. Now, these new arrivals were also looking for their share of the pie. As a result, crime took over entire districts of the city, creating a problem that would plague the city for many decades to come.

EIGHTY ACRES OF HELL

The misery of the Civil War's prison camps came to Chicago in February 1862 when a training camp for Federal soldiers was converted into place of brutal misery for Confederate prisoners. Rumors of crowded and unhealthy conditions, along with death and disease, were widely circulated in the southern press during the war. The camp soon earned what many people would consider a fitting nickname -- "Eighty Acres of Hell".

A sketch of Camp Douglas that was done after the war in 1866.

Camp Douglas was named in honor of Stephen A. Douglas, the famed Illinois legislator and Lincoln rival, who passed away in Chicago in June 1861. Douglas was still well known for his recent Democratic presidential nomination, which he had lost to Lincoln the year before, as well as his previous 25 years in Illinois politics. During the last years of his life, Douglas and his wife had resided at Okenwald, their south side estate. It was located just east of the present-day intersection of Cottage Grove Avenue and 35th Street. Following Douglas' death, the government took control of his property and constructed a training camp that was named in his honor. The camp enclosed about 60 acres, which were further divided by interior partitions to create compounds of various sizes. Each of the compounds, or squares, was named according to the purpose that it was used for.

Garrison Square, which was about 20 acres in size, was lined on all four sides by the officer's quarters and the enlisted men's barracks and had a flat parade ground in the center. Hospital Square was about 10 acres in size and served as a medical facility. Whiteoak Square, which was another 10 acres, originally served as the post's prison. When orders were received to prepare the camp for Confederate prisoners, Whiteoak was merged with portions of other squares, creating Prison Square, a compound of 20 acres.

In the early months of the war, the outpost trained thousands of Union troops under the command of General Joseph H. Tucker. Soon, however, the camp became a place of misery for the Confederate prisoners. The camp received its first prisoners in February 1862, after the Battle of Fort Donelson, and soon overcrowding, starvation, scurvy and a complete lack of medical attention made the place into a living hell. The death toll for the camp, during the last three years of the war, has been estimated at as many as 6,129 men, which is slightly less than one-third of the entire prison population at the camp. Most perished from scurvy and smallpox, despite the best intentions of relief workers, who organized a fund to care for the men in 1862. In 1864 alone, 1,156 inmates died at the camp.

While many left the camp as corpses, others managed to escape. In November 1863, 75 very ragged prisoners managed to tunnel their way beneath the walls. In response, eight companies of the Veteran Reserve Corps and a regiment of Michigan sharpshooters were ordered to the camp for additional protection. There were no more tunnels dug out of the camp.

To make matters worse, a great fear of insurrection at the camp concerned Chicago city officials. The city was filled with "copperheads", spies and southern sympathizers, who might do anything to arm the prisoners at the camp. The compound was only guarded by 450 Union enlisted men and officers. This was not a number large enough to make most Chicago citizens feel safe. Somehow though, the camp managed to make it through the war without serious incident and it was closed down in the summer of 1865. The remaining prisoners were asked to take a loyalty oath to the United States and then set free. For a short time, the post was used as a rendezvous point for returning Federal troops, but by fall, it was deserted. In November, the government sold the property and Camp Douglas ceased to exist. The remaining buildings were demolished a short time later.

Today, the Lake Meadows condominiums are located on the site and a short distance away is a monument to Stephen Douglas that is located on the remains of Okenwald. The burial crypt is located between Lake Park Avenue and the Illinois Central Railroad tracks. The tomb was not completed until 1881 because of the failure to produce backers who would give private funds for its completion. The tomb was eventually funded by the state of Illinois and, as Richard Lindberg in his book *Return to the Scene of the Crime* notes... "the monument is the last visible reminder of Chicago's hidden role in the War Between the States".

THE GREAT CHICAGO FIRE

According to the legend, the Great Chicago Fire was started by a cow that belonged to an Irishwoman named Catherine O'Leary. She ran a neighborhood milk business from the barn behind her home. She carelessly left a kerosene lantern in the barn after her evening milking and a cow kicked over it over and ignited the hay on the floor. Of course, no proof of this story has ever been offered, other than the testimony of a neighborhood liar, but the legend took hold in Chicago and was told around the world. Regardless of how the fire started though, on Sunday evening, October 8, 1871, Chicago became a city in flames.

Mrs. O'Leary's Mythical Lantern

In 1871, Chicago was truly a boom town. It had become one of the fastest growing cities in America during the Civil War and because of this, construction standards had been "loose" to say the least. Beyond the downtown area, the city was miles and miles of rickety wooden structures. Most of the working-class neighborhoods consisted of wooden cottages and tenement houses, all of which made for dangerous fuel in the event of a fire. However, Chicago was not a wooden "shantytown", although even the downtown hotels, banks, theaters and stores needed constant repair. Just a month before the Great Fire, the *Chicago Tribune* had remarked on the shabby construction of the brick and stone downtown buildings. The newspaper warned that they were weak and seemed to be falling apart and mentioned that hardly a week passed when some stone facade or cornice was not falling into the street, narrowly missing the skull of some hapless pedestrian.

And, they said, if the city didn't fall down, it was liable to burn! "The absence of rain for three weeks," reported the newspaper, "has left everything in so flammable a condition that a spark might set a fire that would sweep from end to end of the city".

Although ignoring the legend of the O'Leary cow, the Great Chicago Fire did break out in the vicinity of the O'Leary home at 137 De Koven Street on the west side. The home and barn were located in what was then called the "West Division", an area of the city that was west of the south branch of the river. Whether the cow kicked over the lantern or not, conditions were perfect for a fire. The summer had been dry and less than three inches of rain had fallen between July and October.

There had been other fires in the city already. On the previous day, October 7, four blocks of the city had burned. This conflagration was said to have left the fire department so exhausted that they were slow to respond to another alarm at De Koven Street. By the time they arrived, it was already too late. By 10:30 that evening, it was reported that the fire was officially out of control. A strong, dry wind from the southwest made matters even worse, blowing the fire toward the very heart of the city. In what seemed like minutes, mills and factories along the river were on fire. Additional buildings, hit by fiery missiles from the main blaze, also began burning from top to bottom. The air was filled with sparks and cinders that contemporary accounts described as looking like "red rain".

In just over an hour, the west side of the city was in ashes and the fire showed no signs of slowing down. It hungrily jumped the Chicago River and pushed toward the center of the city. Among the first buildings to be engulfed was the new Parmalee Omnibus and Stage Company at the southeast corner of Jackson and Franklin Streets. A flying brand also struck the South Side Gas Works and soon this structure burst into flames, creating a new and larger center for the fire. At this point, even the grease and oil-covered river caught fire and the surface of the water shimmered with heat and flames.

In moments, the fire also spread to the banks and office buildings along LaSalle Street. Soon, the inferno became impossible to battle with more than a dozen different locations burning at once. The fire swept through Wells, Market and Franklin Streets, igniting more than 500 different buildings. One by one, these great structures fell. The Tribune building, long vaunted as "fire proof", was turned into a smoking ruin as was Marshall Field's grand department store, along with hundreds of other businesses.

Many of the great hotels, like the Palmer House and the Sherman, were reduced to blazing ash. The Grand Pacific Hotel, which had just been completed and was not yet open, crashed down in flames. Another new hotel, the Bigelow, with its art gallery, Turkish carpets and carved wood furniture, was also consumed. The Tremont House burned for the fourth time in its history and the manager, John Drake, left the place in a hurry, carrying the contents of the hotel safe in a pillowcase. Unshaken though, Drake passed by the Avenue Hotel on Congress Street and noting that it was untouched by fire, entered and approached the distracted owner with a startling offer to buy the place, right then and there with $1,000 from the Tremont's safe as a down payment. The deal was made and a hasty bill of sale was written, witnessed by fleeing guests. Drake then departed and went home with his pillowcase full of silver. He knew that he had an even chance of being a hotel owner the next morning. As it turned out, the Avenue Hotel survived but Drake had to insist on his ownership rights with a pistol.

In the early morning hours of Monday, the fire reached the courthouse, which stood in a block surrounded by LaSalle, Clark, Randolph and Washington Streets. A burning timber landed on the building's wooden cupola and the soon turned into a fire that blazed out of control. The building was ordered evacuated. The prisoners, who had begun to scream and shake the bars of their cells as smoke filled the air, were released. Most of them were allowed to simply go free but the most dangerous of them were shackled and taken away under guard. Just after 2:00 AM, the bell of the courthouse tolled for the last time and it crashed through the remains of the building to the ground beneath it. The roaring sound made by the building's collapse was reportedly heard more than a mile away.

Around this same time, the State Street Bridge, leading to the north side, also caught fire and soon the inferno began to devour the area on the north side of the river as well. Soon, stables, warehouse and breweries were also burning. The lumber mills and wood storage yards on the riverbanks were eaten by the fire and many people who were dunking themselves in the water had to flee again to keep from being strangled by the black smoke. Some people threw chairs and sofas into the river and sat with just their heads and shoulders in sight. Many of them stayed in the river for up to 14 hours.

Then, the fire swept into the luxurious residential district surrounding Cass, Huron, Ontario, Rush and Dearborn Streets. Here, stood the mansions of some of Chicago's oldest and most prominent families. By daylight, these beautiful homes were nothing but ruins. The servants of the rich desperately buried the contents of the mansions in hidden places on the grounds. Oddly enough, at least a dozen pianos were later found buried in gardens. Also discovered were family silver collections that, even when buried, had melted into twisted masses.

Members of the Chicago Club, the expensive enclave of the rich, never dreamed that the fire would dare to affect them. Many of them had breakfast while the city burned and they toasted their defiance of the fire. The building burned though, almost as the men lifted their glasses, and they ran for their lives, after having stuffed their coats with wine bottles from the best year's vintages and fine Havana cigars. The club's celebrated red satin lobby sofas were carried in grand fashion down to the lake.

Lincoln Park became one of the macabre locations during the fire as it served as a gathering place for uprooted families and fleeing fire victims. Old graves in the burial ground were in the process of being moved during the fire and now the opened pits and the haphazardly stacked tombstones were being used to sheltered huddled masses of adults and children.

The Chicago Water Tower & Pumping Stations in 1869 (Chicago Historical Society)

By 3:00 a.m. that morning, the pumps at the Waterworks on Pine Street had been destroyed and by Monday evening, the only intact structure for blocks was the gothic stone Water Tower. Somehow, it managed to survive the devastation. Legend has it that this structure is haunted today by the ghost of a man who stayed on the job during the fire, continuing to pump the water as the fire got closer. The story goes that this heroic city worker waited until the last possible minute and then took his own life rather than be engulfed in the flames. His ghost has reportedly been seen hanging through an upper window of the tower.

The flames were not the only thing that residents of the city had to worry about either. In the early hours of the fire, looting and violence had broken out in the city. Saloon keepers, hoping that it might prevent their taverns from being destroyed, had foolishly rolled barrels of whiskey out into the streets. Soon, men and women from all classes were staggering in the streets, thoroughly intoxicated. The drunks and the looters did not comprehend the danger they were in however and many were trampled in the streets. Plundered goods were also tossed aside and were lost in the fire, abandoned by the looters as the fire drew near. Although many were injured, the stories of lawlessness were greatly exaggerated in later accounts. They were overblown into stories of lynchings and murders by "villainous Negroes" and Irishmen. These tales were proved to be absolutely false.

Worse perhaps than the looters were the drivers of wagons and carts who charged outrageous prices to haul away household possessions and baggage. This only added to the misery of the fleeing people and compounded the chaos. In his book, *City of the Century*, author Donald L. Miller described the scene as the streets thronged with people; crying children searched for their parents; processions of refugees milled everywhere; wealthy ladies panicked, wearing all of the jewelry they owned; immigrant women ran, carrying mattresses on their heads; half-naked prostitutes scurried from rented "cribs" on Wells and Clark Streets; people carried the sick and the crippled on chairs or on makeshift litters; even the bodies of the dead were transported in coffins or wrapped in bed sheets -- It combined to create a vision that most of us cannot even imagine today.

Thankfully, the fire began to die on the morning of October 10, when steady and soaking rains began to fall on Chicago. According to the records, the last house in Chicago to burn was a doctor's residence on Fullerton Street. The fire started around 10:30 p.m. but rain began to fall around midnight, turning the blaze into nothing more than cherry red coals just before dawn.

The Great Fire, as it was called from then on, was to be the most disastrous event in America until the San Francisco earthquake and fire of 1906. The people of the city were devastated, as was the city itself. Over 300 people were dead but many more were never reported or their bodies were never found. Another 100,000 people were without homes or shelter. The fire had cut a swath through the city that was four miles long and about two-thirds of a mile wide. Over $200 million in property had been destroyed. Records, deeds, archives, libraries and priceless artwork were all lost although a little of it had survived in public and private vaults. In the destruction of the Federal Building, which, among other things, housed the post office, more than $100,000 in currency was burned.

Chicago had become a blasted and charred wasteland.

In the first days after the fire, wild rumors flew about more looting in the city. It was said that criminals were now breaking into safes and vaults in the ruined business district. Local business owners hired Allan Pinkerton to deploy his detectives around the remains of stores and banks and soon, six companies of Federal troops were deployed under the command of General Phillip Sheridan to assist in maintaining order. Two days later, Chicago's Mayor, Roswell Mason, placed the city under martial law, entrusting Sheridan and his troops to watch over it.

Although Sheridan saw no sign of the reported murders and looting, he did recruit a volunteer home guard of about 1,000 men to patrol unburned areas of the city. He also enforced a curfew, much to the chagrin of Illinois governor John M. Palmer, who felt that martial law was uncalled for and unnecessary. Mayor Mason was heavily influenced by local business leaders however and ignored Palmer's order to withdraw the troops. The state of martial law didn't last for long though. A few days after it went into effect, a local businessman (and one of those responsible for pushing Mason into enacting martial law) was accidentally killed by one of the volunteer home guard. In spite of this, Sheridan did receive orders from President Grant that left four companies of men on active duty in the city through the end of the year.

As terrible as the disaster was, Chicago was not dead, but merely shaken and stunned. Within days of the fire, rebuilding began on a grand scale. The vigor of the city's rebirth amazed the rest of the nation and within three years, it once again dominated the western United States. It soared from the ashes like the fable phoenix and became the home of the first skyscraper in 1885, then passed the one million mark in population five years later. The Great Chicago Fire was the beginning of a new metropolis, much greater than it could have ever become if the horrific fire had never happened at all.

CHICAGO BUSINESS - RIOT & UNREST

In the years after the Great Fire, wealth and prosperity returned to Chicago. According to many reformers and activists though, that wealth remained in the hands of the privileged few. These included men like Marshall Field, Potter Palmer, George Pullman, Cyrus McCormick and others, most of whom had made fortunes in the city even before the fire and the Civil War.

Marshall Field is a Chicago icon and is known as the founder of America's greatest mercantile firm, Marshall Field & Company. Renowned in his day as the "Merchant Prince", Field was then commonly regarded as one of the richest men in the world. After his death in 1905, Field's estate was estimated at over $100 million, according to one authority, and much of it consisted of Chicago real estate. And while he made a fortune from the city of Chicago, he also gave much of it back, including the lake-front museum that was established and named in his honor. He was also largely responsible for the founding of the Art Institute and laid the groundwork for the University of Chicago.

Field came to Chicago in 1856 and went to work as a clerk in a dry goods store with a salary of $400 per year, half of which he saved. A pioneer of new merchandising methods, he went on to coin the ultimate customer service slogan of "Give the Lady What She Wants". He and a partner, Levi Z. Leiter, purchased Potter Palmer's store in 1865 and it became Marshall Field and Company. Even before becoming the premiere dry goods merchant in the country though, he looked for other ways to make money and discovered real estate investment. He was known for being an affable, serious, mild-looking man and was well-liked, even though he never praised his employees and paid them low wages -- never a cent more than he had agreed to pay them, no matter how well they performed. Thanks to this, he did not keep partners for long. At each year's end, he held a dinner in his house for partners and members of the upper management. Over after-dinner brandy, he would make simple announcements to the assembled group as to which of them would not be celebrating the holidays with the company the following year. If an employee had not measured up, he would no longer be required by Marshall Field and Company.

In 1876, Field constructed a luxurious mansion with a prestigious address on Prairie Street. The house cost over $2 million to build and was the first home in Chicago to have electric lights. Field lived here with his wife, the former Nannie Scott of Ironton, Ohio, and she became known as the social queen of the city. Here, the Field's reared their son, Marshall Field, Jr. and their daughter, Ethel. The family entertained both famous and infamous American and European personages and held many notable parties and balls. Perhaps the most noted event was staged in January 1886 and the party was held in honor of the two Field children. More than 500 guests were present and as Gilbert and Sullivan's operetta *Mikado* was then all the rage in the fashionable world, the Field event was designated as a "Mikado Ball". Wealthy children and their parents attended the party in colorful, Oriental costumes and their carriages passed beneath special calcium lights that had been erected for the evening. The ball was said to have cost $75,000 and it was talked about for years afterward.

But not everything connected to the Marshall Field family was bright and filled with joy -- and the Mikado Ball was certainly not the only thing spoken of in the city for years after it took place.

In 1890, Marshall Field, Jr. married a young woman named Albertine Huck and with his father's help, purchased a Prairie Street home just a few doors down from the family mansion. The house had commonly been known in the neighborhood as the William H. Murray House and while it is boarded up and shuttered today, it loomed for many years as a beautiful Queen Anne mansion that held its own with the other architectural wonders on the street.

The Field's lived happily in the house for a number of years, entertaining and welcoming only the best people on the Chicago social register. However, tragedy came to call at the Field mansion on November 22, 1905. Just before dinner that evening, Marshall Field, Jr. fired a bullet into his left side while he was seated in his dressing room. According to the newspapers, the gunshot had been a tragic accident. Field had been examining a loaded revolver in anticipation of an upcoming hunting trip to Wisconsin when the gun went off. It was said that it had accidentally discharged and had inflicted a wound that would eventually prove fatal. Rumors around town told a different story though...

According to the stories, Field had actually been shot by a whore in one of Chicago's most fashionable brothels (the Everleigh Club is usually mentioned) and that his body was then smuggled home to avoid scandal. He was later found in his room "having had an accident while cleaning his gun". But if there was ever any evidence of this having actually happened, it has since vanished.

The police were summoned to the house and the servants were closely questioned but no one had witnessed the shooting and Mrs. Field had been away for the afternoon. The parents of the critically wounded man were vacationing in New York at the time. Satisfied with the "cleaning the gun" story, the police looked no further into the incident.

Marshall Field, Jr. died on November 27, 1905 and a private wake was held in his home. He was buried at Graceland Cemetery and was soon joined there by his father. On January 16, 1906, the "Merchant Prince", still mourning his son, died from complications of pneumonia and old age. Not long afterward, the younger Field's widow disposed of the house where he died and battered by time, it has deteriorated ever since. No shadow remains of the home's former glory.

In an earlier section of this chapter, the strange origins of Streeterville were revealed and readers couldn't help but notice the inclusion of the name Potter Palmer as one of the chief rivals of eccentric Cap Streeter. Potter Palmer was another of Chicago's industrial pioneers, shaping more of the city that most of us can begin to imagine today. He is best recalled for his wonderful hotel, the Palmer House, which continues to provide luxurious accommodations in the city today.

Palmer had good reason to object to the bizarre homesteading that was accomplished by Cap Streeter along Lake Michigan. No man had worked harder to develop the portion of the city that followed the northbound edge of the lake.

A section of the State Street shopping district -- literally created by Potter Palmer (Chicago Historical Society)

He had been a daring merchant in the 1850's, who had sold out to Marshal Field, and who had shocked Chicago in 1865 when he retired from business on the advice of his doctor. He then left for Europe and New York City and the quiet bachelor learned to enjoy his money before returning to Chicago in 1868. Shortly after he came back, he helped to build a baseball park for the Chicago White Stockings, the city's most successful team, and embarked on a new business plan -- one that was so secret that even his closest friends had no idea what he was up to. Palmer's plan was to move the city's main commercial district from Lake Street, which ran east and west, to State Street, which ran north and south and parallel with the lake -- the way Chicago's downtown still runs today. Chicago only learned of his plan when he approached the city council with a request to widen State Street, where, he explained, he had quietly bought almost a mile of frontage.

The council told him that the idea of moving the business district was ridiculous. State Street, which had once been Hubbard's Trail, was little more than a muddy alley, narrow and lined with pawn shops, saloons and boarding houses. Merchants on Lake Street also fought the proposed street widening, as did property owners on State Street, who did not want to have to move their present buildings back. But Palmer was absolutely fixed on the idea and he pushed the bill through the city council without ever resorting to threats or bribery. He was simply a very determined man and he was able to accomplish just about anything that he set his mind to.

But all did not go smoothly. Many of the owners of older buildings along State Street decided to ignore the ordinance and refused to move their buildings. Palmer simply bypassed them, tearing down the old structures that he had purchased along the street and erecting handsome new stores and business buildings. He placed all of them on the new building line so there would be plenty of parking space for the carriage trade and space also for the tracks of additional trolleys. Until all of the main streets were widened to a standard width after the Great Fire, State Street, with its irregular building line, was one of the strangest looking streets in the city. Soon, Lake Street merchants began moving into Palmer's new buildings, despite the higher rents, so that their business rivals could not take possession of the "splendid quarters".

In the summer of 1870, Potter Palmer surprised Chicago again by announcing his engagement to beautiful socialite Bertha Honore, the daughter of the late real estate magnate, H.H. Honore of Louisville, Kentucky. She was 21 years-old at the time of their engagement and Palmer was 44. The two of them had met eight years earlier when Bertha was shopping in Palmer's Lake Street store with her mother. Bertha would become known as an outspoken feminist, the grande dame of Chicago society and later, the official hostess of the World's Columbian Exposition. She would likely be better known to the country than her husband, who returned to his quiet ways after their marriage. At the time of her engagement though, Bertha was more than satisfied to have a loving husband and to be the wife of an "innkeeper".

The "inn" in question was the much praised Palmer House, which was just nearing completion on State Street. The hotel was designed to be Palmer's wedding present to his wife. Even by Chicago standards, a city that was used to extravagant hotels, it was an impressive place. It was eight stories tall and boasted 225 rooms, making it one of the largest hotels in the country. It was decorated with expensive marble, hand woven rugs and antiques and furniture imported from Europe. And it would be staffed, Palmer had proudly announced, by several hundred uniformed Negroes. The hotel was also billed as the only fireproof hotel in America, with alarms in every room, fire hoses on every floor and a large water tank on the roof. Unfortunately, the hotel would prove these claims to be untrue during the inferno of 1871.

In the years after the Great Fire, Chicagoans would date their past with two simple phrases - "before the fire" or "after the fire". The city's history would be written by the Great Fire as both a major dividing point and a transforming event. A new and modern city had been built on the scorched ruins of what was little more than a western boom town. Many tremendous changes came to Chicago "after the fire" and Potter Palmer was responsible for at least one more of them.

In addition to his creation of the new State Street shopping district, Palmer was also the creator of the lavish residential district known as the "Gold Coast". As mentioned already, Palmer was a determined man and he dreamed up an idea of turning the low, treacherous dunes of the lakeside into a housing area for the privileged members of Chicago society. The project was helped by the ambitions of the Lincoln Park commissioners, who were in the early stages of developing Lake Shore Drive. Palmer quitclaimed the land where the drive would run and the park commissioners, who controlled the eastern strip of land, quitclaimed a portion of their property to Palmer. The land itself was then developed by bringing in soil and fill to level out the area. Much of it came from a great distance so that no marsh soil would be included, which was thought to cause malaria. The property was then parceled out to purchasers, who began constructing new homes. The quiet thoroughfare, shaded by rows of trees, paralleled the lake for almost a half mile before reaching Lincoln Park. It was an ideal residential street, fronting an inland sea, and was lined by solid, handsome dwellings and strong iron fences. These dwellings awed visitors for decades and still manage to amaze many of us today.

Just a short time before old Cap Streeter wrecked himself on the Lake Michigan beach, Potter Palmer himself constructed a huge dwelling that captured the imagination of Chicagoans and strangers alike. The Palmer house has long been referred to as a "castle" and it was certainly designed to look the part with imposing heights and battlements that would more befit a medieval fortress than a Chicago residence. The house was designed and built (depending on accounts) in either 1882 or 1885 by prominent architects Henry Ives Cobb and Charles Sumner Frost. The style was "English Gothic" with square windows and was allowed to be covered with ivy, thus securing the look of a British manor house.

The house was built at a cost of nearly $1 million and almost instantly became the showplace of the city. During the 1893 World's Columbian Exposition, it was one of the leading sights for tourists, outside of the fairgrounds themselves. It was during this period of time that the stone castle by the lake was at the peak of its glory. Here, Bertha Palmer ruled as the social queen of America's second largest city and as president of the Board of Lady Managers of the World's Fair, she was the dominant figure of all social events at which American and European celebrities were entertained. Guests included Presidents Grant and McKinley, the Infanta Eulalia of Spain, the Duke and Duchess of Veragua (the duke was a descendant of Columbus), various Russian princes and princesses and many other leaders of the era.

In the years that followed the fair, the house continued to be the social center of Chicago and Mrs. Palmer also maintained homes in both Paris and London. She remained a resident in the house until her death in 1918. Potter Palmer himself died in 1902 and with his passing, a great era in Chicago history came to an end. And whether beloved or hated, it cannot be denied that he left a permanent mark on the history of the city.

Charles Tyson Yerkes came to Chicago in the 1880's for no other reason than to pillage the growing city. The street transit mogul began his business empire at the age of eight when he borrowed $18 from his father and made a deal with a local grocer to sell a certain soap to the grocery at nine cents a pound. Yerkes bought the soap at six cents a pound and started his fortune.

Yerkes was born in Philadelphia as the son of a bank president and left home at 15 to work as an office boy in a grain commission house. He started his own stock brokerage at 22, went into banking three years later and by 34, was in prison. A panic at the Philadelphia stock exchange -- started by market confusion in the aftermath of the Chicago Fire -- found him overextended and unable to deliver the money that he had received from selling City of Philadelphia securities. He was pardoned after seven months and after speculating successfully during the Panic of 1873, he seized control of Philadelphia's Continental Passenger Railway Company. With his profits, he paid off his criminal shortfall to the city, even though the city council had already forgiven his debt.

Within a few years, Yerkes found himself divorced and he relocated to Fargo, North Dakota. He remarried but found that small town life did not suit him. In 1881, he and his wife, with just $40,000 of his own capital, moved to Chicago. Thanks to connections that he maintained in Philadelphia, he managed to establish credentials with the local financial community. After some initial ventures into gas and electricity stocks, he took an option on the North Chicago Street Railway. A year later, he also acquired the West Division Railway Company and his object became clear: he planned to gain a monopoly of all Chicago transit.

Yerkes devoted the next 12 years to his plan, starting in 1886. During this time, he irrevocably wrecked the pattern of Chicago mass transit. The service was poor and at rush hours, there were always fewer seats than passengers. Yerkes didn't care though and in fact, relished the idea of the overcrowded cars. "The strap hangers pay the dividends," he explained.

With shrewdness, cunning, the force of his personality and of course, the ever present Chicago methods of bribery and back door political dealing, Yerkes built a tangled maze of companies that managed to finance his business maneuvering so that he had to invest very little capital of his own. Even so, he was always able to rake in millions. Not only did he control the companies that contracted for his projects (which billed at astronomical rates) but he also took kickbacks from the contractors who were hired.

His clever business dealings not only enriched his pocket book, but they also brought about a change in Chicago transit from horse-drawn cars to cable cars and by the middle 1890's, he was introducing trolley systems to the city and building an elevated transit system as well. The downtown branch of the system was called "The Loop", after the smaller streetcar route that had been there earlier.

He built a magnificent Chicago mansion for himself and his wife but they were never admitted to Chicago high society, which rankled the second Mrs. Yerkes. But even though the couple was not acceptable to Bertha Palmer and the rest of the city's elite, this did not prevent the social register husbands from joining Yerkes in his predatory business forays whenever they smelled a profit. Rumor has it that they did so at some peril however -- when dealing with Yerkes it was always advised to keep a close watch on your wife and daughters! His ever roaming eye was yet another thing that bothered his second wife.

The other Chicago titans used Yerkes for a time but in 1896, decided to try and force him into bankruptcy. A number of merchants and bankers, including meatpacker Phillip D. Armour, decided to try and rid the city of him by calling in his loans, for which he had pledged most of his holdings as collateral. But in the eagerness to destroy the man, they never considered that he could retaliate against their banks and business with the strength of the transit system, virtually bringing Chicago to a screeching halt. Yerkes was given a reprieve on the counsel of Marshall Field. "Leave Mr. Yerkes alone," he reportedly told the others, "and he will come to his own end."

Yerkes dealt through any dirty politicians that he could find and bought favors constantly. In fact, his Chicago mansion, his collection of fine jewelry, his racing stable and his art collection (which had been bought in Europe and contained works by the masters) were all assessed for only $7,000 when tax time rolled around. The *Chicago Tribune* called this the "Chicago system of taxation". And it would not be the only time that this newspaper, and others, attacked Yerkes and his business operations. Much of this came from not only disapproval of the way that he did business, but personal animosity as well. Yerkes methods were not so different from other Chicago businessmen but something about the man (perhaps because his connections were all in the East) was just completely unlikable. For his part, Yerkes returned the editor's dislike. On one occasion, after learning that an article was going to be published about his private life, including innuendoes about his wife, he called on the editor of the paper in question. "The publication of this article will hurt me," he allegedly said, "and I shall be down and out. There will be nothing for me to do. But I'll also inform you that if you publish it, I, myself, personally, will kill you for sure! Good morning!" he then added and walked out the door. It should be noted that the article was never published.

Thanks to the newspapers though, Yerkes had the worst reputation of all of Chicago's robber barons. The crusading British journalist W.T. Stead wrote in his 1894 book *If Christ Came to Chicago* "As the man said when asked if the fox had stolen the goose, 'I would not like to say what I cannot prove, but I saw a good many feathers around his nose when he left the yard'. Mr. Yerkes' nose is well-feathered, indeed."

Thanks to money that was spread throughout the Chicago city council and the state legislature in Springfield, Yerkes was given 12 transit renewals that would have permitted him use of the streets of Chicago for the next 99 years -- without any sort of payment! Illinois Governor John Peter Altgeld vetoed these bills, in spite of Yerkes' offer of a half-million dollar bribe to sign them. Altgeld's successor, John R. Tanner, was not so principled though and he signed a bill that authorized the city council to extend Yerkes' franchises for another 50 years without payment. But this did not go unnoticed by Yerkes' enemies. Banding together with the usually ineffectual Municipal Voters League, they forced Yerkes to mount an expensive defense of his 50-year bill after the first one was defeated.

Yerkes did everything he could to win the public's trust, including the donation of an electrically lighted fountain in Lincoln Park and the construction of the world's largest refracting telescope (later installed at Yerkes Observatory on Lake Geneva in Wisconsin) but the citizens rallied against him anyway. The Municipal Voter's League posted thousands of placards condemning him throughout the city. The newspapers elaborated on charges that he was using public money for private gain, causing ministers to rail against him from church pulpits and mass meetings to be held, where it was half-seriously proposed that he be hanged. Mayor Carter Harrison Jr., then in his first of five terms, vowed that he would "eat my fedora hat" before he would allow Yerkes to win. When the second bill (for the additional 50 years) reached the city council, a mob carrying guns and nooses marched on City Hall to monitor the voting. Not surprisingly, the bill was soundly defeated.

The vote in 1898 ended Yerkes pillaging of Chicago for good. He gave a stirring farewell speech to his transit workers and then left Chicago after disposing of his personal holdings, which were rumored to have put over $20 million in his pockets. He moved to New York and then to London, where he moved socially in the King's circle and headed the syndicate that dug the London Underground transit system.

Yerkes died, at only age 68, in December 1905 while living sick and alone in New York City hotels. He was estranged from his second wife because of his involvement with a married woman -- and her daughter.

His fortune, which had been worth anywhere between $30 million and $70 million, had dwindled to around $2 million at the time of his death, thanks to lawsuits and bad investments. Most of this went to the lawyers when he was gone.

Although seldom remembered in Chicago today, Yerkes lives on in literary history, as he provided the basis for the character of Frank Cowperwood in Theodore Dreiser's two classic novels, *The Titan* and *The Financier*. Yerkes' style lived on in the city for years after his departure as well. His reckless and open manipulation of the system, through bribery and swindles, was a precursor to the gangsters who made Chicago their cashbox in the years that followed him. For that reason, Charles Tyson Yerkes should never be forgotten ...

Cyrus Hall McCormick was born in Virginia in 1809 and came to Chicago in 1845 with only $60 in his pocket. He established a factory here to manufacture a mechanical reaper that he devised and within a few years was a millionaire many times over. It would be this same reaper that would change the face of Chicago forever and would also play a major part in the Union victory in the Civil War. The mechanical efficiency of the reaper on the flat farm lands of the Midwest easily accomplished the work of the half million men in uniform who were away from their farms during the harvest season.

McCormick was a stout man of great temper and perhaps even a greater persistence to succeed. He fought his many competitors with constant lawsuits, widespread advertising and yearly field days when his reapers would be pitted against other models, easy credit, good service and a product that was far superior to anything else on the market. Throughout the 1870's, he sold more than 10,000 reapers and binders a year. The money came pouring into his coffers in such substantial amounts that in 1879 he built a fabulous sandstone mansion on Rush Street that was rivaled in the city by only the castle of Potter Palmer. The house was so mammoth that it contained a 200-seat private theater!

McCormick's claim to being the sole inventor of the reaper was always open to question, even by his own family. However, his assembly procedures, his sales methods that put thousands of reapers into fields where wheat would have rotted before and his constant improvements on the machines did make him a pioneer in the industry. Whatever he may have lacked in actual invention, he more than made up for when it came time to put the machinery to work and to get it into the hands of those who could use it.

Even though he was generous to a number of charities and causes in Chicago, including the Presbyterian Theological Seminary (later named in McCormick's honor), he was mostly known for being tight-fisted with a dollar. Once, when charged what he felt was an unjust $8.70 fee for excessive luggage by the railroad, he sued the company and fought the suit in court after court for 18 years, finally winning it in the Supreme Court. When he took his family to dine at the elegant Palmer House, he insisted on a special rate, which Palmer gave to him because he quickly learned that it was not worth the time to argue the matter. In McCormick's later years, when he was crippled with rheumatism, he became even more difficult and would fire household servants on the spot if he felt they were being impertinent.

Needless to say, such tight handling of the coin did not endear him much to his employees. He worked them hard, including his brother, and for low wages. Like all of the other Chicago titans during America's so-called "Gilded Age", he was puzzled when the employees were not grateful for what they were given and was enraged when they dared to ask, and organize, for more. All of the major employers, including McCormick, saw constant unrest among their workers over job conditions, wages and shorter work days. There was no question that conditions in many plants were questionable at best and men worked 10-12 hours, six days a week, for very little pay. Strikes and protests soon became commonplace.

During the tense summer of 1877, when there were riots in the city that were part of a nationwide strike effort by railroad workers protesting wage cuts, Marshall Field volunteered the use of his delivery wagons to transport policemen from one problem area to another. Three men were killed and eight wounded during a demonstration at a Burlington Railroad roundhouse and the next day, ten more strike sympathizers were killed at the Halsted Street viaduct. Federal troops who came directly from fighting

Indians out west were sent in to restore order. The following year, Field, McCormick and others secretly subscribed to a fund that would furnish Gatling guns and uniforms for the Illinois National Guard. This was done, according to McCormick's assistant, to prepare for "what danger if any was to be anticipated from the communistic element in the city".

Strikes and protests continued but the Haymarket Square Riot in 1886 would change the face of the labor movement forever.

THE HAYMARKET SQUARE RIOT

The events that culminated here had been brewing since the end of the Civil War as trade unions began to organize to protect the rights of workers. It should also be pointed out that many of the organizers were blatant socialists and some were not content to merely let strikes and walk-outs speak for them. Many of them endorsed a more violent form of action. That action reached its peak in Haymarket Square, where rural farmers came to exchange produce for cash, in May 1886.

Recent troubles at the McCormick Reaper Works had turned Chicago into a labor battleground. There was trouble simmering in the city, hidden just below the surface, but threatening to boil over. Between the labor agitators and the city business leaders, something volatile was about to happen. Following a strike at the McCormick factory in 1885, Marshall Field had proposed establishing a U.S. military base near the city, since federal troops had already proven during the railroad strikes that they could be effective in maintaining order. The business leaders had previously been using Pinkerton agents to break unions but the idea that the military could be used instead appealed to all of them. With a donation of land on the north shore of Lake Michigan, Fort Highwood (later re-named Fort Sheridan by General Sheridan himself) was established in 1887.

The bombing that occurred in Haymarket Square in 1886 must have assured business leaders that they had made the right decision. On Tuesday evening, May 4, a mass meeting of workers was called to protest police actions against striking employees at the McCormick factory, who were trying to force an eight-hour work day. Six workers had been killed by plant guards and emotions were running high. A crowd of 20,000 had been expected to turn out but a cool rain kept many in. Eventually, about 2,500 tired spectators showed up to hear the speeches by Albert Parsons, Samuel Fielden and August Spies. All three men were considered "dangerous agitators" and "anarchists" by city business leaders; however Mayor Carter Henry Harrison issued a parade permit for the gathering, believing there was no cause for concern.

Others were not so sure. Responding to pressure from businessmen, Police Inspector John Bonfield called up 600 police reserves into duty that night at the West Chicago, Harrison and Central stations. He led them to believe that a citywide riot might occur. A short time later, 100 more officers were added to the Des Plains station, less than a half block from Haymarket Square.

The rally began at 8:30 p.m. and the crowd was fairly listless, dampened by the drizzling rain. Mayor Harrison rode by on his horse a short time later and was satisfied that it was a peaceable gathering. He ordered Bonfield to send the reserve officers home. The police inspector refused and two hours later, he ordered his men to disperse the crowd. The speakers were approached by Captain William Ward, who commanded the meeting to end in the "name of the people of Illinois".

Suddenly, according to author Richard Lindberg in his book *Return to the Scene of the Crime*, a crudely manufactured pipe bomb was thrown from a vestibule at Randolph and Des Plaines Streets. The bomb exploded in the midst of a 200-man police column. Officer Mathias Degan was killed instantly and six others were mortally wounded. Although momentarily stunned, the officers quickly recovered and began shooting wildly into the fleeing crowd of laborers. The shooting continued for more than five minutes.

While the mayor pleaded for calm, Bonfield and Police Inspector Michael Schaak took it upon themselves to find the culprits who had thrown the bomb, or even who had caused the bomb to be thrown in the first place. The officers began a reign of terror among working class citizens in Chicago. All rights (such as they were then) were suspended and hundreds of suspects were arrested, beaten and interrogated at all hours of the night. False confessions were violently extracted from those who were thought to be "anarchists" or sympathizers of the labor unions. Whoever the bomb thrower actually was, he faded away into history.

Eventually, eight conspirators were brought to trial for the riot and seven of them received the death sentence, while the eighth was given fifteen years in prison. All of them were tried and sentenced on conspiracy charges to incite violence that led to the deaths of the police officers. On November 11, 1887, August Spies, Albert Parsons, George Engel and Adolph Fischer were hanged at the Criminal Courts Building on Hubbard Street. Another of the conspirators died in an explosion and the death sentences of the others were commuted to prison terms. It was said that on the gallows that day, Albert Parsons, when asked if he had any last statement to make, shouted "Let the voice of the people be heard!" Some would say that it was, even though the men apparently had the deck stacked against them from the time of their arrests.

Rumor had it that the jurors in the trial had been given $100,000 by Chicago business leaders and prior to the verdict being read, Marshall Field was already lobbying that the men be hanged. He also reportedly went to City Hall and demanded that the mayor repress free speech in the city, in the interests of public safety. The mayor refused, even after Field informed him that he "represented great interests in Chicago."

The city of Chicago erected a statue of a police officer in Haymarket Square on May 4, 1889 and it became the first such monument in the nation. For many years, the police were seen as the martyrs of the riot but with the rise of the big labor unions, that perception slowly changed. During the 1960's, the statue was defaced, blown up twice, repaired and finally removed to the Chicago Police Training Academy by Mayor Richard J. Daley. Nothing remains to mark this area today, save for the memories of the past.

THE PULLMAN ERA

George M. Pullman never dreamed that anything like the Haymarket Square Riot would affect his company. Pullman was a self-described "humanitarian", who even built a model company town for his employees. He was born in New York and came to Chicago in 1855. As a cabinetmaker and construction engineer, he supervised the raising of many of Chicago's buildings to higher levels and later developed the first railway sleeping car that was suitable for long distance travel. He also developed the dining car and parlor car through the Pullman Palace Car Company, which was organized in 1867. In 1880, he built a factory south of Chicago and during the heyday of his company, created the model town of Pullman around it.

The small town was located ten miles outside of the city proper, next the factory. It consisted of 1,800 brick homes, an arcade with a theater, a library, a hotel, stores, a bank, two churches and a school. However, there were no beer gardens or saloons and alcohol was strictly forbidden. The only bar in town was located in the Florence Hotel and it was reserved for Pullman and his guests.

Rules in the company town were harsh. Any employee who dropped paper in the street and did not pick it up could be fired. Any tenant could be evicted from his home, for any reason, with a ten day notice. No labor organizers were permitted within the town. No improper books or plays were allowed at the library. In addition, rent was higher than in comparable homes in the city and all gas and water was purchased from the company, who made a profit on it. On payday, all debts owed to the company were automatically deducted from what the employee earned. This debt included rent, water, gas or food from the company store. Some families literally ended up with a only few cents left after all of their deductions.

In 1893, Chicago was host to the World's Columbian Exposition, which celebrated the 400th anniversary of Columbus' discovery of America. As author Curt Johnson put in it his book *Wicked City*, the fairgrounds may have been dubbed the "White City" but the whole of Chicago was immersed in the "Black Winter" that year. One of the nation's recurrent financial panics and depressions had struck and in Chicago, people were going hungry and dying from the harsh weather. Soup kitchens were organized and City Hall was used to shelter as many as 2,000 people each night. The saloon keepers of the city were even doing their part, feeding as many as 60,000 jobless men each day, as many of them were unable to afford even the nickel beer that was customary to earn the free lunch.

During this recession, Pullman laid off about one-third of the workforce and wages for those remaining on the job were cut by as much as 40 percent. Many men received nothing, or even went into debt on payday. That winter, some men went so hungry that they fainted on the factory floor. Finally, a delegation of workers went to see George Pullman about the conditions. He refused to meet with them and in fact, fired all of them and evicted them from their homes.

An Indiana man named Eugene Debs organized a group of the Pullman workers in a nearby town and they demanded restoration of their wages from the Pullman Company. Needless to say, the demand was refused. On May 11, the workers went on strike and Pullman was shut down. Soon, members of the American Railway Union began a sympathy strike, which led to violence across the country. President Grover Cleveland intervened and ordered the strike to end, stating that the railway demonstrations interfered with delivery of the mail. Eugene Debs refused to bow to pressure and he was jailed.

By the middle of May, Pullman families were begging for food. Chicago's mayor sent thousands of dollars in groceries to the company town, spending money from his own pocket. Chicago city leaders and politicians from around the country urged Pullman to settle the strike, but he refused. The Union sent him a letter that asked him to meet with the workers, but he would not even open it.

The Union then voted to boycott all Pullman cars on the rail lines and refused to handle them. The United States Attorney General, Richard Olney, saw this as a way to end the strike. Thanks to the previous court ruling, the Union could not interfere with the delivery of the mail, but the ruling said nothing about other trains. They could refuse to work on any train that was not carrying mail. Soon, the railroads began attaching unnecessary Pullman cars to other trains so that Union members would not handle them. In this way, the companies forced the members to break the law by refusing to allow the mail to go through.

With that accomplished, President Cleveland sent troops into Chicago on July 2. The confrontation between the soldiers and the workers turned into a riot and a number of railroad cars were overturned and set on fire. The riots lasted for several days. Twelve men were killed and over $685,000 in property was destroyed.

The Pullman plant re-opened in late August, although with new employees on the payroll. Each of them had to sign a pledge that they would not join the Union. All of the Union workers who were hired back had to surrender their Union cards. However, many of the men were not hired back. This prompted Illinois Governor Altgeld, who had fought against federal interference in the strike, to go to Pullman and personally ask that the men be hired back. He arrived in the company town and was taken on a tour by the Pullman Company vice-president. Pullman himself was too busy to entertain him. The idea was to show the governor what a wonderful place the town was. Instead, Altgeld found more than 6,000 people with no food, families living in poverty and women and children in unsuitable living conditions. He was appalled by the place and realized that Pullman was simply oblivious to the lives of his employees. Altgeld returned to Springfield and quickly dispatched a letter. He asked that Pullman hire back all of the replaced workers and in addition, cancel all rents from October 1 so that the workers could get back on their feet. Pullman refused to accept the letter until he was literally forced to take it by an Illinois National Guard officer. Then, of course, he did nothing.

In 1898, the Illinois Supreme Court ordered the company to sell off its housing stock in the town of Pullman. It was eventually sold and the town became a state landmark in 1969. The Historic Pullman Foundation has preserved the Florence Hotel but was not as lucky in 1998 when a homeless man set fire to the historic railcar factory at 111th Street and St. Lawrence Avenue. He told police that he heard "voices" that compelled him to set the building on fire. Perhaps the voices of lost workers from the company's past?

As for Pullman, his victory in breaking the strike was a short-lived one. He succeeded in losing the love of his daughters, losing the respect of his workers and earned the disdain of most of the national press. He died three years later in 1897 and was buried in Graceland Cemetery. His grave was fortified with railroad ties and reinforced concrete so that "radicals, anarchists and embittered workers" would not be able to violate his crypt.

CHICAGO STOCKYARDS

Many social theorists would sat that the fortunes of Chicago's titans had been amassed at the expense of others, from the labors and, sometimes, from the misery of the lives these men "owned" but never gave the slightest thought to. And if there was a single area that portrayed the greatest contrast between the lifestyles of the company owners and the workers, it was among the packing districts of Chicago. For example, Phillip Armour lived on fashionable Prairie Avenue but his fortune had been created from his meat packing operations in a place called "Packingtown", a tenement area near the stockyards. Because the pay for slaughtering was so low, many of the children in this area scavenged for food from the garbage dumps. Nearby was "Whiskey Row", a district of more than 200 saloons. Here, stockyard workers were often treated to a free lunch, but only on the condition that they bought a drink.

Carl Sandburg called Chicago the "hog butcher for the world" but it was beef that actually made the city wealthy. Until the 1800's, cuts of beef were prepared only by local butchers. However in 1872, a man named Gustavas Swift began buying cattle from the western ranges and shipping sides of beef to the east on express trains that ran in the winter months with their doors open to preserve the meat. Later, Swift developed refrigerated rail cars and soon he and his competitor, Phillip Armour, were shipped most of the nation's beef and pork products.

The slaughterhouses were located on the south side of the city, in Packingtown. The plants were filthy and dangerous workplaces that treated the workers, who were most Eastern European immigrants, with little regard. It was said that the plants used "every part of the hog but the squeal" but there was still waste to be disposed of. The slaughter refuse was dumped into a large, open sewer that ran down the middle of Packingtown. It was dubbed "Bubbly Creek" because it would literally bubble as the bacteria devoured the blood and waste.

The horrible conditions of Packingtown caught the attention of Frank Warren, the editor of a weekly Socialist newspaper. He decided to send one of his reporters, a young man named Upton Sinclair, to Chicago to write a piece on the packing houses. Sinclair was poor himself and so his threadbare clothing fit right in with the immigrants working in Packingtown. He found that by carrying a pail with him, he could go anywhere that he wanted to. He gathered his material and his article ran as a series in the newspaper starting in February 1905. He later gathered the material into a book that would be titled *The Jungle*.

For months, he was unable to find anyone to publish the fictionalized depiction of the area. No one could believe that the conditions he described in Packingtown were accurate. Sinclair insisted that while the Lithuanian family of the book was not real, it had been based on real people and the horrific condition of Packingtown was genuine.

The Jungle was finally published by Doubleday in 1906. It contained graphic details and by the end of the year, it had sold more than 100,000 copies. Author Jack London called it "the *Uncle Tom's Cabin* of wage slavery". Another fan of the book was President Theodore Roosevelt, who had long been a critic of the nation's meatpackers. During the Spanish-American War, he had stated that he would rather eat his old hat as eat the meat that the companies were sending to Cuba. He believed that Sinclair's book could help him do something about the problem.

Roosevelt began actively pursuing government regulations on the meat industry, including inspections. The meat packers opposed the new standards but with meat sales falling in wake of Sinclair's book, they began claiming that the plants were clean and safe. Soon, doctors began supporting Sinclair's claims of unsanitary conditions and the public began turning against the industry. A popular rhyme that made the rounds in Chicago in 1906 went "Mary had a little lamb, and when she saw it sicken, she shipped it off to Packingtown, and now its labeled chicken."

Roosevelt succeeded with his plans and the first meat inspection bill was passed one year later. *The Jungle* had changed an industry and meat packing was never the same. Despite the fact that the meatpackers had strenuously opposed the new regulations at first, they soon embraced them. The federal inspections became a marketing opportunity and meat today is still sold as being "guaranteed pure" by the

US government.

The volatile conditions of the packing industry in Chicago have spawned at least one tale of murder and ghosts in the city. It is a tale that had a lot of people in Chicago avoiding sausages back in 1897!

THE SAUSAGE VAT MURDER

The ghost of Louisa Luetgert still walks the now almost deserted neighborhood where her home once stood, or at least that's what the legends of northwest Chicago say. Louisa was the murdered wife of "Sausage King" Adolph Luetgert, a German meat packer who came to the city in the 1870's. Killed by her own husband in one of the most grisly ways imaginable, her ghost not only haunts the area around Hermitage Avenue but the legends say that she hounded her treacherous husband from Joliet Prison to the grave!

After finding that his German sausages were well-liked in Chicago, Adolph Luetgert built a sausage plant at the southwest corner of Hermitage and Diversey Parkway in 1894. He was so taken with his own success that he also built a three-story frame house next door to the factory, which he shared with his wife Louisa.

Louisa Bicknese was an attractive young woman who was 10 years younger than her husband was. She was a former servant from the Fox River Valley who met her new husband by chance. He was immediately taken with her, entranced by her diminutive stature and tiny frame. She was less than five feet tall and looked almost child-like next to her burly husband. As a wedding gift, he gave her a unique, heavy gold ring. Inside of it, he had gotten her new initials inscribed, reading "L.L.". Little did he know at the time that this ring would prove to be his undoing.

The Infamous Luetgert Sausage Works

According to friends and neighbors, Luetgert's fascination with his beautiful young wife did not last long. The couple was frequently heard to argue and their disagreements became so heated that Luetgert eventually moved his bedroom from the house to a small chamber inside of the factory. Luetgert soon became involved with a girl named Mary Simerling, Louisa's niece and a household servant. This new scandal also got the attention of the people in the neighborhood, who were already gossiping about the couple's marital woes.

Then, on May 1, 1897, Louisa disappeared. When questioned by his sons, Luetgert told them that their mother had gone out the previous evening to visit her sister. After several days though, she did not come back. Finally, Diedrich Bicknese, Louisa's brother, went to the police. The investigation fell on Captain Herman Schuettler, who author Richard Lindberg described as "an honest but occasionally brutal detective".

The detective and his men began to immediately search for Louisa. They questioned neighbors and relatives and soon learned of the couple's violent arguments. They also talked to Wilhelm Fulpeck, an employee of the sausage factory, who recalled seeing Louisa enter the factory around 10:30 in the evening on May 1. Frank Bialk, a night watchman at the plant, confirmed his story. He also added that he saw both Luetgert and Louisa at the plant together. Apparently, Luetgert sent him out on an errand that evening and gave him the rest of the night off.

Schuettler also made another disturbing and suspicious discovery. Just a short time before Louisa's disappearance, the factory had been closed for ten weeks for reorganization. However, the day before Louisa vanished, Luetgert ordered 378 pounds of crude potash and fifty pounds of arsenic. The circumstantial evidence was starting to add up and Schuettler began to theorize about the crime. He became convinced that Luetgert had killed his wife, boiled her in acid and then disposed of her in a factory furnace. With that in mind, he and his men started another hunt through the sausage plant. They narrowed the search to the basement and to a twelve-foot-long, five-foot-deep vat that was located next to the furnaces that smoked the meat. The officers drained the greasy paste from the vat and began poking through the residue with sticks. Here, Officer Walter Dean found a small piece of a skull fragment and two gold rings. One of them was engraved with the initials "L.L.".

On May 7, Adolph Luetgert, proclaiming his innocence, was arrested for the murder of his wife. No body was ever found and there were no witnesses to the crime, but police officers and prosecutors believed the evidence was overwhelming. Luetgert was indicted for the crime a month later and details of the murder shocked the city, especially those on the northwest side. Even though Luetgert was charged with burning his wife's body, local rumor had it that she had been ground into sausage instead. Needless to say, sausage sales declined substantially in 1897.

Luetgert went to trial but the proceedings ended in a hung jury on October 21 after the jurors failed to agree on a suitable punishment. Some argued for the death penalty, while others voted for life in prison. Only one of the jury members thought that Luetgert might be innocent. A second trial was held and on February 9, 1898, Luetgert was convicted and sentenced to life imprisonment at Joliet.

Luetgert was taken away to prison, where he became a shell of his former self. He babbled incoherently to the guards, claiming that his dead wife was haunting him, intent on having her revenge, even though he was innocent of her murder. Luetgert, possibly insane by this time, died in 1900.

And he was not the only one to suffer. His attorney, Lawrence Harmon, believed that his client was telling the truth and that he did not kill his wife. He was sure that she had simply disappeared. In fact, Harmon was so convinced of Luetgert's innocence that he spent over $2,000 of his own money and devoted the rest of his life to finding Louisa. Eventually, he also went insane and he died in a mental institution.

As for Louisa, whether she was murdered by her husband or not, she reportedly did not rest in peace. Not long after her husband was sent to prison, her ghost began to be seen inside of the Luetgert house. Neighbors claimed to see a woman in a white dress leaning against the mantel in the fireplace. Light turned on and off in the abandoned building and passersby complained of eerie noises and moaning sounds. Eventually, the house began to be rented out but none of the tenants stayed there for long. The ghost was also reported inside of the sausage factory but this building burned down in 1902 and was never rebuilt.

Legend has it on the northwest side that Louisa Luetgert still walks. If she does, she probably no longer recognizes the neighborhood where she once lived as the factory is long gone and the houses that once stood here have been replaced by empty lots and an industrial complex. They say though, that if you happened to be in this area on May 1, the anniversary of Louisa's death, there is a chance that you might see her lonely specter still roaming the area where she lived and died.

GHOSTS OF FORT SHERIDAN

Although closed now as an official military installation, Fort Sheridan, which is located along the wild and rocky shoreline of Lake Michigan, was an important part of Chicago's military and social history. Originally developed by members of the city's elite to protect their commercial interests from strikers and labor agitators, it became a respected military installation. It was officially closed down during the first round of military budget cuts in 1990 but continued to serve as a training and administrative base during Desert Storm and Desert Shield. It was closed for good in May 1993 but its legend lives on -- and so do its ghost stories.

The site of Fort Sheridan was located on an old Indian trail that ran between Green Bay, Wisconsin and a French trading post that was established around 1670, near what was to become Chicago. Known as the Green Bay Trail, it extended north through Chicago along what is today North Clark Street. The settlers who later came to the region also began to use the trail and as they were often escorted by soldiers from Fort

Dearborn, it also became known as the Military Road. In 1883, when the last of the Native Americans in region ceded their land in Illinois to the United States, trade increased and as more people began to use the trail, it came to be officially known as the Green Bay Road.

By the late 1860's, Chicago had become a gateway for eastern settlers who were heading west. The Division of the Missouri was quartered in Chicago and was led by Lieutenant General Phillip Sheridan and played a large part in the protection of the settlers heading west. The Division's headquarters were at Washington and LaSalle Streets and from here, Sheridan was charged with not only escorting important travelers but also with making sure that the new settlers obeyed the laws of the frontier territories.

Sheridan was needed almost as soon as his command was established. In October 1871, the Great Chicago Fire swept through the city and in the chaos that followed, Sheridan was asked to assist in maintaining order and to protect the city from looting and pillaging. Chicago's Mayor, Roswell Mason, placed the city under martial law, entrusting Sheridan and his troops to watch over it. Although many felt that martial law was unnecessary, Sheridan was generally praised for his work in restoring law and order and also for the organizing that he did to provide relief for the homeless and the hungry. Martial law was only temporary, it was repealed on October 23, but four companies of men remained on active duty in the city until the end of the year.

General Sheridan remained in Chicago until 1883, when he was reassigned to the War Department in Washington, D.C. By this time he had received the nation's highest military office, Commanding General, United States Army.

With the reputation that he had established as a leader, Sheridan came to mind several years later when Chicago businessmen met to discuss plans for a military installation near the city. Chicago had been suffering from labor unrest throughout the 1870's and 1880's, which ultimately erupted during the Haymarket Square Bombing of 1886. Further riots and strikes, such as those at the McCormick Reaper works, sent feelings of uneasiness through the city's business leaders. The effectiveness of the U.S. troops in controlling matters after the Great Fire had left an impression on Chicago's elite and land was donated on the north side for a permanent base. A proposal was made by the Commercial Club, made up of Chicago's wealthiest residents, and sent to the War Department.

The government accepted the proposal and in July, a team of officers that included General Sheridan, selected a location that came to be known as the Highwood tract. The deed was signed over by the Commercial Club, although legally they could neither own nor donate any property. Because of this, their wives served as intermediaries and as the grantors named in the deed. The post became known as "Camp Highwood".

On November 8, 1887, the first regiment arrived. Eighty-four men were commanded by Major William Lyster and they set up an encampment near the rugged shoreline of the lake. The timing of their arrival was such that the troops arrived at the camp just three days before the execution of the accused Haymarket bombers. In addition to Lyster's men, 1,200 members of the Illinois National Guard were on placed on alert in case of trouble, but the feared crisis passed with no military action. The first winter at the camp was horrible. With five men to a tent, no vegetables and little drinkable water, many of the men were sick and in poor health by the time that spring came.

On February 27, 1888, the camp at Highwood was officially named Fort Sheridan after the general who had played such a significant role in the founding of the fort. General Sheridan visited the post on May 5, 1888, and received his last review of troops. He died August 5, 1888.

Despite the rough conditions starting out, Major Lyster and his men pushed forward with their duties and by the time that his command ended in late summer of 1890, the construction of permanent buildings on the post had begun. Within ten years, Congress had provided the money for structures to house six companies of infantry troops and four of cavalry, as well as a wharf, water tower, cemetery and rifle range. The construction was much harder than first anticipated as water had to be pumped from the lake and taken by wagon to the building sites. Construction materials had to be brought in along always muddy roads and the harsh terrain and the ravines of the area proved to be a challenge for the builders. The Fort was designed by the architectural firm of Holabird and Roche out of Chicago and their work would eventually lead the Fort to obtain status as a National Historic Landmark.

An old postcard view of historic Fort Sheridan

As the builders of the Fort experienced their difficulties, other problems with the post's location were beginning to emerge as well. With the establishment of the Fort came the development of the village of Highwood. Although started in 1868, most of the settlers of the town came to Highwood after being left homeless by the Great Fire. Many of them hoped to start farms along the North Shore. Soon, Highwood became so closely tied to the fort that residents eventually renamed it the village of Fort Sheridan. In the early days many conflicts arose about the sale of liquor in town to the soldiers and construction workers at the fort. Concerned that the town would become a cesspool of vice, they banned the sale of alcohol, although many establishments ignored the new law and kept peddling booze anyway. Finally, liquor licenses were created and were sold at $1,000 each. Anyone willing to pay the price could obtain one, as long as he promised not to sell alcohol to "lunatics, idiots, minors and habitual drunkards". In 1908 though, the local taverns were all shut down and stayed that way until state laws took over liquor sales.

Fort Sheridan's first real military duties were after the Battle of Wounded Knee, which took place in South Dakota in December 1890. A group of the defeated Lakota tribe was imprisoned at the Fort. By 1894, two years after their design work was completed, all of the individual buildings designed by Holabird & Roche were completed. These included the Officers' Housing, Bachelor Officers' Quarters and Mess, the Quartermaster Stables Guardhouse, the Saddler's and Stable Sergeant's Buildings, the Gun Shed, the Army Mess Hall and Central Heating Plant, the Infantry Drill Hall, a Magazine, Ordnance Storehouse, the Dead House (Morgue), a Blacksmith Shop, and the Fire Station.

In June 1894, Fort Sheridan played a role in the Pullman strike when disagreements between union officials and management of the giant railroad car company erupted in violence. The measures taken by the soldiers during the Pullman strike proved to be successful in restoring peace and order but it was the last time Fort Sheridan would serve its original purpose as a watchdog over Chicago business disputes. In 1898, the Fort served as a temporary stop for troops on their way to fight in the Spanish-American War.

In these early years, Fort Sheridan was known locally as a "Cavalry Post." Cavalry officers were always highly regarded and Fort Sheridan became a social spot on the North Shore. There were balls and receptions at the Officers' Club and other social activities including drills and parades, band concerts and even polo matches with nearby wealthy residents. This aspect of military life was limited to the officers though and did not extend to the enlisted men.

In the early 1900's, a considerable amount of construction took place at the Fort. Holabird & Roche did not play a role except for designing wings that added space to the guardhouse in 1905-1906. All of the other new construction was done by the Office of the Quartermaster General except for the Post Office, built in 1907, and the Post Hospital, built in 1893 and 1905-1906. The hospital buildings were built by the Office of the Surgeon General and there is no listing as to who designed the post office. After this, no significant construction was done until the 1930's.

The American military went through many changes in the years after the Spanish-American War and it was becoming evident to national leaders, thanks to the conflicts in Europe and Mexico, that the United States would be playing a greater role in international affairs and would likely be entering into the conflicts in the future. An emphasis started to be placed on training and readiness and on the growing need for a large standby force of men who would be deployed in case of war. Major General Leonard Wood believed that a great part of fighting in future wars would be done by these men and he initiated the reserve training camps that would be independent of the National Guard.

Fort Sheridan served as the site of the nation's first Reserve Officers Training Camp (ROTC) and it was held in the summer of 1917 for 2,500 men. A second one immediately followed and approximately 5,800 men who had completed three months' basic training in the two successive camps were commissioned as officers in the Army Reserve, applying in combat what they had learned in their training at Fort Sheridan. The Reserve Training Camps provided a logical expansion into training centers following the United States entry into World War I in 1917. Fort Sheridan became an induction and Midwest training center for men entering the Army from Illinois, Michigan, and Wisconsin.

As the war in Europe continued and Fort Sheridan remained a training center for soldiers, it also took on several changes including the addition of what was at that time the largest base hospital in the United States, Lovell General Hospital. During its two years of operation the facility treated some 60,000 patients and kept the great influenza epidemic of 1918 from ravaging the entire base.

After World War I, changes came to Fort Sheridan that were brought about by the introduction of automobiles and motorized tanks and trucks. The cavalry was phased out and was replaced by support buildings for cars, machinery and related equipment. A school for automobile mechanics was set up by the Quartermaster Corps in 1941 and this marked the permanent end of a need for blacksmiths, wheelwrights, and wagonmasters on the post.

Between 1920 and 1943, Fort Sheridan remained not only a reserve training facility but a regular army training base as well. The Coast Artillery (for anti-aircraft training) established a major center at the Fort and soldiers who trained in these units lived in a tent village dubbed "Camp Leonard Wood", under harsh conditions until 1939, when a permanent structure was built for them.

Around 1936, Fort Sheridan, like others across the country, prepared for the possibility that the United States might enter the war in Europe. When the peacetime draft was instituted in 1940, Fort Sheridan became one of four Recruit Reception Centers in the country and was expanded to receive huge numbers of new inductees and recruits from Illinois and other surrounding states. In 1944, the Fort also assumed administrative control of prisoner of war camps in Illinois, Michigan, and Wisconsin. A total of 15,000 prisoners under this administrative control performed civilian construction jobs, crop harvesting, kitchen police, and other forms of manual labor. When World War II ended, the POW camp that had been at Fort Sheridan closed, and all but nine of the prisoners returned to their homeland (most were from Germany). Those nine are buried in the post cemetery.

In the years following World War II, the army units stationed at the Fort were sent to other battle areas. During the Korean conflict of the 1950's Fort Sheridan again served as a primary reception center. Fort Sheridan's mission was then expanded to include the support of defense sites protecting a Midwest industrial area that encompassed Illinois, Indiana, Michigan, Wisconsin, and Minnesota. The post became responsible for all logistical support of a network of 33 Nike-Hercules missile sites throughout the country. During the Vietnam conflict, the Fort served as an administrative and logistics center in addition to sending its regular army units into battle areas.

After the Vietnam War, a peacetime army was station at the Fort and the post continued to serve as an administrative center. In the early 1970's, there were several attempts by Congress to close Fort Sheridan. However, the post endured, and by the late 1980's was a center for recruiting activities in eleven states. Regardless, by the end of the decade, the contingent at the Fort dwindled and soon, there no regular combat troops station here at all. The main function of the post was to supervise reserve activities around the Midwest and to coordinate Army recruiting nationwide. It also served as headquarters to the 112th Military Intelligence Command, the Army Criminal Investigation Command, and a detachment of explosives experts.

Fort Sheridan was finally closed for good in 1993, bringing an era of the military in Chicago, and a rich history, to a sudden end.

It should come as no surprise to readers that, after all that has taken place at Fort Sheridan, a contingent of spectral residents from the past have managed to linger here. The post has since been divided into a park, historic site and cemetery but it's likely that the ghosts who remain here will continue to carry on just as they did in days gone by. During the last years when the post was active, stories of ghosts and hauntings were widely reported in the *Chicago Sun-Times* and other places.

What became known as the Fort's most famous ghost was not that of an old soldier but rather that of non-military person instead. She became known as the "Lady in Orange" and was so-named because of the bright, orange dress that she was often seen wearing. She appeared at random events that were held in Building 31, the Community Club Building, which previously housed the officer's mess hall and the officer's club, the El Morocco Lounge.

Peggy Flanigan, once the Fort's unofficial historian and public relations director, had a frightening experience in the building that caused her to go so far as to seek out a psychic for answers. She had heard about other people's sightings of the Lady in Orange, but one night in the building she had a different sort of experience altogether. She stayed the night in Building 31 and was preparing to leave near dawn when she was suddenly overwhelmed by an icy cold feeling that she couldn't explain. To make matters worse, the lights in the room abruptly went out! She managed to make her way out of the building but did not return for a couple of weeks. When she did, she brought a respected psychic with her -- who knew nothing about the history of the sightings that had taken place in the building. She told Peggy that she sensed a woman in a "bright dress, possibly orange" and that she was the wife of a senior officer, "possibly a general" and that she also resembled Mamie Eisenhower. Flanigan was chilled by this revelation and later stated that when they left the club, she "caught a flash of something orange out of the corner of my eye, like a wisp of orange in the air."

Interested by what the psychic had told her, Flanigan began doing some research. She discovered a group of photographs that had been taken in the officer's club and found a woman in the photos that looked a great deal like Mamie Eisenhower. To her continued astonishment, she discovered that during the 1950's, there had been a base general's wife who came to the dining room everyday to talk to the cooks and give orders as to how the food should be served. She habitually hung around the kitchen, drinking martinis, and enjoying the company of the staff. It's possible that she liked the place so much that she never chose to leave it. When she died, she was buried in the post cemetery, across from the club, but her flamboyant personality lived on -- possibly manifesting as a woman in a bright orange dress.

The sightings of the figure continued for years after this discovery and while the lady never did anything frightening, she did like to be noticed, as was evidenced by her behavior with the lights in the room where Peggy Flanigan was. However, there was one officer who apparently the ghost never really liked. According to his story, he could never make it from the kitchen to his office, no matter how fast he walked, without his hot cup of coffee turning ice cold. No one else seemed to have this problem but he could never shake off the feeling that the spectral presence in the building had it in for him for some reason.

The Fort hosted a plethora of other ghostly inhabitants as well. Building I, the Fort's old hospital, was said to be haunted by not only a custodian who continued to attend to his duties after death but a phantom nurse as well. The custodian was believed to have been a civilian worker at the post from the early 1900's. He died after being shot by accident but apparently never left. He was seen for years sweeping hallways and was often heard walking in empty corridors and tapping on pipes. According to the stories, the nurse was also a former staff member but her identity remains unknown. She was sometimes seen looking out a window on the top floor of the building.

Across the road and behind the old hospital was the post's morgue or "Dead House". For years after the building fell out of use, soldiers complained of strange sounds and feelings of cold dread in and around the small stone building. The Dead House was designed with sealed windows that were fixed with raised crosses and the inside was a cramped area with a sink and a table for autopsies. Could the sounds reported coming from the building have been merely the imaginations of soldiers who knew what the place had once been used for -- or something else?

There seems to be no question as to the "something else" when looking into the accounts of military police officers from Fort Sheridan. Over a period of several years, there several reports of unauthorized entry into the post's hospital by what was described as a "stocky man". Although officers searched for the man repeatedly, he was nowhere to be found. They also reported footsteps that would echo in the corridors of locked barracks and believing that someone else was inside, would search the building and find it to be deserted. There are were also stories of officers hearing the sound of what seemed to be a drill sergeant bellowing out orders to new recruits and voices speaking in German. One officer also told of hearing the strains of accordion music coming from where the German POW camp was once located. It's hard to imagine that these two events are not connected in some way.

The Fort was also plagued by rumors and legends of a phantom cavalry officer who would gallop along the roads, a soldier in clothing from the Spanish-American War era who would appear on a flight of stairs, a young man who was killed during the construction of the post but returned haunt the water tower and even a one-time sighting of a blacksmith who walked into the home of an officer as he and his wife were watching television one night. He turned and then vanished without a trace.

Once again, history teaches a valuable lesson with the rise and fall of Fort Sheridan. Everything that we do in life leaves an echo behind and what may have seemed like a minor occurrence may someday return as a haunting. The history of Fort Sheridan lives on, not only through its military legacy -- but in its ghost stories and lore as well.

CROOKS, CRIMINALS & CORRUPTION
THE LEGACY OF CHICAGO POLITICS

"Vote early ... and vote often."
A FAMOUS CHICAGO POLTICAL SLOGAN

There is no city in America that has been as maligned as Chicago when it comes to the city's politics, politicians, corruption and questionable voting practices. Even Chicago's most famous nickname of the "Windy City" comes from the hot air that is expelled by the city's politicians, rather than for the speed of the local air currents. This is a city that is known for its back room politics, favors and bribes and its politicians have long been colorful characters.

Chicago's mayors have always been men of importance. It's true that the early pioneer mayors are barely remembered today but later on, as the mayors became more entrenched in the city's political system, they became capable of causing riots and firing the entire police force. Some of them were controlled by gamblers, befriended by gangsters or manipulated behind the scenes by merchants and businessmen. Occasionally, good men would be elected to office and each would try valiantly to clean up the town. They would start reform movements to purge the city of corrupt officials, to close down saloons on Sunday and brothels on weeknights and to raid all of the gambling dens within spitting distance of City Hall. But in most cases, these good men were not supported by an honest administration and soon, the people of Chicago would be drawn to another man, who spoke louder and made more promises than the rest. For the most part it seems that the best Chicago mayors have been the ones who have more or less let the city run them, rather than to try and run the city, and have enforced the laws to the point that respectable citizens could walk the streets but never caused enough trouble to scare off the tourists and local folks who wanted to drink, gamble or carouse a little.

Some authors have said that Chicago is a religious town but I wouldn't say it's religious in any traditional way. The town has a moral façade that it maintains to disguise its sinful activities. The city loves the money that its reputation for being a bloody city that is tied to gangsters and ghosts brings in -- but the "official" stance on the subject rejects this image. Many of the mayors of the city have epitomized this attitude. They made deals with crooks and gangsters, while issuing self righteous statements about how awful crime was.

The first mayor of Chicago was a man named William Ogden, who made an amazing impact on the early city. In addition to being the first mayor, he was also the first president of the Union Pacific Railroad, built the first drawbridge across the Chicago River, helped to create the Illinois-Michigan Canal, was the first president of Rush Medical College, invested heavily in local real estate and bankrolled International Harvester when he gave Cyrus McCormick $25,000 so that he could build his reaper works in Chicago. He didn't start out with such grand plans however. In fact, some of his relatives had purchased a large amount of property during one of the city's first real estate booms and Ogden had been sent to the region to look it over. He looked out over the muddy wasteland and wrote to his family that they had "been guilty of the grossest folly."

He soon changed his mind though. Later that summer, he sold a third of the land and gained back the entire initial investment. He began to believe that Chicago had a future and soon his own investments in land and business convinced him of the fact.

He was elected mayor on May 2, 1837, defeating John Kinzie's son for the position. Even then, the local Democratic Party was accused of "large scale election fraud". Ogden weathered problems and scandals during his time, including the period when the state of Illinois went bankrupt. Ogden refused to allow the fledgling city to ignore its debts and arranged for special scrip to be issued that would get Chicago through this rough series of years. Later, Ogden and his friend, Walter L. Newberry, were instrumental in the building of Holy Name Cathedral, the city's most illustrious church. But the two men did not do so for religious reasons. They actually donated the block where the church stands in exchange for the Catholic vote for a new bridge over the Chicago River. The bridge was needed so that land owned by Newberry and Ogden could be developed and sold.

In the early 1850's, a wave of sentiment that claimed to be patriotic swept the country and out of this came the "Know Nothing" political party. Its slogan was: "Put none but Americans on guard", meaning that only native born Americans should serve on the police force and in politics. Dr. Levi Day Boone, grand nephew of famous Indian fighter Daniel Boone, was the head of the Know Nothing party in Chicago and somehow managed to get himself elected mayor, despite the fact that the city was made up of mostly Irish and German immigrants.

He implemented his new political policy and demanded that all applicants for city employment, especially those on the new police force, be able to prove that they were born on American soil. Many in Chicago were angry about this but not as angry as they were about the enforcement of the old (but seldom enforced) law that forced saloons to be closed on Sunday. This might have still been acceptable except for Boone's peculiar manner of enforcing it. Only beer halls, which were mainly located on the north side with its German population, would be closed. Saloons that sold whiskey, on the south side, could remain open. Boone also recommended that licensing fees for beer halls be raised from $50 to $300 each year.

The owners of the German beer halls and gardens refused to close and they refused to pay the higher fee. More than 200 people were arrested over this and put on trial. The hearing was scheduled for April 21, 1855 but on that morning, a mob of over 400 Germans marched on the court house. Their representatives entered the courtroom and announced to Judge Henry C. Rucker that if any of the defendants were found guilty, a riot would commence. The mob then left the courthouse and stopped all traffic on Randolph and Clark Streets until a legion of police officers could be summoned. The officers, led by Captain of Police

Luther Nichols, charged into the mob with clubs, causing the Germans to break ranks and to run. Shots were fired but no one was injured.

Meanwhile, the mob retreated to the north side to make new plans. They returned to the area around the courthouse that afternoon with over 1,000 men and they had armed themselves with shotguns, rifles, pistols, clubs, butcher knives and hammers. Mayor Boone countered this by bringing every police officer in town to the area, plus about 150 deputies. He even ordered that cannons be brought to the courthouse.

The rioters soon marched on the Clark Street Bridge and as they approached it, the mayor ordered that the bridge be opened so that the group would be unable to cross. The mob shouted and yelled until (for some inexplicable reason) the bridge was put back into place. They swarmed across the river and collided with the police officers on the other side. Shots were fired and knives flashed -- and all for the right to drink beer on Sunday! In fact, the pitched battle lasted for almost an hour and a number of injuries were later reported, along with a single death. One of the Germans, Peter Martin, fired off a shotgun and Patrolman George Hunt lost his arm from the blast. Martin was then killed where he stood. Rumor persisted for some time that more than one man was killed but this was never confirmed as the Germans were close-mouthed about their injuries and fatalities. Hunt was later arrested for the murder but then was released and given a $3,000 reward by the city council.

In the end, 60 people were arrested for their part in the Lager Beer Riots but only 14 of them were tried and only two were found guilty of anything. They were later granted new trials but nothing ever came of it.

Eventually, the story faded away into memory -- just as the Know Nothing party did. Boone was not re-elected as mayor and two months after the riot, the voters soundly defeated a prohibition law in Chicago.

Long John Wentworth was undoubtedly the most colorful of all of Chicago's mayors. During his tenure in office, he fired the entire city police force, personally caught and arrested gamblers, tore down advertising signs that personally offended him and illegally leveled an entire neighborhood. As author Norman Mark noted, "if he were any more colorful, Chicago might not have been standing after he finished his terms as mayor."

Wentworth was 21 years-old when he arrived barefoot in Chicago. It was October 1836 and the young man had almost nothing to his name. Somehow though, within four weeks, he was the owner of the local newspaper and by 28, was in Congress. He soon was offered his first bribe -- by the people of Wisconsin. They badly wanted to become a state but needed the population of Chicago to do so. They told Wentworth that if he would vote to have the boundaries of Wisconsin redrawn down to the southern tip of Lake Michigan, swallowing up Chicago, they would make him their first senator. Wentworth refused, having no interest in becoming a citizen of Wisconsin.

Mayor "Long John" Wentworth
(Chicago Historical Society)

Long John certainly earned his nickname. He stood six feet, six inches tall and weighed over 300 pounds. He would usually order as many as 30 courses for a single dinner and would insist that everything be placed on the table before him when he was ready to eat, from soup to dessert. He always sat alone at a table that had been made for four or five and would spin the table around so that whatever dish he wanted to eat from next was always within reach.

He became mayor of Chicago in March 1857, taking office after a violent campaign that saw one man killed and several others wounded near polling places. Early in his administration, he decided that he didn't like low advertising signs. Since he constantly bumped his head on them, he decided that they should be removed. On June 18, 1857, he gathered all of the police officers and express drivers in the city and prepared them for their mission by personally pouring them all shots of bourbon. He then ordered them to remove "every swinging sign, awning post or box found protruding two feet or more beyond the front of buildings." All of the signs were thrown into a large pile on State Street and their owners were allowed to retrieve them if they wished -- and to hang them somewhere else.

This would not be the only time that Wentworth would create his own laws and it was certainly not the last time that he enforced them. According to Herbert Asbury, Wentworth went along on a raid when two police officers entered the second floor window of Burrough's Place, a notorious gambling den. When the gamblers inside sounded the alarm, the customers and dealers went running out the front door and into the waiting arms of the city's giant mayor. Wentworth personally supervised the booking of 18 of the prisoners who were captured that night. Later, the gambler's lawyer, a man named Charlie Cameron, appeared at the jail and demanded to speak to his clients. His request was denied so he crept around to the back of the building and whispered a conversation through the barred window. Enraged, Wentworth grabbed the attorney and locked him up too. Police returned to the gambling parlor and stripped the place and Burrough's never re-opened.

That same year, Wentworth went beyond just closing a gambling den and decided to level an entire neighborhood instead. For years, an area known as the Sands, had been a blight on downtown Chicago. This vice district was located along a stretch of lake that was just north of the Chicago River, and had originally been the site of a few lodging houses and some saloons. Gradually it enlarged to between 20 and 30 ramshackle buildings where gambling parlors, saloons and brothels could be found. The *Chicago Tribune* called it "decidedly the vilest and most dangerous place in Chicago." Little could be done about this area because the ownership of the property was tied up in court battles -- or at least that was the case until Long John Wentworth decided to get involved in the matter.

Wentworth led a procession of about 30 policemen, and hundreds of well-meaning citizens, across the Clark Street Bridge one afternoon. They managed to tear nine buildings down with hooks and chains that afternoon and by the time that darkness was starting to fall, they began burning the rest of the district to the ground. Unfortunately, the plan to clean up vice in Chicago backfired though. Once the Sands was destroyed, the gamblers, criminals and whores simply spread out all through the city.

This event managed to anger many people in the city and they began to question the authority that Wentworth actually had, especially when it concerned the police force. The mayor was so busy making his own arrests, writing laws and designing uniforms and badges that many had to wonder how he was managing to run the city. Wentworth had overstepped his bounds, many believed, and so local citizens convinced the state legislature to create a board of three police commissioners to take control of the Chicago police force out of the mayor's hands.

Undaunted, the mayor then decided to fire the entire police force in protest. On March 26, 1861, the force was assembled as one in the court house and Wentworth discharged them from duty, leaving the streets unprotected and the stations empty and abandoned. Of course, it was all done for show as Wentworth left custodians in all of the police stations and told the men to be ready to be called to action if the town bells were sounded. Symbolically though, Chicago had been turned over to the criminals!

How long the city was actually unprotected is open to debate. Some say that it was for as short a time as 12 hours, while others say that it was for as long as 36 hours before the police board began to rehire the officers. There are those who say that the old police force was so inept though that no one ever knew the difference!

One of the most famous statements that Wentworth ever made during his tenure occurred during Chicago's first royal visit. The distinguished guest was the Prince of Wales, who later became King Edward VII. When he came to Chicago in 1860, Wentworth introduced the royal guest from a hotel balcony to a crowd that was gathered on the street. He slapped the Prince on the back and said, "Boys, this is the Prince of Wales. He's come to see the city and I'm going to show him around. Prince, these are the boys!"

But Wentworth's ego knew no bounds, even when it came to the Prince of England. When he was asked how he felt sitting next to the future king of England, he corrected the questioner by saying "I was not sitting beside the Prince. He sat beside me." An author once submitted to him a new history of Chicago for his approval and Wentworth scratched out all of the entries in the book that did not pertain to him and handed it back. "There is a correct history of the city," he reportedly said.

Wentworth was even filled with himself when it came to his death. Before he died, he bought a huge burial plot at Rosehill Cemetery that took up nearly two-thirds of an acre. He died on October 16, 1888 and was buried beneath a 70-foot monument of his own design. It remains the largest in the cemetery and for years, had no inscription on it. When he was asked about this peculiarity, he replied that if nothing was placed on the stone, people would ask whose monument it was and when told, they would "ransack the libraries to find out who John Wentworth was". Years later though, someone decided that too few people were asking who the stone belonged to and so they inscribed his name and a list of accomplishments on the monument. It didn't seem to help though for few people remember Long John Wentworth today -- and even fewer are ransacking the libraries in search of his history.

Aside from the Daley's, there have been two other mayors in Chicago history that have had the same name. The two men, both named Carter Harrison, were father and son and they held office between them for more than two decades. The elder Harrison was elected first in 1879 and the last time in 1893, just in time to preside over the city during the Columbian Exposition. It was believed that Harrison got the job thanks to the criminal element in the city, who bribed him to allow gambling and prostitution to continue unmolested in Chicago. He may have done so to the city's benefit however. The story persists that he made a deal with Mike McDonald, a long time leader in the vice community, that agreed that no one's pocket would be picked at the entrance to the fair. The agreement specified that any pickpocket who was arrested at the gates would have to either return the money to their victim and would have to pay a fine of $10. In exchange, any pickpocket arrested in the city's central area during daylight hours would be immediately released from the Central Station House.

The fair was considered to be a great success, by all accounts, and marked the crowning achievement of the elder Carter Harrison's career. Unfortunately though, he met with a tragic and premature end. He was at home one day during the waning days of the fair and because he had no bodyguards of any sort, a man named Patrick Eugene Joseph Prendergast was able to walk right into the house. Before visiting Harrison, Prendergast had visited Adolph Kraus, the Corporation Counsel for the city. Kraus had already received several threatening postcards from Prendergast, who wrote in red ink: "I want your job." "Do not be a fool. Resign" and "Third and final notice. You either resign or I will remove you."

When Prendergast arrived at his home, Kraus immediately humored him by telling him that the job was now his. Unsure of what to do, Prendergast became flustered and insisted that he did not want the job that day. Confused, he wandered out of the house. Obviously unbalanced, Prendergast fancied himself a religious man and a politician but a more apt description would have been "fanatic". He believed that it was his divine duty to force the elevation of street car tracks in the city. When he arrived at Harrison's home, he walked in and fired three bullets into the mayor's chest. Hearing the shots, Preston and Sophie Harrison ran to their father's side, while the mayor's valet, William Chalmers, rushed in pursuit of the killer.

Prendergast, firing over his shoulder, ran down the street and vanished. He paused long enough to put away his gun and to climb into a street car, which he rode until reaching Des Plaines Avenue. Less than 15 minutes after Harrison had been shot, Prendergast strolled into a police station, handed his weapon to the desk sergeant and surrendered. At almost the same moment, Carter Harrison died.

Prendergast was put through two exhausting trials with his sanity being called into question by his attorneys and by Clarence Darrow, who spoke for two hours at the man's sentencing hearing, begging for the killer's life. However, the assassin remained unrepentant and flippant throughout the trials, even while his lawyers were testing the insanity defense for the first time in Illinois criminal history. The jury was unconvinced that he was insane though and Prendergast was sent to the gallows on July 13, 1894. He made the sign of the cross just before the trapdoor sprung open and ended his life.

By most of the accounts, the second Carter Harrison was not as easily swayed by the questionable elements of the city as his father was. For one thing, he was the man really responsible for bringing down the Chicago transit monopoly of Charles Yerkes when he refused the man's bribe to extend his contracts with the city. During his first mayoral campaign in 1897, he was pictured with both of his hands in his pockets, leading citizens to laugh that they might actually get a mayor who could keep his hands in his *own* pockets for a change.

But Harrison never had a chance when it came to really cleaning up the city though, and he was not adverse to admitting it. When he took office, he described the city council as being a " 'motley crew' of saloon keepers, proprietors of gambling house and undertakers". They had no outstanding characteristics except for an "unquenchable lust for money". Those interesting characters included "Hot Stove" Jimmy Quinn, who claimed that his cronies would steal anything they could get their hands on; Johnny Powers, who bought the votes of fellow councilmen for about $10 each; "Umbrella Mike" Boyle, who collected bribes in an umbrella; and Mike McInerney, who once said that the smoke from the stockyards was good for babies.

And these were the men running the city! It is any wonder that Harrison later suggested that good citizens might want to "carry revolvers strapped outside of their clothing" for protection?

Even so, Harrison did manage to clean things up as well as could be expected. By the last year of his final administration, in 1915, Chicago was as free of vice as it ever had been. His administration had been free from official corruption and none of his friends had gotten rich from bribes or at the expense of the public. But this state of affairs would not continue in city government for long....

Between the second Carter Harrison's first terms and what was perhaps the most corrupt administration in Chicago history, there was really only one mayor of note, Fred A. Busse, a bar brawler, drunk and personal friend of well-known Chicago gangster. He was a man of few words and never took criticism with style. Once when questioned by a reporter about his close ties to business in the city, he simply smirked and said "Go to Hell." That summed up his feelings to that!

Busse did achieve some worthwhile accomplishments during his time as mayor, although suspending the closing time of his favorite saloon and raiding the Illinois Athletic Club after he was insulted there during a card game were not among them. He also took some criticism for his relationship with gangster Christian "Barney" Bertsche, who killed a detective and two police officers shortly after Busse took office in 1907. In spite of this, Busse did help to create the Chicago Plan Commission, which eventually saved the lakefront for the people and reluctantly supported the massive 1911 Vice Commission Report. Ironically, that report was considered "pornographic" at that time and was banned by the U.S. Postal Service. Busse also ended the infamous First Ward Ball, a genuine annual orgy that involved many Chicago politicians.

He was considered a "reform mayor" during his time but most recalled him as a crude, overweight ice and coal merchant who had little time for anyone. He never even bothered to make speeches during his campaign and yet somehow managed to get elected. No real scandals rocked his term in office but it should be noted that when Busse died, his safe-deposit box was opened to reveal a huge block of stock that indicated his ownership in the company that sold all of the manhole covers to the city! Any question as to how they managed to get that particular contract?

William Hale "Big Bill" Thompson served as the mayor of Chicago during what was likely the city's worst and most violent period. When he finally left office after three terms, the *Chicago Tribune* wrote that Thompson's rule had meant "filth corruption, obscenity, idiocy and bankruptcy" for Chicago. They added that he had "given the city an international reputation for moronic buffoonery, barbaric crime, triumphant hoodlumism, unchecked graft and dejected citizenship. He nearly ruined the property and completely destroyed the pride of the city".

In Thompson's defense though, he did serve as mayor through the most difficult era in Chicago history.

In those days, Chicago seemed to be filled with gangsters - gangsters that slaughtered one another (214 dead in four years); gangsters killed by the police (160 during the same period); gangsters shooting up buildings, throwing bombs and speeding in big automobiles; gangsters bribing city officials, ward bosses and aldermen; gangsters dining in expensive restaurants and attending plays, operas and baseball games; gangsters with shotguns, rifles and machine guns, convoying beer trucks; pretty much gangsters everywhere -- except in jail!

"That's all newspaper talk," scoffed Mayor Big Bill Thompson. Although, just for the record, according to the Illinois Crime Survey, gangster Al Capone was one of the largest contributors to Thompson's mayoral campaign and at his headquarters in the Lexington Hotel, Capone sat under framed portraits of George Washington, Abraham Lincoln -- and Big Bill Thompson. But how corrupt was Thompson? Did he purposely allow the criminal element of Chicago to run unchecked during his terms of office? Or was he just so inept that he had no idea of the lawlessness around him. Who can say? But we should note that when he first started his political career, one of his supporters stated that "the worst thing that you can say about him is that he's stupid."

Bib Bill Thompson crowing the Queen of the Stockyards in 1921 (Chicago Historical Society)

Author Norman Mark wrote that Thompson's early life was spent avoiding education. He went out west as a young man to become a cowboy but returned to Chicago after the death of his father. He later achieved a small amount of fame as captain of the Chicago Athletic Club's water-polo team, which was his only qualification for office when he ran for the first time! He first ran for alderman in 1900 after making a $50 poker bet with friends who said that he was too afraid to run. His speeches were dull, his delivery was listless and he had little idea what he was talking about. In fact, he was so clueless that when it was time for him to smile or laugh, a friend would let a brick fall to the floor as a signal.

Thompson ran for mayor with the naiveté of a champion athlete on the side of truth, justice and the American way. He actually vowed in this first campaign that "I am going to clean up Chicago" but by this third campaign, his picture was hanging in Capone's office and the gangster was donating as much as $260,000 for Thompson's re-election. After winning that first election, Chicago became a wide open town as far as vice and crime were concerned.

But Thompson's ability to win elections did not always come from Chicago's criminals. In 1915, he was largely elected due to his pro-German stance. In fact, he was often nicknamed "Kaiser Bill". A short time later, his stance caused a great amount of controversy when he refused to invite Marshall Joffre, hero of the Marne, and Rene Vivani, the French Minster of Justice, to Chicago as part of their national tour to drum up American support for their side in the Great War. Thompson noted that Chicago was the "sixth largest German city in the world" and added that he didn't think many of the residents would be interested in having the Frenchmen here. Joffre and Vivani were finally given the invitation but not before Theodore Roosevelt was heard to say "We'll hang old Thompson to a sour apple tree."

Even after the visit though, Thompson continued to oppose the United States getting involved in the war. A bishop from Texas was quoted: "I think that Mayor Thompson is guilty of treason and ought to be shot... what this country needs is a few first class hangings, then we could go one with our work without fear of being stabbed in the back."

Scandals continued to plague Thompson through his first two terms as mayor. He employed a henchman of Al Capone as city sealer, the person in charge of honest weights and measures, and a local court once ruled that he and his associates owed the city over $2 million, an amount they had allegedly plundered. Thompson almost had a nervous breakdown over this decision until it was thrown out on appeal.

After his first two terms (he was elected in 1915, 1919 and 1927), there was so many scandals, indictments of friends and signs of obvious corruption that Thompson believed that he would never be able to run again. He decided to leave town and look for headlines instead. He found them by organizing an expedition to the South Seas in search of the legendary "tree climbing fish". Thompson set sail on a ship called the *Big Bill*, with a crew that included a theater owner who wore nothing but a jockstrap on most days. The expedition ended before the *Big Bill* ever left the Mississippi River.

Thompson decided to run again in 1927 and it was his final campaign and term that marked Big Bill was the most irresponsible, dangerous and corrupt mayor that ever presided over Chicago politics -- and that's saying a lot in this city! The 1927 campaign was so out of control that it was only exceeded by Thompson's losing 1931 primary effort.

Thompson was so immersed in the corruption that had plagued his former terms in office by this time that he was oblivious to what was going on around him. He had lost his mentor, Fred Lundin, who ran his campaigns and bossed his patronage throughout most of his career, and also Dr. John Dill Robertson, a long time supporter. The two men had become supporters of Thompson's rival in the Republican primary, Edward R. Litsinger, and Thompson was not above "slinging mud" in every direction. At one point, he appeared at a theater for a campaign rally and was accompanied by two caged rats that he called "Fred" and "Doc". He also noted that Litsinger "lived back of the gashouse, and when he moved to the North Side, he left his old mother behind". His opponent seemed nonplussed by his comments and simply said that Thompson had "the carcass of a rhinoceros and the brains of a baboon."

During that same campaign, Thompson also spent a lot of time maligning the King of England, who was assuredly not interested in being the mayor of Chicago. He even boasted that he would punch the monarch in the nose if he ever dared set foot in Chicago. No one seems to know where this bizarre obsession with England came from but even after he was elected, he spent a lot of time trying to get allegedly pro-British history books banned from the Chicago Public Library. A henchman named Urbine J. "Sport" Herrmann even threatened to burn all of the offensive books at the lakefront until a court order stopped him. It wouldn't haven't been much of a fire anyway since Thompson only found four offending volumes in the library's collection and one of them was dedicated to George Washington.

Thompson's election night victory celebration was as big a farce as his campaign had been. He and his cronies ended the night aboard his *Fish Fan Club* ship, drinking illegal hooch. The 1,500 followers who came so overloaded the boat that the ship actually sank in six feet of water. This was perhaps a precursor of things to come, for Thompson nearly sunk the city during his term in office and he assuredly sunk his own career.

All of his terms were marked with criminal activity, especially during election time. The most stunning events occurred during the so-called "Pineapple Primary" in 1928, when "pineapples" (hand grenades) were used to convince voters of which way to cast their ballots. A series of bombings occurred in Chicago when Senator Charles S. Deneen's faction of the Republican Party opposed the faction headed by Thompson and State's Attorney Robert E. Crowe. Thompson's political machine was so powerful by this time that they controlled practically all of the jobs and patronage in the city, county and in association with Governor Len Small, the state as well.

Several bombs were exploded during the early days of the campaign, mostly directed against supporters of Thompson and Crowe. On March 21, 1928, assassins killed Diamond Joe Esposito, a racketeer who was behind the Genna gang of bootleggers. Esposito was also a close friend of Senator Deneen and one of his most influential supporters. On the morning of his funeral, bombs were also set off at the homes of Senator Deneen and Judge John A. Swanson, Deneen's candidate for State's Attorney.

The bombings prompted Crowe to make a huge blunder. He issued a statement saying that he was "satisfied that the bombings were done by the leaders in the Deneen forces... and were done mainly to discredit Mayor Thompson and myself". The mayor made a similar statement a short time later but the reaction against Crowe was tremendous. Newspapers, which had been supporting him, now turned against him, saying that "the callous, cynical note in this led to public exasperation." Meetings were held to denounce his candidacy and the Chicago Crime Commission, which had been friendly to him, now released a letter recommending his defeat. The Deneen faction managed to carry the election and this began to spell the beginning of the end of the rampant days of crime in Chicago.

In 1931, Thompson tried to maintain his hold on the office but failed. He lost to Anton J. Cermak, his Democratic rival. This ended his political career but it did not end the rumors and scandals that would plague him -- even after his death. Thompson passed away on March 19, 1944 and it was thought that his estate amounted to about $150,000, which would have indicated that, despite the stories, his claims of being honest were true and that it had been the newspapers creating scandalous tales about him all along. However, when his safe-deposit boxes were opened, cash literally came tumbling out. One box held $1,466,250 in cash, plus stocks, bonds and gold certificates. Another had $112,000 in stocks and bonds and two other boxes contained nearly $250,000 in stocks and cash made up of $50 and $100 bills. In the end, his estate totaled well over $2 million. No one had any idea how the money had gotten there -- but there were plenty of theories, as the reader can imagine.

To make matters worse, his death also sparked a battle between his mistress of a dozen years, Ethabelle Green, who settled for $250,000 and his wife, Maysie, who got most of the estate. By the time that she paid off all of her attorney bills though, she managed to end up with just $100,000.

The *Daily News* sounded the last note on Thompson in that he "was not a great man, he was highly successful in his field. He was not a statesman, he was a consummate politician. His success was based on deception and distraction. He was the most amazingly unbelievable man in Chicago's history."

As the reader has undoubtedly discovered already, it's possible that the section on Chicago politicians might be better served in this book to be moved to the section on Chicago crime instead. And this will become even more apparent in the pages that follow, which reveal some of the most colorful (and powerful) politicians in the city who never served as the city's mayor. You see, the real control over politics in the city of Chicago is held by those who control the jobs. He who controls the jobs has the loyalty of the people and the votes on election day. It's no wonder that such men are so well remembered in the city today -- for better or for worse.

Chicago's South Side Levee District took shape during the Columbian Exposition in 1893, when thousands of people from all over the world descended on the city. Many believe that the growth of a vice district on the south side may have been what spurred Potter Palmer to flee the region and to build his castle on North Lake Shore Drive, far from the illicit goings-on. And he was not the only one of the wealthy to flee either. Prairie Avenue soon fell into gradual ruin as the Levee began to grow and prosper in the early 1900's.

Visitors to the district could partake of just about every form of vice imaginable from drinks to women and it became a seedbed of crime that would go on to spawn men like Al Capone, Johnny Torrio and the generations that followed them and who became the modern Chicago "outfit". Three vice rings formed the criminal organization that ruled the Levee and which provided the areas various forms of "entertainment".

James Colosimo, an old-world Italian brothel keeper, controlled the street sweeper's union and was linked to the legendary Black Hand. After striking it rich selling the services of young women in two of his bordellos (one of which was named in honor of his wife!), he opened a famous café on South Wabash Avenue that attracted both society patrons and gangsters to its doors. Italian opera stars often dropped in to sample Colosimo's famous pasta, and to rub shoulders with dangerous Levee characters, as well. The café was closed only twice during Prohibition and remained in business long after the proprietor was dead. Colosimo himself was shot to death inside of the vestibule of the restaurant on May 11, 1920 and his garish funeral procession included three judges and nine aldermen as pallbearers. The café was taken over by Mike "The Greek" Potson, a former Indiana saloon keeper. He kept the restaurant going but after Colosimo was killed, he reportedly gained a new business partner -- Al Capone.

Another Levee vice ring was controlled by Maurice Van Bever and his wife Julia, who operated an interstate white slavery ring that extended from St. Louis to Chicago. The ring inspired the passage of the Mann Act in 1910. The act was introduced by Representative James Robert Mann of Illinois and it made it illegal to transport women across state lines for immoral purposes. It was believed that operators in the Levee had imported more than 20,000 young women into the United States to work in their brothels.

The third vice ring was operated by Charley Maibum, who ran a "pay by the hour" hotel where the local streetwalkers could take their clients for a quick rendezvous.

In addition to these, there were scores of independent operators in the district. The Levee arcade featured a number of "dollar a girl" joints, where the women provided services on a volume basis. Many of these unfortunate young ladies ended up on the Levee thanks to the smooth charm of oily con men, who lured them away from small-town life with promises of romance and marriage in the big city. Instead of a love and excitement, they ended up robbed, beaten and "broken in" at the hellish dives of the Levee. In those days, most could see the need for organized prostitution but saw the methods used to induce women to become prostitutes as far more unwholesome. In Chicago (and in every other major city of the day), vice operators had no problem paying off police officers and politicians for permission to run houses of prostitution. However, the officials were less tolerant of what was called the "procuring" of the girls, although the right amount of money could always get them to look the other way. Chicago's vice trade required so many women that procurers operated here with or without approval and the city became a supply point for other cities in the Midwest.

But not all of the bordellos in this part of town were cheap dives that were filled with "white slavery" victims and broken down old whores. Located at 2131 was the famous Everleigh Club, believed to be the most garish and opulent bordello in the city. Ada and Minna Everleigh recruited refined and cultured young women and charged their wealthy patrons as much as $500 a night for their entertainment. The Everleigh opened in 1900 and hired chefs, porters and servants to provide background staffing for the six parlors and 50 bedrooms located on the premises. The rooms were amazingly furnished with tapestries, oriental rugs, impressionist paintings and fine furnishings and there was even a huge library for the education of the young women who worked there. There was a waterfall in one room and orchestras often appeared in the drawing rooms. Upstairs, the Gold Room featured gold-rimmed fish bowls, a miniature gold piano and gold spittoons. The basement was arranged to duplicate the sleeping arrangements of Pullman cars.

The Everleigh circulated brochures all over the Midwest and the bordello attracted a famous, and infamous, trade. The sisters paid an extravagant sum for police protection and this may have been the reason why Captain Patrick J. Harding ignored a direct order from Mayor Carter Harrison II to shut the place down. It did get padlocked in 1911 however and the sisters, who had amassed a personal fortune in jewelry, stocks and bonds, moved on to the city's west side. The ladies were driven out by their indignant neighbors though and retired to private life in New York. The club was demolished in 1933 to make room for the Hilliard Homes, a public housing project.

The rest of the South Side Levee only lasted a year longer than the Everleigh Club. A massive civil welfare parade that was organized on September 29, 1912 spurred grand jury indictments and complaints to be filed against property owners in the district. This resulted in the end of "segregated vice" in Chicago but the Levee did not completely disappear. Many of the famous resorts from this area were bulldozed, as they stood in the way of an important east-west railroad corridor, but others remained and became the jazz clubs of the 1920's. A number of deadly occurrences still plagued the district in the years to come but when Colosimo's was finally closed in 1945 (Mike "The Greek" was convicted for income tax evasion) and demolished in 1957, an era in Chicago's sorted history finally came to a close.

The point of this history lesson on the vice of the South Side Levee district is to explain who the real "bosses" behind the Levee were. Michael "Hinky Dink" Kenna and "Bathhouse" John Coughlin, Chicago politicians, ran the notorious, gangster-infested First Ward for almost four decades, between 1897 and 1938.

They made a legendary team, collecting graft and doling out favors in the area to those who paid the most. In 1911, when Mayor Harrison gave the word to Captain Patrick J. Harding to order his divisional inspector John Wheeler to close down the Everleigh Club, the inspector did nothing until he received the okay from aldermen Kenna and Coughlin.

Coughlin was known as "Bathhouse" because he had once been a masseur in a Turkish bath and he was a large, poetry-spouting buffoon. He was known for being outgoing and good-hearted and a bizarre dresser, sporting garishly colored waistcoats. His poetry often appeared in Chicago newspapers and in his public statements, many mistook him for being simple-minded. Mayor Harrison once asked his partner, Kenna, if Bathhouse was crazy or taken with drugs. Kenna replied that he was neither. "To tell you the god's truth, Mayor, they ain't found a name for it yet."

"Hinky Dink" Kenna & "Bathhouse" John Coughlin (Chicago Historical Society)

Kenna was Coughlin's mirror opposite. He was small, glum and quietly dressed and was known for being shrewd and close-mouthed. At Kenna's Workingman's Exchange on Clark Street, patrons were served what was referred to as the "Largest and Coolest Schooner of Beer in the City" and the best free lunch around too. There were no orchestras here, no women, no music and no selling to minors. Here, for more than 20 years, the bums, the homeless and the jobless of the First Ward ate and drank for a nickel. Kenna also found jobs for the down and out and often rescued them from trouble with the police.

But he also told them how to vote -- in more than 40 years, he never lost an election or primary. He and Bathhouse created this astonishing record by marshaling the ward's party workers on election day to get votes from railroad hands, tramps, thieves and any other warm bodies that were available. They were taken to a polling place and were given already marked ballots that were deposited in a box. When they returned with the unmarked ballots (taken from the polling place), they could turn them in for a fee of 50 cents or a dollar. Those ballots were then marked and used at another polling place, where the whole scheme was repeated.

The two men made an unlikely pair but were a highly effective and increasingly wealthy duo. In addition to the other services they offered, such as guaranteed voting in the First Ward, they also provided protection for a variety of illicit enterprises. They exacted regular and weekly tributes that ranged from $25 per week from the small houses and as much as $100 from the larger ones. They also received an additional fee if drinks were sold or gambling occurred there. They also offered fees for legal work as well, such as stopping indictments for charges of grand larceny, pandering, theft or kidnapping. These fees could range as high as $500 to $2,000.

They were able to provide such services thanks to the fact that Coughlin and Kenna had men who were beholden to them in every city, county, state and federal office in the city. They controlled the jobs of city workers, including inspectors and the police, and were also, as aldermen, in a position to grant favors to respectable businessmen in Chicago. They could usually count on a routine take of between $15,000 and $30,000 per year, over and above the stipend of $3 per council meeting that they received from the city. Special votes that were purchased bought them in anywhere from $8,000 to $100,000 each, depending on the importance of the matter. The two men went carefully about their business filling the requests that the financiers of Chicago were willing to pay for, such as zoning variances, permits, tax deductions, licenses and other amenities.

However, things didn't always go smoothly and the two men did manage to get attention brought to them, both personally and professionally. For instance, one of Bathhouse's pet projects was the construction of a zoo on land that he owned in Colorado Springs in 1902. The zoo featured a refugee elephant from the

Lincoln Park Zoo who had managed to lose part of her trunk in a trap door. Princess Alice, as she was called, was purchased by Coughlin and shipped to Colorado, where she caught a severe cold in the winter of 1906. Coughlin suggested that she be given whiskey, which cured his own ailments, and so keepers gave the elephant an entire quart, which quickly cured her cold. After that, Princess Alice acquired a serious taste for the hard stuff and began searching the zoo looking for visitors with flasks. She would beg for drinks from them and when whiskey was given to her, she would sip it daintily and then go off somewhere and pass out.

As mentioned, Bathhouse was also noted for his horrible poetry. Epics that he penned included titles like "She Sleeps by the Drainage Canal", "Ode to a Bathtub", "Why Did They Build the Lovely Lake So Close to the Horrible Shore", "They're Tearing Up Clark Street Again" and others. It was later revealed though that John Kelley, a reporter for the *Chicago Tribune*, was the actual author of many of Coughlin's poems, which he read regularly at city council meetings. But only Coughlin would have taken credit for a terrible song that he wrote called "Dear Midnight of Love", which was performed for the first and last time at the Auditorium Theater in October 1899.

Bad poetry aside though, it was not weak prose that brought Coughlin and Kenna to the attention of the public and to every reform organization in Chicago from 1897 onward. It was constantly, and justifiably, assumed that the two of them were corrupt, although nothing was ever proven against them. Their most famous exploit was a party and it was one that was such an outstanding example of public debauchery that it was eventually shut down.

The First Ward Ball, which they organized, was referred to as an "annual underworld orgy". It was required that every prostitute, pimp, pickpocket and thief had to buy at least one ticket, while the owners of brothels and saloons had to purchase large blocks of them. The madams usually had their own boxes, where they could rub shoulders with city officials and politicians. The ball continued a tradition that started around 1880, when there was a charity party to honor Lame Jimmy, a pianist who worked for the renowned madam, Carrie Watson. They continued on until 1895, when a drunken detective shot another police officer at the party.

After the end of the charity gatherings, Coughlin and Kenna took responsibility for throwing the annual affair. It grew larger every year until the two aldermen were making as much as $50,000 from the party. They held the ball at the Chicago Coliseum and after one spectacle; the *Tribune* wrote that "if a great disaster had befallen the Coliseum last night, there would not have been a second story worker, a dip or pug ugly, porch climber, dope fiend or scarlet woman remaining in Chicago."

The 1907 First Ward Ball was perhaps the most widely reported and for this reason, seemed to raise the most ire among the various reform movements in the city. By the time, the ball opened that year, there were 15,000 people jammed into the Coliseum. One newspaper reported that there were so many drunks inside that when one would pass out, they could not even fall to the floor. In addition, women who fainted were passed over the heads of the crowd to the exits. As the event opened, a procession of Levee prostitutes marched into the building, led by Bathhouse John, with a lavender cravat and a red sash across his chest. Authors Lloyd Wendt and Herman Kogan described the parade: "On they came, madams, strumpets, airily clad jockeys, harlequins, Diana's, page boys, female impersonators, tramps, pan handlers, card sharps, mountebanks, pimps, owners of dives and resorts, young bloods and 'older men careless of their reputations'..."

At this point, the party really got started as women draped themselves over railings and ordered men to pour champagne down their throats. "The girls in peekaboo waists, slit skirts, bathing suits and jockey costumes relaxed and tripped to the floor where they danced wildly and drunkenly ... drunken men sought to undress young women and met with few objections ..." This seems to also be the first mention of Chicago's "drag queens" of the era too and reformers later described the antics of these men in women's costumes as "unbelievably appalling and nauseating."

Even though there had been 100 policemen detailed to the party, there were only eight arrests and one conviction -- that of Bernard Dooley, who was fined for entering the party without paying!

The Chicago Coliseum - Home of the First Ward Ball for years (Chicago Historical Society)

Hinky Dink Kenna later called the party a "lallapalooza" and added that "Chicago ain't no sissy town!"

Reform elements had attempted every year to stop the ball from taking place but had never succeeded. After the 1907 affair though, they were even more determined. In 1908, the rector, warden and vestry of the Grace Episcopal Church asked the Superior Court for an injunction against the event but the court simply stated that the affair was not within its jurisdiction. On December 13, just two days before the ball was to be held, a bomb exploded in the Coliseum, wrecking a two-story building that was used as a warehouse and breaking windows as far as two blocks away. The police who investigated said that it had been the work of "fanatical reformers" and the ball was given as scheduled. In fact, Bathhouse John told reporters that it was the "nicest Derby we ever had."

Reverend Melbourne P. Boynton of the Lexington Avenue Baptist Church, who apparently attended, said that it was "unspeakably low, vulgar and immoral". Public opinion sided with the minister and the 1908 First Ward Ball was the last. When Coughlin announced plans for the event in 1909, such a storm of opposition arose that Mayor Fred Busse refused to issue a liquor license. On December 13, Coughlin and Kenna gave a concert in the Coliseum but less than 3,000 people attended and police were on hand to make sure that no liquor was served and that no one got out of hand. It was the dullest affair that the Levee had ever seen and there has been no attempt to hold the First Ward Ball since.

The end came for Chicago's two most colorful aldermen not with a bang, but with a sad whisper. Bathhouse John Coughlin died on November 8, 1938, an old and fading politician and a veteran of 46 years on the city council. After all of the money that had had made over the years, he died more than $50,000 in debt, thanks to bad gambling debts.

Hinky Dink took care of his old friend's funeral arrangements but there were few people around to do the same thing for Kenna when he passed on in 1946. After more than 50 years as boss of the First Ward, there were only three cars with flowers at the graveside and the mayor didn't even attend. Unlike Coughlin though, Hinky Dink died a millionaire, leaving behind piles of cash (mostly in $1000 bills), two pints of vintage 1917 bourbon, 11 suits of woolen long underwear and a 1930 Pierce Arrow Limousine. After Coughlin's death though, he rarely ever left his suite at the Blackstone Hotel and toward the end, he never left it all. He died mostly forgotten and if not for the blatant corruption that reigned during his tenure as an alderman, and the debauchery of the First Ward Ball, it's likely he would not be remembered at all.

THE COLUMBIAN EXPOSITION OF 1893

The World's Columbian Exposition, celebrating the 400th Anniversary of Christopher Columbus' landing in America, was held in Chicago in 1893 -- one year later than the actual anniversary. Chicago, New York, Washington and St. Louis all competed vigorously for the honor of being host to the fair and it was during this jockeying that the city of Chicago actually gained the title of the "Windy City". As Chicago was doing more boasting about its landscape and amenities than any of the other cities, Charles A. Dana, editor of the *New York Sun*, advised his readers to ignore the "nonsensical claims of that windy city". This was the first use of the term and as mentioned already, has nothing to do with wind gusts along Lake Michigan. Chicago's lobbyists eventually won out and on April 25, 1890, President Benjamin Harrison signed the act that designated Chicago as the site of the exposition. It took three frantic years of preparation to produce the fair and although dedication ceremonies were held on October 21, 1892, the fairgrounds were not actually opened to the public until the following May.

By all accounts, the fair was a great success for both the city and the local criminal element as well. Attendance at the gin joints and brothels of the Levee tripled and everyone seemed to be making money. The city also attracted many famous, and infamous, visitors, including Gentleman Jim Corbett, Diamond Jim Brady, John Phillip Sousa, Lillian Russell and many others. Scandal was even provided Princess Eulalia of Spain, who snubbed Bertha Palmer, the queen of Chicago society, when she was invited as a guest to the Palmer Castle. She turned up her nose and stated that she preferred "not to meet with an innkeeper's wife." However, she did later turn up at the castle after breakfasting with the Carter Harrison's but there was little exchange between Bertha and the Princess. Years later, while in Paris, Mrs. Palmer got her revenge when she was invited to meet with the Princess. She politely sent her regrets: "I cannot meet with this bibulous representative of a degenerate monarchy", she said.

President Grover Cleveland arrived in Chicago in May 1893 to open the fair and nearly 400,000 people turned out to cheer and enjoy the event. The fairgrounds that had been constructed were made up of 630 acres and between May and October of that year, they attracted 25,836,073 people -- a number that equaled nearly half of the population of America at that time. The grounds included palaces, lagoons and immense buildings of plaster. Many of them became electrically lighted fantasies at night and so gleamed in the daylight sun that the grounds were dubbed the "White City".

Cleveland arrived riding in front of 23 horse-drawn carriages that conveyed the city's most solid and influential citizens. Thousands crushed into the area near the main speech stand and their cries and shouts were nearly drowned out by an orchestra that blared the "Columbian March". Crushed children wept, women screamed as their dresses were torn and some even fainted and had to be rescued from being stomped into the muddy lawns. Out of the chaos though, the fair was opened with the press of an electric key by President Cleveland. The president's high silk hat had been damaged in all of the excitement but he placed it aside and made a speech that could not have been heard by the gathered throng. He pressed the key with enthusiasm though and the flags of the United States and the red banner of Spain were run up their masts. Fountains began to spurt water and throughout the fair, vast and mysterious machines began to turn. Across the lake, the banging of guns from the warships assembled there began to sound and the fair was officially opened.

The main site of the fair was bounded by Stony Island Avenue on the west, 67th Street on the south, Lake Michigan on the east and 56th Street on the north. The Midway, which was one of the most popular attractions of the fair, was a narrow strip of land that ran between 59th and 60th Streets and extended west from Stony Island to Cottage Grove Avenue. Frederick Law Olmstead, who was America's foremost landscape architect, was responsible for the design of the fairgrounds. Jackson Park, which remains from those efforts, is still regarded as one of the city's most beautiful. A distinguished group of architects was assembled to create the buildings, including Henry Ives Cobb, Richard Morris Hunt, Charles McKim, George B. Post and Louis Sullivan. Sophie Hayden, the first woman awarded a degree in architecture from the Massachusetts Institute of Technology, designed the famous Women's Building.

The planners selected a classical architectural theme for the fair buildings, over the strenuous objections of the more innovative Chicago architects. In fact, Louis Sullivan later predicted that "the damage wrought by the World's Fair will last for half a century from its date, if not longer". Some have shared these feelings but others have pointed to the fact that the exposition's positive contributions to city planning led to the "City Beautiful" movement that followed.

In truth, most feel that the buildings that were created tended to be on the amazing side, if for nothing other than sheer size alone. Although the classical buildings were detailed and high decorated, they were made from temporary materials and were not substantial at all. The buildings were made from "staff", which was plaster and a mixture of fibers that would harden and be adaptable, like wood. By pouring the staff into glue molds, many ornamental pieces, which appeared to be hand made, could be achieved in a short time. The structure underneath the material was always steel or wood so that the buildings would not collapse.

Only one of the 200 buildings that were constructed for the fair, the Palace of Fine Arts, remains today. Like most of the others, this building was also a temporary structure that was made from staff but it housed the Field Columbian Museum after the fair's closing until 1920. During the late 1920's, the building was reduced to its steel skeleton and rebuilt with stone. It was opened again in 1931 as the Museum of Science and Industry.

The buildings on the grounds housed 65 exhibits that followed the theme of each building. Some of the most popular exhibits were curiosities, rather than serious displays of technology or progress. These included a hygienically stuffed whale that attendees could walk through, an 11-ton piece of cheese, a 1,500 pound replica of the Venus de Milo that was made from chocolate and a 70-foot tower of light bulbs in the Electricity Building.

There was always something to see on the fairgrounds and in those simpler times, the sights amazed the visitors, whether they had come from the city or the farms. There were movable sidewalks; the giant Yerkes telescopes; replicas of Columbus' three ships that has actually sailed from Spain in 1892; an Irish Village; Blarney Castle, with an appropriately fake Blarney stone that was actually a Chicago paving stone; and even a Nicola Tesla high current wire that powered a long-distance telephone line to New York. Visitors could also see real Parisian fashions; Miles Standish's pipe; a full-sized replica of Washington's Mount Vernon; the Liberty Bell; and an a presentation by a woman named Susan B. Anthony, who cherished a seemingly hopeless dream of a woman's right to vote.

The Columbian Exposition was the first world's fair to ever feature a separate amusement and entertainment area, dubbed the Midway. The noisy and distracting attractions here were concentrated in a central area so that not to disturb the park-like setting of the rest of the exposition. The Midway's features ranged from a replica "Streets of Cairo" to carnival rides and was the greatest attraction of the fair to those often referred to as the "great unwashed." It was here that the world's first Ferris Wheel was exhibited, invented by George W. Ferris. The 250-feet high steel structure had 36 cars, carrying 60 persons in each one. It was here also that a visitor could be treated to a cold beer, good food and could have your pocket picked by the best "dips" in the city.

It was along the "Streets of Cairo" exhibit that fair goers could see what became the most popular, and the most legendary, attraction of the fair. This was the first amusement to introduce the art of exotic dancing to America. While shocking to many, the exhibit proved to be the most successful Midway attraction and its investors realized more than double the profit on their investment. Without a doubt, the sensation of the exhibit (and the fair) was Fahreda Mahzar, who was better known as "Little Egypt". Fahreda was a belly dancer and with the diamonds on her garter, colorful brassiere and suggestive dance fascinated the "rubes" and easily gained the title of sexiest dancer at the fair. Little Egypt later became the wife of a Chicago restaurant owner and while her clothing would have been tame by modern standards, she was remembered for years as the most beautiful and wondrous attraction of the entire exhibition.

But not everything was shiny and beautiful with the Columbian Exposition. Despite the public face that had been put on the event, a darker side shimmered just below the surface. The area was a prime target for confidence men, pea-shell and three-card monte men, and thieves of every kind. Newspapers (mostly from out of town) reporting muggings and robberies and country yokels who were conned by loaded dice, marked cards, the gin joints and the painted ladies who could easily be found within walking distance of the fairgrounds.

And, as will be reported later, America's first real serial killer was operating in the Englewood neighborhood on the city's far south side, luring fair visitor's to his "hotel", where scores of them vanished without a trace --- never to be seen again.

Among its other problems, the fair also happen to be held during a panic on Wall Street and a depression that severely affected the city of Chicago and the rest of the nation. The Chemical National Bank, with a branch at the fair, failed just eight days after the exhibition opened.

The Jewelry Exhibition, a supposedly impregnable repository, was broken into and two large diamonds were stolen, along with a riding whip that was owned by King Leopold of the Belgians.

A tragic fire also struck during the fair. Some of the most popular buildings at the fair were the attractions that introduced many to the progress being made in the electrical field. Thomas Edison showed off his moving picture machine and enormous nighttime shows of artificial lighting were provided by George Westinghouse. It had been these strange and mysterious contraptions that had hummed to life with the press of the switch by President Cleveland. In addition to these exhibits, the fairgrounds boasted restaurants, cafés and support buildings. One of these utility buildings was the fair's cold storage warehouse. It was dubbed the "greatest refrigerator on earth", thanks to its massive size and it was located at 64th and Stony Island Avenue. Although it was not officially a part of the fair, it had its own ice skating rink and had been built specifically to manufacture ice and to store perishable items used by fair vendors.

The cold storage building had one fatal flaw in its design. Its iron chimney, fitted at its base to a series of boilers, was 200 feet high and because it was considered to be unsightly, a large wooden, decorative tower, topped with an ornate cupola, was built to enclose the chimney and hide it from view. For some reason, the cupola had been built just a few feet above the chimney and thus created a fire hazard. This should have caused concern with fire officials, especially after flames broke out in the tower. On June 17, the tower caught fire but the blaze was quickly put out by the Columbian Exposition Fire Brigade. On July 10, the firefighters (the Chicago Fire Department also maintained a battalion on the fairgrounds) were called back to the storage building when another fire started in the tower. This time, the blaze was not so easy to extinguish.

Led by Captain James Fitzpatrick, 20 men rushed to the top of the tower, climbing interior stairs that took them to platforms above the hot metal smokestack. Using ropes, the men hauled their equipment up, including a hose and a portable ladder. At this same time, hot coals started falling onto a platform below the firefighter's position, starting a secondary fire that began to burn upward. It quickly ate through the tower, cutting off the escape for the firefighters. The men were now trapped and were also faced with a loss of pressure in their hose, which nearly cut off their water supply.

The stranded men were left with just one option and that was tying off their hose line and trying to slide down it and escape from the flames, which were still climbing the tower. Two of them managed to escape, although they were badly burned in the process. When a third man followed their lead, he fell to his death when the hose burned through and snapped. The remaining firefighters either jumped or fell to their deaths. More than 40,000 spectators watched in disbelief as the men died. More than two hours passed before 30 responding fire companies were able to put out the fire. Another three days passed before the bodies of the firefighters, including Captain Fitzpatrick, could be found. Tragically, Fitzpatrick had survived the fall but had died soon after when his body fell through the roof and was buried in debris. Five of the other firefighters were badly injured and one was crippled for life. Two cold storage employees and one electrician working in the building had also been killed.

The tragedy marred the fair and it was not the only tragedy to occur during the fair's 183-day run. "Chicago Day" at the fair was a great success and its acceptance by the local residents was said to be a display of affection for Mayor Carter Harrison, who organized the day and welcomed all manner and class of people to the fairgrounds. Soon after the day was held though, Harrison received a visitor in his home, Patrick Eugene Joseph Prendergast, who shot the mayor to death.

The fair flags were lowered to half-mast at the news of the murder and on the Midway, minor rioting broke out and whiskey bottles were shattered on the facades of the white buildings. And not since the arrival of Abraham Lincoln's funeral train had there been such a weeping and thronging procession of mourners as when the mayor lay in state at Chicago's city hall. It was, some have said, a fitting climax to the soon-to-be-closing fair.

As the lights went dark on the fairground, many breathed a sigh of relief that the element that had been attracted to the city would finally be sent on its way. The Midway was scattered among the variety shows and museum circuits around the country, including the exotic dancers, which some called one of the worst "abominations ever invented". Little Egypt's imitators were now loose in America and for years afterward, small-time carnival midways were sure to feature "the Original Little Egypt -- direct from the Chicago Exposition".

All in all though, Chicago fared well during the fair. If not for the exposition, it's likely that the local economy would have been hit even harder than it was by the depression of the day. The gate receipts brought in more than $10 million and the concession receipts at least $4 million more. This did not include the millions made from souvenir books, coins and other items that were sold or even the bank interest that was earned on the deposits that were made. It was thought that at least $3 million was leftover to divide between the investors, a not insubstantial sum in those days.

But the glory of the Columbus Exposition was a transient one for Chicago. The vice dynasties that had been in existence, and those created during the fair, ran as wildly as they had in the past. And even darker days were ahead for the city ...

THE 1919 WHITE SOX SCANDAL

Civil War General Abner Doubleday has long been considered the inventor of baseball and while he may have popularized the pastime, he certainly did not create it. Based on the British sport of cricket, the official rules were set down in New York by Alexander Cartwright in 1845. The next year found the first game of record to be played in Hoboken, New Jersey with the New York Nine defeating the Knickerbockers in four full innings with a score of 23 to 1. The first professional team, the Cincinnati Red Stockings, appeared in 1869 and the rest, as they say, is history.

From these humble beginnings, baseball evolved into a major league sport and became big business. And when sports began to make money, the sportsmen began to brush shoulders with gangsters and gamblers. Prior to 1919, the fixing of baseball games for betting purposes was by no means unheard of, but it was in that year that it went too far and resulted in the most famous scandal in baseball history. Eight players of the Chicago White Sox (later nicknamed the Black Sox) were accused of throwing the World Series that was being played against the Cincinnati Red Legs, five games to three.

The details of what actually happened during the series are unclear and it's still unknown just how deeply the accused men were actually involved. It was, however, front page news around the country and even though they were acquitted of criminal charges, the players were all banned from professional baseball for life. The eight men included the great "Shoeless" Joe Jackson; pitchers Eddie Cicotte and Claude "Lefty" Williams; infielders Buck Weaver, Arnold "Chick" Gandil, Fred McMullin and Charles "Swede" Risberg; and outfielder Oscar "Happy" Felsch.

In those days, baseball was truly and American sport and almost everyone in the country watched their local games or followed some favorite team. The events that took place in Chicago, as the days of summer, faded into fall, shook the country to its core. Having just weathered a great world war, and now standing on the eve of Prohibition, when lawlessness would become a way of life to even the average person, the White Sox scandal can actually be seen as the final loss of innocence for the celebrated American way of life.

The White Sox during the 1919 World Series
(Chicago Historical Society)

The White Sox were formed in 1900 as a franchise in the American Baseball League and were owned by Charles A. Comiskey. They were originally called the White Stockings but the name was changed in 1902. In the team's first year, they won the league championship and the following year, the American and National Leagues agreed to meet in an end of the season play-off that had been dubbed the "World Series". In 1906, the White Sox won the championship by defeating the Chicago Cubs, four games to two. This would be the last of the team's victories for a while though and over the course of the next eight years, they lost many more games than they won.

In 1901 however, Comiskey decided to build a new ballpark on Chicago's south side and he dedicated himself to building a strong ball club. In 1915, he purchased the contracts of three stay players: outfield Joe Jackson, second baseman Eddie Collins and center fielder Happy Felsch. Comiskey was closely involved with the changing of the team and in fact, as a former first baseman, is credited with being the first to teach his players to adjust their field positions according to the habits of the batter. In 1917, the Sox won the World Series and by 1919 had the best record in the American League. Comiskey had succeeded in building baseball's most powerful team.

But despite their success on the field, the White Sox were a troubled and unhappy team. They may have played better than every other team in 1919 but were the worst paid in both leagues. Many have stated that they believe Comiskey himself was really the one responsible for the World Series scandal. If he had not grossly underpaid his players and had not treated them so unfairly, it's likely that none of them would have agreed to throw the series. He was able to get away with paying them so poorly because of a "reverse clause" that has been put into their contracts. This clause prevented the players from changing teams without the permission of the owner and with no union, the players had no bargaining power at all.

Comiskey also made frequent promises to the players that he did not keep. For instance, he once promised them that they would receive a large bonus if they won the pennant. When they did win it though, the bonus turned out to be nothing more than a case of cheap champagne. He even charged the players for laundering their uniforms, so in protest, the players wore the same uniforms for several weeks. Comiskey finally had the filthy uniforms removed from their lockers and cleaned, then fined the players for their demonstration.

To make matters even more volatile, the White Sox team members did not get along well with each other either. Their constant bickering was marked by jealousy and verbal abuse, dividing the team into separate factions, one led by second baseman Eddie Collins and the other by first baseman Chick Gandil. Collins' group was educated, sophisticated and able to negotiate salaries as high as $15,000. Gandil's less polished faction, who earned only about $6,000, bitterly resented the disparity.

All of these things combined to make for a bad situation in 1919. The year before, with the country disrupted by World War I, interest in baseball dropped to a record low. By the time of the World Series in 1919 though, baseball and America were back on track. In fact, baseball was more popular than ever and the enthusiasm for it took everyone by surprise. Fans eagerly followed the games and national interest in the World Series was so great that baseball officials decided for the first time to make it a best of nine series, instead of the traditional best of seven.

This probably explains the marked interest with gamblers in the game as well. Gamblers were often visibly present at the ballpark and there had been rumors of games being fixed for many years. Rumors even circulated that players were supplementing their incomes by throwing games and some of them had gained reputations for working closely with the gamblers. One small time Chicago gambler, Joseph Sullivan, had allegedly made money using inside information from Sox player Chick Gandil. Sullivan's bets were always safer when he knew a pitcher or hitter was sick, injured or even just having an off week. Many of the team owners attempted to curb the presence of gamblers in the ballpark. Comiskey posted signs throughout the stadium that stated "No Betting Allowed in this Park" but unfortunately, the signs were not enough. Player resentment was high and the gambler's offers, which were usually several times a player's usual salary, were often too tempting to refuse.

Over the years, the facts behind the throwing of the World Series have become quite cloudy but those who have researched the case believe that it was likely Arnold "Chick" Gandil who was the ringleader. A few weeks before the 1919 World Series, Gandil approached gamblers Joseph "Sport" Sullivan and William "Sleepy Bill" Burns of New York about fixing the series. He allegedly told them that for $10,000, Gandil and several of his teammates could make sure that the White Sox lost the series. Because the gamblers felt that they needed more capital to finance a huge win, they approached the country's leading gambler, Arnold "The Brain" Rothstein. It is unknown whether or not Rothstein entered into the plot or if he turned them down and then simply went ahead and bet at least $60,000 on Cincinnati (he collected $270,000) because he knew the fix was in and saw no need to pay the bribe money himself. Whatever actually happened, the main operator behind the fix became Abe Attell, a former featherweight boxing champion.

After Gandil gained the support of the gamblers, he went to work getting the cooperation of his teammates. Gandil was known as a rough character and had been in trouble before. At the age of 33, he was getting ready to retire but wanted to make one last shot at big money before he went. He had been linked to gamblers in the past and had been suspended temporarily earlier that same season. The White Sox had been playing the Cleveland Indians at Comiskey Park and Gandil had become annoyed with the Indians' Tris Speaker. In the eighth inning, Speaker had smacked a grounder to Gandil at first and then had come sliding into first base with his spikes flying. Gandil's shins were cut and at the end of the inning, when Speaker came out of the dugout to take his place in center field, the two men got into a brawl. They hammered at one another for several minutes before seven police officers were able to separate them. The fans were upset and began to throw soda bottles at the Indians until Sox manager, William "Kid" Gleason, walked out onto the field with a police officer. He asked them to stop before someone got hurt or the game ended up being forfeited. They settled down and the Sox won the game. Both of the players were temporarily suspended the next day by Bancroft B. Johnson, the president of the American League.

And Gandil was heading for bigger trouble than this. He needed to recruit as many of his fellow players to the scheme as possible. If the gamblers were going to put up $100,000, Gandil needed to make sure that a sufficient number of players would go along with the fix. Two of the Sox pitchers, Cicotte and Williams (some say that Williams became the go-between for the players and gamblers) had won 52 games between them in the 1919 season and Gandil needed their participation to succeed. Cicotte had his own grudge against Comiskey too. The team owner had once promised Cicotte that if he won 30 games, he would receive a $10,000 bonus. When Cicotte won 29 games, Comiskey benched him with an excuse that he needed to rest up for the pennant games to come. Comiskey never did give him the money. That was surely on his mind when he told Gandil that if he wanted him to go along with the scheme, Cicotte would need $10,000 up front. Williams and Risberg were also interested and McMullin, who overheard Gandil talking to Risberg, also wanted in.

Jackson and Weaver are the two players whose involvement in fixing the series is most disputed. According to Jackson, when Gandil offered him $10,000 in exchange for helping to throw the games, Jackson turned him down. Gandil upped the amount to $20,000 but Jackson still refused. Gandil then supposedly told Jackson that he could take it or leave it because the fix was already going to happen as long as the gamblers came up with the money. Jackson's refusal was a problem though, as he was the team's star player and it's likely that the gamblers would have wanted his involvement. Most believe that Gandil simply lied to them and told them that Jackson was part of the scheme, even though he actually wasn't. As for Weaver, he attended several meetings of the players who planned to fix the games but he also apparently refused to be a part of the actual conspiracy.

When the series finally kicked off, the White Sox were matched up against the Cincinnati Reds and were favored to win. They were almost the identical team from the 1917 championship and the 1919 World Series should have been easily won. It was said that most people came to the games not to see if the Sox won, but how they actually went about it. Early odds favored Chicago 5 to 1 but the day before the series started in Cincinnati, rumors of a fix were flying. As soon as the big money started changing hands, the odds began to shift toward the Reds.

On the night before the first game, Cicotte found $10,000 waiting for him in his hotel room.

Chicago lost the first game with a score of 9 to 1 but the players did not receive the $20,000 in cash that Gandil had promised them for losing the game. They were willing to lose game two, they told him, but only as long as the money came in at the end of the next day. They lost that next game 4 to 2 and needless to say, Sox players not involved in the fix began to get suspicious. Catcher Ray Schalk knew that something was wrong with the pitching and he and Kid Gleason reportedly got into fights with Gandil and Williams over their pathetic performances. After the game, Gandil went searching for Abe Attell, looking for the $40,000 that he and his fellow conspirators were owed for throwing the two games. He received only $10,000 though and now the players were having second thoughts about losing.

Angry at being stiffed for the initial amount they were promised, the players put an extra effort into the next game and managed to win. The gamblers who had been betting on individual games lost a bundle and feeling betrayed, Attell refused to pay any more. Sullivan however, came up with $20,000 before the fourth game and at least some of the conspirators were still willing to lose. Cicotte made several clumsy but crucial errors and the Reds won the game 2 to 0. Chicago lost game five as well, with a final score of 5 to 0.

By now, the gamblers had missed another payment and the players decided that it just wasn't worth it to lose. At least if they won the series, they would take home $5,000 each. The White Sox then managed to win game six with a score of 5 to 4 and the seventh game, 4 to 1. The team was back to playing to the best of their abilities and it seemed inevitable that the championship title would go to Chicago. But then any chance of winning was curbed by Arnold Rothstein, who had not bet on the individual games but on Cincinnati to win the entire series. With his investment now at risk, he sent one of his men to go and have a talk with Claude Williams, who would be pitching the eighth game. He "explained" to Williams that Rothstein wanted the series to end the following day and he got his point across by telling the pitcher that his wife would pay the price for his refusal to obey orders. Terrified, Williams pitched the worst game of his career and Chicago lost 10 to 5. Cincinnati had just won the World Series.

During the series, a sports writer for the *Chicago Herald & Examiner*, Hugh Fullerton, was paying close attention to the rumors that he heard about a fix. He had hinted about the potential problems with the series in his columns and used the rumors to encourage team owners to do something about the involvement of gamblers in baseball. His columns met with little response though. The public never dreamed that anyone could, or would, fix the World Series. The owners however, feared that it could be done but they also believed that if the public found out, they would turn their backs on baseball for good. They refused to acknowledge the problem and hoped that it would either stay silent or simply go away. Fullerton suspected that something shady had occurred during the 1919 World Series, but he could never put his finger on just what it was or who was actually involved.

And the whole thing might have faded from memory if the gambler's involvement in the sport had not continued to cause problems. During the 1920 season, players on other teams began to take advantage of the offers made to them by gamblers. Widespread rumors began to surface about games being thrown by players with the New York Giants, the Yankees, the Atlanta Braves and the Cleveland Indians.

Finally, in September 1920, a Cook County grand jury convened to look into allegations that the Chicago Cubs had thrown games that were played against the Philadelphia Phillies. The investigation grew and eventually extended to the 1919 World Series and baseball gambling in general. The White Sox were enjoying a good season in 1920 when the grand jury began calling players, owners, managers, writers and gamblers to testify about what had taken place the year before. At the urging of Comiskey, who was trying to cover up his knowledge of the conspiracy, Jackson and Cicotte were the first to admit what they knew about the fix.

When the grand jury concluded its investigation, indictments were handed down against eight White Sox players, as well as Abe Attell, Joe Sullivan and several of Rothstein's men. Rothstein, who made a reported $270,000 on the series, was never indicted. He later moved on to bootlegging during Prohibition, then drug dealing and labor racketeering. Years later, he was murdered by a rival gambler that Rothstein had accused of fixing a poker game.

The trial of the accused White Sox players began in June 1921. The players had not even been suspended until they were only three games left to play in the 1920 season. By this time, the confessions of three of the players forced Comiskey to act. When the trial got started, it was discovered that the grand jury records, including the confessions of Jackson, Cicotte and Williams, were missing. (Note: they turned up four years later in the possession of Comiskey's lawyer, George Hudnall, who never explained why he had them) After a month of hearing testimony, it took the jury just two hours and 47 minutes to acquit all of the defendants. The lack of any real evidence, and the missing confessions, resulted in a not-guilty verdict. The trial never really answered any of the lingering questions in the case and the facts, which were never really clear cut in the first place, continued to be manipulated and distorted into outright lies.

After the 1920 season, club owners realized that if they were going to regain the public trust in baseball, they were going to have to clean things up. The three-man national commission was replaced by a single, independent commissioner with dictatorial power over baseball. Federal Judge Kenesaw Mountain Landis was appointed commissioner and he acted quickly to restore the public trust in the sport. Immediately after the accused White Sox players were acquitted of all criminal charges, Landis banned all eight players from the game -- for life. An outcry went up from certain quarters but Landis refused to budge. He said: "regardless of the verdict of the juries, no player who throws a ball game, no player who undertakes or promises to throw a ball game, no player who sits in confidence with a bunch of crooked players and does not promptly tell his club about it, will ever play professional baseball." And true to his word, Landis never allowed any of the eight men to play professional ball again.

Although banned from baseball, several of the so-called Black Sox were unwilling, or unable, to give up the game entirely. Not only did they love the sport but for several of them, it was the only profession that they had ever known. While some of the players distanced themselves from sports, Joe Jackson, Eddie Cicotte and Swede Risberg continued to play the game in outlaw leagues or semi-professional teams. When

Shoeless Joe Jackson
(Chicago Historical Society)

Joe Jackson was unable to play ball anymore, he owned and operated a liquor store. He died in 1951, shortly after being inducted into the Cleveland Baseball Hall of Fame. Eddie Cicotte became a game warden and security guard and died in 1970. Swede Risberg worked for many years on a Minnesota dairy farm and died in California in 1975. Third Basemen Buck Weaver attended meetings where the fix was planned but refused to participate and he made a number of attempts to appeal to Judge Landis for reinstatement to the game. They were all unsuccessful and he ended up running a drugstore and died of a heart attack in 1956.

Fred McMullin died in California in 1952. Lefty Williams ran a poolroom for a while and then moved to California, where he ran a landscaping business. He died in 1959. Happy Felsch operated a tavern in Milwaukee until his death in 1964.

As the years passed, the story of the Black Sox scandal became a tragic part of baseball history --- and a heartbreaking piece of American folklore as well. The story goes that when several of the accused players left the grand jury room at the start of the investigation, a small group of young boys were waiting for them. One of them spoke up to Shoeless Joe Jackson. "It ain't true, is it, Joe?" one of them asked.

"Yes, boys," the outfielder replied sadly. "I'm afraid it is."

"Say it ain't so, Joe," the boy cried and his words have yet to be forgotten.

TRAGEDY AND DEATH

Over the years, Chicago has been plagued by many tragedies and scores of lives have been lost in fires, accidents and disasters. Many of these horrible events have left an impression behind -- not only with the ruined lives and broken families -- but as hauntings as well.

Fires have taken many lives in Chicago and have left a mark on the city. While the Great Chicago Fire was the most famous blaze in the city's history, it was certainly not the deadliest, nor, some might say, was it the most heartbreakingly tragic.

That soul-crushing fire took place on December 1, 1958 when 92 children and three nuns died at the Our Lady of Angels School on the west side. This horrible event has been called the "fire that refuses to die" as many lives were shattered on that fateful day and the neighborhood where the school once stood has never fully recovered.

The fire is painstakingly documented in the book *To Sleep with the Angels* by David Cowan and John Kuentsler and it describes a quiet Catholic parish around 3820 West Iowa Street (where the school was located) of about 4,500 families of mostly Irish and Italian backgrounds. Many of them lived modestly in apartments and brick bungalows and after the fire, many of these hardworking families abandoned the neighborhood, never to return.

The fire began at around 2:40 p.m. on December 1, about 20 minutes before school was let out for the day. Like many other schools at that time, Our Lady of Angels was tragically without many of the safety measures that exist today. There were no smoke detectors, no sprinkler systems, no outside fire alarm and the entire school had only one fire escape. Unbelievably though, the school had just passed a fire inspection two months before. By 1958 standards, the building was legally safe.

It is believed that the fire started in a trash can at the bottom of the basement stairwell. Here, it smoldered all day and then spread to the stairs, thanks to air from an open window. Once it was ignited, the fire quickly spread and burned up to the second floor, devouring the building as it went. By the time the first fire trucks arrived, the upper floor of the north wing was engulfed in flames. The fire had already been burning for a number of minutes before the alarm was sent and more precious time was lost when the fire department trucks pulled up the church rectory and not the school. The dispatchers had been given the wrong address by the person who phoned in the report. Then, when the first trucks arrived at the school, they had to break through a locked gate to get inside.

Inside of the classrooms, which were rapidly filling with smoke, the students heard the sound of the fire trucks approaching but then nothing, as the trucks went to the rectory instead. At that desperate moment, the nuns asked the children to simply bow their heads in prayer. When the trucks finally arrived, and the extent of the blaze was realized, another alarm was sent out, ordering all available vehicles to the scene. Before it was over, 43 pieces of fire equipment were at the scene.

As more time passed, the fire escape had become unreachable through the burning hallways. The only way out was through the windows and soon, screaming children were plunging to the frozen ground below. The firemen behaved heroically and as desperate as the situation had become, the firefighters managed to save 160 children by pulling them out the windows, passing them down ladders, catching them in nets and breaking their falls with their own bodies. One rescuer who climbed a ladder up to the building's second floor was Lieutenant Charles Kamin. When he reached the window of Room 211, he found a number of 8th graders were crammed together and trying to squeeze out. He reached inside and, one a time, began grabbing them, swinging them around his back and dropping them onto the ladder. He saved nine children, mostly boys because he could grab hold of their belts. He was only stopped when the room exploded and the students fell back out of his reach.

More confusion, and despair, was added to the scene as spectators began to arrive. They rushed the police lines, hysterically trying to reach their children who were trapped in the building, and hampered the efforts of the firefighters. It took the crews a little more than an hour to put out the fire and when they entered the second-story classrooms, they made a number of heartbreaking discoveries. Flames had consumed everything and had claimed the lives of dozens of children and nuns.

For the hundreds of parents and relatives who stood outside, the huge loss of life was soon apparent as cloth-covered stretchers began to emerge from the smoldering building. A long line of ambulances and police squadrons slowly collected the bodies and took them to the Cook County morgue, where family members could identify them. For many parents standing outside, the tragedy was made worse because many of them did not know if their children were dead or alive. Although a number of parents located them in the streets outside the school or in homes nearby, others were left to search the seven hospitals were the injured were taken --- or worse yet, the morgue.

Chicago was stunned by the appalling loss and word of the disaster spread around the world. In Rome, Pope John XXIII sent a personal message to the archbishop of Chicago, the Most Reverend Albert Gregory Meyer. Four days later, he would conduct a mass for the victims and their families before an altar set up at the Northwest Armory. He called the fire "a great and inescapable sorrow".

Nearly as tragic as the fire itself is the fact that no blame was ever placed for the disaster. In those days, there was no thought of suing those responsible for the conditions that allowed the fire to happen. Outwardly, the families accepted the idea that the fire had been simply "God's will" but it cannot be denied that a number of those involved left the church, their faith was shattered as their lives. No one dared to challenge the church over what happened and life moved quietly on.

But in January 1962, the fire was news again when police in Cicero, Illinois questioned a 13 year-old boy about a series of fires that had been set in the city. When they learned that he had been a troubled student at Our Lady of Angels at the time of the fire, their interrogations took another direction. His mother and stepfather hired an attorney, who recommended that the boy submit to a polygraph test.

In the interview, polygraph expert John Reid learned that the boy began starting fires at the age of five, when he set fire to his family's garage. He had also set as many as 11 fires in buildings in Chicago and

Cicero, usually by tossing burning matches on papers at the bottom of staircases. This was exactly how most believed the Our Lady of Angels fire started and so Reid pressed him harder. The boy denied starting the fire at first but test results pointed to the fact that he was lying. Later, the boy admitted that he had set the blaze, hoping for a few extra days out of school. He also hated his teachers and his principal because they "always wanted to expel me from school". His attendance record had been poor and his behavior was "deplorable".

In his confession, he said that he had started the fire in the basement after going to the bathroom. He threw three matches into a trashcan and then ran upstairs to his second-floor classroom, which was soon evacuated. When Reid asked him why he had never told anyone about setting fire to the school, the boy replied: "I was afraid my dad was going to give me a beating and I'd get in trouble with the police and I'd get the electric chair or something."

Reid turned the confession over to the police and the boy was placed in the Audy Juvenile Home. Charges were filed against him but after a series of hearings that ended in March 1962, Judge Alfred Cilella tossed out the boy's confessions, ruling that Reid had obtained it illegally. Also, since the boy was under the age of 13 at the time of the fire, he could not be tried for a felony in Illinois. He did charge the boy with starting the fires in Cicero though and he was sent away to a home for troubled boys in Michigan. Whatever became of the boy after that is mystery.

Even after all of the time that has passed, the fire has never been forgotten. A new parish school was constructed on the site in 1960, but it was closed down in 1999 because of declining enrollments. The only memorial to the victims of the fire is located in Queen of Heaven Cemetery in Hillside, where 25 of the victims were buried. It was constructed from private donations in 1960 and to this date, no official recognition or memorial to the fire has been erected.

But no matter how you look at it, the fire may have another legacy that has endured. Thanks to the horror at the Our Lady of Angels, the lives of future children may have been saved. Even though this is small comfort to the families of those who perished, the new safety regulations that went into effect because of the fire, including alarm boxes and sprinkler systems, have most likely saved the lives of thousands of children over the years. Regardless, those who lost their lives in this tragedy will never be forgotten.

THE IROQUOIS THEATER FIRE

Another terrible blaze occurred at the Iroquois Theater on December 30, 1903 as a fire broke out in the crowded theater during a performance of a vaudeville show, starring the popular comedian Eddie Foy. The fire was believed to have been started by faulty wiring leading to a spotlight and claimed the lives of hundreds of people, including children, who were packed into the afternoon show for the holidays.

The Iroquois Theater, the newest and most beautiful showplace in Chicago in 1903, was believed to be "absolutely fireproof". The Chicago Tribune called it a "virtual temple of beauty" but just five weeks after it opened its doors, it became a blazing death trap.

The new theater was much acclaimed, even before it opened. It was patterned after the Opera Cominque in Paris and was located downtown on the north side of Randolph Street, between State and Dearborn. The interior of the four-story building was magnificent, with stained glass and polished wood throughout. The lobby had an ornate 60-foot-high ceiling and featured white marble walls fitted with large mirrors that were framed in gold leaf and stone. Two grand staircases led away from either side of the lobby to the balcony areas as well. Outside, the building's front façade resembled a Greek temple with a towering stone archway that was supported by massive columns.

Thanks to the dozens of fires that had occurred over the years in theaters, architect Benjamin H. Marshall wanted to assure the public that the Iroquois was safe. He studied a number of fires that had occurred in the past and made every effort to make sure that no tragedy would occur in the new theater. The Iroquois had 25 exits that, it was claimed, could empty the building in less than five minutes. The stage had also been fitted with an asbestos curtain that could be quickly lowered to protect the audience.

And while all of this was impressive, it was not enough to battle the real problems that existed with the Iroquois. Seats in the theater were wooden and stuffed with hemp and much of the precautionary fire equipment that was advertised to have been installed, never actually made it into the building. The theater had no fire alarms and in a rush to open the theater on time, other safety factors had been forgotten or simply ignored.

The horrific events began on a bitterly cold December 30 of 1903. A holiday crowd had packed into the theater on that Wednesday afternoon to see a matinee performance of the hit comedy *Mr. Bluebeard*. Officially, the Iroquois seated 1,600 people but with school out for Christmas break, it is believed there was an overflow crowd of nearly 2,000 people filling the seats and standing four-deep in the aisles. Another crowd filled the backstage area with 400 actors, dancers and stagehands hidden from those in the auditorium.

Around 3:20 p.m., at the beginning of the second act, stagehands noticed a spark descend from an overhead light, and then some scraps of burning paper that fell down onto the stage. In moments, flames began licking at the red-velvet curtain and while a collective gasp went up from the audience, no one rushed for the exits. It has been surmised that the audience merely thought the fire was part of the show.

Although in his dressing room, applying his final makeup for the act, Eddie Foy heard the commotion outside and rushed out onto the stage to see what was going on. He implored the audience to remain seated and calm, assuring them that the theater was fireproof and that everyone was safe. He signaled conductor Herbert Gillea to play and the music had a temporary soothing effect on the crowd, which was growing restless. A few moments later, a flaming set crashed down onto the stage and Foy signaled a stagehand to lower the asbestos curtain to protect the audience. Unfortunately though, the curtain snagged halfway down, leaving a 20-foot gap between the bottom of the curtain and the wooden stage.

The other actors in the show remained composed until they too realized what was happening. Many of them panicked and several chorus girls fainted and had to be dragged off-stage. The audience began to scream and panic too and a mad rush was started for the Randolph Street exit from the theater. Foy made one last attempt to calm the audience and then he fled to a rear exit. With children in tow, the audience members immediately clogged the gallery and the upper balconies. The aisles had become impassable and as the lights went out, the crowd milled about in blind terror. The auditorium began to fill with heat and smoke and screams echoed off the walls and ceilings. Through it all, the mass continued to move forward but when the crowd reached the doors, they could not open them as they had been designed to swing inward rather than outward. The crush of people prevented those in the front from opening the doors. To make matters worse, some of the side doors to the auditorium were reportedly locked. Many of those who died not only burned, but suffocated from the smoke and the crush of bodies as well. Later, as the police removed the charred remains from the theater, they discovered that a number of victims had been trampled in the panic. One dead woman's face even bore the mark of a shoe heel.

Backstage, theater employees and cast members opened a rear set of double doors, which sucked the wind inside and caused flames to fan out under the asbestos curtain and into the auditorium. A second gust of wind created a fireball that shot out into the galleries and balconies that were filled with people. All of the stage drops were now on fire and as they burned, they engulfed the supposedly noncombustible asbestos curtain and when it collapsed, it plunged into the seats of the theater.

The scene outside of the theater was completely normal and most accounts say that the fire was burning for almost 15 minutes before any smoke was noticed by those passing by. Because there was no fire alarm box outside, someone ran around the corner to sound the alarm at Engine Co. 13. Things were so quiet in front of the Iroquois though that the first firefighters to arrive thought it was a false alarm.

This changed when they tried to open the auditorium doors and found they could not --- there were too many bodies stacked up against them. Another alarm was sounded as the firemen tried to get into the building. They were only able to gain access by actually pulling the bodies out of the way with pike poles, peeling them off one another and then climbing over the stacks of corpses. It took only ten minutes to put out the remaining blaze, as the intense heat inside had already eaten up anything that would still burn. The firefighters made their way into the blackened auditorium and were met with only silence and smell of death. They called out for survivors but no one answered their cry.

The gallery and upper balconies sustained the greatest loss of life as the patrons had been trapped by locked doors at the top of the stairways. The firefighters found 200 bodies stacked there, as many as 10 deep. Those who escaped had literally ripped the metal bars from the front of the balcony and had jumped onto the crowds below. Even then, most of these met their deaths at a lower level.

A few who made it to the fire escape door behind the top balcony found that the iron staircase was missing. In its place was a platform that plunged about 100 feet to the cobblestone alley below. Across the alley, behind the theater, painters were working on a building occupied by Northwestern University's dental school. When they realized what was happening at the theater, they quickly erected a makeshift bridge using ladders and wooden planks, which they extended across the alley to the fire escape platform. Reports vary as to how many they saved, but it's thought that it may have been as many as 12, although it's also believed that at least seven people fell to their deaths from the "bridge". Others say that many times that number jumped from the ledge or were pushed by the milling crowd that pressed through the doors behind them. The passageway behind the theater is still referred to as "Death Alley" today, after nearly 150 victims were found piled here -- stacked by the firemen or having fallen to their fates.

When it was all over, 572 people died in the fire and more died later, bringing the eventual death toll up to 602, including 212 children. For nearly five hours, police officers, firemen and even newspaper reporters, carried out the dead. Anxious relatives sifted through the remains, searching for loved ones. Other bodies were taken away by police wagons and ambulances and transported to a temporary morgue at Marshall Field's on State Street. Medical examiners and investigators worked all through the night.

The next day, the newspapers devoted full pages to lists of the known dead and injured. News wires carried reports of the tragedy around the country and it soon became a national disaster. Chicago mayor Carter Harrison, Jr. issued an order that banned public celebration on New Year's Eve, closing the night clubs and making forbidden any fireworks or sounding of horns. Every church and factory bell in the city was silenced and on January 2, 1904, the city observed an official day of mourning.

Someone, the public cried, had to answer for the fire and an investigation of the blaze brought to light a number of troubling facts. The investigation discovered that two vents of the building's roof, which had not been completed in time for the theater's opening, were supposed to filter out smoke and poisonous gases in case of a fire. However, the unfinished vents had been nailed shut to keep out rain and snow. That meant that the smoke had nowhere to go but back into the theater, literally suffocating those audience members who were not already burned to death. Another finding showed that the supposedly "fireproof" asbestos curtain was really made from cotton and other combustible materials. It would have never saved anyone at all. In addition to not having any fire alarms in the building, the owners had decided that sprinklers were too unsightly and too costly and had never had them installed.

To make matters worse, the management also established a policy to keep non-paying customers from slipping into the theater during a performance --- they quietly bolted nine pair of iron panels over the rear doors and installed padlocked, accordion-style gates at the top of the interior second and third floor stairway landings. And just as tragic was the idea they came up with to keep the audience from being distracted during a show. They ordered all of the exit lights to be turned off! One exit sign that was left on led only to ladies restroom and another to a locked door for a private stairway. And as mentioned already, the doors of the outside exits, which were supposed to make it possible for the theater to empty in five minutes, opened to the inside, not to the outside.

The investigation led to a cover-up by officials from the city and the fire department, who denied all knowledge of fire code violations. They blamed the inspectors, who had overlooked the problems in exchange for free theater passes. A grand jury indicted a number of individuals, including the theater owners, fire officials and even the mayor. No one was ever charged with a criminal act though. Families of the dead filed nearly 275 civil lawsuits against the theater but no money was ever collected. The Iroquois Theater Company filed for bankruptcy soon after the disaster.

The Iroquois Theater Fire ranks as the nation's fourth deadliest blaze and the deadliest single building fire in American history. Nevertheless, the building was repaired and re-opened briefly in 1904 as Hyde and Behmann's Music Hall and then in 1905 as the Colonial Theater. In 1924, the building was razed to make room for a new theater, the Oriental, but the façade of the Iroquois was used in its construction. The Oriental operated at what is now 24 West Randolph Street until the middle part of 1981, when it fell into disrepair and was closed down. It opened again as the home to a wholesale electronics dealer for a time and then went dark again. The restored theater is now part of the Civic Tower Building and is next door to the restored Delaware Building. It reopened as the Ford Center for the Performing Arts in 1998.

But this has not stopped the tales of the old Iroquois Theater from being told, especially in light of more recent -- and more ghostly events. According to author Ursula Bielski, and current accounts from people who live and work in this area, "Death Alley" is not as empty as it appears to be. The narrow passageway, which runs behind the old Oriental Theater, is rarely used today, except for the occasional delivery truck or a lone pedestrian who is in a hurry to get somewhere else. It is largely deserted, but why? The stories say that those a few who do pass through the alley often find themselves very uncomfortable and unsettled here. They say that faint cries are sometimes heard in the shadows and that some have reported being touched by unseen hands and by eerie cold spots that seem to come from nowhere and vanish just as quickly.

One man that I spoke with attended college nearby and lived at that time in a building that was located along "Death Alley". He, and others who resided in the building, often spoke of strange things that took place in their apartments, including doors that opened and closed, inexplicable sounds and on one occasion, an apparition that appeared standing in a doorway one evening. Residents of the building came to believe that the weird happenings were a result of the long ago fire and were caused by the spirits of those who did not survive the tragedy.

Could the alleyway, and the surrounding area, actually be haunted? And do the spirits of those who met their tragic end inside of the burning theater still linger here? Perhaps, or perhaps the strange sensations experienced here are "ghosts of the past" of another kind --- a chilling remembrance of a terrifying event that will never be completely forgotten.

THE FATEFUL HAND OF DEATH

The story of Frank Leavy's handprint has long been one of my favorite weird tales of Chicago. It is a tale that involves a portent of doom, a tragic fire and a ghostly handprint that could not be explained.

On the afternoon of Good Friday, April 18, 1924, the members of the Chicago Fire Department's Engine Co. 107 were going about their usual routine. Even though it was holy day, it would be a day like any other to the firefighters who were on call. They still had to eat, clean and make sure their equipment and trucks were always ready. And cleaning the large firehouse seemed to be a never-ending task for the men. One of firefighters was a man named Francis X. Leavy and on this particular day, he had drawn the duty of cleaning the building's first floor windows.

Leavy was a good Irish family man and had been with the fire department for 13 years, after an eight-year tour with the Navy, which he had joined at age 14. He and his wife Mary were the parents of two children, Frank Jr. and daughter June. On this day, the usually jovial Leavy was strangely sullen and quiet. He couldn't seem to shake whatever was bothering him and this put his friends on edge.

Also troubling was the news that was coming over the telegraph system in front of the firehouse. A four-alarm fire had started in the Union Stockyards and even though Engine Co. 107 was too far away from it and not expected to respond, the idea that a large fire was burning just a few miles away bothered all of them.

Leavy seemed to be lost in his own thoughts, keeping his attention on the window that he was washing. For some reason though, he paused in his work and with his left hand resting against the pane of glass, spoke aloud: "This is my last day on the fire department."

Leavy spoke to no one in particular but several men heard him. This, along with his sudden change in personality, puzzled the others, including Edward McKevitt, who had been standing next to Leavy. He started to ask what his friend meant by this but just then, the station received an alarm call. They were told to go to Fourteenth and Blue Island because the stations that normally covered that area were tied up with the stockyards fire. Just as the other men did, Leavy put on his helmet, coat and boots and jumped onto the back of the truck that had been assigned to Engine 107.

The burning building they were sent to was Curran Hall, a 50 year-old brick building that was located on South Blue Island, southwest of the Loop. During its heyday, it had been a popular dance hall but had closed down because of Prohibition. Several small businesses were now operating out of it.

The fire crew stretched a hose up the fire escape and into the building's second story. They crawled through the smoke and fire to aim the water stream at the flames that were roaring inside. They had no breathing apparatus in those days and so the men had to crawl back and forth to a door or window, following the hose line, to get fresh air. They fought the fire for about a half hour before one of the building's outer walls suddenly buckled, knocking down the entire structure and trapping the firefighters inside. The collapse knocked out the electricity in the area and the remaining crew had to search for the buried men with flashlights. For hours they dug by hand, ignoring the risk of another collapse, but it was not until cranes were brought in that the bodies of the eight men were discovered.

One of the dead men was Frank Leavy. His eerie prophecy had been fulfilled.

Edward McKevitt had been outside when Curran Hall collapsed and the following day, he told the other firefighters about Leavy's weird premonition at the window. As he told the story, he looked up at the window that Frank had been cleaning and saw what appeared to be an unusual stain on the glass. It appeared to be in the same spot that Leavy had placed his hand when he made the dire prediction about his own future. McKevitt showed it to the other man and asked whether they thought it could be Leavy's handprint? They tried scrubbing it away and searched for ways to erase the print, but it was no use --- it seemed to be etched into the glass!

The story began making the rounds and firefighters from all over the city dropped in at the station to see the mysterious handprint. A number of suggestions were made as to how to remove the image but it refused to come off. Not a single effort, including the use of ammonia and scraping the glass with a razor blade, ever succeeded. At one point, an expert from the Pittsburgh Plate Glass Company brought in a special solution, guaranteeing that it would remove the print, but it didn't work. It only succeeded in making the handprint more famous.

Hoping to dispel the story, a city official visited the station house after obtaining a copy of Frank Leavy's thumbprint. He planned to compare the print with that on the window and prove once and for all that this was only an anomaly and not the handprint of a dead man. Unfortunately for him, his plan failed for when the fingerprint comparison was concluded, it revealed that the two thumbprints matched perfectly. There was no doubt about the fact that the handprint on the window belonged to Frank Leavy.

But what could have caused it? Was it a supernatural occurrence that was left to remind the firemen of their own mortality? Or did the print have a scientific explanation? Some believe that Leavy's fear of a coming tragedy may have caused his body to create a chemical that left a permanent stain behind through his sweat.

No one will ever know for sure though. The handprint continued to defy all explanation for the next two decades and provided an attraction for visitors to the fire house. Then, on the morning of April 18, 1944 a careless paper boy tossed the morning edition at the fire house and shattered the window where Frank's handprint had been. The glass was broken and the shards were scattered about on the ground, destroying not only the strange window but also any hope that the mystery of the handprint would ever be solved.

Even more eerie than the precise throw of an unknowing paperboy though was the date on which the broken window occurred. It was April 18, 1944 --- exactly 20 years to the day of when Frank Leavy died!

THE EASTLAND DISASTER

One of the most devastating, and haunting, tragedies to strike Chicago was the capsizing of the *Eastland* steamer on July 24, 1915, between the Clark and LaSalle Street bridges. The horrific accident not only claimed the lives of scores of people but it also left an impression behind that still resonates in downtown Chicago tale. The *Eastland* disaster is a tale of terror, death and ghosts...

Although it had only just departed the dock when the tragedy occurred, the steamer was bound for Michigan City, Indiana where a picnic had been planned for the workers of Western Electric and their families. There were four vessels chartered to take the estimated 7,000 people on their journey across the lake. One of these vessels was the *Eastland*, a rusting Lake Michigan steamer owned by the St. Joseph-Chicago Steamship Company. It was supposed to hold a capacity crowd of 2,570 but it is believed that at least 3,200 were on board. Besides being overcrowded, the vessel had a reputation for being notoriously unstable.

The *Eastland* was moored on the south side of the river and after the passengers were loaded on board, the dock lines were loosed and the ship prepared to depart. What followed was a nightmare...

The overflow crowd, dressed in their best summer attire, even on this drizzly morning, jammed onto the decks, waving handkerchiefs and calling out to those still on shore. The ship eased away from the dock and immediately began to list to the post. As more passengers pushed toward that side of the deck, the boat tilted dangerously. What the passengers were unaware of was that the crew of the steamer had emptied the ballast compartments (designed to provide "stability" for the craft) so that more passengers could be loaded aboard. This would be the undoing of the *Eastland*, as moments later, the ship simply toppled over!

Rescue workers hurried to save victims from the Eastland disaster after it capsized in this period postcard.

The passengers above deck were thrown into the water and the river became a moving sea of bodies. Crews on the other boats threw life preservers into the river, while onlookers began throwing lines, boxes and anything else that would float to the floundering passengers. To make matters more difficult, the river was now surging, thanks to the wake caused by the overturned ship. Many of the luckless passengers were pulled beneath the water by the current, or swamped by the crashing waves.

Worst of all was the fate of those passengers who had remained inside of the ship when it had departed. These unlucky victims were first thrown to one side of the ship as it turned over and then they were covered with water as the river rushed inside. A few of them managed to escape to the upturned end of the ship, but most didn't, becoming trapped in a tangled heap at the lowest point of the *Eastland*.

Firefighters and rescue workers arrived within minutes and began cutting holes in the wood above the water line and in the steel hull below it. In the first fateful minutes, a number of passengers managed to escape, but soon, it was simply too late. The rescue workers had to resign themselves to fishing corpses out of the water, which they wrapped in sheets and transferred to the *Roosevelt*, another vessel that had been rented for the excursion. The big downtown stores sent wagons and trucks to ferry the injured and dead to nearby hospitals and makeshift morgues. Large grappling hooks were also used to pull bodies from the water. By late that afternoon, nearly 200 bodies had been taken to the 2nd Regiment Armory on West Washington Blvd, which was used as a temporary morgue.

According to newspaper accounts, a police diver who had been hauling bodies up from the bottom of the river since mid-morning suddenly broke down and became crazed. He had to be subdued by several of his friends and fellow officers. City workers began dragging the river far south of where the ship had capsized, using large nets to stop the bodies from washing out into the lake. By the time that it was all over, 835 of the ship's passengers perished, including 22 entire families.

The mystery of the *Eastland* was never solved. There was never a clear cause that could be reached that accounted for the capsizing of the vessel. Several hundred lawsuits were eventually filed but almost all of them were thrown out by the Circuit Court of Appeals, who held the owners of the steamship blameless in the disaster. The *Eastland* was later sold at public auction in December 1915. The title was later transferred to the government and it was pressed into duty as the gunboat *USS Wilmette*. In 1946, it was sold for scrap metal. But the story of the *Eastland* does not end there.

The first bodies that were recovered on the day of the tragedy were taken to the nearby Reid-Murdoch Building, where Chicago's Traffic Court is now located, or were taken to local mortuaries. The only public building nearby that was large enough to serve as a morgue was the Second Illinois Regiment National Guard Armory on Carpenter Street, between Randolph and Washington Blvd. The bodies were carried into the building, one after another, for hours. They were laid out in rows of 85 and assigned numbers. Any personal possessions that came in with them were placed in envelopes and then marked with the corresponding number of the corpse. Loved ones and family members searched through the rows in search of familiar faces but in 22 cases, entire families perished, leaving no one to identify them. The cries and wails of the bereaved echoed off the walls of the armory for days and the Red Cross treated 30 women for exhaustion and hysteria during the ordeal.

The last of the bodies was identified on Friday, July 30. Seven year-old Willie Novotny of Cicero, number 396, was the last. There was no one remaining from his immediate family, as both his parents and older sister has also perished. His identification finally came from extended family members, nearly a week after the disaster took place.

As the years passed, the need for an armory so close to downtown Chicago passed. Threats to public order, like the beer riots or the Haymarket Square bombing were long past. The military closed the armory and the building was sold off. It was used a number of times over the years as a stable and a bowling alley. In recent years though, the armory building has been incorporated into Harpo Studios, the production company owned by Oprah Winfrey. As one of Chicago's greatest success stories, Oprah came to Chicago in 1984 to host the WLS-TV talk show "AM Chicago". Within a few years, she had recreated the program and it was re-named the "Oprah Winfrey Show". She has since gone on to become the host of the most popular talk show in television history, a film star, producer and well-known personality.

But all of the success and attention that the show has brought to the former armory building has done nothing to put to rest the spirits of the *Eastland*. Many who work here claim that the ghosts of the perished passengers are still restless in the new studios. According to Dale Kaczmarek's book, *Windy City Ghosts*, many employees have had strange encounters that cannot be explained, including the sighting of an apparition that has been dubbed the "Gray Lady". In addition, staff members hear whispering voices, the laughter of children, sobbing sounds, old-time music, the clinking of phantom glasses and marching of invisible footsteps. The footsteps (which sound as though they belong to a large group) are frequently heard on the lobby staircase and nearby doors often slam shut without assistance. A large number of the staff members believe this to be a very haunted place!

The site of the disaster is not without its chilling stories either. Today, the site is marked by a historical plaque, commemorating the memories of those whose lives were lost. Some say it is marked by other things as well, namely cries of terror from the victims of the tragedy. For many years, passersby on the Clark Street

Bridge claimed to hear cries and moans coming from the river, along with the bloodcurdling sound of terrified screams. Perhaps the horror of the event impressed itself on this place, where it continues to replay itself over and over again. The *Eastland* disaster continues to be remembered, in more ways than one!

THE TROLLEY OF DEATH

The fates of 33 people were tragically changed in Chicago in 1950 because of a rainstorm. On the night of May 24, a sudden and torrential downpour flooded the 63rd Street underpass at State Street, making the road impassable for the electric CTA trolley cars. No one knew what horrific events would follow this rainstorm or how simply missing a signal would send the occupants of a Green Hornet trolley along a path of no return.

During the first half of the Twentieth Century, electric streetcars were a familiar sight on Chicago streets. Trolleys had first appeared in the Windy City, pulled by horses, back in 1859. By the 1890's, electricity had replaced the horses and the cars began to travel along steel rails that had been fitted into the city streets. The system was so popular that during World War I, Chicago operated the largest streetcar operation in the country.

And while many riders relied on the trolleys to get them to and from work each day and to allow them to travel throughout the city, the vehicles did have their drawbacks. The most obvious problem was that they lacked the ability to maneuver around accidents and flooded areas, causing the cars to have to be diverted to alternate routes. For this reason, among others, trolleys were eventually replaced by buses. The fact that the trolleys were unable to change routes with ease would later lead to the "worst loss of life involving a motor vehicle in America".

On the morning of Thursday, May 25, the low-lying underpass at State Street remained flooded with rain water from the storm and so throughout that day, a flagman detoured southbound cars to a turnaround track on the east side of State Street, making 63rd Street the temporary end of the line. By rush hour, the area remained closed but this fact was apparently missed by the driver of the Green Hornet, Paul Manning. The trolley that he was driving was known for being one of the newest and sleekest vehicles on the CTA line and it was in perfect working order. Only a terrible mistake could be blamed for what happened that night.

Manning was driving the Green Hornet at a speed that was estimated to be about 35 m.p.h., which was considered to be dangerously fast for the wet conditions. The CTA flagman was still in place at 62nd, one block north of the turnaround, and when he saw Manning's trolley come into view, he frantically began signaling the driver to slow down. Instead of slowing though, the streetcar continued speeding along the street. The flagman continued to wave and attempted to warn the driver that a switch in the track was open for a turn that would put the Green Hornet directly into the path of oncoming northbound travel.

In the opposite lane, heading north, a semi-trailer truck that was driven by Mel Wilson was also quickly approaching the viaduct. The semi-truck happened to be hauling 8,000 gallons of gasoline that was destined for south side filling stations.

How Manning failed to see the flagman's signal is unknown, but we do know that he was unaware of the closed underpass and also unaware of the open switch that was being used to bypass the trolleys. It's likely that he simply thought that the car would clip right along on the route that he normally took. However, when the trolley hit the open switch track, it violently swung to the left, throwing the passengers aboard to the floor. Manning was last seen throwing up his hands and screaming in terror as the streetcar hurled through the intersection and rammed into the tanker truck. The impact ripped open the tanker's steel skin, creating a shower of sparks that immediately ignited the gasoline that was now flooding onto the street. The two vehicles erupted into a single fireball and incinerated the trolley.

At the time of the accident, every seat on the Green Hornet had been filled. The aisles had been filled with the people who had been jolted by the sudden turn and they suddenly felt the tremendous heat as the fire swept through the car. In the terror and confusion that followed, the trapped and charred victims pushed against the side doors, but they refused to open. The windows were covered with steel bars, making them useless as an escape route. Somehow, 30 people managed to crawl away from the scene, leaving 33 others behind to die. Those fortunate few who survived were all treated for severe burns at Provident Hospital.

Meanwhile, the explosion shook the entire neighborhood and the flames soared two and three stories high. The burning gasoline managed to engulf seven buildings on State Street and the fire was so hot that it twisted metal, fused windows and melted sections of asphalt on the street. The walls of several of the buildings collapsed, although the occupants managed to escape. Drivers who had been lined up in traffic were able to leave unharmed as well.

More than 30 fire companies were called to the scene and it took more than two hours to get the worst of the fire under control. It would be a long time before a sense of calm could be restored to the area though and the smell of scorched flesh hung in the air long after the debris was cleared away. According to newspaper reports, as many as 20,000 people lined the streets, craning to catch a glimpse of the fire, the destroyed vehicles and the blackened bodies that were taken away to the morgue.

It's likely that some of the emergency workers who had to deal with the carnage would have gladly traded places with the curiosity-seekers. When they forced open the rear doors of the trolley, they were met with a ghastly scene. "In some cases we found only the skulls and parts of limbs," Fire Marshall Albert Peterson later recalled. "We had to remove all of them and make a temporary morgue on the sidewalk."

A number of the passengers escaped the trolley thanks to a 14 year-old girl who had thought quickly enough to pull down a red safety knob that opened the center doors. However, the rear doors had no such device and were in fact designed to be entry doors only, not opening from the inside. This created a bottleneck when the panicked passengers tried to get out of them. When the firefighters had opened the doors, they found a mass of bodies that had been literally fused together by the heat.

In the investigation that followed, it was found that the Green Hornet had been in perfect working order, as had the gasoline truck. Mel Wilson, the driver of the truck, had also been burned to death in the accident. Most pointed fingers of blame at Paul Manning, who had been involved in 10 minor accidents during his career, but the real problems were the design flaws in the trolley itself. These included the lack of safety pulls (now standard equipment on buses and elevated lines), the steel bars that blocked an emergency escape through the windows and doors that would not open from either side. It took the senseless slaughter of 33 innocent victims to learn what should have been a simple lesson from the start.

In the years that followed the Green Hornet crash, trolleys slowly began to disappear from Chicago streets and were replaced by buses. The final run of a Green Hornet trolley took place on June 21, 1958 and another chapter closed in Chicago's history of disasters.

LINGERING SPIRITS OF FLIGHT 191

Before the horrific events of September 11, 2001, the worst airline-related disaster in American history occurred on Memorial Day weekend of 1979 in Chicago. On Friday, May 25, American Airlines Flight 191 literally fell from the sky, killing all of the 271 passengers and crew on board. The flight was meant to be a non-stop journey from Chicago to Los Angeles --- but as fate would have it, the plane would never leave the Windy City.

It was a beautiful holiday weekend in Chicago and throngs of people filled O'Hare International, the world's busiest airport. The passengers of Flight 191, including a number of Chicago literary figures who were bound for Los Angeles and the annual American Booksellers Association conference, boarded the McDonnell-Douglas DC-10 shortly before 3:00 in the afternoon. There seemed to be nothing out of the ordinary about the flight. The DC-10 was a top of the line aircraft and this particular model had logged more than 20,000 trouble-free hours since it left the assembly line. The crew was top-notch as well, including Captain Walter Lux, a 22,000 hour pilot who had been flying DC-10's since their introduction into service eight years before, and First Officer James Dillard and Flight Engineer Alfred Udovich, who had nearly 25,000 flight hours between them.

At one minute before 3:00, the plane was cleared to begin its taxi to the runway's holding point. Then, at 3:02 pm, Flight 191 started down the runway. All went smoothly until a point about 6,000 feet down the runway, just prior to rotation. The tower controller saw parts of the port engine pylon falling away from the aircraft and a "white vapor" coming from the area. A moment later, the aircraft pitched into rotation and lifted off. As it did so, the entire engine and pylon tore loose from its mounting, flipped up and over the wing and crashed down onto the runway.

Immediately, the tower controller tried to raise the plan on the radio. "American 191, do you want to come back? If so, what runway do you want?"

Flight 191 as it began to wheel sideways and then to cartwheel into a crash. (AP Photos)

There was no reply from the aircraft but it proceeded to climb out normally, only dipping the left wing for a moment. It quickly stabilized and the plane continued its descent. About ten seconds later though, at a height of around 300 feet, the aircraft began to bank to the left, first slightly, then sharply. The nose of the plane dipped and as the aircraft began to lose height, the bank to left increased until the wings were past vertical --- then it fell to the earth!

The left wingtip hit the ground first and the rip of the metal was followed by a massive explosion that erupted throughout the plane. The fireball went down about a half mile northwest of O'Hare and slammed into an abandoned hangar on the site of the old Ravenswood Airport on Touhy Avenue, just east of a mobile home park. It was mostly vacant ground, although the plane narrowly missed some fuel storage tanks on Elmhurst Road and the busy I-90 Expressway. However, 2 people were killed on the ground and several homes were damaged in the trailer park. As for the crew and passengers on the aircraft --- all 271 of them had been killed instantly.

The enormity of the tragedy was felt throughout the country and people everywhere demanded answers from the airline, the airport and the National Transportation Safety Board. How could something like this have happened? It is a standard in the industry for planes to be able to finish a flight with only one engine, so how did the loss of one engine seal the fate of Flight 191? The long and grueling investigation that followed revealed a stress crack in a flange that held the engine pylon, flawed maintenance methods and a problem with the supposedly serviceable DC-10. These answers were long in coming but even when they came, did not solve the mysteries that were plaguing Chicagoans who lived in the vicinity of the crash.

Ghostly tales soon began to spring up about the site. According to Des Plaines police officers, motorists began reporting odd sights within a few months of the crash. They called in about seeing odd, bobbing white lights in the field where the aircraft had gone down. First thought to be flashlights that were carried by ghoulish souvenir hunters, officers responded to the reports to find the field was silent and deserted. No one was ever found, despite patrols arriving on the scene almost moments after receiving a report.

More unnerving though were the accounts that came from the residents of the nearby mobile home, which was adjacent to the crash site. Many of these reports came within hours of the crash, when residents claimed to hear knocking and rapping sounds at their doors and windows. Those who responded, including a number of retirees and off-duty police and firefighters, opened their doors to find no one was there. Dogs in the trailer park would bark endlessly at the empty field where the plane had gone down. Their masters could find no reason for their erratic behavior. This continued for weeks and months and even escalated to the point that doorknobs were being turned and rattled, footsteps were heard approaching the trailers, clanging on the metal stairs, and on some occasions, actual figures were confronted. According to some reports, a few residents opened their doors to find a worried figure who stated that he "had to get his luggage" or "had to make a connection" standing on their porch. The figure then turned and vanished into the darkness.

The tragedy, and the strange events that followed, caused many of the residents to move out of the park but when new arrivals took their place, they too began to report the weird happenings. A fairly recent sighting was described by a man who was walking his dog one night near the area where Flight 191 went down. He was approached by a young man who explained that he needed to make an emergency telephone call. The man with his dog looked at this person curiously for he seemed to reek of gasoline and also appeared to be smoldering. At first, he just assumed the man had been running on this chilly night and steam was coming from his clothing, but when he turned away to point out a nearby phone and then turned back again --- the man had vanished! The man with the dog had heard stories from other local residents about moans and weird cries emanating from the 1979 crash site but he never believed them until now. He was now convinced that he had encountered one of the restless passengers from Flight 191 for himself!

And he's likely not the only one, for the stories of weird knockings, inexplicable sounds and even apparitions continue to this day. One long-standing incident, which is often repeated, comes from the terminal at O'Hare itself. According to travelers, many have purported to see a man making a telephone call from a booth that is located close to the departure gate that was used by Flight 191. Those who have seen him say that is quite normal-looking, except for the fact that his business attire seems oddly out of date. He allegedly steps away from the telephone booth, manages a few steps and then vanishes into thin air. Is he one of the doomed passengers from Flight 191 --- or another phantom altogether?

CHAPTER TWO
GHOSTLY GREETINGS FROM THE GRAVEYARD

THE MYSTERIES OF CHICAGO'S HAUNTED BURIAL GROUNDS

One may, then, look back and see the lower part of the noble playground as a shelf of gloomy sand flat and scrub oak, upon which the waves worked their will, and into which, year after year, were lowered the bodies of pioneers who had died in their adopted city.
HENRY JUSTIN SMITH

My own interest in cemeteries springs most emphatically --- and quite naturally, from a frantic interest in the business of the living. Chicago is often called a city of neighborhoods, but what of these silent boroughs? As we attend to the daily grind, millions sleep the eternal sleep all over the city, scattered like gems in the urban landscape.
URSULA BIELSKI

There is not a single person among us who has not contemplated the mystery of death at one time or another. We all wonder, no matter what we believe in, what will happen to us after we pass on from this world. Some believe that everything comes to an end, that life in this world is our only existence. Others feel that we are born again, as an old soul in a new body; while others believe that our spirits pass on to another place -- or perhaps even remain behind as ghosts.

We all wonder about such things and perhaps this is the reason that we have dreamed up so many rituals and practices dealing with death. Death has been celebrated and feared since the beginning of time itself. We have immortalized it with cemeteries, grave markers and of course, with our darkest and most frightening legends and lore.

It is a common belief among experts of the occult that cemeteries are not usually the best places to find ghosts. While most would fancy a misty, abandoned graveyard to be the perfect setting for a ghost story, such stories are not as common as you might believe. A cemetery is meant to be the final stop in our journey from this world to the next, but is it always that way?

Nearly every ghost enthusiast would agree that a place becomes haunted after a traumatic event or unexpected death occurs at that location. History is filled with stories of houses that have become haunted after a murder has taken place there, or after some horrible event occurs that echoes over the decades as a haunting.

But what of a haunted cemetery? Do such places really exist? Most assuredly they do, but ghosts who haunt cemeteries seem to be a different sort than those you might find lingering in a haunted house. Most of these ghosts seem to be connected to the cemetery in some way that excludes events that occurred during their lifetime. As most spirits reportedly remain in this world because of some sort of unfinished business in life, this seems to leave out a cemetery as a place where such business might remain undone.

Graveyard ghosts seem to have a few things in common. These spirits seem to be connected to the burial ground because of events that occurred after their deaths, rather than before. In other cases, the ghosts seem to be seeking eternal rest that eludes them at the spot where their physical bodies are currently found. Cemeteries gain a reputation for being haunted for reasons that include the desecration of the dead and grave robbery, unmarked or forgotten burials, natural disasters that disturb resting places, or sometimes even because the deceased was not properly buried at all!

With that said, it's not surprising that Chicago has more than its share of haunted graveyards, tombs and even roadways connected to the cemeteries themselves. For one thing, one of the cities most famous burial grounds was created from a smaller cemetery when the remains were transferred to a new location -- of course, leaving some of the original bodies behind. Unmarked graves abound, along with strange stories, mysterious figures and vanishing hitchhikers. All of the things that have occurred in these locations, according to cemetery lore, can cause graveyards to become haunted.

There are stories here that will have you watching your rearview mirror as you travel down the street or perhaps wondering what might be buried just beneath your feet!

AMERICA'S GARDEN CEMETERIES

The city of Chicago can boast some of the most beautiful cemeteries in the Midwest, and perhaps America. Those readers who have been fortunate enough to visit either Graceland or Rosehill Cemetery can attest to the glory of the open expanses, the shaded walkways and the incredible artwork that went into creating the monuments to the dead that cover the grounds. But it wasn't always this way, for years ago, cemeteries were a hellish and often frightening place.

Death, as they say, is the final darkness at the end of life. It has been both feared and worshipped since the beginnings of history. For this reason, our civilization has dreamed up countless practices and rituals to deal with and perhaps understand it. We have even personified this great unknown with a semi-human figure, the "Grim Reaper", and have given him a menacing scythe to harvest human souls with. Yet, death remains a mystery.

Maybe because of this mystery, we have chosen to immortalize death with stones and markers that tell about the people who are buried beneath them. We take the bodies of those whose spirits have departed and place them in the ground, or in the enclosure of the tomb, and place a monument over these remains that speaks of the life once lived. This is not only out of respect for the dead because it also serves as a reminder for the living. It reminds us of the person who has died -- and it also reminds us that someday, it will be our bodies that lie moldering below the earth.

The stone monuments became cemeteries, or repositories of the dead, where the living could come and feel some small connection with the one that passed on. The earliest of the modern cemeteries, or what is referred to as a "garden" cemetery, began in Europe in the 1800's.

Before the beginning of the Garden cemetery, the dead were buried strictly in the churchyards of Europe. For the rich, burial within the church itself was preferred. For those who could not be buried inside of the church, the churchyard became the next best thing. Even here, one's social status depended on the section of the ground where you were buried. The most favored sites were those to the east, as close as possible to the church. In such a location, the dead would be assured the best view of the rising sun on the Day of Judgment. People of lesser distinction were buried on the south side, while the north corner of the graveyard was considered the Devil's domain. It was reserved for stillborns, bastards and strangers unfortunate enough to die while passing through the local parish.

Suicides, if they were buried in consecrated ground at all, were usually deposited in the north end, although their corpses were not allowed to pass through the cemetery gates to enter. They had to be passed over the top of the stone wall. During the late Middle Ages, the pressure of space finally "exorcized" the Devil from the north end of the churchyard to make way for more burials.

As expected, it soon became nearly impossible for the churchyards to hold the bodies of the dead. As towns and cities swelled in population during the 1700's, a chronic shortage of space began to develop. The first solution to the problem was simply to pack the coffins more closely together. Later on, coffins were stacked atop one another and the earth rose to the extent that some churchyards rose twenty feet or more above that of the church floor. Another solution was to grant only limited occupation of a grave site. However, it actually got to the point that occupancy of a plot was measured in only days, or even hours, before the coffin was removed and another was put in its place.

It became impossible for the churchyards to hold the dead and by the middle 1700's, the situation had reached crisis proportions in France. Dirt and stone walls had been added around the graveyards in an attempt to hold back the bodies but they often collapsed, leaving human remains scattered about the streets of Paris. The government was finally forced into taking action. In 1786, it was decided to move all of the bodies from the Cemetery of the Innocents and transport them to catacombs that had been carved beneath the southern part of the city. It was a massive undertaking. There was no way to identify the individual remains, so it was decided to arrange the bones into rows of skulls, femurs and so on. It has been estimated that the Paris catacombs contain the bodies of between 3 and 6 million people.

In addition to the catacombs, four cemeteries were built within the confines of the city. One of them Pere-Lachaise has become known as the first of the "garden" cemeteries. It was named after the confessor priest of Louis XIV and is probably the most celebrated burial ground in the world. Today, the walls of this graveyard hold the bodies of the most illustrious people in France and a number of other celebrities as well. The dead include Balzac, Victor Hugo, Colette, Marcel Proust, Chopin, Oscar Wilde, Sarah Bernhardt and Jim Morrison of the Doors (if you believe he's dead, that is).

Pere-Lachaise became known around the world for its size and beauty. It covered hundreds of acres and was landscaped and fashioned with pathways for carriages. It reflected the new creative age where art and nature could combine to celebrate the lives of those buried there.

Paris set the standard and America slowly followed. In this country, the churchyard remained the most common burial place through the end of the 1800's. While these spots are regarded as picturesque today, years ago, they varied little from their European counterparts.

After the founding of the Pere-Lachaise Cemetery in Paris, the movement toward creating "garden" cemeteries spread to America. The first of these was Mount Auburn Cemetery in Cambridge, Massachusetts, which was consecrated in 1831. It was planned as an "oasis" on the outskirts of the city and defined a new romantic kind of cemetery with winding paths and a forested setting. It was the opposite of the crowded churchyard and it became an immediate success, giving rise to many other similar burial grounds in cities across the country. In fact, they became so popular that they served as not only burial grounds, but as public recreation areas as well. Here, people could enjoy the shaded walkways and even picnic on weekend afternoons. The Garden cemetery would go on to inspire the American Park movement and virtually create the field of landscape architecture.

The idea of the Garden cemetery spread across America and by the early 1900's was the perfect answer to the old, overcrowded burial grounds. Many of these early cemeteries had been established close to the center of town and were soon in the way of urban growth. Small towns and large ones across the country were soon hurrying to move the graves of those buried in years past to the new cemeteries, which were always located outside of town.

In Chicago, one burial ground actually created several Garden Cemeteries, although the most spectacular of them is undoubtedly Graceland Cemetery. Graceland and several others came about thanks to the closure of the old Chicago City Cemetery around 1870.

The City Cemetery was located exactly where Chicago's Lincoln Park is located today. Before its establishment, most of the early pioneers simply buried their dead out in the back yard, leading to many gruesome discoveries as the downtown was developed years later. Two cemeteries were later set aside for both Protestants and Catholics, but both of them were located along the lake shore, leading to the frequent unearthing of caskets whenever the water was high. Finally, the city set aside land at Clark Street and North Avenue for the Chicago City Cemetery. Soon, many of the bodies were moved from the other sites to this central and often troubling one.

Within ten years of the opening of the cemetery, it became the subject of much criticism. Not only was it severely overcrowded from both population growth and cholera epidemics, but many also felt that poorly carried out burials here were creating health problems and contaminating the water supply. To make matters worse, both the city morgue and the local Pest House, a quarantine building for epidemic victims, were located on the cemetery grounds. Soon, local families and churches were moving their loved ones to burial grounds considered to be safer and the City Cemetery was closed down in 1859. Little was done to enforce this prohibition however until 1866, when a final ban was put in place against more burials.

This ended the practice of the dead being carried to the City Cemetery but the removal of bodies to Graceland, Rosehill and other spots was a slow process. Monuments and slabs had to be moved too and the owners of lots had to have an exchange with lots in other cemeteries and some of those who wished to sell held out for high prices. This further exasperated the process and distressed the city planners, who hoped to turn the former cemetery into a park. One account describes the area at that time: "We saw countless open graves," wrote Mrs. Joseph T. Bowen, "with a piece here and there of a decayed coffin... the whole place looked exactly as if the Judgment Day had come."

The cemetery that benefited the most from the closure of the graveyard was Graceland Cemetery, located on North Clark Street. When it was started in 1860 by real estate developer Thomas B. Bryan, it was located far away from the city and over the years, a number of different architects have worked to preserve the natural setting of its 120 acres. It is regarded as one of the most beautiful burial grounds in all of Chicago today --- and as we'll see later in the chapter, one of those considered to be haunted as well.

Bachelor's Grove Cemetery (Photo Courtesy of Robert Johnson)

BACHELOR'S GROVE CEMETERY
The Most Haunted Place in Chicagoland

Located near the southwest suburb of Midlothian is the Rubio Woods Forest Preserve, an island of trees and shadows nestled in the urban sprawl of the Chicago area. The rambling refuge creates an illusion that it is secluded from the crowded city that threatens its borders, and perhaps it is. On the edge of the forest is a small graveyard that many believe may be the most haunted place in the region. The name of this cemetery is Bachelor's Grove and this ramshackle burial ground may be infested with more ghosts than most can imagine. Over the years, the place has been cursed with more than 100 documented reports of paranormal phenomena, from actual apparitions to glowing balls of light.

There have been no new burials here for many years and as a place of rest for the departed, it is largely forgotten. But if you should ask any ghost hunter just where to go to find a haunting, Bachelor's Grove is usually the first place in Chicago to be mentioned!

The history of Bachelor's Grove has been somewhat shadowy over the years but most historians agree that it was started in the early part of the 1800's. In August 1933, the famous *Ripley's Believe it or Not* column featured a short piece on Bachelor's Grove Cemetery, stating that it was so unusual because even though it had been set aside as a burial ground for "bachelors only", there were also women buried here. Unfortunately though, the column was inaccurate and this has been just one of the many myths and misconceptions created about the cemetery over the years. The name of the cemetery came not from the number of single men buried here but from the name of a family who settled in the area. The lore about the "bachelor burial ground" dates back to 1833 or 1834 when a man named Stephen H. Rexford settled in the region with a number of other unmarried men. Allegedly, they began calling the place "Bachelor's Grove" but this has been widely disputed by historians, who believe the name "Batchelor's Grove" was already in use at the time.

They believe that the name of the cemetery came from a settlement that was started in the late 1820's that consisted of mostly German immigrants from New York, Vermont and Connecticut. One family that moved into the area was called "Batchelder" and their name was given to the timberland where they settled, just as other timber areas like Walker's Grove, Cooper's Grove and Blackstone's Grove were named after families and individuals.

Regardless, the small settlement continued for some years as Batchelor's Grove, until 1850, when it was changed to "Bremen" by postmaster Samuel Everden in recognition of the new township name where the post office was located. In 1855, it was changed again to "Bachelder's Grove" by postmaster Robert Patrick but the post office closed down just three years later. Officially, the settlement ceased to exist and was swallowed by the forest around it.

The cemetery itself has a much stranger history -- or at least a more mysterious one. The land was apparently first set aside to be used as a burial ground in 1844, when the first recorded burial took place here, that of Eliza (Mrs. Leonard H.) Scott. The land had been donated by the property owner, Samuel

Everden, and it was named "Everden" in his honor. Strangely though, this first burial is disputed by an article that appeared in the *Blue Island Sun-Standard* in August 1935. According to this story, the first burial was that of a man named William B. Nobles, who died in 1838. The last burials to take place are believed to be that of Laura M. McGhee in 1965 and Robert E. Shields, who was cremated and buried in the family plot here in 1989.

Regardless of exactly when the cemetery started, the first legal record of it appeared when Edward Everden sold the property to Frederick Schmidt in 1864. A notation in the records stated that all of the land would be sold excepting "one acre used as a grave yard". This makes it clear that the cemetery was already in existence and had been created by Everden, not, as the Schmidt family later tried to claim, by Frederick Schmidt. However, the Schmidt's did intend to expand the original property later on, but there is no evidence that this was ever done.

The last independent caretaker of the cemetery was a man named Clarence Fulton, whose family were early settlers in the township. According to Fulton, Bachelor's Grove was like a park for many years and people often came here to fish and swim in the adjacent pond. Families often visited on weekends to care for the graves of the deceased and to picnic under the trees. Things have certainly changed since then!

Problems began in and around the cemetery in the early 1960's, at the same time that the Midlothian Turnpike was closed to vehicle traffic in front of the cemetery. Even before that, the cemetery had become a popular spot along a "lover's lane" and when the road closed, it became even more isolated. Soon it began to show signs of vandalism and decay and a short time later, became considered haunted. Although the amount of paranormal activity that actually occurs in the cemetery has been argued by some, few can deny that strange things do happen here. When the various types of phenomenon really began is unclear but it has been happening for more than three decades now. Was the burial ground already haunted? Or did the haunting actually begin with the destructive decades of the 1960's and 1970's?

The vandals first discovered Bachelor's Grove in the 1960's and probably because of its secluded location, they began to wreak havoc on the place. Gravestones were knocked over and destroyed, sprayed with paint, broken apart and even stolen. Police reports later stated that markers from Bachelor's Grove turned up in homes, yards and even as far away as Evergreen Cemetery! Worst of all, in 1964, 1975 and 1978, graves were opened and caskets removed. Bones were sometimes found to be strewn about the cemetery. Desecrated graves are still frequently found in the cemetery.

Was the haunting first caused by these disturbances? Most believe so, but others cite another source for the activity. Near the small pond that borders the cemetery, forest rangers and cemetery visitors have repeatedly found the remains of chickens and other small animals that have been slaughtered and mutilated in a ritualistic fashion. Officers that have patrolled the woods at night have reported seeing evidence of black magic and occult rituals in and around the graveyard. In some cases, inscriptions and elaborate writings have been carved in and painted on trees and grave markers and on the cemetery grounds themselves. This has led many to believe that the cemetery has been used for occult activities.

If you combine this sorted activity with the vandalism that has nearly destroyed the place, you have a situation that is ripe for supernatural occurrences. Could this be what has caused the blight on Bachelor's Grove? Even the early superstitions of the tombstone give credence to the idea that man has always felt that desecration of graves causes cemeteries to become haunted. Grave markers began as heavy stones that were placed on top of the graves of the deceased in the belief that the weight of it would keep the dead person, or their angry spirit, beneath the ground. Those who devised this system believed that if the stone was moved, the dead would be free to walk the earth.

There is no question that vandals have not been kind to Bachelor's Grove, but then neither has time. The Midlothian Turnpike bypassed the cemetery and even the road leading back to the graveyard was eventually closed. People forgot about the place and allowed it to fade into memory, just like the poor souls buried here.

Today, the cemetery is overgrown with weeds and is surrounded by a high, chain-link fence, although access is easily gained through the holes that trespassers have cut into it. The cemetery sign is long since gone. It once hung above the main gates, which are now broken open and lean dangerously into the confines of Bachelor's Grove.

The first thing noticed by those who visit here is the destruction. Tombstones seem to be randomly scattered about, no longer marking the resting places of those whose names are inscribed upon them. Many of the stones are missing, lost forever and perhaps carried away by thieves. These macabre crimes gave birth to legends about how the stones of the cemetery move about under their own power. The most disturbing things to visitors though are the trenches and pits that have been dug above some of the graves, as vandals have attempted to make off with souvenirs from those whose rest they disturb.

The original sign to Bachelor's Grove Cemetery -- long since destroyed by vandals (courtesy Dale Kaczmarek)

Near the front gate is a broken monument to a woman whose name was heard being called repeatedly on an audio tape. Some amateur ghost hunters left a recording device running while on an excursion to Bachelor's Grove and later, upon playback of the tape, they discovered that the recorder had been left on the ruined tombstone of a woman that had the same name as that being called to on the tape. Coincidence? Perhaps, but it hardly seems likely.

Just beyond the rear barrier of the cemetery is a small, stagnant pond that can be seen by motorists who pass on 143rd Street. This pond, while outside of the graveyard, is still not untouched by the horror connected to the place. One night in the late 1970's, two Cook County forest rangers were on night patrol near here and claimed to see the apparition of a horse emerge from the waters of the pond. The animal appeared to be pulling a plow behind it that was steered by the ghost of an old man. The vision crossed the road in front of the ranger's vehicle, was framed for a moment in the glare of their headlights, and then vanished into the forest. The men simply stared in shock for a moment and then looked at one another to be sure that had both seen the same thing. They later reported the incident and since that time, have not been the last to see the old man and the horse.

Little did the rangers know, but this apparition was actually a part of an old legend connected to the pond. It seems that in the 1870's, a farmer was plowing a nearby field when something startled his horse. The farmer was caught by surprise and became tangled in the reins. He was dragged behind the horse and it plunged into the small pond. Unable to free himself, he was pulled down into the murky water by the weight of the horse and the plow and he drowned. Since that time, the vivid recording of this terrible incident has been supernaturally revisiting the surrounding area.

In addition to this unfortunate phantom, the pond was also rumored to be a dumping spot for murder victims during the Prohibition era in Chicago. Those who went on a "one-way ride" were alleged to have ended the trip at the pond near Bachelor's Grove. Thanks to this, their spirits are also said to haunt the dark waters.

Strangely though, it's not the restless spirits of gangland execution victims that have created the most bizarre tales of the pond. One night, an elderly couple was driving past the cemetery and claimed to see something by the bridge at the edge of the pond. They stopped to get a closer look and were understandably terrified to see a huge, two-headed man come out from under the bridge and cross the road in the light from their headlights! Whatever this creature may have been, it quickly vanished into the woods.

Incredibly, even the road near Bachelor's Grove is reputed to be haunted. Could there be such a taint to this place that even the surrounding area is affected? The Midlothian Turnpike is said to be the scene of vanishing "ghost cars" and phantom automobile accidents. No historical events can provide a clue as to why this might be, but the unexplained vehicles have been reported numerous times in recent years. The stories are all remarkably the same too. People who are traveling west on the turnpike see the tail lights of a car in front of them. The brake lights go on, as if the car is planning to stop or turn. The car then turns off the road. However, once the following auto gets to the point in the road where the first vehicle turned, they find no car there at all! Other drivers have reported passing these phantoms autos, only to see the car vanish in their rearview mirrors.

One young couple even claimed to have a collision with one of these phantom cars in 1978. They had just stopped at the intersection of Central Avenue and the Midlothian Turnpike. The driver looked both ways, saw that the road was clear in both directions, and then pulled out. Suddenly, a brown sedan appeared from nowhere, racing in the direction of the cemetery. The driver of the couple's car hit the brakes and tried to stop, but it was too late to avoid the crash. The two vehicles collided with not only a shuddering impact, but with the sound of screeching metal and broken glass as well. To make the event even more traumatic, the couple was then shocked to see the brown sedan literally fade away! They climbed out of their car, which had been spun completely around by the impact, but realized that it had not been damaged at all. They had distinctly heard the sound of the torn metal and broken glass and had felt the crush of the two cars coming together, but somehow it had never physically happened!

It remains a mystery as to where these phantom cars come from, and where they vanish to. Why do they haunt this stretch of roadway? No one knows...

For those searching for Bachelor's Grove, it can be found by leaving the roadway and walking up an overgrown gravel track that is surrounded on both sides by the forest. The old road is blocked with chains and concrete dividers and a dented "No Trespassing" sign that hangs ominously near the mouth to the trail. The burial ground lies about a half-mile or so beyond it in the woods.

It is along this deserted road where other strange tales of the cemetery take place. One of these odd occurrences is the sighting of the "phantom farm house". It has been seen appearing and disappearing along the trail for several decades now. The reports date back as far as the early 1960's and continue today. The most credible thing about many of the accounts is that they come from people who originally had no idea that the house shouldn't be there at all.

The house has been reported in all weather conditions and in the daylight hours, as well as at night. There is no historical record of a house existing here but the descriptions of it rarely vary. Each person claims it to be an old frame farm house with two-stories, painted white, with wooden posts, a porch swing and a welcoming light that burns softly in the window. Popular legend states that should you enter this house though, you would never come back out again. As witnesses approach the building, it is reported to get smaller and smaller until it finally just fades away, like someone switching off an old television set. No one has ever claimed to set foot on the front porch of the house.

But the story gets stranger yet! In addition to the house appearing and disappearing, it also shows up at a wide variety of locations along the trail. On one occasion it may be sighted in one area and then at an entirely different spot the next time. Author Dale Kaczmarek, who also heads the *Ghost Research Society* paranormal investigation group, has interviewed dozens of witnesses about the paranormal events at Bachelor's Grove. He has talked to many who say they have experienced the vanishing farm house. He has found that while all of their descriptions of the house are identical, the locations of the sightings are not. In fact, he asked the witnesses to place an "X" on the map of the area where they saw the house. Kaczmarek now has a map of the Bachelor's Grove area with "X's" all over it!

Also from this stretch of trail come reports of "ghost lights". One such light that has been reported many times is a red, beacon-like orb that has been seen flying rapidly up and down the trail to the cemetery. The light is so bright, and moves so fast, that it is impossible to tell what it really looks like. Most witnesses state that they have seen a "red streak" that is left in its wake.

Others, like Jack Hermanski from Joliet, have reported seeing balls of blue light in the woods and in the cemetery itself. These weird lights have sometimes been reported moving in and around the tombstones in the graveyard. Hermanski encountered the lights in the early 1970's and chased a number of them. All of the lights managed to stay just out of his reach. However, a woman named Denise Travers did manage to catch up with one of the blue lights in December 1971. She claimed to pass her hand completely through one of them but felt no heat or sensation.

Besides the aforementioned phenomena, there have been many sightings of ghosts and apparitions within Bachelor's Grove Cemetery itself. The two most frequently reported figures have been the "phantom monks" and the so-called "Madonna of Bachelor's Grove".

The claims of the monk-like ghosts are strange in themselves. These spirits are said to be clothed in the flowing robes and cowls of a monastic order and they have been reported in Bachelor's Grove and in other places in the Chicago area too. There are no records to indicate that a monastery ever existed near any of the locations where the "monks" have been sighted though, making them one of the greatest of the area's enigmas.

The most frequently reported spirit though is known by a variety of names from the "Madonna of Bachelor's Grove" to the "White Lady" to the affectionate name of "Mrs. Rogers". Legend has it that she is the ghost of a woman who was buried in the cemetery next to the grave of her young child. She is reported to wander the cemetery on nights of the full moon with an infant wrapped in her arms. She appears to walk aimlessly, with no apparent direction and completely unaware of the people who claim to encounter her. There is no real evidence to say who this woman might be but, over the years, she has taken her place as one of the many spirits of this haunted burial ground.

And there are other ghosts as well. Legends tell more apocryphal tales of a ghostly child who has been seen running across the bridge from one side of the pond to the other, a glowing yellow man and even a black carriage that travels along the old road through the woods.

Many of these tales come from a combination of stories, both new and old, but the majority of first-hand reports and encounters are the result of literally hundreds of paranormal investigations that have been conducted here over the last forty years. Many of the ghost hunters who come to this place are amateur investigators, looking for thrills as much as they are looking for evidence of the supernatural, while others, like Dale Kaczmarek and the *Ghost Research Society,* are much more on the serious side.

Kaczmarek and his investigators have turned up many clues and pieces of evidence that seem to fit randomly into the mystery of Bachelor's Grove. These mysterious bits of evidence, while showing that strange things do happen here, never really seem to provide the hard evidence that these researchers look for. Even the photographs collected during their outings tantalize the investigators. For example, a series of photos taken by the group in 1979 show a monk-like figure standing near the cemetery fence. The figure appeared to be wearing a hooded robe and holding a baby in its arms. Oddly, this was three years before the *Ghost Research Society* collected any accounts of the "White Lady"!

Perhaps the most stunning photograph from Bachelor's Grove was taken in August 1991, during a full-fledged investigation of the cemetery. *Ghost Research Society* members came to the burial ground in the daytime and covered the area with the latest in scientific equipment, cameras, tape recorders and video cameras. All of the members were given maps of the cemetery and instructed to walk through and note any changes in electro-magnetic readings or atmosphere fluctuations. After the maps were compared, it was obvious that several investigators found odd changes in a number of distinct areas. A number of photos were taken in those areas, using both standard and infrared film. Nothing was seen at the time the photographs were taken, but once they were developed, the investigators learned that something had apparently been

The now famous image of the ghostly figure in Bachelor's Grove (Photo by Mari Huff)

there!

In a photo, taken by Mari Huff, there appeared the semi-transparent form of a woman, who was seated on the remains of a tombstone. Was this one of the ghosts of Bachelor's Grove? Skeptics immediately said "no", claiming that it was nothing more than a double exposure or an outright hoax.

Curious, I asked for and received a copy of the photograph and had it examined by several independent photographers. Most of them would have liked to come up with a reason why the photograph could not be real, but unfortunately they couldn't. They ruled out the idea of a double exposure and also the theory that the person in the photo was a live woman who was placed in the photo and made to appear like she was a ghost. One skeptic also claimed that the woman in the photo was casting a shadow, but according to the photographers who analyzed the image, the "shadow" is actually nothing more than the natural shading of the landscape. Besides that, one of them asked, if she is casting a shadow in that direction, then why isn't anything else in the frame? Genuine or not (and I think it is), this photograph is just one of the hundreds of photos taken here that allegedly show supernatural activity. While many of them can be ruled out as nothing more than atmospheric conditions, reflections and poor photography, there are others that cannot.

In the end, we have to ask, what is it about Bachelor's Grove Cemetery? Is it as haunted as we have been led to believe? I have to leave that up to the reader to decide, but strange things happen here and there is little reason to doubt that this one of the most haunted places in the Midwest.

But haunted or not, Bachelor's Grove is still a burial ground and a place that should be treated with respect as the final resting place of those interred here. It should also be remembered that the cemetery is not a private playground for those who are intrigued by ghosts and hauntings. It is first and foremost a repository for the dead and should be protected as such by those who hope to enjoy it, and possibly learn from it, in the years to come. Thanks to the efforts of local preservation groups, it appears that Bachelor's Grove is not beyond restoration, but it should still be protected against the abuses that it has suffered in the past. It is a piece of our haunted history that we cannot afford to lose.

GHOSTS OF GRACELAND

While Bachelor's Grove Cemetery certainly captures much of the attention paid to ghosts and hauntings in Chicago graveyards, it is certainly not alone when it comes to the area's ghostly burial grounds.

As mentioned earlier, Graceland Cemetery came about because of the closure of the Old City Cemetery, which is now Lincoln Park. The cemetery was started in 1860 by real estate developer Thomas B. Bryan and it was located far away from the city proper along North Clark Street. Over the years, a number of different architects have worked to preserve the natural setting of its 120 acres. Two of the men largely responsible for the beauty of the place were architect William Le Baron Jenney and another architect named Ossian Cole Simonds, who became so fascinated with the site that he ended up turning his entire business to landscape design. In addition to the natural setting, the cemetery boasts a number of wonderful monuments and buildings, including the cemetery chapel, which holds city's oldest crematorium, built in 1893.

There are a number of Chicago notables buried in Graceland, including John Kinzie, Marshall Field, Phillip Armour, George Pullman, Potter Palmer, Allan Pinkerton, Vincent Starrett, writer and creator of the "Baker Street Irregulars", architect Louis Sullivan and many others.

Graceland is also home to several ghost / supernatural stories. One of these legends however, remains puzzling to both cemetery buffs and ghost hunters alike. It involves the strange story of the ghost who has been seen in the vicinity of the underground vault belonging to a man named Ludwig Wolff. The tomb has been excavated from the side of a mildly sloping hill at the south end of the cemetery and according to local legend, it is supposedly guarded by the apparition of a green-eyed dog that howls at the moon. There are those who believe this creature is some form of supernatural entity, while others dismiss it as nothing more than a story created from the name of the man buried in the crypt. Who can say for sure?

There are two very different stories connected to "haunted" grave monuments in Graceland. While one of them has widely become accepted as a folk legend, the other one finds a surprisingly receptive, and believing, audience.

The first tale concerns the statue that was placed over the resting place of a man named Dexter Graves. He was a hotel owner and businessman who brought an early group of settlers to the Chicago area in 1831. He passed away and was buried but his body was moved to Graceland in 1909. At that time, a statue that was created by the famed sculptor Lorado Taft was placed on his grave. Taft christened the statue "Eternal Silence" but the brooding and menacing figure has become more commonly known as the "Statue of Death".

The figure was once black in color but over the years, the black has mostly worn away, exposing the green, weathered metal beneath. Only one portion of it remains darkened and that is the face, which is hidden in the deepest folds of the figure's robe. It gives the impression that the ominous face is hidden in shadow and the look of the image has given birth to several legends. It is said that anyone who looks into the face of the statue will get a glimpse of his or her own death to come. In addition, it is said that the statue is impossible to photograph and that no camera will function in its presence. Needless to say though, scores of photos exist of the figure so most people scoff at the threats of doom and death that have long been associated with "Eternal Silence".

Without a doubt, the most famous sculpture (and most enduring ghost) of Graceland is that of Inez Clarke. In 1880, this little girl died at the tender age of only six. Tradition has it that she was killed during a lightning storm while on a family picnic. Her parents, stunned by the tragic loss, commissioned a life-size statue of the girl to be placed on her grave. It was completed a year later, and like many Chicago area grave sculptures, was placed in a glass box to protect it from the elements. The image remains in nearly perfect condition today. Even in death, Inez still manages to charm cemetery visitors, who discover the little girl perched on a small stool. The likeness was cast so that Inez is seen wearing her favorite dress and carrying a tiny parasol. The perfectly formed face was created with just the hint of a smile. It is not uncommon to come to the cemetery and find gifts of

The face of Inez Clark (Photo by Michelle Bonadurer)

flowers and toys at the foot of her grave. The site has become one of the most popular places in the cemetery, for graveyard buffs and curiosity seekers alike.

You see, according to local legend, this site is haunted. Not only are their stories of strange sounds heard nearby, but some claim the statue of Inez actually moves under its own power. The most disconcerting stories may be those of the disembodied weeping that is heard nearby but the most famous are those of the statue itself. It is said that Inez will sometimes vanish from inside of the glass box. This is said to often take place during violent thunderstorms. Many years ago, a night watchman for the Pinkerton agency stated that he was making his rounds one night during a storm and discovered that the box that holds Inez was empty. He left the cemetery that night, never to return. Other guards have also reported it missing, only to find it back in place when they pass by again, or the following morning.

Does the spirit of little Inez still manifest in this part of the cemetery? Recent accounts say that occasional visitors to Graceland will spot a child who sometimes disappears in the vicinity of her monument. Perhaps she is still entertaining herself, just on the other side?

PHANTOMS OF ROSEHILL

Rosehill Cemetery began in 1859, taking its name from a nearby tavern keeper named Roe. The area around his saloon was known for some years as "Roes Hill". In time, the name was slightly altered and became "Rosehill". After the closure of the "dreary" Chicago City Cemetery, where Lincoln Park is now located, Rosehill became the oldest and the largest graveyard in Chicago and serves as the final resting place of more than 1,500 notable Chicagoans, including a number of Civil War generals, mayors, former millionaires, local celebrities and early founders of the city. There are also some infamous burials here as well, like that of Reinhart Schwimmer, the unlucky eye doctor and gangster hanger-on who was killed during the St. Valentine's Day Massacre. Another, more mysterious grave site, is that of young Bobby Franks, the victim of "thrill killers" Nathan Leopold and Richard Loeb. After his death, Bobby Franks was buried at Rosehill with the understanding that his lot number would never been given out to the curious. To this day, it remains a secret, although visitors will sometimes find the site by accident among the tens of thousands of graves in the cemetery.

There are also a number of deceased Chicagoans who are not peacefully at rest here and they serve to provide the cemetery with its legends of ghosts and strange happenings.

Perhaps the most famous ghostly site on the grounds is the tomb belonging to Charles Hopkinson, a real estate tycoon from the middle 1800's. In his will, he left plans for his mausoleum to serve as a shrine to the memory of himself and his family. When he died in 1885, a miniature cathedral was designed to serve as the tomb. Construction was started and then halted when the property owners behind the Hopkinson site took the family to court. They claimed that the cathedral tomb would block the view of their own burial sites. The case proceeded all of the way to the Illinois Supreme Court, which ruled that the other families had no say over what sort of monument the Hopkinson family built and that they should have expected that something could eventually block the view of their site. Shortly after, construction on the tomb continued and was completed. Despite the fact that the courts ruled in the favor of Hopkinson, it is said that on the anniversary of the real estate investor's death, a horrible moaning sound can be heard coming from the tomb, followed by what appears to be sound of rattling chains.

Ghost lore is filled with stories of the dead returning from the grave to protest wrongs that were done to them in their lifetime, or to continue business and rivalries started while they were among the living. Such events have long been a part of the lore of Rosehill's community mausoleum.

The Rosehill Cemetery Mausoleum was proposed in 1912 and the cemetery appealed to the elite businessmen of the city for the funds to begin construction. These men were impressed with the idea of a large and stately mausoleum and enjoyed the thought of entire rooms in the building that could be dedicated to their families alone and which also could be decorated to their style and taste. The building was designed Sidney Lovell and is a massive, multi-level structure with marble passageways and rows upon rows of the dead. It is filled with a number of Chicago notables from the world of business and even architect Sidney Lovell himself.

One of the funding subscribers for the mausoleum was John G. Shedd, the president of Marshall Field from 1909 to 1926 and the man who donated the wonderful Shedd Aquarium to Chicago. He guaranteed himself immortality with the development of what he dreamed would be the world's largest aquarium. Even though Shedd died four years before the aquarium would open, his directors remained loyal to his plans and created an aquatic showplace. A little of that extravagance can be found in the Rosehill mausoleum, as Shedd's family room is one of the most beautiful portions of the building. The chapel outside the room features chairs that are carved in images depicting shells and sea horses and the window inside bathes the room with a blue haze that makes the chamber appear to be under water. For this window, Shedd commissioned the artisan Louis Comfort Tiffany and made him sign a contract that said he would never create another window like it.

There have been no ghost stories associated with John Shedd, but there are others entombed in the structure who may not have found the peace that Shedd has found. Two of the men also laid to rest in the building are Aaron Montgomery Ward and his bitter business rival, Richard Warren Sears. One has to wonder if either of these men could rest in peace with the other man in the same structure, but it is the ghost of Sears who has been seen walking through the mausoleum at night. The business pioneer has been spotted, wearing a top hat and tails, leaving the Sears family room and walking the hallways from his tomb to that of Ward's. Perhaps the rivalry that plagued his life continues on after death?

Another otherworldly manifestation comes to us as a protest over an unmarked grave. Ghostly lore is filled with such tales and Rosehill boasts at least one legend of this type. In October 1995, a groundskeeper at the cemetery reported that he had seen a woman wandering about in the graveyard at night. She had been standing next to a tree, not far from the wall that separates the cemetery from Peterson Avenue. The staff member stopped his truck and got out. The cemetery was closed for the night and he was going to tell the woman that she had to leave and offer to escort her to the gate. When he approached her, he realized that the woman, who was dressing in some sort of flowing white garment, was actually floating above the ground! Before his eyes, she turned into a mist and slowly vanished. Not surprisingly, the groundskeeper wasted no time in rushing to the cemetery office to report the weird incident.

Strangely, a woman from Des Plaines, Illinois called the cemetery office the following day and requested that a marker be placed on the grave of her aunt, Carrie Kalbas, who had died in 1933. The grave site had previously been unmarked but the night before, the woman claimed that her aunt had appeared to her in a dream. She asked her niece to be sure that her burial place was marked because she wanted to be remembered. The aunt's grave was located in an old family plot and staff members went out to the site to verify the location and to see what type of monument was needed. They were amazed to find that the grave was located in the exact spot where the apparition had been reported the night before! The grave stone was ordered and the ghost was never seen again.

Rosehill has been plagued with odd monuments and unusual stories connected to them. One of them is a monument that was erected in the cemetery by the Lincoln Park Masonic Lodge. Strangely, the charter for the group was revoked by the Grand Lodge of Joliet when allegations were made that the Lincoln Park masons were dealing in the black arts. The defunct lodge's monument features a large sphere that is affixed to its pinnacle. Although it weighs several tons, the sphere reportedly falls from the monument about every decade, as if signifying that the stories told about the lodge were true.

Another legend that attracts visitors to a Rosehill monument is connected to the tombstone of Mary Shedden, who was allegedly poisoned by her husband in 1931. Those who find the stone may have to use their imaginations a little but they will likely see two startling visions within the stone of the monument itself. One is the young and happy face of Mary Shedden --- and the other is her grinning and cadaverous skull! Skeptics dismiss the tale, saying that the illusion of "faces" is nothing more than the stone's material playing tricks on the eye, but others are not so sure.

Lulu Fellows
(Photo by Michelle Bonadurer)

One of the most famous mortuary statues in the cemetery, or at least one of the most visited, is the monument to Lulu Fellows, a young woman who died at age 16 in 1833. Visitors who come here often leave behind coins, toys and tokens to the girl whose monument bears the words *Many Hopes Lie Buried Here*. A number of visitors claim that they have encountered the smell of fresh flowers around this life-like monument -- even in the winter, when no fresh flowers are present.

Another "statuary spirit" that comes from Rosehill Cemetery and while this burial ground boasts a number of ghosts, perhaps the most romantic and tragic tale involves the grave of Frances Pearce. This striking monument was moved from the old Chicago City Cemetery to Rosehill many years ago and depicts the life-sized images of Frances and her infant daughter. Both of them are reclining, with the little girl in the arms of her mother, atop the stone. The figures are encased inside of one of the already described glass boxes.

Frances was married to a man named Horatio Stone around 1852. The two of them were said to be very much in love and lived a happy life together. Then, in 1854, Frances tragically died at the age of twenty from tuberculosis. To make matters worse, her infant daughter followed her to the grave four months later. Horatio was nearly destroyed by these terrible events and he commissioned sculptor Chauncey Ives to create a memorial sculpture to be placed on their graves in the City Cemetery. Later, both the remains and the memorial were moved to Rosehill.

According to local legend, on the anniversary of their deaths, a glowing, white haze fills the interior of the glass box. The stories go on to say that the mother and daughter are still reaching out from beyond the grave for the husband and father they left behind.

Another doomed lover at Rosehill is the specter of Elizabeth Archer, an attractive young woman who committed suicide after high school sweetheart, Arnold Fischel, was killed in an accident. The two of them had been students together at North Side Senn High School and even though they were young, no one could deny the connection they obviously shared. Grief-stricken by the death of his daughter, Elizabeth's father erected what is called the Archer-Fischel Monument, where Elizabeth is sometimes seen lurking on cold nights during the month of November.

An unknown pair of lost lovers has been seen on many occasions between the Smith Column in Section 11 and the Smith Memorial Bench a short distance away. No one knows for sure who they are but traditions state that the seemingly distraught figures are the ghosts of a couple buried nearby. According to the lore, they killed themselves during a suicide pact that was meant to keep them together forever. When approached by concerned visitors to the cemetery (who can't help but notice how upset they seem to be), the couple simply explain that they are unable to leave --- and then they vanish! The mystery of their identity remains but their reality seems assured by the number of witnesses who have encountered them, including a Catholic priest and a funeral director.

Another sad and tragic figure here is that of Philomena Boyington, the granddaughter of architect William W. Boyington, who designed the gothic gates that lead into the cemetery. According to the stories, people who sometimes pass by the cemetery at night will see the face of Philomena peering out at them from the window to the left and just below the bell tower of the Ravenswood gates. It has been said that the young girl often played near the site when the gates were being constructed back in 1864. She died of pneumonia not long after the structure was completed and she has haunted the place ever since.

Rosehill Cemetery also has a couple of tombs that are worthy of interest to readers with a penchant for the strange. The first belongs to a man named Gerhardt Foreman, a friend and contemporary of the famed occultist, Alistair Crowley. Foreman studied with the so-called "wickedest man in the world" for several years and when he returned to America, was instrumental in spreading the word of the Golden Dawn throughout the country and in the founding of the Ancient and Mystical Order of the Rosicrucians. Entombed here in Rosehill, Foreman's mausoleum is said to have been chained shut in order to keep Gerhardt from wandering about.

The Egyptian themed tomb of Darius Miller

Also entombed in Rosehill is Darius Miller, whose keen interest in Ancient Egypt is readily apparent from the unique design of his mausoleum. His monument was constructed as a replica of the Egyptian Temple of Anubis but it is Miller's cause of death that is of keen interest to supernatural enthusiasts -- and the stories that surround this marvelous tomb.

In November 1922, Darius Miller was the curator of Egyptology at Chicago's Field Museum of Natural History and happened to be in Egypt at the time when Howard Carter and Lord Carnarvon opened the fabled tomb of Pharaoh Tutankhamen in the Valley of the Kings. And while this must have been the experience of a lifetime, it also made Miller susceptible to what some have dubbed "The Curse of the Pharaoh" and he died the following spring.

When Carter and Carnarvon opened the tomb, they created a great mystery, as several of those connected with the discovery died violent, unusual or at least, untimely deaths. The sinister superstition of the curse started on the very day that the two archaeologists penetrated the entrance to the tomb. As the last man climbed back into the sunshine, a sandstorm is said to have come up suddenly, swirling over the mouth of the cave. As it died away, a hawk (the royal emblem of Egypt) was allegedly seen soaring over the tomb to the west -- in the direction of the afterworld in Egyptian belief. The spirit of the dead pharaoh, some believed, has left his mark on those who violated his tomb. There were also stories that said that on the entrance to the tomb had been an inscription that read something like "death comes with wings to those who violate this tomb" but this story has never been confirmed.

Regardless, five months later, in April 1923, Lord Carnarvon was bitten on the left cheek by a mosquito. The bite became infected and then weakened by blood poisoning, he contracted pneumonia. He died in Cairo at 1:55 in the morning and at the moment of his death, all of the lights in the city went out. At the same time, back on his estate in England, Carnarvon's dog suddenly began to inexplicably howl. Moments later, he fell to the ground and died.

The curse was also blamed for the deaths of others, including Darius Miller. One of the first to die was the Canadian archaeologist Le Fleur, a close friend of Carter's who had come to assist in the excavation of the tomb. He was struck down just a few weeks after his arrival by a mysterious illness.

The next victim was English archaeologist Arthur C. Mace, who had helped Carter remove the door to the burial chamber. Soon after Carnarvon's death, Mace reportedly became very anxious and his strength simply ebbed away. He finally just lost consciousness and died, in the same hotel as Lord Carnarvon, for no apparent reason.

His death was followed by that of American millionaire and railway tycoon George Jay Gould, one of Carnarvon's oldest acquaintances. He had come to Egypt to pay last respects to his friend but fascinated by the discovery of the tomb, he went out to the desert and asked Carter for a tour. The next day, Gould suffered a violent attack of fever and died that same evening.

Dr. Evelyn White, a well-known archaeologist and friend of Carter, began suffering from bouts of depression shortly after the discovery of the tomb. He was driven to suicide and hanged himself in his hotel room. In his farewell note, he reportedly wrote: "I am a victim of the curse, which has forced me to take my life."

Alfred Lucas, Douglas Derry and Miller also died, sending a current of fear though those who had been a part of the tomb's discovery. Shortly after, Carnarvon's half brother, Aubrey Herbert, died of peritonitis and in February 1929, Lady Alminia, wife of Lord Carnarvon, died under strange circumstances. An insect bite, according to doctors, had resulted in her death. That same year, Richard Bethell, Carter's former secretary and the man responsible for cataloging many of the treasures in the tomb, was found dead in his bed at the age of 49. A few months later, in February 1930, his father, Lord Westbury, hurled himself to his death from the window of his London apartment. An alabaster vase from the Pharaoh's tomb was in his bedroom. During his funeral, the hearse accidentally ran over two small boys and one of them died on the way to the hospital.

In the seven years after the discovery of the tomb in 1922, a dozen people who had been concerned with it one way or another had died strange deaths -- but the number would continue to grow and would include doctors, archaeologists and even those who examined the body of Tutankhamen. The 27th victim of the "curse" was James Breasted of the University of Chicago, who had spent quite a lot of time in the tomb with Carter. He contracted a mysterious ailment that doctors could find no explanation for but included high fevers, a swelling of the throat and piercing headaches. He eventually fell into a coma and never awakened.

But was there really a curse, or was these tragic events merely a series of odd coincidences that played into hands of occultists? Howard Carter scoffed at the idea of any curse and he should have been the man most affected by one if it actually existed. However, he died from natural causes in 1939. Many modern scholars have come to believe that the "curse" was merely the result of decay inside of the tomb that affected many of the discoverers as an ancient disease would have after being exposed to air -- and to the systems of those who had never encountered anything like it before. This might explain the mysterious ailments, the depressions and suicides, high fevers and more. But how do we explain what seem to be the untimely deaths of those who merely examined the body of the Pharaoh, catalogued items from the tomb or simply came into contact with the treasure? Merely a coincidence -- or something more?

No one can say for sure what may have been the ultimate cause of death for Darius Miller but legends persist to say that his tomb in Rosehill Cemetery is haunted. According to the legend, a blue light can be seen coming from inside his tomb during the early morning hours every May 1. Is it Miller's spirit still calling out from the other side, more than eight decades after his death?

THE ITALIAN BRIDE

In Hillside, Illinois, just outside of Chicago, is Mount Carmel Cemetery. In addition to being the final resting place of Al Capone, Dion O'Banion and other great Chicago mobsters, the cemetery is also the burial place of a woman named Julia Buccola Petta. While her name may not spring to mind as a part of Chicago history, for those intrigued by the supernatural, she is better known as the "Italian Bride". Julia's grave is marked today by the life-sized statue of the unfortunate woman in her wedding dress, a stone reproduction of the wedding photo that is mounted on the front of her monument. The statue marks the location where Julia's apparition is said to appear. Not surprisingly, the ghost is clad in a glowing, white bridal gown.

Julia Buccola grew up on the west side of Chicago and when she and her husband married, they moved to a more upscale Italian neighborhood. Eventually, she became pregnant with her first child but complications set in and she died giving birth to a stillborn child in 1921. Because of the Italian tradition that dying in childbirth made the woman a type of martyr, Julia was buried in white, the martyr's color. Her wedding dress also served as her burial gown and with her dead infant tucked into her arms, the two of them were laid to rest in a single coffin

Julia's mother, Filomena, angrily blamed her daughter's husband for the girl's death and she claimed the body and buried her with the Buccola's at Mount Carmel Cemetery. Shortly after Julia was buried though, Filomena began to experience strange and terrifying dreams every night. In these nightmares, she envisioned Julia telling her that she was still alive and needed her help. For the next six years, the dreams plagued Filomena and she began trying, without success, to have her daughter's grave opened and her body exhumed. She was unable to explain why she needed to do this, she only knew that she should. Finally, through sheer persistence, her request was granted and a sympathetic judge passed down an order for Julia's exhumation.

 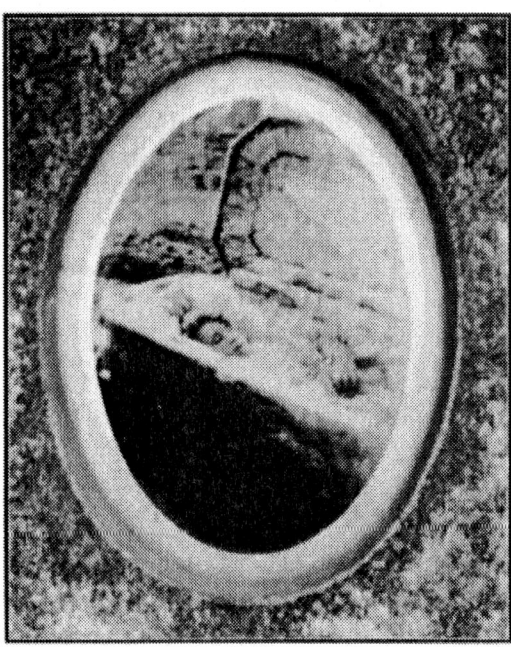

Two Photographs from the grave marker of Julia Buccola Petta show her on the day of her wedding, wearing the bridal gown that she was buried in and the condition of her body when it was exhumed six years after her death.

In 1927, six years after Julia's death, the casket was removed from the grave. When it was opened, Julia's body was found not to have decayed at all. In fact, it was said that her flesh was still as soft as it had been when she was alive. A photograph was taken at the time of the exhumation and shows Julia's "incorruptible" body in the casket. Her mother, and other admirers, placed the photo on the front of her grave monument, which was constructed after her reburial. The photograph shows a body that appears to be fresh, with no discoloration of the skin, even after six years. The rotted and decayed appearance of the coffin in the photo however, bears witness to the fact that it had been underground for some time. Julia appears to be merely sleeping. Her family took the fact that she was found to be so well preserved as a sign from God and so after collecting money from other family members and neighbors, they created the impressive monument that stands over her grave today.

What mysterious secret rests at the grave of Julia Petta? How could her body have stayed in perfect condition after lying in the grave for six years? No one knows, but not surprisingly, reports have circulated for years claiming that a woman in a bridal gown haunts this portion of the cemetery.

Some of the stories come from students at Proviso West High School, which is located just east of the cemetery on Wolf Road. They have reported a girl walking in the cemetery at night and they are not alone. A number of people in a car traveling down Harrison Street were startled to see a woman passing through the tombstones one night. Thinking that it was simply a Halloween prank, they stopped the car for a closer look. They did not become unnerved until they realized that, even though it was pouring down rain, the girl was perfectly dry. They didn't choose to investigate any closer and immediately drove away!

THE MIRACLE CHILD OF CHICAGO

Another grave, located in the Chicago suburb of Worth and at Holy Sepulchre Cemetery, is said to have mysterious benevolent properties. In fact, it is said be able to heal the sick and the dying. Many people feel that this is a sacred place and is made so because the grave holds the final remains of a young girl named Mary Alice Quinn. Over the years, hundreds have claimed to experience miraculous healings here, while others speak of strange occurrences that can only be paranormal in nature. Because of this, Mary's grave and tombstone have been the subject of visits by religious pilgrims and supernatural enthusiasts alike.

Mary was a quiet child who died suddenly in 1935, when she was only 14. Born in 1920, she was one of three children of Daniel and Alice Quinn. As a young girl, she was diagnosed with a heart condition and became devoutly religious, devoted to St. Theresa, who claimed to have a mystical experience when she saw a religious image appear on her wall. After that, she became known in her neighborhood for curing the sick. While on her deathbed, Mary told her parents that she wanted to come back and help people after her death. The faithful say that she has done just that. Soon after her death, she was said to have mysteriously appeared to a number of people in the Chicago area. Throughout the 1930's and 1940's, it was not uncommon to hear of new Mary Alice Quinn sightings.

On one occasion, a sick nun at Mary Alice's former school claimed that she was visited by an apparition of the girl and cured. Others who claimed to see her said that her apparition had a glowing veil over her face. This was attributed to being a "veil of grace", a supernatural manifestation that is found in cases of people who are saints. Witnesses also began to tell of the spectral scent of roses that surrounded the healings and the apparition sightings. This is noteworthy because of Mary Alice's devotion to St. Theresa, whose motto had been "I will let fall from heaven a shower of roses." For years after their daughter's death, Daniel and Alice Quinn hoped that the numerous reports of healings and strange phenomena attached to their daughter would attract the attention of the Catholic Church and that the girl might someday be considered for sainthood herself. They distributed literature and holy cards and helped to provide documentation for the few articles that were written about Mary Alice in Catholic journals.

The Grave Site of Mary Alice Quinn

And while there has been no official interest from the church, Mary Alice's following continues to grow among believers. Today, her healing powers are said to have taken on another manifestation and one that surrounds her grave marker. When she passed away, she was secretly buried in a cemetery plot that belonged to the Reilly family. It was thought that this might keep her burial place a secret and prevent the graveyard from being overrun by curiosity seekers intent on finding her resting place. Word soon spread though and a gravestone was eventually cut with her name on it. Since that time, thousands have come to the site, many of them bringing prayer tokens, rosaries, coins and photos to leave as offerings and to ask that Mary intercede for them in prayer. Many claim to have been healed of their afflictions after visiting the grave and others have been healed by extension. They claim to have found relief from one of the many spoonfuls of dirt that has been taken from Mary's burial site.

Strangely, the phantom scent of roses has been reported filling the air around the gravestone, even when there are no roses anywhere around. The smell is said to be especially strong in the winter months, when the scent of fresh roses would be impossible to mistake. Many visitors have alleged this smell over the years and some of them even say that it is overwhelming. The faithful claim that this unexplainable odor is proof that Mary's spirit is still nearby and interceding on their behalf. Her love and charity continues, even decades after her death.

SPECTRAL FIGURES OF CHICAGO GRAVEYARDS

In addition to the ghosts, Chicago area graveyards have been plagued by other, perhaps even more mysterious creatures --- from pale men in black to what appear to be hooded monks. These creatures seem to exist in places where they should not and history cannot provide us with answers when it comes to their existence. For while ghostly monks seem to have long been a part of Chicago lore, there is no record to say that a monastery ever existed here at all. So who are these strange figures, what do they want --- and are the best avoided on a dark night? My answer to that question is definitely "yes"!

American history is not filled with cases of vampirism, although some cases do exist to show that the lore of the vampire was alive and well in the colonies, as well as in Europe. Most "vampire" outbreaks in America could be traced to epidemics of tuberculosis or the "white death", as it was called. In the 1800's, the symptoms of this disease, which would often wipe out entire families, mirrored closely with the vampires of legend. And while European vampires were seen as romantic creatures, the colonials did not see these monsters as graceful "creatures of the night". The vampire was a death-bringer and something to be feared. An unsuspecting community that fell under the spell of one of these monsters could very well be destroyed. You see, in historic America, vampires were not mythical creatures from books and folklore, they were unquestionably real!

And these are not the only types of vampires to appear in the annals of the unexplained. More traditional "phantom attacker" types make their appearances as well. In Spring Valley, Illinois, there was a local graveyard around which rumors of a resident vampire lingered for years. Many witnesses claimed to find dead dogs there on occasion, always drained of their blood. In 1967, teenagers broke into the tomb of three brothers, the Massock's, who had once been well-known butchers in the area. It was from this crypt that the cemetery's vampire was said to emerge. After the teenagers entered the tomb, they stole the head from one of the corpses entombed there. The boys were later caught and punished and their vandalism did nothing to dispel the stories and the incidents continued.

According to Rosemary Ellen Guiley, a hardened Vietnam veteran went out to the cemetery one night in the 1980's to see if the stories of the creature were true. He and several friends approached the tomb and here, encountered a gaunt and pale figure that seemed to "radiate evil". The veteran reportedly shot the creature five times as close range, but the bullets seemed to have no effect. As it lurched toward them, the group ran from the cemetery.

Not long after, a Chicago writer allegedly gathered a party and investigated the cemetery. The group rapped on the door of the crypt in question but received no response. They then tried poked a wooden rod into a small vent on the side and when they did, something "black and wormy" shot out from the hole and twisted onto the ground. Unnerved, the investigators took off running, although they returned later that afternoon, around dusk, and emptied a bottle of holy water into the vent. They were startled to hear a "painful groaning" coming from inside. Since that time, reports of vampires from Spring Valley have been eerily silent.

Another figure, this time much more menacing in that it was frequently seen, began to be reported around St. Casimir's Cemetery on the south side of Chicago in the middle and late 1970's. The first sighting occurred in 1978 when a man was driving past the cemetery on Pulaski Road one night and spotted a figure standing just inside of the cemetery fence, draped in a long, black cape. The figure had its back to the driver, but the young man couldn't help but slow down to get a closer look. As he did, the man turned around to face him, revealing a ghastly white face above the neck of the cloak. The sinister looking man bared his teeth at the driver and the fellow in the car sped off.

Around June 14 and 15, the figure was seen again, this time by neighborhood teenagers, who added that he was now seen in the same cape, but also with a top hat on his head. The local police believed that it was nothing more than a prank to frighten the local children, but they became concerned after two police reports stated that the man had approached, chased and threatened youths on two separate occasions. According to the reports, the man was described as being "six feet tall, extremely thin with broken teeth and wearing dirty, muddy clothing." Both reports also said that he had a "disgusting odor" about him, to go along with the hat, cape and makeup. The sightings were apparently kept quiet in the 1970's to "prevent hysteria" but similar sightings continue today.

A number of people traveling southbound on Kostner Avenue near the cemetery arrive at the stoplight at 111th Street and see their headlights illuminate the front gates of the cemetery. It has become common for these motorists to claim to see a thin man with a pale face, dressed in black and wearing a cape, peering out at them from the graveyard. Before the traffic light changes, the man apparently fades away. He does not leave -- he simply vanishes! Others claim to be walking or riding a bicycle past the gates to see the same figure. In addition to the sighting though, they are also subjected to a menacing hiss or growl before the creature disappears.

One of the most frightening encounters though took place in 1979 when a woman was driving south on 115th Street, approaching the railroad tracks on the western edge of Restvale Cemetery. She stated later that a man who matched the earlier, vampire-like descriptions suddenly appeared on the street in front of her car. To avoid hitting the man, she swerved into oncoming traffic and then veered back into her own lane just in the nick of time. She immediately stopped and looked in the rearview mirror but the man was gone! There was no place that he could have gone to, he simply vanished.

Another encounter took place in the backyard of an elderly woman who lived near the cemetery. She opened the sliding patio door of her home to let her dog outside but no sooner had the poodle stepped out, that it began to bark loudly. Startled, the woman switched on the back patio light to see what was bothering the dog and was terrified to see a figure lying in the grass. He immediately turned and she got a long look at his white face and bared teeth. He let out a loud hiss and then got up and began to run. According to her statement, he then jumped over a four foot fence without even touching it. When he landed on the other side, he vanished.

Who is this strange creature and why does he appear here? No one can say for sure, but author Dale Kaczmarek researched the story and discovered that, around the time of the original sightings, there was a mildly retarded young man who lived near the cemetery. He often jogged and walked alongside the road at night and one evening was killed by a passing car. Could this young man have been the thin "man in black" who was reported here in the 1970's? He could have been playing a prank on people who passed by the cemetery -- and perhaps that "prank" continues after his death. Perhaps it is his ghost who appears at St. Casimir's now? Whether it is or not, keep a watchful eye out when passing these gates by night for those who have encountered this unnerving phantom have certainly never forgotten it!

Another mysterious figure, with another possible connection to the past, haunts a stretch of roadway that leads into the gates of Calvary Cemetery, located along the North Shore in Evanston. This old Catholic Cemetery rests on the edge of Lake Michigan and is located between two large universities, Loyola in Chicago and Northwestern in Evanston. For this reason, students from both of these colleges have been unlucky enough to travel Sheridan Road at night and to encounter the phantom as he crosses the roadway to the graveyard gates.

According to the story, motorists following the "S" curve that passes between the cemetery on one side and Juneway park and beach on the other are often startled by a disheveled, wet and tired-looking figure as he pulls himself from the rocky water and staggers across the road to the graveyard. He often stumbles from the water and barely pulls himself across the road. In some reports, he even drags a strand of seaweed behind him, further adding to his drowned appearance.

While a legend among those who live along the North Shore, his identity remains unknown. The tales have it that the man was a drowning victim who met his death in Lake Michigan many years ago (the sightings began in the 1950's). His body was apparently washed ashore near this site and his ghost has remained here ever since. Some believe that perhaps he is buried in Calvary Cemetery and his spirit is now trying to make its way to his grave -- or that the man was never buried at all and for this reason, struggles to make it to consecrated ground. Regardless, who he really is remains a mystery, although this has never stopped anyone from speculating.

Some believe that the phantom may be connected to a plane crash that occurred in nearby Lake Michigan in May 1951. An instructor from the Glenview Naval Air Station experienced engine problems and had to bail out of his aircraft. He landed in the lake just a short distance from Northwestern University. He was spotted alive and waving his arms as a signal for help, but unfortunately, he drowned before anyone could get to him. Two days later, his body was found washed up on the rocks near the cemetery. Could it be this lost soul who now haunts the roadway leading into the cemetery. Many local residents believe so and in fact, have even dubbed the ghost "the Aviator".

Others believe that while this figure did haunt the roadway for a number of years, sightings abruptly came to an end in the 1960's and that he has not been seen since. Apparently though, while sightings have been few and far between in recent years, they do continue. I recently spoke to a young woman who saw a figure cross the roadway in August 1997. She was driving to a friend's house in Evanston one night and traveled along Sheridan Road at about 9:45 pm. Just as she was coming up on the cemetery, her headlights illuminated a shambling figure as he lurched from one side of the road to the other. She immediately stomped on the brake pedal and her car fishtailed and came to a stop. The figure ahead of her kept moving slowly, unfazed by the lights or by the screech of brakes on the pavement.

The young woman described to me what she saw: "It was definitely a man and he was tall and thin and really sort of sickly looking. I couldn't tell much about his clothing because it was still pretty dark but I can say that he did look like he had been wet. His hair was all plastered onto his head ... it stuck out in all directions. He never really looked at me, so I don't know what he looked like really, just pale. I was really upset that I had almost hit him ... I never even dreamed that he might be a ghost."

After the man reached the other side of the road, she pressed on the accelerator and slowly moved forward. She was angry at the fact that the man had walked out in front of her without looking and she planned to say something to him as she went by but he never even glanced in her direction. She rolled her window down anyway and was suddenly struck by a very cold chill. The air temperature outside was much too cold for August and she knew that it was certainly colder than it had been when she had gotten into the car. Her air conditioning was on, she told me, and it was colder outside than in. Unnerved by this, and by the idea of confronting the strange man on a dark road at night, she rolled up her window and drove on.

It was not until she reached her friend's house that she learned that the man she had encountered might not have been of this world. "When I told my friend about what had happened, she started really freaking out," she recalled to me later. "She told me all about this ghost story about the drowned man and the cemetery and by the time she finished, I was pretty scared.

"I have been to her house many times since then," she added, "but I can tell you that I have never taken that particular route to get there again!"

Another Chicago area burial ground, Bethania Cemetery in Justice, boasts at least two mysterious figures that haunt the grounds and the streets nearby. Bethania is a largely German cemetery and it is located just southwest of famous Resurrection Cemetery. As this graveyard is located along the very haunted Archer Avenue (as we'll explore further in this chapter), it's no wonder that strange happenings occur here.

One of the most common phantoms to appear here is seen on the 79th Street side of the cemetery. Just past the maintenance entrance to the grounds, motorists have often reported seeing the harmless figure of an elderly man as he rakes and burns leaves along the side of the road. These sightings normally occur during the fall, so it's not the time of year that it happens that seems so odd to the people who spot this scene -- it's the time of day! Those who are driving by are often puzzled as to why this old man would be out working in the cemetery between 2:00 and 4:00 in the morning. However, as the witnesses slow down to have a look in the rearview mirror, or even glance back in his direction, they discover that not only is the old man gone, but so are the piles of burning leaves. So far, no one has been able to provide an explanation as to why this odd figure is being seen here, nor even who he might be.

Bethania's other phantom figure is more on the unnerving side. He haunts the far southwestern edge of the cemetery, located along Cork Avenue. Several reliable witnesses have reported to author and ghost hunter Dale Kaczmarek that they have seen a blood-covered man running from a nearby model home and waving a flashlight as he goes. He flees the edge of the graveyard towards oncoming traffic, whirling the flashlight as he goes, as if trying to flag down one of the passing cars.

One witness told Kaczmarek that the bloody man had run right out in front of his car, forcing the witness to swerve wildly to avoid hitting what he believed was a flesh and blood person. The sighting was so real that he could see the injuries to the man, the blood on his clothing and at one point, the light from the phantom flashlight temporarily blinded the driver. The witness regained control of his car and as he swerved back into his lane, he quickly looked back in his rearview mirror. Amazingly, he was stunned to see the bleeding man stumble into the path of another car, still waving the flashlight. The second driver did not react as quickly though and the first witness watched in shock as the car passed directly through the figure without even slowing down. The bloody man then staggered to the side of the road, crossed a shallow ditch and then vanished as he reached the cemetery fence.

The identity of this strange figure also remains a mystery and no research has even been able to discover if a murder or accident occurred near here that might explain the horrific apparition.

Another Calvary Cemetery, this time in Steger, Illinois, is home to yet another mystery figure. Again, the figure haunts the roadway in front of the cemetery gates and may just be re-playing an incident from the past. The burial grounds are located on the north side of Steger Road and near the south edge of the Sauk Trails Woods Forest Preserve. It's a fairly secluded area and roads here are often shrouded in darkness from the overhanging trees. Which makes the strange occurrences along the roadway all the more unnerving...

According to witnesses, sightings of the cemetery's phantom figure occur after turning east on Steger Road from Western Avenue. This is a dark, rural roadway and there are no streetlights of any kind here until the driver actually enters a residential area further up the road. It's along this dark stretch of drive though, near the cemetery entrance, where the motorists suddenly encounter the figure of a young boy who is a riding his bicycle in the middle of the road! Everyone who experiences this phantom never imagine that he is anything other than a careless little boy -- until they realize he is apparently out riding his bike in the middle of the night!

These late night encounters nearly always end up in near collisions and accidents as the driver tries to avoid hitting the boy. They are stunned as he appears out of the darkness, riding casually down two lanes of traffic, and often have to slam on their brakes or swerve quickly. After recovering from their near miss, they attempt to find the boy and reprimand him for his dangerous behavior but there is never any boy to be found. He has simply vanished into the night.

Who this phantom boy might be is unclear but many believe that he may be the spirit of a child who was killed on this same roadway in the past. Perhaps he was struck and killed by a passing motorist one night and is now replaying his final moments again and again -- or perhaps the figure appears a warning. Perhaps the ghost is appearing to drivers to caution them to look for other children who might share his same fate someday if a motorist comes over one too many hills in the darkness, only to find another careless bicyclist on the other side?

A "woman in white" haunts one of the area's most foreboding graveyards, a place called Archer Woods Cemetery. For years, the female phantom has been reported at this wooded burial ground, especially back in the days when it was a desolate spot along Kean Road. She does not wander the roadway flagging down passing motorists however, although she is usually spotted by those who drive by the cemetery at night.

Those unwitting travelers, passing along Kean Road, are often greeted by the sound of a woman loudly sobbing in despair. When they stop their vehicles for a closer look, they see a woman in a white gown wandering near the edge of the graveyard. She is always said to be weeping and crying and covering her face with her hands. She is normally only seen for a matter of seconds before she disappears.

In addition to the "Weeping Woman", Archer Woods is also said to be home to another, more terrifying, specter, an old-fashioned hearse. This black coach is said to be driverless but pulled by a team of mad horses. The hearse itself is made from black oak and glass and carries the glowing coffin of a small child as cargo. Residents of the area have been reporting this bizarre "ghost hearse" for years and it is often seen along nearby Archer Avenue. The origins of the hearse vary, but one thing is sure -- no one wants to encounter it while traveling through the shadows along Kean Road after dark!

HAUNTING ALONG CUBA ROAD

The graveyard ghosts of Chicagoland are strange and often perplexing and as you can see from the preceding pages, the many stories run the entire gamut between entertaining folklore and authentic accounts of the supernatural. One such account, which seems to combine elements of both, involves a place called White Cemetery in northern Illinois. This small graveyard, and the surrounding Cuba Road area near Barrington, has gained a rather strange reputation in recent years.

White Cemetery is a small burial ground that is located just east of Old Barrington Road. It dates back as far as the 1820's, but no records exist to say when it started to gain the attention of those with an interest in the unexplained.

For many years, it has been reportedly haunted by eerie, white globes of light that have been seen to hover and float among the tombstones. Witnesses to these anomalies have ranged from teenagers to average passersby, many of whom have gone to the local police and have described not only the glowing lights, but hazy figures too. The lights are said to sometimes float along through the cemetery, drift over the fence and then glide out over the surface of the road. The hazy human-like figures have been spotted along the edge of the fence and lingering near stands of trees. They tend to appear and then vanish at will. Both types of the phenomenon have been investigated and studied by ghost hunters and researchers for some time, but no explanation has been discovered as to their source.

There have also been many stories told about nearby Cuba Road itself. Most of them involve a phantom black automobile that appears near the cemetery and an old house that is seen and then vanishes nearby. The house is believed to have actually existed many years ago and legends say that it burned down under mysterious circumstances. It has been repeatedly spotted over time, often by people who have no idea that the house no longer exists. Some of the sightings also involve a spectral old woman that carries a lantern and flags down passing motorists. When someone stops and tries to help her, she disappears along the edge of the roadway.

In her book *More Chicago Haunts*, author Ursula Bielski adds another element to the strange legends of Cuba Road. According to local historians, nearby Barrington and Lake Zurich were often visited by gangsters during the Prohibition era. Looking for a little peace and quiet, they would come to the small towns to rest, fish, sun and often, to cause a little trouble. Local folks were afraid of these Chicago tough guys and the author believes that this unease remains in one of the ghostly encounters said to occur along Cuba Road. The stories say that the spectral image of a cigar-chewing gangster sometimes appears in the rearview mirror of drivers who pass along this roadway. Who this mobster might be is unknown, but those drivers who have seen him can testify to the fact that he was there!

Strange things, as they say, happen along Cuba Road.

MYSTERIES OF ROBINSON WOODS

One of the last places in the busy city of Chicago that you would expect to find a Native American Burial Ground would be along a busy stretch of roadway, but that's exactly where you will find Robinson Woods. And the graves of the Robinson family may not be the only thing that you find there either. Some have found their ghosts also are present as well!

Andrew Robinson was the son of an Ottawa Indian woman and a Scottish trader and may have been one of the most influential early leaders of Chicago. During the War of 1812, Robinson sided with the American troops and stayed hidden during the conflict, avoiding the local Indians and helping those who were sequestered inside of Fort Dearborn when possible. He is credited with saving the lives of many of those who survived the massacre and was later rewarded for his efforts with land and a yearly stipend. Robinson became a permanent resident of Chicago in 1814 and cultivated good relationships with the mixed culture of the region. He was highly regarded by the local tribes and by the white settlers who were beginning to arrive.

In 1826, Robinson married Catherine Chevalier and became the son-in-law of the Potawatomi chief, Shobonier. A short time later, after the death of the chieftain, Robinson assumed the role of chief, taking the name of Che-che-pin-quay, which means "winking eye". He worked as a translator for Chicago Indian agent Alexander Wolcott and continued to make friends among both the white residents and the Native Americans in the region. When the Potawatomi gave up a large portion of their land in the Treaty of Prairie du Chien in 1829, a large section was set aside for Robinson at Lawrence Avenue and River Road along the Des Plaines River. In addition, he was awarded a lifetime benefit of $200 per year, an amount that was later increased to $500.

In 1830, Robinson opened a saloon in the city and five years later departed for Iowa. He lived away from Chicago for a few years and then returned with the departure of the remaining regional Indian tribes. He lived in Chicago until his death in 1872, signing away huge portions of land to the arriving settlers and attempting to make the transition of Chicago from a small settlement to a growing city a smooth one.

In the early 1900's, the remaining Robinson family continued to be a visible presence in the city. There were many stories about the Robinson house, located in the woods off of Lawrence Avenue, which told of wild living and unseemly parties. In spite of their reputation, the family continued to live in the house in the woods until 1955, when the structure burned to the ground.

A short time after the fire, another, more horrifying event took place here. In October 1955, the bodies of John and Anton Schuessler and Robert Peterson were discovered bound and naked in a ditch at the edge of the woods. The case stunned the city and would remain unsolved for almost 40 years. Not surprisingly, this event may have also left a dark stain on the atmosphere of Robinson Woods.

Several members of the family remained on the property until 1958, when the construction of O'Hare airport allowed the land to be annexed to Chicago as part of the link between the airport and the city. The last Robinson descendant died in 1972 and while an agreement was made that would allow him to be buried on the remaining property with the rest of his family, the city later denied his wishes.

Robinson Woods still remain today, just off Lawrence Avenue. If you go there and leave the street, walking a short distance, you will see a large stone that serves as a burial monument to Andrew Robinson and his family. Their bodies lie here underneath the earth, where they rest peacefully. Or do they?

Strange events have been reported here for many years and first-hand accounts claim the sightings of apparitions that look like Native Americans, along with odd lights that have been spotted in the woods by passing motorists. Other claims the sounds of drums beating and disembodied voices that seem to come from out of the air. Investigations by the Chicago-based *Ghost Research Society* have traced reports where people claim to be overwhelmed by the scent of flowers in the air, even in the winter, when no plants or trees are in bloom!

A dozen paranormal experiments carried out here in 1974-1975 managed to pick up some of the strange sounds that people reported hearing on audio tape. What resulted sounded exactly like Indian tribal drums and the sounds of chopping wood. This may have been common sounds for this area many years ago, but there is no reason why they should still be heard today.

HAUNTS ALONG ARCHER AVENUE

Perhaps the greatest cemetery ghost story of Illinois (and perhaps of all time) is centered around a stretch of roadway on the south side of Chicago called Archer Avenue. Before we get to this story, and to the tales of other phantom hitchers in the Chicago area, we should take a closer look at some of the hauntings along Archer Avenue, especially the reported paranormal events at the St. James-Sag burial ground.

Archer Avenue seems to be the perfect location for a haunting. There are a number of locations along this road, including cemeteries, homes and businesses, which boast more than their share of ghosts. The paranormal activity on the roadway seems to be anchored at both ends by cemeteries, both of which have their own ghost stories. One of them is the famous Resurrection Cemetery and the other, lesser-known, burial ground is St. James-Sag.

But what makes Archer Avenue so haunted? In the early days of Chicago, the road was an Indian trail that stretched all of the way from Fort Dearborn and the old mouth of the Chicago River to what is now the southwest suburbs. The trail linked to the Saucunasi trail that led south and to the Joliet trail that led to the southwest. An Indian village was located just north of the trail's end, across what would be the Illinois & Michigan Canal and along Mud Lake. Some have suggested that the original inhabitants forged a path here because of some mystical, magnetic force that connected it to the next world. They say that paranormal energies would also be attracted to this magnetism and this would explain the hauntings in the area.

Some have also suggested that Archer Avenue may be connected to what are called "ley lines". The idea that a number of unusual spots are often located in a particular area, or along a straight line, was suggested by Alfred Watkins in 1925. The idea came to him when he was examining a map of Herefordshire, England and noticed an alignment of ancient sites. He gave such alignments the name of "ley", a Saxon word that meant "a clearing in the woodland". Since that time, the idea has been expanded beyond ancient sites and has enveloped strange and haunted sites as well. Many believe that these ley lines cross the entire world and feel that locations where the lines cross are especially energy-filled. This might explain what seems to attract such a large number of hauntings to the vicinity of Archer Avenue.

It has also been theorized that this area is so haunted because of its proximity to water. Archer Avenue is nearly surrounded by water sources like the Cal-Sag Channel, the Des Plaines River, the Illinois and Michigan Canal, the Chicago Sanitary and Shipping Canal and even Maple Lake, which reportedly is the scene of "ghost lights" activity. (See Chapter 9)

But no matter what the reason, Archer Avenue may be the most haunted street in Chicago! The Indian trail that it used to be was turned into an actual road in the 1830's. Irish workers on the Illinois-Michigan Canal completed the construction. Most of them lived near Lemont, at the southern end of Archer Avenue. Here is located the St. James-Sag Church and burial ground, which dates back to around 1817, a few years before Archer Avenue was built to follow the route of the canal. Most of the men who worked on the road and canal moved out of Chicago and became parishioners of the church. Legend has it that they settled into a small, nearby community, which was cursed by an early rector of St. James-Sag because the residents were lax in their attendance at services. The story has it that the curse caused the community to die out and no trace of it can be found today.

The site of the church and burial grounds has a long history in Chicago. The site marks the second oldest Catholic Church in northern Illinois and dates back to 1833. Before that, Marquette and Jolliet were the first white men to see this area, later known as the Sag Ridge and when they arrived in 1673, the local Indians were using it as a burial ground. For this reason, the site was already sacred ground when Marquette offered a mass here in the year of his arrival. The site became a mission and a French signal post in the late 1600's. The present parish was established not by the French, but by the Irish when, as mentioned earlier, so many of them moved into the region as workers on the canal.

A campaign for the construction of the canal began back in 1814, when President James Madison asked Congress to authorize the construction of a ship canal from the Chicago River to the Illinois River, thus connecting Lake Michigan with the Mississippi. Madison's recommendation was ignored but the scheme was kept alive by supporters in Congress for 13 years, mainly through the efforts of Nathaniel Pope, the Territorial Delegate for Illinois and Representative Daniel Cook, for whom Cook County was named. In 1827, Congress finally authorized the canal and agreed to give the state of Illinois every alternate section on a belt of land six miles wide on either side of the chosen route. Two years later, the Illinois and Michigan Canal Commission began financing the project, the purchase of land, the layout of towns along the route and the plotting of building lots.

The project began in 1833 with an appropriation of $25,000 to build a suitable harbor at or near Chicago. The work began on July 1 after a delay that was caused by a controversy between Stephen A. Douglas and a young Army officer named Jefferson Davis. Douglas insisted that the harbor be constructed at the mouth of the Calumet River, 14 miles south of Chicago, while Davis contended the reasonable and logical location for it was the mouth of the Chicago River. Davis' recommendations were eventually adopted and by the spring of 1834, two 500-foot piers had been built, creating a new channel for the river. On July 11, 1834, the first large vessel to enter the river, the *Illinois*, sailed into the new harbor.

Actual construction work on the ship canal was delayed until 1836 though and in that same year, Archer Avenue, named after Colonel William B. Archer, one of the promoters of the canal, was laid out and placed over and existed Indian trail. The first water traffic began on the canal in April 1848, some 15 years after the church on the Sag Ridge had been constructed.

The first church was constructed in 1833 and was a simple log cabin that stood on the highest point of the ridge. In 1850, it was replaced by the limestone building that is still in use today. The pale yellow building stands on top of the hill, just a short distance from the newer rectory and stands watch over the hundreds of graves scattered about on the hills below. It is an idyllic scene and could easily be part of the Irish countryside, rather than a landscape from the southwest side of Chicago.

Supernatural events have been reported at St. James-Sag since around 1847. It was at this time when the first sightings of the "phantom monks" took place here. These stories continued for decades and there were many reliable witnesses to the strange activity. One of them, a former rector of the church, admitted on his deathbed that he had seen ghosts roaming the cemetery grounds for many years.

One cold night in November 1977, a Cook County police officer was passing the cemetery and happened to turn his spotlight up past the cemetery gates. He claimed to see nine hooded figures floating up the cemetery road toward the rectory. Knowing that no one was supposed to be in the cemetery, he stopped and yelled out the window at them to come back toward the road. If they did not, they would be arrested for trespassing. The figures simply ignored him and continued up the road toward the church and rectory.

Quickly, he grabbed his shotgun and ran around the gate and into the graveyard. He pursued what he first thought were pranksters into the graveyard but while he stumbled and fell over the uneven ground and tombstones, the monk-like figures eerily glided past without effort. He said that he nearly caught up with them when "they vanished without a trace". Unable to believe what had just happened, he searched around the area for any trace of the figures but found no one. Finally, he returned to his squad car to write up his report. The paperwork that he filed merely stated that he had chased some trespassers through the cemetery but he always maintained that what he had seen was beyond this world.

Another legend of St. James-Sag is likely what gave the burial ground its ghostly reputation in the first place. This story concerns a phantom hearse that is possibly the same vehicle seen on Kean Road and at nearby Archer Woods Cemetery. The description of the vehicle is the same, from the black horses to the glowing coffin of a child, and was first reported back in 1897. According to a report in the *Chicago Tribune*, two musicians spent the night in a recreation hall that is located at the bottom of the hill below the St. James-Sag rectory. They were awakened in the early morning hours by the sound of a carriage on the stones outside. They looked out and saw the macabre hearse. They became the first to report the eerie vehicle, but they would not be the last.

And in addition to the many alleged haunted houses, businesses and graveyards along this stretch of roadway, Archer Avenue has also become home to one of Chicago's longest standing tales of diabolical delight. It was to a ballroom along Archer Avenue where the devil himself came to dance many years ago. Local tradition in the Bridgeport neighborhood recalls that this supernatural event occurred at Kaiser Hall, just west of Loomis Street on Archer Avenue.

The story recalls that a young woman became entranced one night with a handsome and dashing stranger that she met on the dance floor. As they danced the night away, she happened to glance down at the stranger's feet -- turning her cries of pleasure into a horrified scream! Assuming that the stranger had made an inappropriate advance toward the girl, the neighborhood men angrily pursued the man, who quickly fled from the room. He refused to fight and instead managed to get himself cornered near a second-story window. Suddenly, he leapt out of the window and surprised everyone by landing on his feet on the sidewalk below. When the crowd rushed to the window to peer after him, they discovered him running away.

The folks from the neighborhood followed the man outside (wisely using the staircase) and were amazed to see the real reason for the young woman's scream. Pressed into the concrete, just where the stranger had landed, they found the unmistakable mark of a hoof print!

What is it about this strange and haunted place called Archer Avenue? Is it really connected to the world beyond, or is there a natural explanation for the ghost sightings linked to the region? Are they truth or legend? That remains to be seen, but there may be more to this seemingly innocent roadway than meets the eye!

CHICAGO'S PHANTOM HITCHERS

Without a doubt, the most famous ghostly hitchhiker in the Chicago area is the young girl who has been connected to Resurrection Cemetery and Archer Avenue for a number of decades. Her story will appear later in the chapter, but there are other restless and roaming ghosts of Chicago cemeteries as well.

Undoubtedly, the greatest piece of American cemetery lore is that of the "phantom" or "vanishing" hitchhiker. There is not a region of the country that does not boast at least one tale about a pale young girl who gets a ride with a stranger, only to vanish from the car before they reach their destination. Many, but not all, of these stories seem to also revolve around cemeteries and in some versions of the story, a graveyard plays a very prominent role.

Most stories of phantom hitchhikers go something like this:

On a cold and rainy night, a young man is on his way to a party at a local dance hall and on his way there, he happens to offer a ride to an attractive young woman who agrees to go with him to the dance. Everyone at the party found her to be very charming and after the dance was over, the young man offered to drive her home as the night had turned quite chilly. She accepted and because it was so cold out, he gave her his coat to wear.

He asked for her address and she gave it to him and a short time later, they pulled into the driveway of the house where the girl said that she lived and the driver turned to tell her that they had arrived. To his astonishment, she was gone! The passenger seat of the car was empty, although the door had never opened - the girl had simply vanished.

Not knowing what else to do, the man went up to the door and knocked. An elderly woman answered the door and he explained to her what had happened. Right away, she seemed to know exactly what he was talking about. The young girl he had taken to the dance was her daughter - but she had died ten years before in an auto accident.

The horrified young man didn't believe her, even though the name of the girl he had taken to the dance and the woman's daughter were the same. In order to convince him, the old woman even told him where to find the grave of the dead girl in the local cemetery. The young man quickly drove there and following the directions he had been given, found the stone with the girl's name on it. Folded neatly over the top of the marker was the coat that the girl had borrowed to ward off the night chill!

Stories just like that one have been with us for many years and tales of these spectral passengers (usually young women) are often attached to bridges, dangerous hills and intersections and graveyards. There were stories of "vanishing hitchhikers" being told as far back as the late 1800's, when men would tell stories of ghostly women who appeared on the back of their horses. These spectral riders always disappeared when they reached their destination and would often prove to be the deceased daughters of local farmers. Not much has changed in the stories that are still told today, outside of the preferred method of transportation.

As most readers are well aware, such tales are usually referred to as "urban legends". They are stories that have been told and re-told over the years and in most every case have been experienced by the proverbial "friend of a friend" and have no real basis in fact -- or do they?

There are a number of stories of alleged vanishing hitchhikers that have been attached to various highways and roadways in America, including in Chicago. But are all of these stories, as some would like us to believe, nothing more than folklore? Are they simply stories that have been made up and have been spread across the country over a long period of time? Perhaps this is the case, or perhaps not.

There is no question that many ghostly stories do not purport to be true. They are often tales told by people, who believe them to be true, which makes them legends or oral folklore. However, I cannot help but wonder how many of these stories actually got started in the first place. Could any of them have a basis in truth? What if an incident like one of these actually happened somewhere and then was told and re-told to the point that it lost many of the elements of truth? As the story spread, it was embraced by people all over the country and it became a part of their local lore. It has long been believed that people provide an explanation for something that they cannot understand. This is usually done by creating mythology that made sense at the time. Who knows if there may be a very small kernel of truth hidden inside of the folk tales that sends shivers down your spine?

So I will ask you to keep an open mind and look at the heart of every legend and peel away the outer layer of fiction to see if there remains anything at the center. As you might imagine, in some of these stories, there is little of relevance that does remain. The stories often occur to "friends of friends" or happened "many years ago" in an unnamed place to unknown people. Could any of these types of stories be true? It's unlikely, but not all of the stories are the same. In fact, some of them are not only filled with details, but actually list names, dates and locations. What do we make of these tales? And what do we make of those who claim to have experienced these phantoms?

Could all of these people be (as the debunkers would have us believe) drunk, stupid or insane? How do we explain independent sightings by witnesses who are not connected to one another and yet who all claim to experience the same thing? And what about incidents of vanishing hitchhikers who leave real physical evidence behind? I don't mean the proverbial scarves and jackets of the urban legends, but real signs of the fact that they exist -- as you will find the ghost known as Resurrection Mary did later on in this chapter?

If there is a point to this cautionary introduction, it is this -- be careful about disregarding a story that sounds entirely too good to be true. There may be more to the story than first meets the eye!

Chicago has been known as being home to not only the typical vanishing hitchhikers but also to reports of what some have dubbed "prophesying passengers" -- strange hitchhikers who are picked up and then pass along odd messages, usually involving the end of the world or something almost as dire. Many of them are described as looking "Christ-like" or like biblical prophets and in fact, one such enigmatic figure was even nicknamed the "Hitchhiking Jesus" by the press in Palatine, Illinois as they reported alleged encounters with the man. He was always dressed in white clothing and had long hair and a beard. If someone offered him a ride he would climb into the back seat and after riding in silence for a time would shout "the end is near" or "sinner repent" or some such thing. Then, he would simply vanish.

There is also a tale of a prophesying nun from Chicago. A cab driver once told a strange and unsettling fare that he had picked up in December 1941. He was cruising the downtown streets in his cab one night and he pulled over to let in a nun who was dressed in the traditional garb of a Catholic order. She gave him the address that she wished to be taken to and they drove off. The radio was on and the announcer was discussing the events that had taken place at Pearl Harbor a short time before and the preparations that the United States was making for war.

The nun suddenly spoke up from the back seat. "It won't last more than four months", she said and then didn't speak again for the rest of the ride.

When the cabbie pulled up to the address, he got out to open the door for the sister. He was surprised to discover that she wasn't there! Afraid that the little old lady had forgotten to pay her fare, the driver climbed the steps of the address she had given him and discovered that it was a convent. He knocked on the door and was brought to the Mother Superior. He then explained his predicament to her. "What did she look like?" he was asked. She told him that none of the sisters had been downtown that day.

As the driver began to describe her, he happened to look up at a portrait that was hanging on the wall behind the Mother Superior's desk. "That's her," he said, obviously thinking that he was going to get his fare after all -- but he couldn't have been more wrong. The Mother Superior smiled and quietly said, "But she has been dead for ten years."

And the nun, like those passengers who tell of the end of the world, was incorrect in her prediction. One has to wonder if these beings are truly supernatural, then perhaps they should consider another source for their upcoming events! Another passenger from the Windy City had her own strange prediction to make.

During Chicago's Century of Progress Exposition in 1933, a group of people in an automobile told of a strange encounter. They were traveling along Lake Shore Drive when a woman with a suitcase, standing by the roadside, hailed them. They invited her to ride along with them and she climbed in. They later said that they never really got a good look at her because it was dark outside.

As they drove along, they got into a conversation about the Exposition and the mysterious woman oddly told them that the "fair is going to slide off into Lake Michigan in September". She then gave them her address in Chicago and invited them to call on her anytime. When they turn around to speak to her again, after this doom-filled warning, they discovered that she had disappeared!

Unnerved, they decided to go to the address the woman gave them and when they did, a man answered the door. They explained to him why they had come to the house and he merely nodded his head. "Yes, that was my wife", he told them. "She died four years ago."

Another most standard hitcher, a sort of "sister ghost" to Resurrection Mary, haunts the vicinity of Jewish Waldheim Cemetery (now re-named Waldheim Cemetery), located at 1800 South Harlem Avenue in Chicago. This is perhaps one of the more peaceful and attractive of the city's downtown graveyards and is easily recognizable from the columns that are mounted at the front gates. They were once part of the old Cook County Building, which was demolished in 1908. This cemetery would most likely go quietly on through its existence if not for the tales of the "Flapper Ghost". While little background can be discovered about this spirit, it remains a fascinating story.

The story of the ghost states that she was a young Jewish girl who attended dances at the Melody Mill Ballroom, formerly on Des Plaines Avenue. The place was one of the area's favorite spots for ballroom dancing, from the 1920's to the middle 1980's. The brick building was topped with a miniature windmill, the ballroom's trademark. The girl who became the spirit was said to be a very attractive brunette with bobbed hair and a dress right out of the Roaring 20's, hence the spirit's nickname of the "Flapper Ghost". This fetching phantom has been known to hitch rides on Des Plaines Avenue and most often has been seen near the cemetery gates. Some travelers passing the cemetery even claimed to see her entering a mausoleum that is located off Harlem Avenue.

The ghost seems to have had a real-life counterpart, although her name has been lost to time. She was a lovely girl and a regular at the Melody Mill Ballroom until she died of peritonitis, the result of a burst appendix. The girl was buried at Jewish Waldheim and she likely would have been forgotten, to rest in peace, if strange things had not started to happen a few months later. The events began as staff members at the Melody Mill began to see a young woman who looked just like the deceased girl appearing at dances at the ballroom. A number of men actually claimed to meet the girl here (after her death) and also to have offered her a ride home. During the journey, the young woman always vanished.

Although recent sightings have been few, the ghost was most active in 1933, during the Century of Progress Exhibition, and again in 1973. In the early 1930's, she was often reported at the ballroom, where she would dance with young men and ask for a rides to her home at the end of the evening. Every report was basically the same. A young man agreed to drive the girl home and then she would give him directions to go east on Cermak Road, then north on Harlem Avenue. When they reached the cemetery, the girl always asked for the driver to stop the car. The girl would explain to them that she lived in the caretaker's house (since demolished) and then get out of the car. One man stated that he watched the girl go towards the house but then duck around the side of it. Curious, he climbed out of the car to see where she was going and saw her run out into the cemetery and vanish among the tombstones.

Another young man, who was also told that the girl lived in the caretaker's house, decided to come back during the day and to ask about the girl at the house. He had become infatuated with her and hoped to take her dancing again on another evening. His questions to the occupants of the house were met with blank stares and bafflement. No such girl lived, or had ever lived, at the house.

More sightings took place in the early 1970's and one report even occurred during the daylight hours. A family was visiting the cemetery one day and was startled to see a young woman dressed like a "flapper" walking toward a crypt, where she suddenly disappeared. The family hurried over to the spot, only to find no girl and nowhere to which she could have vanished so quickly.

According to author Dale Kaczmarek, another strange sighting took place in 1979 when a police officer saw a beautiful girl walking near the ballroom on a rainy night. He asked her where she was going and she replied "home". He offered her a ride and she directed him to go east on Cermak Road. He later reported that he asked her a number of questions but she always just changed the subject and steered the conversation to how much she liked to dance and how much she enjoyed going to the Melody Mill. The girl then directed him to an apartment building near the cemetery entrance. After the girl got out of the car, she vanished near a covered doorway and the policeman, shocked, got out and went after her. He was sure that she could not have gotten into the building so quickly and was even more surprised to see no wet footprints on the dry sidewalk below the building's awning.

Since that time, sightings of the "Flapper" have been few, and this may be because the old Melody Mill is no more. The days of jazz and big bands were gone by the 1980's and attendance on weekend evenings continued to slip until the place was closed down in 1985. It was later demolished and a new building was put up in its place two years later. Has the Flapper Ghost simply moved on to the other side since her favorite dance spot has disappeared? Perhaps -- and perhaps she is still kicking up her heels on a dance floor in another time and place, where it's 1933 every day!

Another phantom hitcher haunts the roadways near the Evergreen Cemetery in Evergreen Park, a Chicagoland community. For more than two decades, an attractive teenager has been roaming out beyond the confines of the cemetery in search of a ride. A number of drivers claim to have spotted her and in the 1980's a flurry of encounters occurred when motorists in the south and western suburbs reported picking up this young girl. She always asked them for a ride to a location in Evergreen Park and then mysteriously vanished from the vehicle at the cemetery.

According to the legends, she is the spirit of a child buried within the cemetery, but there is no real folklore to explain why she leaves her grave in search of travelers, nor what brings her to the suburbs and so far from home. She is what some would call the typical "vanishing hitchhiker" but there is one aspect to this ghost that sets her apart from the others. In addition to seeking rides in cars, she is resourceful enough to find other transportation when it suits her.

In recent years, encounters with this phantom have also taken place at a bus stop that is located directly across the street from the cemetery. Many have claimed to see a dark-haired young girl here who mysteriously vanishes. On occasion, she has also climbed aboard a few Chicago Transit Authority buses as well.

One evening, a young girl climbed aboard a bus and breezed right past the driver without paying the fare. She walked to the back portion of the vehicle and sat down, seemingly without a care in the world. Irritated the driver called out to her, but she didn't answer. Finally, he stood up and walked back toward where she was seating. She would either pay, he thought, or have to get off the bus. Not surprisingly though, before he could reach her, she vanished before his eyes!

According to reports, other shaken drivers have had the same eerie experience at this bus stop. The other drivers have also seen this young girl and every single one of them have seen her disappear as if she had never been there in the first place.

One of the most intriguing of Chicago's phantom hitchers was the spirit dubbed the "Kennedy Road Phantom" around Christmas time in 1980. This mysterious female ghost was first seen around Byron, Illinois during the frigid months of December and attracted so many curiosity-seekers that traffic was often bumper-to-bumper along Kennedy Road. My guess would be that many of these would-be ghost hunters were male -- for this slender young woman was allegedly dressed, despite the cold weather, in very little clothing!

The sightings continued for several weeks and a number of reliable witnesses came forward to police officers and newspaper reporters, all claming to have seen the phantom. One witness, Dave Trenholm, stated that he was driving along Kennedy Road with Guy Harriett of Oregon at about 9:00 p.m. on the night of January 2, 1981. He told the *Chicago Tribune* that he saw the girl step out from behind some bushes at the side of the road and that he had to look twice to really see her because he was so shocked by her appearance. He couldn't believe his eyes! He described her as being "tall, slender, nice-looking, about 20. All she was wearing were some black panties and some kind of scarf around her neck." The woman seemed to be unaffected by the cold weather (it was about 10 degrees that night) and after she spotted the car, she turned and ran towards a nearby farmhouse --- and then vanished.

There were a number of theories as to who the woman might be, ghostly or otherwise. Some thought that she was a lost mentally handicapped girl who had been reported missing by her parents in Oregon around Christmas. This turned out not to be the case and after all of the standard theories of pranksters were dismissed (for what woman would go to the length of standing on the side of the road nearly naked in December for a joke?), many ideas turned to the supernatural.

Initial thoughts were that she was a car accident victim who had been killed along Kennedy Road and had now come back to haunt the highway. Others speculated that she was the ghost of a person who had been buried in a nearby abandoned cemetery, which had been destroyed.

Regardless of who she was, additional sightings continued through January and began to include reports in which the phantom varied her clothing and description. One man stated that she was wearing a pair of light-colored shorts and a sweatshirt, shorts and a light jacket and even a skimpy halter-top. Again, this was the dead of winter and a remote rural roadway. It didn't seem to be a joke or a hoax, so what was going on?

In late January 1980, the *Rockford Register Star* published a report that a mysterious woman was run over by an Ogle County Sheriff's car around 8:00 in the evening. The woman had suddenly appeared in the middle of the road and the squad car had slammed into her. According to the officers, the woman was pulled beneath the car and they heard her bones crunch and felt the impact of the tires rolling over the body. Needless to say, they quickly came to a stop and jumped out of the car to investigate and to assist her if possible. But when they ran back up the road, they found no body and no woman lying there. A police lieutenant called the story "crazy and untrue" but the stories and the strange sightings continued.

By the end of January, the stories started to die out and finally, despite many people still looking for her, the ghostly woman had faded out of existence. Does she still haunt this lonesome stretch of road? No one knows for sure for she has certainly not been seen in quite awhile -- although I doubt that any male ghost hunters have stopped looking for her!

The Willowbrook Ballroom - Did Resurrection Mary Really Dance Here?

RESURRECTION MARY
My Favorite Ghost Story

It is a cold night in late December on the south side of Chicago. A taxicab travels along Archer Avenue as rain and sleet pelt the windshield. The driver reaches over to crank the heater up one more notch. It is the kind of night, he thinks, that makes your bones ache.

As the car rolls past the Willowbrook Ballroom, a pale figure, blurry though the wet and icy glass of the window, appears along the roadside. The driver cranes his neck and sees a young woman walking alone. She is strangely dressed for such a cold and wet night, wearing only a white cocktail dress and a thin shawl over her shoulders. She stumbles along the uneven shoulder of the road and the cabbie pulls over and stops the car. He rolls down the window and the young girl approaches the taxi. She is beautiful, he sees, despite her disheveled appearance. Her blond hair is damp from the weather and plastered to her forehead. Her light blue eyes are the color of ice on a winter lake.

He invites her into the cab and she opens the back door and slides across the seat. The cabbie looks into the rearview mirror and asks her where she wants to go. He offers her a free ride. It's the least that he can do in this weather, he tells her.

The girl simply replies that he should keep driving down Archer Avenue, so the cabbie puts the car into gear and pulls back onto the road. He notices in his mirror that the girl is shivering so he turns up the heater again. He comments on the weather, making conversation, but she doesn't answer him at first. He wonders if she might be a little drunk because she is acting oddly. Finally, she answers him, although her voice wavers and she sounds almost fearful. The driver is unsure if her whispered words are directed to him or if she is speaking to herself. "The snow came early this year," she murmurs and then is silent once more.

The cabbie agrees with her that it did and attempts to make more small talk with the lovely young girl. He soon realizes that she is not interested in conversation. Finally, she does speak, but when she does, she shouts at him. She orders him to pull over to the side of the road. This is where she needs to get out!

The startled driver jerks the steering wheel to the right and stops in an open area in front of two large, metal gates. He looks up and realizes where they have stopped. "You can't get out here," he says to the young woman, "this is a cemetery!"

When he looks into the rearview mirror, he realizes that he is in the cab alone -- the girl is no longer in the backseat. He never heard the back door open or close, but the beautiful girl has simply disappeared.

One must wonder if it finally dawned on him just who he had taken for a ride in his cab. She is known all over the Chicago area as the region's most enigmatic and sought after ghost. Her name is "Resurrection Mary".

Chicago is a city filled with ghosts, from haunted houses to ghostly graveyards. But of all of the tales, there is one that rises above all of the others. I like to think of Resurrection Mary as Chicago's most famous ghost. It is also probably my favorite ghost story of all time. It has all of the elements of the fantastic from the beautiful female spirit to actual eyewitness sightings that have yet to be debunked. There is much about the story that appeals to me and I never tire of hearing or talking about Mary, her sightings and her mysterious origins.

Although stories of "vanishing hitchhikers" in Chicago date back to the horse and buggy days, Mary's tale begins in the 1930's. It was around this time that drivers along Archer Avenue started reporting strange encounters with a young woman in a white dress. She always appeared to be real, until she would inexplicably vanish. The reports of this girl began in the middle 1930's and started when motorists passing by Resurrection Cemetery began claiming that a young woman was attempting to jump onto the running boards of their automobiles.

Not long after, the woman became more mysterious, and much more alluring. The strange encounters began to move further away from the graveyard and closer to the O Henry Ballroom, which is now known as the Willowbrook. She was now reported on the nearby roadway and sometimes, inside of the ballroom itself. On many occasions, young men would meet a girl at the ballroom, dance with her and then offer her a ride home at the end of the evening. She would always accept and offer vague directions that would lead north on Archer Avenue. When the car would reach the gates of Resurrection Cemetery, the young woman would always vanish.

More common were the claims of motorists who would see the girl walking along the road. They would offer her a ride and then witness her vanishing from their car. These drivers could describe the girl in detail and nearly every single description precisely matched the previous accounts. The girl was said to have light blond hair, blue eyes and was wearing a white party dress. Some more attentive drivers would sometimes add that she wore a thin shawl, or dancing shoes, and that she had a small clutch purse.

Others had even more harrowing experiences. Rather than having the girl vanish for their car, they claimed to actually run her down in the street. They claimed to see a woman in a white dress bolt in front of their car near the cemetery and would actually describe the sickening thud as she was struck by the front of the car. When they stopped to go to her aid, she would be gone. Some even said that the automobile passed directly through the girl. At that point, she would turn and disappear through the cemetery gates.

Bewildered and shaken drivers began to appear almost routinely in nearby businesses and even at the nearby Justice, Illinois police station. They told strange and frightening stories and sometimes they were believed and sometimes they weren't. Regardless, they created an even greater legend of the vanishing girl, who would go on to become Resurrection Mary.

But who is this young woman, or at least who was she when she was alive?

Most researchers agree that the most accurate version of the story concerns a young girl who was killed while hitchhiking down Archer Avenue in the early 1930's. Apparently, she had spent the evening dancing with a boyfriend at the O Henry Ballroom. At some point, they got into an argument and Mary (as she has come to be called) stormed out of the place. Even though it was a cold winter's night, she thought, she would rather face a cold walk home than another minute with her boorish lover. She left the ballroom and started walking up Archer Avenue. She had not gotten very far when she was struck and killed by a passing automobile. The driver fled the scene and Mary was left there to die.

Her grieving parents buried her in Resurrection Cemetery, wearing a white dress and her dancing shoes. Since that time, her spirit has been seen along Archer Avenue, perhaps trying to return to her grave after one last night among the living.

It has never been known just who the earthy counterpart of Mary might have been, but several years ago, a newspaper report confused things so badly that a number of writers and researchers ended up creating their own "Mary". She was another girl who was tragically killed, but had nothing to do with the woman who haunts Archer Avenue. In the quest to learn Mary's identity, speculation fell onto a woman named Mary Bregovy, who is also buried in Resurrection Cemetery. Unfortunately, there are too many factors that prevent her from being Resurrection Mary.

Even though Bregovy was killed in an auto accident in 1934, it is unlikely that she was returning home from the O Henry Ballroom, as some have claimed. The accident in which she was killed took place on Wacker Drive in downtown Chicago. The car that she was riding in collided with an elevated train support and she was thrown through the windshield. This is a far cry from being killed by a hit-and-run driver on Archer Avenue.

Bregovy also did not resemble the phantom that has been reported either. According to memory and photographs, she had short, dark hair, which is the opposite of the fair-skinned blond ghost. Besides that, the undertaker who prepared Bregovy for her funeral, John Satala, recalled that she was buried in an orchid-colored dress, not the white one of legend. However, John Satala does add an interesting note to the story. In fact, he may have been the person who caused the confusion between the spectral "Mary's" in the first place. In a newspaper interview many years ago, Satala mentioned a caretaker at Resurrection Cemetery who told him that he had seen a ghost on the cemetery grounds. The caretaker believed the ghost was that of Mary Bregovy.

So, if Resurrection Mary was not Mary Bregovy, who was she?

More compelling evidence of the ghost's identity was compiled by Frank Andrejasich of Summit, Illinois. According to his materials, he discovered that some people believed the story of Resurrection Mary could be traced to the early 1940's and to an automobile accident that occurred near Resurrection Cemetery at that time. A young Polish woman had taken her father's car in the early morning hours to visit her boyfriend. She received fatal injuries in the accident and was buried in a term grave at the nearby cemetery. While an interesting tale, it does not explain how motorists and young men were encountering the ghost in the 1930's.

He also uncovered another version of the "real" Resurrection Mary from a man who claimed that he and his fiancée witnessed an accident along Archer Avenue in 1936. A black Model A sedan collided with a farm truck, killing three of the four passengers. The man was sure that one of the victims, a young woman, spawned the ghostly legend of Mary. Another woman claimed that Mary was actually the ghost of a young woman named Mary Miskowski, who was killed crossing the street one night in October 1930 on her way to a costume party.

Andrejasich sifted through all of these accounts (and many others) and came to believe that Mary was actually the spirit of a 12-year-old girl named Anna Norkus. Born in 1914, she was a vivacious young girl whose middle name had been "Mary", named for the Blessed Mother. She was slim, blonde and loved to dance and on the eve of her 13th birthday, she convinced her father to take her to the O Henry Ballroom to celebrate. They left home on the evening of July 20, 1927 and were accompanied by her father August's friend, William Weisner and Weisner's date.

On their way home, around 1:30 in the morning, they passed Resurrection Cemetery on Archer Avenue, then turned east on 71st Street and then north on Harlem to 67th. Moments later, the car overturned sideways into an unseen railroad cut and Anna was killed instantly. The grieving family made plans to have Anna buried in one of three newly purchased lots at St. Casimir Cemetery and she was buried there -- unless the theories of Andrejasich are correct.

According to the stories of the time, strikes were often common among Chicago gravediggers and during these strikes, bodies were usually buried for safekeeping until a proper internment could take place. Andrejasich learned that a man named Churas had once lived in a brick bungalow across the street from Resurrection Cemetery and that part of his employment involved retrieving bodies from cemeteries where workers were on strike. They would be temporarily placed in Resurrection Cemetery for a short time until the strike was over. However, in cases where the strikes continued for an extended time, the temporarily buried bodies could be forgotten or misplaced. This is exactly what Andrejasich believes happened in the case of Anna Norkus. His theory is that her body was left behind at Resurrection Cemetery and for this reason, her spirit still wanders Archer Avenue.

And while this is a compelling idea, once again, the reality of the situation differs greatly from the theory. If the stories of countless witnesses can be believed, then the Resurrection Mary of legend looks nothing like a 12 (or even almost 13) year-old girl.

But if Mary is not one of these, then who can she be? Some have speculated that she never really existed at all. They have disregarded the search for her identity, believing that she is nothing more than an "urban legend" and a piece of fascinating folklore. They believe the story can be traced to nothing more than Chicago's version of the "vanishing hitchhiker".

While the story of Resurrection Mary does bear some resemblance to the tale, the folklorists have forgotten an important thing that Mary's story has that the many versions of the other stories do not -- credible eyewitness accounts, places, times and dates. Many of these reports are not just stories that have been passed from person to person and rely on a "friend of a friend" for authenticity. In fact, some of the encounters with Mary have been chillingly up close and personal and remain unexplained to this day. Besides that, as you will soon see, Mary is one of the few ghosts to ever leave physical evidence behind!

Aside from harried motorists who encountered Mary along Archer Avenue, one of the first people to ever meet her face to face was a young man named Jerry Palus. His experience with Mary took place in 1939 but would leave such an impression that he would never forget it until his death in 1992. Palus remained an unshakable witness and appeared on a number of television shows to discuss his night with Resurrection Mary. Regardless, he had little to gain from his story and no reason to lie. He never doubted the fact that he spent an evening with a ghost!

Palus met the young girl at the Liberty Grove and Hall, a dance hall that was near 47th Street and Mozart. He had apparently seen her there on several occasions and finally asked her to dance one night. He did note in later interviews that he did not recall ever actually seeing the girl come into the dance hall. He looked away and then looked back a few moments later and she just seemed to appear near the wall. Jerry asked the young woman to dance. She accepted and they spent several hours together. Strangely though, she seemed a little distant and Palus also noticed that her skin was very cold, almost icy to the touch. When he later kissed her, he found her lips were also cold and clammy.

At the end of the evening, the young woman asked Palus for a ride home and when they got to his automobile, she directed him to drive down Archer Avenue. Palus admitted to being confused. Earlier in the evening, the woman had told him where she lived and he knew that it would be far out of the way for them to travel there via Archer. When he asked her about it, she simply told him again that she wanted to go down Archer Avenue.

As they drove down the street, they approached the gates to Resurrection Cemetery and she asked him to pull over. She had to get out here, she told him. Again, Jerry was confused, not being able to understand why she would want to get out at such a spot. He agreed that he would let her out, but only if she allowed him to walk her across the street. She refused to allow this though. The beautiful girl turned in her seat and faced Palus. "This is where I have to get out," she spoke softly, "but where I'm going, you can't follow."

Palus was bewildered by this statement, but before he could respond, the girl got out of the car and ran toward the cemetery gates. She vanished before she reached them -- right before Jerry's eyes! That was the moment when he knew that he had danced with a specter.

Determined to find out what was going on, Palus visited the address the girl had given him on the following day. The woman who answered the door told him that he couldn't have possibly been with her daughter the night before because she had been dead for several years. However, Palus was able to correctly identify the girl from a family portrait in the other room.

Needless to say, Palus was stunned by this revelation but apparently, the address and identity of the woman were forgotten over the years. Some time later, when Palus was contacted again about his story (when the passage of time had renewed interest in the elusive ghost) he was unable to remember where he had gone on the day after his encounter. Despite this memory lapse, Palus' story remains the most credible of all of the Resurrection Mary encounters.

This was only the beginning for Mary and from that time period on, she began making regular appearances on Archer Avenue. Stories like the one told by Jerry Palus have become commonplace over the years, but his account remains among the most convincing. Since that time, dozens of other young men have told of picking up the same girl, or meeting her at the ballroom, only to have her disappear from their car. The majority of the reports seem to come from the cold winter months, like the account passed on by a cab driver. He picked up a girl who was walking along Archer Avenue one night in 1941. It was very cold outside, but she was not wearing a coat. She jumped into the cab and told him that she needed to get home very quickly. She directed him along Archer Avenue and a few minutes later, he looked back and she was gone. He realized that he was passing in front of the cemetery when she disappeared.

In 1973, Mary was said to have shown up at least twice at a nightclub called Harlow's on Cicero on the southwest side. She danced alone in a faded white dress and despite the fact that bouncers checked the I.D.'s of everyone who came through the door, no one ever saw the girl enter or leave. Later that same year, an annoyed cab driver entered Chet's Melody Lounge, located across Archer from the gates to Resurrection Cemetery, looking for a fare that had skipped off without paying. The young blond woman that he reportedly picked up was nowhere to be seen. The manager explained that no blond woman had entered the bar.

During the middle 1970's, the number of Mary sightings began to increase. People from many different walks of life, from cab drivers to ministers claimed they had picked her up and had given her rides. It was during this period that Resurrection Cemetery was undergoing some major renovations and perhaps this was what caused her restlessness.

Other accounts also began to surface at this time, which had Mary being struck by passing cars. Drivers started reporting a young girl in white who ran out in front of their automobile. Occasionally, the girl would vanish when she collided with the car and at other times, would crumple and fall to the road as if seriously injured. When the motorist stopped and went to help the girl, she would disappear.

On August 12, 1976, Cook County police officers investigated an emergency call about an apparent hit and run victim near the intersection of 76th Street and Roberts Road. The officers found a young female motorist in tears at the scene and they asked her where the body was that she had allegedly discovered beside the road? She pointed to a wet grass area and the policemen could plainly see a depression in the grass that matched the shape of a human body. The girl said that just as the police car approached the scene, the body on the side of the road vanished!

In May 1978, a young couple was driving down Archer when a girl suddenly darted out in the road in front of their car. The driver swerved to avoid her but knew when he hit the brakes that it was too late. As they braced for impact, the car passed right through the girl! She then turned and ran into Resurrection Cemetery, melting right past the bars in the gate. Another man was on his way to work in the early morning hours and spotted the body of a young girl lying directly in front of the cemetery gates. He stopped his truck and got out, quickly discovering that the woman was apparently badly injured, but still alive. He jumped into his truck and sped to the nearby police station, where he summoned an ambulance and then hurried back to the cemetery. When he came back, he found that the body was gone! However the outline of her body was still visible on the dew-covered pavement.

The stories continued but perhaps the strangest account of Mary was the one that occurred on the night of August 10, 1976. This event has remained so bizarre after all this time because on this occasion, Mary did not just appear as a passing spirit. It was on this night that she left evidence behind!

A driver was passing by the cemetery around 10:30 that night when he happened to see a girl standing on the other side of the gates. He said that when he saw her, she was wearing a white dress and grasping the iron bars of the gate. The driver was considerate enough to stop down the street at the Justice police station and alert them to the fact that someone had been accidentally locked in the cemetery at closing time. Two officers responded to the call but when they arrived at the cemetery gates, was no one was there. The graveyard was dark and deserted and there was no sign of any girl.

But his inspection of the gates, where the girl had been seen standing, did reveal something unusual. The revelation chilled both of the men to the bone! They found that two of the bars in the gate had been pulled apart and bent at sharp angles. To make things worse, at the points on the green-colored bronze where they had been pried apart were blackened scorch marks. Within these marks was what looked to be skin texture and handprints that had been seared into the metal with incredible heat.

The marks of the small hands made big news and curiosity-seekers came from all over the area to see them. In an effort to discourage the crowds, cemetery officials attempted to remove the marks with a blowtorch, making them look even worse. Finally, they cut the bars off and installed a wire fence until the two bars could be straightened or replaced.

The twisted and scorched bars of Resurrection Cemetery (Courtesy Dale Kaczmarek)

The cemetery emphatically denied the supernatural version of what happened to the bars. They claimed that a truck backed into the gates while doing sewer work at the cemetery and that grounds workers tried to fix the bars by heating them with a blowtorch and bending them. The imprint in the metal, they said, was from a workman trying to push them together again. While this explanation was quite convenient, it did not explain why the marks of small fingers were clearly visible in the metal.

The bars were removed to discourage onlookers, but taking them out had the opposite effect and soon, people began asking what the cemetery had to hide. The events allegedly embarrassed local officials, so they demanded that the bars be put back into place. Once they were returned to the gate, they were straightened and painted over with green paint so that the blackened area would match the other bars. Unfortunately though, the scorched areas continued to defy all attempts to cover them and the twisted spots where the handprints had been impressed remained obvious until just recently, when the bars were removed for good.

On the last weekend in August 1980, Mary was seen by dozens of people, including the Deacon of the Greek Church on Archer Avenue. Many of witnesses contacted the Justice police department about their sightings. Squad cars were dispatched and although the police could not explain the mass sightings of a young woman who was not present when they arrived, they did find the witnesses themselves. Many of them flagged down the officers to tell them what they had just seen.

On September 5, a young man was leaving a softball game and driving down Archer Avenue. As he passed the Red Barrel Restaurant, he spotted a young woman standing on the side of the road in a white dress. He stopped the car and offered her a ride and she accepted, asking that he take her down Archer. He tried to draw her into conversation, even joking that she looked like "Resurrection Mary", but she was not interested in talking. He tried several times to get her to stop for a drink, but she never replied. He was driving past the cemetery, never having stopped or even slowed down, when he looked over and saw that the girl was gone. She had simply vanished!

In October 1989, two women were driving past Resurrection Cemetery when a girl in a white dress ran out in front of their car. The driver slammed on the brakes, sure that she was going to hit the woman, but there was no impact. Neither of the women could explain where the apparition had disappeared to.

During the 1990's, reports of Mary slacked off, but they have never really stopped altogether. Many of the roadside encounters happened near a place called Chet's Melody Lounge, which is located across the road and a little south of the cemetery gates. Because it is open into the early morning hours, it often becomes the first place where late night drivers look for the young girl who vanished before their eyes.

A number of shaken drivers have stumbled into the bar after their strange encounters, as did a cab driver in 1973. He claimed that his fare, a young woman, jumped out of the back seat of his cab without paying. She ran off and he came into Chet's because it was the closest place that she could have gone to. He told the bartender that she was an attractive blond and that she had skipped out on her fare, but imagine his surprise when staff members told him that no young woman had come in.

Another bizarre encounter took place in the summer of 1996 when the owner of the lounge, the late Chet Prusinski, was leaving the bar at around four in the morning. A man came running inside and told Chet that he needed to use the telephone. He excitedly explained that he had just run over a girl on Archer and now he couldn't find her body. Chet was skeptical about the man's story until a truck driver came in and confirmed the whole thing. He had also seen the girl but stated that she had vanished, "like a ghost". The police came to investigate but, not surprisingly, they found no trace of her.

Even though sighting and encounters have slacked off in recent years, they still continue to occur today. While many of the stories are harder to believe these days, as the tales of Mary have infiltrated our culture to such a degree that almost anyone with an interest in ghosts has heard of her, some of the stories still appear to be chillingly real.

In July 2001, I was contacted by a witness that wished to remain anonymous but who stated that he and his girlfriend had spotted Mary along Archer Avenue. The young woman that the witness was dating at the time was from Lithuania and spoke only broken English. She had no information about the legend of Resurrection Mary, which makes her account of the bizarre sighting even more believable.

The couple was traveling along Archer Avenue, to take the young woman home, and spotted an odd figure near Resurrection Cemetery. The witness noted that, just before the sighting, he spotted a police officer who had pulled over a motorist on the left side of the street (down a side street). He would later use the police car as a point of reference when he and his girlfriend came back for a second look.

As they drove past, both of them spotted a woman walking northbound on the road with her back to their oncoming car. She was wearing a white gown that blew crisply in the wind. After the sighting had registered, the witness quickly related the legend of Mary to his girlfriend and he also called his sister on his cell phone, marking the moment of the sighting. After he explained to his date what they had seen, she insisted that they go back for another look. The witness turned around and headed in the direction they had come from, keeping their eyes open for the woman coming toward them. In a few moments, they had passed the police car that they had seen earlier, but there was no sign of the woman in the white dress.

Suddenly, the figure seemed to lurch out from along the roadway. The witness stated that she seemed to simply appear but he couldn't be sure. She was standing along the shoulder of the road, three to five feet from the pavement, and facing toward their vehicle. She was dressed in a faded and discolored gown and was carrying what appeared to be a bouquet of dark flowers. "She wasn't looking at us," the witness later recalled," she was just staring to the south. She looked somewhat young with the blankest expression that I have ever seen on her face."

Was this Resurrection Mary or was the woman in white a part of some elaborate hoax? As far as the witness was concerned, he didn't care. "After that July, I refuse to drive by the cemetery alone," he said. "I take another route if I ever have to go that way."

So, who is Mary and does she really exist? Many remain skeptical about her, but I have found that this doesn't really seem to matter. You see, people are still spotting Mary walking along Archer Avenue at night. Drivers are still stopping to pick up a forlorn figure who seems inadequately dressed in the winter months, when encounters are most prevalent. Curiosity-seekers still come to see the gates where the twisted and burned bars were once located and some even roam the graveyard, hoping to stumble across the place where Mary's body was laid to rest.

Who is she? No one knows but that has not stopped the stories, tales and even songs from being spun about her. She remains an enigma and her legend lives on, not content to vanish, as Mary does when she reaches the gates to Resurrection Cemetery. You see, our individual belief, or disbelief, does not really matter. Mary lives on anyway. I doubt that we will ever know who she really was, or why she haunts this peculiar stretch of roadway.

In all honesty, I don't suppose that I ever really want to know who she was. I guess that prefer Mary to remain just as she is, a mysterious, elusive and romantic spirit of the Windy City.

CHAPTER THREE
SCHOOL SPIRITS

HAUNTINGS OF CHICAGO'S SCHOOLS & COLLEGES

As a "ghost writer", I have collected tales from haunted colleges and schools all over the Midwest and beyond. I have found that there are halls of learning that boast more than their share of ghosts, including a number in the Chicago area. It is rare to find a school that does not boast a tale or two floating around the campus. Many of them are familiar tales of murdered coeds, whose spirits have returned to their former residences after death.

But how much truth is there to these stories? Are they merely legends that have been told over and over again for the purpose of getting a cute sorority girl to squeeze just a little closer while walking through a particularly spooky spot on campus? Or could there be something more? What if these tales of slain students just happen to be true? Are those tales so easily to dismiss?

Many have surmised that most campus ghost stories are simply the product of overactive imaginations. These same people say they are the result of students who are far too susceptible to the trappings of the supernatural. But what about the stories of ghosts that have been passed on, not only by students, but also by teachers, professors, maintenance workers and in some cases, people who claim to not even believe in ghosts? Are these school spirits simply imaginations working overtime?

Perhaps some of these stories are simply the mixture of fact and fancy. It seems that few of us can deny that we have chuckled a little over yet another report of a ghostly coed who was murdered years before and now haunts her former dorm room. In so many cases, a simple check of the local newspaper files reveals that no coed was ever murdered at the school. So how then do we explain the activity that has been reported there?

In other words, what if these academic ghosts are real? What if the energy produced by hundreds of students in one location attracts spirits who are seeking such energy to exist? Perhaps some of these ghosts really are the spirits of former students, teachers and janitors who left some sort of unfinished business in this world. Or perhaps the proverbial murdered students are sometimes real! What if their traumatic deaths have really caused them to linger behind?

Many would argue and say that these stories couldn't possibly be true but in the coming pages, I will show you that some of these stories just may be! And some of the readers know, if they have ever had their own brush with the supernatural, that there may be more to the local college campus or school building than is readily available on the surface! Something just may lurk in the shadows here -- but whether it is the cold image of truth or the stuff of legend is up to you to decide!

BARAT COLLEGE

Located among the forests and rolling hills of Lake Forest, Illinois, an old and affluent suburb that is north of Chicago on Lake Michigan, is Barat College. The school began as an academy for young women in 1858 and was named for St. Madeleine Sophie Barat, who founded the Society of the Sacred Heart in 1800. The Sacred Heart education was unique at that time in that it was created to provide a formal, religious-based education for women with the idea that these women would assume leadership roles in their family and in society. Needless to say, in 1800, this idea was far ahead of its time but in spite of that, the Society of the Sacred Heart has established schools and colleges all over the country and the world over the last two centuries.

The original Barat College was located in Chicago but in 1904, moved to the current campus in Lake Forest. In 1918, it was chartered by the state of Illinois as a four-year college and 50 years later, passed from the Society of the Scared Heart to an independent board of trustees that is no longer under the financial support of the Catholic Church. Barat has continued to grow over the years and in 1982, became a co-educational institution that formed an education alliance with DePaul University in 2001.

Over the years, much has changed at Barat College, although the education goals of the Society of the Sacred Heart have remained in place as time has gone by. And so have other things, including what many believe are the school's resident spirits...

The haunting at the school appears to be centered around the Old Main Building, the college center that houses some of the faculty and administration offices, as well as most of the classrooms and the original chapel. It is the chapel where most of the strange occurrences here take place. This portion of the school is probably linked to the college's past more than any other place on campus, as it has changed little since the building's construction. The chamber is a vintage Catholic chapel with a carved wood altar, a restored pipe organ, wooden pews and traditional religious statues of saints and holy figures that are set into the walls. The room also has a high, vaulted ceiling and large stained glass windows. The chapel has seen much in the way of history during its years at Barat College and it continues to be used today for spiritual and cultural services.

Many students and visitors who have approached the chapel have been nearly overwhelmed by the smell of flowers that appears along a corridor just outside of it. The odd scent manifests in this stretch of hallway, and nowhere else, and cannot be connected to any real flowers, candles or sprays in the area. It is present in only this small area and does not slowly dissipate as the visitor walks away from any source. It simply seems to have no source! It is very strong when encountered and can suddenly disappear no more than a few steps away, not fading but just vanishing completely.

It is thought that the catalyst of the phantom scent may be linked to a ceremony that was held at Barat College each season years ago. A student named Catherine McCole was so intrigued by the ghostly smell outside of the chapel that she decided to research the chapel's history on a quest for a cause behind the odd happening. During the course of her research, she spoke to one of the older nuns at the school and she explained to McCole that Barat College had decades of traditions that involved flowers. One of the most beloved however began in the 1930's and was recalled as the Daisy Chain Ceremony. During this, a long chain of real daisies was woven with ferns and it was carried through the corridors of Old Main, out the front doors and up to the Sacred Heart statue that was located on the front lawn. The senior and junior girls would form a circle around the statue and the seniors would then symbolically pass the daisy chain to the junior class. The ceremony was very formal and symbolized the passing of the future into the hands of the younger women.

This tradition was later transformed into the "rose and candle ceremony", when the seniors would pass lighted candles to the juniors to symbolically pass on "the light of knowledge." They also carried roses as well and these were also passed on to the younger students to signify the "growth and beauty that would be unfolding in the future". The students would carry the lighted candles and the flowers down the stairs from the chapel and into the corridor where the phantom scents are continuing to be encountered today.

So, could these ceremonies be the cause for the unexplained phenomenon in the chapel corridor? Perhaps so and perhaps the wonderful traditions of the past have left an impression here as a "residual haunting" (discussed in the introduction), when events from history replay themselves over and over again as sights, sounds and in this case, odors from days gone by. The events of the past truly do create the hauntings of today!

And while the phantom scent of the Chapel corridor may be the most famous haunted event at Barat College, it is not the only one. One of the strangest stories involves the ghost of a little girl who is often seen on the fourth floor of Old Main. According to students, a young girl was playing with a ball on the fourth floor one day and somehow plunged to her death in the elevator shaft. There is no explanation as to why the elevator doors were open, but her ball managed to bounce away from her and to fall down the shaft. She chased after it and without thinking, stumbled and fell from the precipice herself.

As recently as 2002, students and staff members have spotted the small girl, seen wearing a pink dress and playing with a ball, on the fourth floor. She darts in and out of the rooms and her footsteps are often heard tapping down the empty corridors. According to Nick Olivero, a student and employee in the student's activities office at the college, a number of art students who have been working late at night have encountered the girl. They have said that "it'll suddenly turn cold and footsteps are heard," Olivero explained. "Then the little girl shows up and just stares at the people in the rooms, then walks away. It's kind of creepy."

If the little girl truly haunts this building, then she may not walk the halls here alone. The story goes that a nun who worked in the rectory at the college fell in love with a resident priest at the college. The two became romantically involved and the nun became pregnant. Terrified of what might happen if anyone found out, the nun decided to end the pregnancy in secret but she was so overwhelmed with guilt over the abortion that she committed suicide in her room at the college. Some would say that she thus compounded her sin -- which may be why she continues to haunt Barat today.

The story of the nun would have been forgotten, except for the fact that an unnamed security guard who patrolled the fourth floor of Old Main used to spend time talking to the woman's ghost during his rounds. Nick Olivero said that the guard would get off the elevator on the fourth floor and would immediately hear a second set of footsteps walking behind him. There is nothing to say that he ever actually saw the nun, but he always sensed her close by and heard her footsteps and the rustle of her habit as she moved.

"He used to talk to her about everything happening in life," Olivero said. "She used to walk with him throughout the entire floor. Then, when he made it back to the elevator, he would tell her that she had to stay there. Then, the footsteps would wander off."

The security guard long ago retired from the college but the nun remains on the fourth floor. Witnesses now claim that her apparition can be seen looking down on the courtyard from the window of the music room --- the same room where the woman lived and died years ago.

LAKE FOREST COLLEGE

Barat College is not the only haunted hall of higher learning in Lake Forest. Located on North Sheridan Road, is Lake Forest College, a liberal arts school that was founded in 1857. The college wanted to achieve a park-like setting for its campus and has been very successful with this, framing the beautiful buildings here with trees and expanses of lawn that provide a tranquil place to study and learn. The original yellow-brick buildings here were constructed during the early days of the school between 1876 and 1890 but the Gothic and Tudor style buildings (Holt Chapel, Reid Hall, Durand Commons, and Carnegie Hall) reflect the adoption of a liberal arts plan around 1900. Expansion and newer buildings on the campus followed World War II but the college's history remains an integral part of the school.

The college started as Lake Forest Academy in 1858, located in the then fledging town of Lake Forest.

Instruction began in 1860 but halted during the Civil War and then began again in the middle 1860's. An academy building (on the site of the present Durand Art Institute), a small Presbyterian church, and several homes formed a sort of village centered at the corner of Deerpath Road and what now is Sheridan Road. This included the home of Sylvester Lind, who had pledged $80,000 to launch the University, which was called "Lind University" in the original charter. It was changed to Lake Forest University in 1865 and remained with this name through the rest of the century.

In 1876, Mary Eveline Smith Farwell of Lake Forest, the wife of U. S. Senator Charles B. Farwell, decided that her daughter, Anna, should remain at home while pursuing a college degree. However, she found none of the regional schools to be suitable to her tastes, so she started Lake Forest College, a division of the University, in a wooden lakefront gingerbread-style hotel that had gone out of business in 1873. She hired faculty and gave scholarships to some capable Chicago high school students and soon the new school was in business.

During the second winter in the unheated resort hotel, a fire that was started in a student's room for warmth got out of control and burned down the building. In the summer of 1878 though, a new building called College Hall (now Young Hall) was built. This building, with its library, laboratories, chapel, and dormitory rooms formed the center of the university. In Lake Forest, the University charter now served as an umbrella for an educational institution including the Academy (boys) and Ferry Hall (girls) at the pre-college level, the College itself with some graduate offerings, and various professional schools in Chicago such as those that would become Rush Medical School, Chicago Kent Law School, and Northwestern University Dental School.

By the 1890's, liberal arts colleges were becoming the fashion and Lake Forest continued with the times. After 1900, the new college took shape with the construction of new buildings and a movement to bring in new ideas and standards that continue to serve the school well today. The college continues the founder's needs for order and tradition also provides a place away from the struggles of the city to the south.

Lake Forest College - Class of 1891

Part of the tradition at the school is the haunting that occurs in the Reid Memorial Chapel, a Gothic-style building (with tower and battlements) that was built in 1899. The story of the first encounters with the ghosts date back many years but it was said that by the 1920's, students and staff members were starting to notice odd sounds and lights in the building. One incident that occurred a few years later involved a night watchman who was making his rounds during the early morning hours of a winter's night. As he trudged along through the snow, he lit up a fresh cigar, which he placed on a ledge outside of the door before he entered the chapel. According to the story, he peered in through the front door and was startled by the appearance of a ghostly, blue figure that was hovering in the corner of the chapel, shimmering in the dim light, suspended in the air. The watchman said that he felt the figure sensed that he was there because it turned in his direction, looked at him and then vanished into the brick wall. Not surprisingly, the watchman turned and fled from the building. As he rushed out the front door, he paused just long enough to look for his cigar -- which had inexplicably disappeared! He kept on running and vowed that he would never go into the building again.

In the years that have followed, students and faculty members have claimed to hear the sounds of an organ being played in the building at night. On some occasions, lights burn in the windows of the chapel at the same time the music is heard. Even though this always occurs in the middle of the night, officers on the security staff suspected prank-playing students of the activity -- until they burst into the building to find it suddenly dark and abandoned. Searches of the chapel revealed no one around and the organ appeared to be untouched.

Who is the ghost who haunts that chapel? Some believe that the spirit might be a church organist who used to practice in the building late at night. He passed away in the early 1900's but apparently never left the place that he loved so much. He continues to practice from beyond the grave!

And he apparently loves a good cigar as well. In addition to the vanishing cigar of the night watchman, visitors to the chapel will sometimes encounter the unmistakable odor of a cigar in the vestibule. According to the reports, they say that the smell is just like walking into a cloud of smoke that someone just exhaled from a fine cigar -- and perhaps that's exactly what it is!

MORTON COLLEGE

While only on its current campus since 1975, Morton College in Cicero has served students from the surrounding communities since 1924. It is the second oldest two-year college in Illinois and a leader in the community college movement. The school got its start in the middle 1920's when 11 teachers began instructing just 76 young men and women from around the Cicero area. For nearly 50 years, classes for the college were held at Morton East High School and in local churches and storefronts. A bond referendum held in December 1966 allowed a much-needed campus to be built on undeveloped land near the Stevenson Expressway. The land was readily available, even though the Jewel Supermarkets chain had been planning to use the property for a new shipping center. However, something took place in 1969 that stigmatized the land to the point that the proposal was withdrawn...

Ground was broken for the new college campus in December 1973 but it took almost two years for the construction to be completed. The first classes began in September 1975 -- but even before the school was finished, it was already thought to be haunted.

In the years before Morton College constructed its campus on the land along South Central Avenue in Cicero, the property was a swampy open lot that was considered an eyesore by local residents. The land went from being a nuisance to a murder site though in the fall of 1969.

Emily M. Keseg was an 18 year-old business administration student at Morton College and a resident of neighboring Berwyn. She was an average girl from a middle class background, somewhat quiet and shy, and she lived with her parents on Maple Avenue. The day of Friday, October 17 began as any normal day for Emily. As he did each weekday, her father dropped her off for her classes, then being held at Morton East High School, at 8:30 am. She followed her usual schedule and according to her friends, nothing seemed to be bothering her. The only out of the ordinary event to occur that day was an incident between Emily and her estranged 16 year-old boyfriend. They got into an argument about a ring that he had given her and now wanted returned.

After her classes ended for the day, Emily met a girlfriend who lived in Cicero at about 6:00 p.m. to make plans for their Friday night. She called her parents at about 8:00 p.m. and told them that she was going out for pizza with friends and would be home around midnight. This is the last time that they would ever hear from their daughter.

Emily and three friends met at Pat's Pizzeria on South Roosevelt Road and according to reports, stayed there until after 1:00 a.m. She and her girlfriend were spotted leaving the pizza parlor with two male friends. As they were leaving, Emily asked the young man who was driving to take her past her boyfriend's house on Central Avenue. She saw him sitting in a parked car in front of his house and was dropped off so that she could talk to him. Strangely though, the boyfriend and his parents claimed that they never saw Emily that night.

The last person believed to have spoken with Emily that night, besides her killer, was a 21 year-old motorist who saw a young woman walking west on 35th Street near 56th Court at about 2:20 a.m. He recognized Emily because he lived near her in Berwyn and he later told police that he stopped and offered her a ride home but she declined.

A short time later, she was also spotted by witnesses standing near a pay phone at the northwest corner of 35th Street and 58th Court (a short distance from the last sighting). Police investigators later discovered Emily's fingerprints on the receiver so it's known that she used the telephone, although unknown who she may have called. Some blood spatter was found on the ground near the pay phone, leading to a small pool of blood that was found around the corner and down an alley. They also found a purse and a shoe that belonged to Emily here as well.

Prior to this discovery though, a Cicero woman reported the sound of a woman moaning coming from an alley near 35th Street and 59th Avenue. When her son returned home from his paper route, she sent him to investigate and he found a wig and a dollar bill with blood on it lying on the ground. His discovery would be followed by a short time later by two telephone repairmen who were working in the area. Just a short distance from the alley, they found several pieces of bloody clothing and Emily's student ID. The police were notified and a search began around 8:00 a.m.

Investigators combed the area and at a little before 1:30 p.m., Emily's naked body was found lying in a muddy field on the site of what would someday be Morton College. The cause of death was determined to be strangulation but Emily's face and head had been badly beaten and there was a hole that had been punched in at the base of her skull. The medical examiner stated that she had been dead about 10-12 hours when found. Her father later identified her bruised and bloody body at MacNeal Memorial Hospital.

The case had an amazing number of contradictions and loose ends. The chronology of the eyewitness accounts really didn't fit the medical examiner's time of death. The police canvassed the neighborhood but could find no other leads and no motive for the girl's murder. She had been carrying little money at the time of her death, which seemed to rule out robbery but it was speculated that perhaps she had rejected advances by an assailant while walking home. However, based on the damage done to her face and head, it seemed to be a crime of passion, committed by someone who knew her. A number of suspects were proposed but no one was ever arrested or indicted for the crime.

The final lead came three days after Emily's body was discovered. They checked a charity donation bin that stood in a grocery store parking lot on 35th Street and found the rest of the girl's belongings inside, including the mate to the shoe that had been found in the alley.

No trace was ever found of Emily's killer though and to this day, the case remains unsolved and remains one of the area's most baffling modern mysteries.

The property where Emily's body was found remained vacant for several years after her murder. At the time of her death, Jewel was reportedly making plans to open a shopping center on the site, but thanks to the stigma of the girl's murder, they withdrew their offer to buy the land. Nothing was done with the site until the new campus for Morton College was constructed here.

As mentioned though, when work was still being done on the buildings, workmen began reporting strange activity. One day during the construction, a worker saw a girl in a white dress walking along the edge of the roof. He called out to her but moments later, she jumped from the roof! He ran as quickly as he could, fearing that she was dead after falling from such a height, but when he looked down, there was no one there. Still sure that she must have been killed, he scrambled to the ground level and searched the area at the base of the building -- but there was no sign of the young woman that he had seen.

Since that time, a ghostly form is still sometimes seen on the roof, but more common are the stones and pebbles that fly from the top of the building and strike unwitting passersby. Custodians who have witnessed this happening often investigate, only to find that the roof is abandoned and the door leading up to it is closed and locked.

Campus elevators also have a habit of operating on their own, running up and down after classes have ended for the day and there is no one but security guards in the buildings. These same guards have heard the sounds of doors slamming shut in B and C buildings and in D Building, have heard the sound of running footsteps on an upper floor, as if someone were dashing back and forth down the hallways. They find the upper floors to be quiet and empty when they investigate the sounds but often hear them again when they return to the first floor.

Building E has also been the scene of water taps that turn on and off by themselves and toilets that flush without assistance. The theater and the library have also been plagued by unexplainable events. Lights often turn out or dim in the theater and problems with the sound system are always blamed on "Emily". Staff members claim to have seen shadows moving about in the library and to have encountered cold chills that should not exist. On one occasion, a dedicated staff member who had recently revamped the entire library, had gotten the facility into the Suburban Library System and, among other duties, organized the student workers and all scheduling, abruptly resigned from her position. She had been in the restroom and had been overwhelmed by a flowery smell that she was sure was the ghost. She became too frightened to work there any longer and quit her job.

Apparently, based on the long list of strange events that have occurred here, a ghost has taken a liking to Morton College. Most believe that this restless spirit is that of Emily Keseg, whose body was found on the site more than three decades ago. Perhaps she stayed behind at the scene of her horrific death -- or perhaps she returned to a place that she loved when she still among the living. The current campus was only a dream at the time she was slain but who can say whether she may have followed the students to the new school after it was built? The answer to the question of the ghost here remains nearly as puzzling as the mystery behind Emily's death.

BENEDICTINE UNIVERSITY

Benedictine University, which was formerly known as Illinois Benedictine College, was originally founded in Chicago as St. Procopius College by the Benedictine monks of St. Procopius Abbey in 1887. It secured a charter from the State of Illinois in 1890 and was originally founded to educate men of Czechoslovak descent. Most students were Czech in the early years.

The Benedictine Order bears the name of St. Benedict, born in 480, who is acknowledged as the father of Western monasticism. In 528, he established the famed monastery of Monte Casino. In the Middle Ages, Benedictine monasteries expanded all over Europe, preserving ancient learning and written languages. The order has a long and respected history within the Catholic Church and Benedictine University of today is allied with 14 other schools and colleges that were founded by the order across the country.

In 1901, the college moved to the quiet western suburb of Lisle, Illinois. The first building on campus, now Benedictine Hall, was dedicated in September of that same year. New buildings were added to the campus in the 1920's and the school became co-educational in 1968. It was re-named Illinois Benedictine College in 1971 and became Benedictine University in 1996.

Over the years, a number of ghostly tales and strange reports have emerged from the campus, including stories of a haunted cemetery, haunted halls, possession and eerie tales of Ouija board sessions gone awry. Many of the tales here seem to fall into that shadow land between legend and truth but have become such a part of campus lore that they have to be included here. As I have mentioned before, I will leave the reader to decide the veracity of the stories.

One of the ghosts here reportedly haunts a stretch of roadway located between the school and the Abbey. According to the story, a student committed suicide along this road years ago by lying down directly in the path of oncoming automobiles. Several vehicles managed to swerve around him at the last minute but one unlucky driver was not so fortunate. He struck the suicidal student and the boy's body managed to get caught underneath the car. He was dragging along the road for the distance it took for driver to jam on his brakes and stop. Since that time, his ghost has been said to make his presence known along the road and in Jaegar Hall, where he had been living at the time of his death. The specter is often seen walking along the road but when drivers who pass him look back in the rearview mirror, the figure has vanished. He has also been spotted roaming the corridors of Jaeger Hall as well. When approached, he will abruptly vanish. One student claimed to see the figure of a young man round a corner but when he followed him, there was no one there.

Other stories have centered around a stretch of woods that is located on the outskirts of the campus. This swampy area contains a small cemetery that holds the graves of the school's founding brothers and other members of the Procopian community. There have been many of the common tales of satanic rituals carried out here over the years and while this may be little more than legend, no can deny the fact that the body of a murdered DuPage County woman was found in the graveyard a few years ago. Not surprisingly, her ghost is believed to haunt the cemetery and the woods around it.

The cemetery was also the scene of one of the strangest events ever reported at Benedictine University as well. During the early 1990's, Ouija boards were quite popular on college campuses as a way for students to entertain themselves and to toy with what they believed was the unknown. But in 1990 or 1991, several students got more than they bargained for when they took a Ouija board into the locked campus cemetery one night. One of the young men who participated in the session allegedly became "possessed". He started screaming and howling uncontrollably and his companions were unable to calm him down or even restrain him from kicking, biting and flailing about. Campus police were said to have assisted in getting the young man back to his room in Kholbeck Hall and a priest was called in to offer prayers for him and to counsel everyone involved. The boy ended up being taken to an area hospital, where he was sedated and treated.

The story of the incident was told, re-told and embellished around campus over the course of the next few days and interesting elements began to be added to the tale. One of the most popular was that the boy was taken to Benedictine Hall and locked in a room all night, in hopes that he might tire himself out. When the door was unlocked, he was sitting quietly in a chair and looking out a window that was covered with swarming flies! Unfortunately, the real story was not so chilling or exciting. According to reliable sources, the boy simply freaked himself out during the Ouija session, which had been conducted in hopes of reaching the spirit of the DuPage County woman whose body had been found in the graveyard. The spooky setting and the excitable nature of the boy combined for a disaster when one of his friends decided to play a prank and make everyone think the ghost was close by. The young man became hysterical and the events that followed were a result of his own overactive imagination.

Rather than the story of the "possessed" boy being a cautionary tale, Ouija boards became even more popular on campus in the weeks that followed. Some credited the boards with terrible powers, including one girl who blamed her séance for a mysterious fire that started in her room on Neuzil Hall. She had left her Ouija board sitting on her sofa when she went to dinner but was called back to her room when the sofa somehow went up in flames. After the fire was put out, no trace could be found of the Ouija Board!

CHANNING MEMORIAL ELEMENTARY SCHOOL

The Channing Memorial Elementary School was built in 1968 in Elgin, Illinois and what should have been an ordinary construction project turned macabre when a number of skeletons that belonged to Elgin's earliest residents turned up during the excavation of the new school's basement. The construction crew quickly discovered that the site had once been the city's first cemetery -- and that a number of the residents had been left behind.

Bluff City Cemetery was located on the same hill as the school from 1845 to 1945. In the 1940's, city planners decided to move the burial ground and replace it with an athletic field. This area was later turned into a park and in the 1960's, the site was chosen for the location of Channing Elementary School. The remains from the cemetery had all been moved back in the late 1940's, or so it was thought. Unfortunately, the early records had not been complete and quite a number of the graves were unmarked and as it turned out, left behind in the move.

As construction began on the new school, workers made a gruesome discovery when they began digging the basement. Caskets and loose bones were uncovered and horrified officials called for their immediate removal. Most don't believe that, even after a second attempt, all of the bodies have been removed though. Rumors persist that the construction workers made only a half-hearted attempt at the job and worse, were disrespectful of the remains. It was not uncommon for pranksters on the site to put bones into their buddy's lunchbox or for a man to go to his car at the end of the day to find a grinning skeleton propped behind the wheel.

Ever since the school has opened, some staff members and many of the children who attend here have come to believe that the disturbed dead beneath their feet do not rest in peace. And although the children's ghostly stories were dismissed in the past, as the years went by, teachers, parents and staff members began to have their own unsettling encounters within the walls of the modern brick building. Whatever presences walk here do not seem to be hampered by doors, separate floors or solid walls -- and no one seems to be immune to their effect.

Reports have filtered out of an elevator that goes from floor to floor by itself, without ever being summoned by the call button, and of a huge wooden door that operates by a hydraulic device and yet manages to open and slam shut under its own power. They also tell of hearing footsteps pounding across the roof and a night custodian named Ricky Bell, who heard these sounds, even called the police. When officers came to investigate, they found no one in (or on) the building.

The building's chief custodian, Joe Gutierrez, once reported that he heard his name being called when he was alone on the third floor and he and others have also reported the sounds of laughter coming from empty classrooms. On the occasion that he heard his name being called, he went to investigate and found nothing from the direction of the voice. However, he then heard a loud sound coming from the room that he had been working in and re-entered it to find that a ceiling panel that he had moved to work behind was now shifted back into its original position. There had been no one else in the room! The previously mentioned laughter has plagued many of the night workers in the school, who have also reported seeing shadowy figures in the hallways. One custodian was so frightened by the laughter that he heard one night that he locked himself in the principal's office and called Gutierrez at home, actually weeping over the telephone and begging for him to come back to the school and help him.

A former principal named Clark White, along with several of the teachers, also reported hearing what seemed to be scratching and clawing coming from inside the walls of the school. Some dismiss this as being nothing more than "squirrels in the wall" but others are not so sure. The sheer number of reports, dating back more than three decades, seems to give some credibility to the idea that something strange is going on at Channing Elementary. What that is remains to be seen, but one thing is sure, not too many people want to stay around there at night to find out!

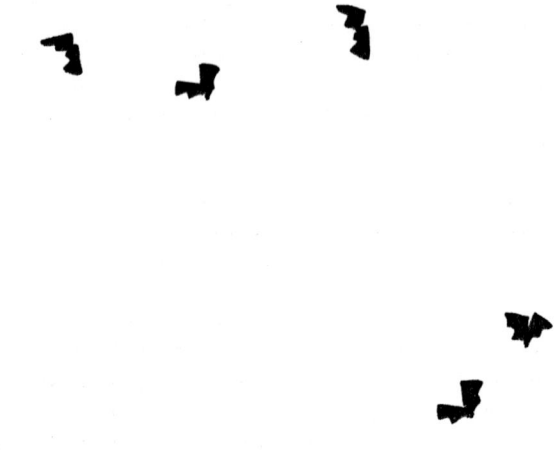

CHAPTER FOUR

DINNER & SPIRITS

GHOSTS OF CHICAGO'S HAUNTED PUBS, RESTAURANTS & TAVERNS

Then stand to your glasses steady and drink to your comrade's eyes; here's a toast to the dead already, and hurrah to the next who dies.

POPULAR DRINKING SONG AT CHICAGO'S WHITECHAPEL CLUB

Years ago, when traveling in Mexico, I was eating dinner and talking with a local man who lived in a small town between Mexico City and the Pacific Ocean. We were discussing the areas where we grew up and I was trying to explain to him where Illinois was located. My description was falling upon deaf ears until I mentioned "Chicago". At that, his face lit up and he grinned. "Chicago!" he laughed, "ah yes, Al Capone and pizza!"

And he was right. Outside of Chicago's bloody history of mob warfare, there is perhaps no greater legendary connection for people who have never traveled to the Windy City (except perhaps the ghosts!) than the food. There also seems to be no greater culinary contribution to American culture that Chicago's deep-dish pizza and hot dogs either. Both are dishes that are best served as a "hands-on" experience and I admit that, while I hate to encourage the stereotype about Chicago food, I never fail to sample either of them with each trip to the city. It doesn't matter if you go somewhere else and they call their pizza or hot dogs "Chicago style", there is no fooling the real connoisseur of Windy City delicacies -- nobody else has the real thing!

With that said, the reader should probably know that the history of food and drink in the city is closely linked to the history of Chicago itself, which likely explains the number of haunted restaurants, taverns and pubs that can be found in the region. Chicago has gained national attention for its food and drinks over the years, as proven by the earlier section on the glories of deep-dish pizza, including the violent battles over beer and alcohol during the years of Prohibition (which we'll look at more closely in a later chapter). Television audiences all over America are also familiar with at least one Chicago restaurant landmark too.

In the 1970's, the famous Billy Goat Tavern became the inspiration for sketches on *Saturday Night Live* that were penned by two Chicago comics, John Belushi and Dan Ackroyd, who were lunchtime regulars here before becoming well known. The tavern and grill is located on lower Michigan Avenue, near the loading docks of the Tribune Tower. As you descend the steps, it's quite possible that you'll hear the trademark lines made famous on television: "cheezborger, cheezborger, cheezborger, no Pepsi - Coke". On any given day, you're liable to rub elbows here with local (or even national celebrities) and certainly with local journalists and writers.

One of the biggest draws here for tourists (and supernatural enthusiasts) is the memorabilia on display that relates to the "curse on the Cubs" that has long been celebrated at the Billy Goat Tavern. The curse dates back to the tavern's original founder, William Sianis. In 1934, he opened a bar and grill on Madison Street, near the old Chicago Stadium. A beloved and eccentric character, he often traveled about town with his trademark, a pet goat that he called "Billy Goat". He often was seen about town, at sporting events and even concerts with the goat in tow.

In 1945, the Chicago Cubs were playing the Detroit Tigers in the World Series and Sianis had tickets for game three at Wrigley Field, one for himself and the other for the goat. When he showed up at the ballpark with his guest, the ushers refused to allow him inside with the animal. To compound matters, owner P.K. Wrigley sent down word from his private box: "Don't bring that goat in here. That goat smells."

Sianis left the ballpark and went back to his bar, where he listened to the game on the radio. When the Cubs lost, he sent a telegram to Wrigley. "Who Stinks Now?" it asked. The Cubs then proceeded to lose the World Series and have never made it back into the series since. It's been said that by refusing to admit Sianis' goat, Wrigley brought a curse down on the Cubs that has never been lifted.

In 1964, the Billy Goat moved from Madison Street to Michigan Avenue but it's still a great place to come for food, drinks and atmosphere. The place is now owned by Sam Sianis, the founder's nephew and is certainly still an important part of downtown Chicago. The walls are covered with photos, news clippings and numerous tributes to William Sianis that were written after his passing in 1970. The mementoes about the infamous "curse" take center stage, even though Sam has tried to lift the curse several times over the years. He tried bringing a goat to a Cubs game in 1973 but was not allowed inside. However, in both 1984 and 1989, Cubs management invited Sam and the goat to opening day festivities and while the team's luck changed a little for the better, it's never been enough to get them to the World Series again.

But that's probably because of the curse, right? If I were a Cubs fan, that's certainly the excuse that I would use!

CHICAGO'S "MICKEY FINN"

Although few likely remember the names of most tavern owners from Chicago history, there is one man, the proprietor of the Lone Star Saloon and Palm Garden, whose name has been immortalized in the American language and his name has likely been spoken by literally hundreds of people who have no idea that he was an actual person. This terrible little man, who stood only five feet, five inches tall and weighed less than 140 pounds, was named Mickey Finn and his name is now used everywhere as a synonym for a knockout drink.

Little is known about the history of Mickey Finn but he was born in either Ireland or Peoria, depending on his mood, and he first came to Chicago during the 1893 World's Fair as a "lush worker", which meant that he robbed drunks in the Bad Lands and the Little Cheyenne vice districts of South Clark Street. Not long after, he began working in a bar owned by Toronto Jim in the Custom House Levee District but only lasted here for a few months. Finn was too tough for even this notorious hangout for hoodlums and thieves and was constantly fighting with customers. He was finally fired after knocking out a man's eyeball with a board when the customer failed to produce the money to pay for a round drinks that he had ordered.

For the next year or two, Finn operated as a pickpocket and as a fence for small-time thieves and burglars. In 1896, he opened the Lone Star Saloon and Palm Garden at the southern end of Whiskey Row. This infamous area was a stretch that ran along the west side of State Street from Van Buren to Harrison and where for almost 30 years, every building was occupied by a saloon, wine room, gambling house or all three combined. A police inspector named Lavin once called the place "a low dive, a hangout for colored and white people of the lowest type." Finn ran the Lone Star for about eight years and during most of this time, continued working as a fence too, handling stolen goods. He also took in money instructing pickpockets in the "art of the lift" and taught thievery to streetwalkers, who he encouraged to rob the men they picked up at the Lone Star.

Finn's wife, Kate Roses, also handled "house girls" for the place who were supposed to induce the customers to drink and to entertain them in any other manner for which they were willing to pay. Two of the in-house prostitutes, Isabelle "Dummy" Ffyffe and "Gold Tooth" Mary Thornton, would later be Finn's downfall when they testified against him during a 1903 vice investigation.

But the saloon's claim to fame came from Finn's novel approach to fleecing his customers. From the beginning, the Lone Star Saloon and Palm Garden (the garden was a back room that was decorated with a sickly palm tree in a pot) was a robbing den. For the first year or two, Finn and his associates contented themselves with picking pockets and rolling drunks but they soon moved on to bigger things. In 1898, Finn met a black "voodoo doctor" named Hall, who sold love potions and charms to girls in bawdy houses and sold cocaine and morphine to dope addicts. From the voodoo man, Finn purchased a bottle that contained "some sort of white stuff". The police never identified it but it was probably chloral hydrate.

With the "white stuff" as the prime ingredient, Mickey Finn invented two knockout drinks that would become his trademark. One of them, the "Mickey Finn Special", was made from raw alcohol, water in which snuff had been soaked and a liberal amount of the voodoo powder. The other, which he dubbed "Number Two", was beer that was mixed with the powder and fortified with the snuff water. Finn brazenly put up a sign behind the bar that said "Try the Mickey Finn Special" and the house girls and whores who worked for him were instructed to push the concoction on every man with whom they drank. Finn was so proud of the drink that he named in his own honor that even the luckless customers who insisted on drinking beer only were given the "Number Two" in retaliation.

A customer who might be given one of the paralyzing potions usually just slumped over and slumbered in his chair until he could be given the proper attention by the proprietor. The bartender or one of the house girls would then drag the man into one of the rear rooms behind the Palm Garden, which Finn called his "operating room". The actual robbing would be done by Finn and Kate Roses. Finn would always put on a derby hat and a clean white apron and would go to work on the man, first stripping him to the skin and searching for a money belt or anything in his pockets. If his clothing was of good quality, Finn would take that too and substitute rags in its place. After that, the man would be tossed into the alley out back or left on the floor of the "operating room" until the next morning. The victims were not hard to handle when awakened and were usually befuddled for a day or two afterwards as well. Few of them ever remembered where or when they were robbed.

Occasionally though, a few of the men gave Finn problems and he always kept a club at hand in case one started to show signs of stirring. Dummy Ffyffe stated that Finn was "terribly brutal" with the men that he doped but Gold Tooth Mary later testified that things sometimes took a darker turn. "I saw Finn take a gold watch and $35 from Billy Miller, a trainman," she told the vice commission. "Finn gave him a dope and he lay in stupor in the saloon for twelve hours. When he recovered he demanded his money, but Finn had gone... Miller was found afterward along the railroad tracks with his head cut off." Mary also talked of many other men that she had seen drugged and robbed in the Lone Star and explained that she had quit working in the bar in the fall of 1903 because of Finn's increasing violence.

She also reported to the commission that (not surprisingly), Finn told her that he would never be arrested because he paid the police for protection and possessed influence with corrupt aldermen Hinky Dink McKenna and Bath House John Coughlin. Strangely, no one was ever asked by the graft commission to explain or deny these boastings by Finn. Not long after the prostitutes appeared before the commission, the police raided the Lone Star but found nothing but a few bottles of liniment and some cough medicine. With no real evidence, they said, they were unable to arrest Finn. The only action the commission could take was to revoke Finn's saloon license and on December 16, 1903, the doors of the Lone Star were closed.

Mickey Finn left Chicago for a few months but returned in the summer of 1904. He tended bar in a place on South Dearborn Street and while he refrained from administering it himself, he sold the formula for his "Special" to a number of ambitious saloon-keepers throughout the city. To the underworld, the potion was known simply as a "mickey finn" and to this day, it's a name that's applied to knockout drinks of every type.

THE WHITECHAPEL CLUB

My favorite drinking establishment from Chicago history was not so much a tavern as it was a private club. Although located in the basement of Henry Koster's saloon at the southwest corner of Calhoun Place and LaSalle Street, the Whitechapel Club operated in a world all its own. In fact, author John Drury once said that he had never found anything to equal it. "It was the weirdest, most fantastic organization I ever heard of," he said. "It even went to the extent of becoming gruesome."

The club was founded by an eccentric and good-humored band of Chicago authors, newsmen, artists and essayists in 1889, the year after Jack the Ripper began his murderous crime spree in London's Whitechapel District. The serial killer does not seem to figure too prominently into the name of the club though. It seems the name really came from the murder of Dr. Patrick Henry Cronin in Chicago in May 1889. Charles Goodyear Seymour, a noted *Chicago Herald* writer, and his colleagues on the crime beat were looking for an out of the way place to compare notes on the murder, and the public stir around it, over beer and sandwiches. It was in tribute to the hated English that these Irishmen named the place "Whitechapel".

The "blood and guts" drinking club was born and 94 men were welcomed into membership. These men included poet and novelist Wallace Rice; *Chicago Tribune* artist John T. McCutcheon; Frederick Upham Adams; Eugene Field; humorist George Ade; Opie Read; Alfred Henry Lewis; Hobart Chatfield-Taylor and many others. The only entrance to the club was through a heavy wooden door that led into the basement of Koster's Saloon. The saloon was located on a corner of Calhoun Place, the western exposure of which was then known as "Newsboy's Alley" in honor of the reporters, editors and illustrators from the nearby *Herald* and *Times* offices. Above the door of Kostner's, a stained-glass window was inscribed with the words: "Abandon hope, all ye who enter here!"

The interior of the club was decorated with all sorts of odd and bizarre artifacts from various collections and from Chicago crime history. Crime reporter John Kelley started this decorating theme by donating a rare, twelve foot snakeskin that could be hung on the wall. After that, members worked to outdo one another with their ghoulishness, bringing in guns, knives, swords, hangman's ropes, exotic weapons, weird photos and illustrations and even a bullet that was removed from the corpse of "Doc" Haggerty, who had been killed in a duel with criminal "Bad" Jimmy Connerton.

Dr. John C. Spray of the Elgin State Mental Hospital gave a collection of skulls to Whitechapel member Chrysostom "Tombstone" Thompson and he immediately incorporated them into the décor of the club. Dr. Spray had used the skulls to compare the differences in size and shape between insane and "normal" people and Thompson converted the skulls into globes for gas jets by drilling holes into the top of them. Another skull, which became known as the most famous piece in the club, was that of "Waterford Jack", a Civil War era madame named Frances Warren, who supervised a stable of girls working the back alleys near the Chicago River.

The members of the club gathered around a large table that had been fashioned in the shape of a coffin to smoke and drink. During the years it was in its heyday, the club welcomed two future presidents, William McKinley and Theodore Roosevelt, and a number of celebrity guests like bare-knuckle fighter John L. Sullivan, author Rudyard Kipling and others. The club's glory days began to wind down in 1892 when Koster moved down the alley to a larger location. And when *Chicago Herald* publisher James Wilmot Scott died in 1895, the club went dark. Scott had paid the rent on the location each month since Whitechapel Club members maintained a policy of "No gas, No water, No police, No Rent, No Taxes." Scott never minded this and considered the rent a small price to pay for the entertainment that he enjoyed meeting with his friends and colleagues in such an unusual setting. With his death, the club died too and in 1902, its corporate charter was canceled. Seven years later, Koster's original saloon was torn down to make way for the LaSalle

Hotel.

In 1921, the superior court of Cook County formally dissolved the Whitechapel Club but years later, what was left of the grisly artifacts, the beer glasses and photographs were set up again in the lobby of the LaSalle, where a "Whitechapel Pub" was established as a tribute to the old days.

The LaSalle has since gone the way of the Whitechapel Club. In 1946, a carelessly tossed cigarette ignited a fire in the pit of the Number Five elevator shaft of the hotel. Within minutes, the building, which was essentially a "fire trap", was burning out of control. The flames shot upwards through the elevator shaft and sent fire along the ceiling from the north elevator to the mezzanine. The flames then spread further up, to the seventh floor, where they stopped. Deadly smoke filled the hallways though, reaching the top floor. Many of the guests, thinking that cries of "fire" were a prank, remained in their rooms. They ended up suffocating from the thick smoke.

As the fire spread, escape routes were cut off and desperate guests threw SOS notes to the street below, begging for rescue that never came. In those days, fire ladders only extended to the eighth floor, making rescue impossible. Many of the guests hurled luggage from their windows and into the streets below, while others took the fatal plunge themselves. In the end, the fire could be blamed on the owners themselves, who had shown a shocking lack of interest in safety. Amazingly though, the hotel later re-opened, only to be demolished in 1976 and an office building erected in its place.

THE RED LION PUB

While most visitors to Chicago would never believe it, there just happens to be an authentic British pub located on the North Side, just across North Lincoln Avenue from the famed Biograph Theater. For many years, it has gained a reputation for being the most haunted eating and drinking establishment in the Chicago area -- a reputation earned from the sheer number of haunts and the number of reports that have emerged from the place.

Although the pub opened in 1984, the two-story building that houses it dates back to 1882. Over the years, it has reportedly had many uses, including a grocery store, a country and western bar called "Dirty Dan's" and an illegal gambling parlor. The top floor was originally used as apartments and it's possible that some of these former occupants may have stayed behind. Even before the Red Lion opened, neighbors along the street already recognized the place as being haunted. The owner's son was told that when the place was a country bar, the owner used to talk to what he called his "invisible friends". Even so, when the current owners moved in, they had no expectations of anything out of the ordinary lurking in the building. They were soon in for a surprise!

John Cordwell bought the building and planned to refurbish it as a pub. Since he passed away, the place has been operated by his son, Colin, and his son-in-law, Joe Heinen. As they began the renovations, one of the men occupied an upstairs apartment during the work and when going out for any reason, would securely lock the doors behind him. When he returned, he would find often find that work he had done had been ruined in his absence. At other times, he would find his tools either missing or scattered about. There was never any indication that anyone had been inside of the building but somehow, these things continued to happen. In spite of this, the work was completed and the pub was opened for business, serving what is (in my opinion) some of the best, and certainly the most authentic, pub fare in the city.

During the renovations, Cordwell installed a stained glass window over the main stairway. Beneath the window, he added a plaque to commemorate his father, who had died in England and had been buried with no grave marker. Shortly after, people passing by the window were suddenly overcome with a light-headed feeling and many others claimed to sense a presence nearby. Cordwell also sensed a strong feeling near the window and became convinced that it was the spirit of his father. Could Cordwell's father have made his way to his son's restaurant, joining several other spirits who already seemed to be in the place?

The strange manifestations in the pub began shortly after opening for business. As mentioned, the idea that the place might be haunted never entered anyone's mind until reports from staff members and customers began to point to the idea that odd things were happening in the pub. The place certainly does not look haunted -- as the first floor is a warm and inviting place with a long bar and a number of tables for drinking and dining. Not long after the Red Lion opened, it was obvious that the first floor alone would not be able to handle the bustling business, so the second floor apartments were removed to make way for additional tables and a second, smaller bar. When this floor was altered, the ghostly activity markedly increased.

One of the happenings most often noticed are the heavy footsteps that trudge across the upper floor, moving from west to east. Customers and staff members often hear the sound, even though everyone present is well aware that no one is upstairs. When anyone goes to check on the sounds, they find the second floor to indeed be abandoned. The phantom footsteps are most active during the cold weather months but they have been known to occur at other times of the year as well. The footsteps are sometimes joined by what sounds like tables and chairs being overturned in the small bar area. Alarmed, staff members would often run upstairs to see what was going on -- only to find the second floor empty and quiet and the chairs and table untouched.

One night, Colin Cordwell, and several others on the first floor, heard a terrific crash from upstairs. Colin put down what he was doing and dashed up the stairs to see what was going on. However, the second floor was darkened and silent. As he searched the room through, he discovered a cricket bat lying on the floor. It had somehow been thrown from where it had been hanging on the wall to a location about 20 feet away! There was no explanation for how this could have happened, other than to say that it occurred by unexplainable means!

Who the ghosts are in this building is unknown for certain but there suspects. There are a couple of confirmed deaths that have taken place in the building, including those of an elderly couple who once lived in one of the second floor apartments. Years earlier, their daughter died as well. Her name was reportedly "Sharon" and, according to the remembrances of those who have lived in the neighborhood for years, she was mentally disabled. They remembered her often sitting on the front stoop of the building, chatting with passersby. I have been unable to find just how Sharon may have died but many believe that she remains behind here and that she manifests herself through a strong, sweet smell of lavender perfume. This old fashioned scent appears and vanishes at will, mainly on the second floor.

Joe Heinen has experienced the phantom smell on many occasions. They have usually occurred on the upper floor and most often happen during the early morning hours after the pub has closed for the night. While standing at the bar counting the receipts, the smell has washed over him -- only to disappear without explanation a short time later.

There is also another manifestation connected to this same spirit. Many staff members and customers have reported walking into an icy cold spot just as they walk into the smaller bar area upstairs. There is no air-conditioning duct to explain why this cold air appears and it seems to come and go at will. According to the oral history of the place, this spot marked the location of Sharon's bedroom before the upper floor was remodeled. It's believed that perhaps she now returns to the place where she was most comfortable in life.

Although it is a rare occasion when it occurs, ghosts are sometimes seen in the pub. There are reports from customers and employees who claim to have seen a blond-haired man that mysteriously vanishes, a bearded man in a black hat and a man seen walking down the steps and through the downstairs bar area. On one other occasion, a woman reported seeing a man in cowboy clothing. He was wearing a hat, boots and cowboy gear and appeared to be in his middle 20's. The woman had never been in the pub before and had no idea that the place had once been a country and western bar. It's thought that this ghost might be the specter of "Dirty Dan" himself, Dan Danforth, a reputed troublemaker who swore revenge over his eviction from the building. It was this ghost with whom John Cordwell had his only negative encounter in the Red Lion. As he was going up the stairs one day, he felt a hard push on his chest, which knocked him back down the steps. Since this was so out of character with the rest of the hauntings in the place, Cordwell was convinced that it was the hard-drinking Danforth who was looking to carry out on his threats of revenge.

Even though Danforth was said to be a nasty character however, none of the other events that have occurred at the Red Lion have been particularly threatening or dangerous. In fact, John Cordwell always enjoyed telling the stories of the place to anyone who would listen. I met this gentleman once several years ago and was delighted with his patience and kind attention to someone who assuredly was annoying him with the same questions he had heard a thousand times before. He was a class act and his pub is certainly the same way. Just remember when visiting here though --- that the spirits in your glass may not be the only spirits you find!

The Red Lion Pub on Chicago's north side
(Photo by Michelle Bonadurer)

OLD ST. ANDREW'S INN

Although it's known today as the Ole St. Andrew's Inn, this Scottish themed pub first gained its ghostly notoriety as one of Chicago haunted drinking establishments as the "Edinburgh Castle Pub". The place has operated as a Scottish bar since 1961 but before that, the place was simply a neighborhood bar owned by a colorful character named Frank Giff. Frank had a taste for playing pool, joking and chatting with the customers and for vodka (although not necessarily in that order). He loved to sample the wares of the tavern and dipped into the stock every evening, drinking with the customers until he would become even more loaded than they were. Sadly, one night in 1959, Frank drank himself to death. The lovable prankster was found slumped onto the floor behind the bar one morning by his wife. Frank Giff had died -- but his spirit never left his beloved bar!

Frank's wife, Edna, operated Giff's for a time but it was never the same without Frank and she eventually put the bar up for sale. The pub was purchased in 1961 by Jane McDougall, a native of Glasgow, Scotland, and she converted the bar into a Scottish establishment. She brought in tartan carpet, Scottish memorabilia and a line of ales and whiskeys from the old country and dubbed the place the Edinburgh Castle Pub. But even with all of the changes, one thing about the place remained the same -- Frank Giff!

As time passed, Jane began to notice large quantities of vodka were disappearing from the stock. As first, she suspected that the bartenders were stealing from her and thinking that she would catch them in the act, she started covertly marking the level in the bottles with a wax pencil. She was shocked to find that the levels were still dropping and even more shocked when she realized that this was occurring at night, when the bar was empty and no one was in the building! She was not a believer in ghosts but this weird happening was quickly starting to convince her that the pub was haunted. And she began to believe that it was haunted by a man she knew -- Frank Giff -- for she recalled his tragic death and his love for vodka.

Soon, other events began to lead her to believe that she was right. Glasses started habitually flying across the room and mysteriously breaking. Several times, the glasses were actually taped down to the rack where they hung above the bar. These glasses were hurled with such force that the bases of the glasses were snapped off and left in place, while the rest of the glass was tossed away. At other times, drinks were disappearing almost in front of startled customers. These drinks, which had been left unattended, would suddenly be drained dry. Ashtrays slid down the bar without assistance. Cash registers and other electronic items would often stop working, or at least behave erratically, when they were first brought into the bar. Later, they would be left alone -- as if Frank had gotten used to them being there.

The pub has been remodeled a number of times since 1961 and each time it has been done, Frank has managed to make his objections to the changes widely known. Perhaps the most active spot in the bar is right around the area where Frank died. As things have been changed around quite a bit since Frank's day, the spot can now be found in the dining area of the pub. There is a booth that marks the location and many people who have eaten here complain of a shifting cold spot that sometimes occurs, as well as a numbness that seems to spread through the legs and feet of the unknowing customers.

Sometimes, attractive young women who sit in this area (or even just generally visit the bar) encounter the friendly spirit of the place. Except in these cases, the spirit may be just a little too friendly! Some of these ladies have reported feeling a cold hand that grabs hold of their shoulder, knee or even a more sensitive part of the anatomy. They describe it as being like fingers that lightly grasp or brush against their skin or clothing, as if they are being gently caressed. The majority of the women who have reported this sensation have been blonds or redheads and Jane McDougall believed that Frank might be mistaking these women for his wife, Edna, who was a strawberry blond. And perhaps she was right. It's possible that Frank's spirit is not aware of the fact that many years have passed since his death and perhaps he still believes that Edna is around.

The haunting has continued here over the years, despite the changes in ownership of the pub and even the name of the place. Jane McDougall retired from the bar business and passed away in 1996 but Frank still remains here -- greeting customers from the other side. In his time and place, perhaps little has changed here at all or perhaps the afterlife offers an endless party for Frank and his spectral drinking buddies. So, if you make it down to the Ole St. Andrew's Inn one evening, be sure to lift a glass in honor of Frank Giff.

And do me a favor -- have one for me too!

BUCKTOWN PUB

One of the most unique haunted bars in Chicago is the Bucktown Pub, an eclectic neighborhood place that is not only a nice place to come to for a drink, but it's a pop art museum as well. The décor includes original poster art, both musical and political, from the 1960's and 1970's, autographed photos of celebrities and rare pieces of underground comic book art that you'll find nowhere else. However, the ghost who haunts this place is not a collector or an artist but merely a former owner -- who never fails to make his continuing presence known!

Today's trendy Bucktown neighborhood has changed much since the early days of Chicago. There are a couple of different versions as to how the region gained its name but most believe that it was coined in the 1830's. Many of the Polish settlers who lived here raised goats (the male is called a buck) and the number of animals in the vicinity inspired the name. Another version, which is less credible, states that young toughs, members of a turn-of-the-century Polish gang, were called "bucks." The term faded away and emerged again in the 1920's. The area known as Bucktown is bounded roughly by Fullerton on the north, on the east by the Kennedy Expressway, the Milwaukee Road railroad tracks on the south, and on the west by Milwaukee

Avenue to Western, and Western north to Fullerton.

Bucktown's history predates that of the city of Chicago. One of the earliest settlements outside of Fort Dearborn was located here. Many Polish immigrants fled their war torn homeland in 1831 and migrated to America, some to Chicago. They settled into an area that later came to be known as Holstein. It was ideally situated near the river and not far from Fort Dearborn, which was easily accessible by a well-used Indian trail that later became Milwaukee Avenue.

By the 1840's, the area had its own post office and hotel, the Powell House, at Milwaukee and Armitage. That Milwaukee Avenue, then the Northwestern Plank Road, ran in front of the Powell House was no accident. Mr. Powell, after erecting a flagpole in front of the hotel, announced to the road-building crew that if they aimed in the direction of the pole, he would provide whiskey for the entire group of workers. Both parties upheld their respective ends of the bargain.

The Bucktown Pub has been located on a corner along Cortland Street for many years and there have been records of a bar operating here since 1933. Prior to this, most believe the location was a speakeasy during Prohibition and this goes well with the fact that there are a number of known gangster sites in the neighborhood, including the site of the St. Valentine's Day Massacre, which occurred just east of here. Before the current owner, the Pub was previously owned by a cantankerous old man named Wally. He was described as being opinionated and loud and would sit on a bar stool and direct the operations of the bar, bellowing orders at his employees as they hustled to keep up with the customers and his shouts. Wally and his wife, Annie, lived in an apartment above the barroom and it was here that Wally committed suicide one day in 1986. In a second floor bedroom, over the bar, he placed a gun to his head and pulled the trigger. After that, the place stood empty for a few years until it was purchased by Krystine Palmer in 1991. She transformed the place into its current incarnation -- one that Wally apparently does not approve of.

Once the new place was set up, strange events began to occur. The morning after the place opened as the new Bucktown Pub, bottles were found to be rearranged and changed, as if Wally wanted them to be put back the way they were when he owned the place. Similar things began to occur during the nights that followed as napkins, coasters and glasses began to move about without assistance. Bottles were changed and moved about and found in different positions each morning. Occasionally, customers and staff members would catch the movement of a person on a nearby bar stool, but when they turned their heads to look closer, the person would always be gone.

At other times, the jukebox would behave strangely and songs would be rejected for no reason other than perhaps Wally didn't like them. The entire jukebox would often shut off on its own or would suddenly come to life, even though no one had been near it.

The bartenders and the staff members here seem to be the main targets of the ghostly activity. One new employee who came to work at the Bucktown Pub several years ago was a complete skeptic when it came to ghosts. Not only did she state loudly that she did not believe the place was haunted but she even went so far as to dare Wally (as if he really existed, she laughed) to do something to prove that he was there. Wally was quick to oblige! There came a loud noise from above the bar and a beer statuette vaulted off its shelf on the wall and came crashing down, narrowly missing the young woman's head! He certainly got her attention and she never talked badly about Wally again.

EXCALIBUR

Built in 1892 as the home for the Chicago Historical Society, the building that now houses the popular night spot Excalibur has seen more than its share of history, and some would say hauntings, over the years. The building was designed by the famous architect Henry Ives Cobb for the Historical Society, which occupied the building until 1931.

After the Historical Society moved to their new location near Lincoln Park, the castle-like structure saw a number of occupants, including the Loyal Order of the Moose, the prestigious Institute of Design, recording studios for blues performers in the 1950's and 1960's, the WPA, the Illinois Institute of Technology and even

The building that now houses Excalibur as it looked in 1896 (Chicago Historical Society)

swanky *Gallery* magazine. More recently though, it has been used as a nightclub. The place began operating as the Limelight in 1985 but was changed to the Excalibur after new owners purchased the building in 1989.

Shortly after the Limelight opened, it started to be widely reported that the place was haunted. At first, they were just little events that were experienced by the staff after hours but soon customers began to notice odd things too. Items often fell over under their own power, or moved about, glasses shattered or rolled off tables and onto the floor. Tom Doody was the special events and public events coordinator for the club for several years and quickly came to believe that the building was infested with ghosts. He witnessed much of the reported poltergeist phenomena for himself, as well as many of the mysterious late night happenings. One of the most active spots that Doody recalled was the VIP lounge, where there were several pool tables. One evening, a pool table had been set up and was left racked and ready to play on. Then suddenly, the balls began rolling all over the table, as if someone had just broken -- even though no one was in the room.

Sometimes during the early morning hours, after all of the customers were gone, staff members who were closing the place down would hear their names being called. When they would search to see where the voices were coming from, they would find no one. They stated that the voices sounded familiar, as if coming from a person they knew. However, they could never place just who the person was and certainly found no one hiding out, trying to play a prank on them.

Staff members also told of hearing what appeared to be large crates or boxes being dragged around in a downstairs storage room but when the room was opened, nothing was found disturbed. The room only had one way in or out and the sounds were often heard when the door was in full view of the employees outside.

The Limelight closed down in 1989 and the new owners opened the Excalibur in its place. They spent several million dollars to renovate and update the building, adding nearly 17,000 square feet to the design of the place. The name of the club obviously came from King Arthur's magical blade but the owners also opened an offshoot from the rest of the club called "Aura" in the former lecture hall of the Historical Society. This area is often called the "Dome Room" because of the lofty ceiling dome here. Inside of the dome is a breathtaking mural of the mythical god Zeus, angrily glaring down at the customers below him. If that's not unsettling enough -- you also have the ghosts!

There have been many strange happenings in the Dome Room over the years and many legends have been associated with this part of the building, including that a number of the bodies that went down with the *Eastland* were brought to the Historical Society so that it could serve as a temporary morgue. There is no documentation to say that this is true, but still the story persists. If there is any truth to this, it might explain why so many ghosts haunt this place. Others have pointed to the fact that the original building on this site was destroyed during the Great Chicago Fire in 1871. They believe that some lives may have been lost during the fire and they it might be their ghosts who still linger here. This may have come from a report from a former creative director named Tom Neubauer, who was overwhelmed by the stench of burning flesh one night. The smell was so strong that he nearly passed out.

No matter who the ghosts are though, they remain very active here as time goes by. Staff members have complained that even though motion detectors and alarms systems have been left on in the building at night, beer glasses are still found to be scattered about, bottles to be opened and alcohol to be missing.

There have also been sightings of the spirits as well, including those of a small girl, a glowing blue figure who was seen floating up the stairs on two occasions and a man in a tuxedo standing behind a bar. Cold spots have also been reported in the upstairs women's restroom, which has also been plagued by the sound of crying and water faucets that turn on and off.

I had the chance to speak to a bartender who was working the upper level of the Dome Room back in the fall of 2000. He confirmed that strange events were still talking place in the club and even told me of an experience that he had witnessed himself just a few weeks before. He had been working at his station around 11:30 p.m. and heard the sound of a woman crying for help. The bartender realized that it was coming from the upstairs women's restroom and he hurried over in that direction to see what he could do. When he reached the door, he could hear the sound of a woman crying inside. She was pounding frantically on the door, begging to be let out. A little unnerved by the ghostly reputation of the building, he cautiously reached over and eased the door open. As he did so, a female customer literally came tumbling out into his arms. She was breathing heavily and her eyes were red-rimmed from crying.

When the bartender asked her what was wrong, she said that someone had been outside of the bathroom door, holding it shut and wouldn't allow her to leave. Surprised, the bartender said that he had been working just a short distance away and had seen no one outside of the door and certainly no one holding it closed. The woman was adamant about what had happened though and she left very upset.

The staff member told me that he later mentioned this incident to a co-worker and she told him that this same thing has happened before and that on each occasion, the customer had unlocked the door and had tried to open it, only to have it held inexplicably shut. No explanation had been found as to why this occurs.

The building that holds Excalibur remains a fascinating place, no matter what business is located here, and it's obvious that the ghosts are an integral part of the history of the place. While music and dance are the primary functions of the building today, ghost hunters who come here are never disappointed either.

AL CAPONE'S HIDEAWAY & STEAK HOUSE

Anyone looking for a good drink, a great steak and a little of Chicago's Prohibition-era ambiance needs look no further than Al Capone's Hideaway and Steak House, near St. Charles, Illinois. Located in a secluded area along the Fox River, the restaurant's location remains one of the best-kept secrets in the region. Back in the 1920's, when this place was a rollicking speakeasy, the seclusion was essential to keep the illegal booze flowing through the place. Today though, it merely adds to the atmosphere as travelers go in search of the place along back roads and through stretches of scenic forest. It's well worth the search though, for if you are looking for "dinner and spirits" (of any kind!), then Al Capone's Hideaway and Steak House is the place to be!

In 1917, the now popular restaurant opened as Reitmayer's Beer Garden. Proprietor James Reitmayer made his own beer and gained a reputation for having a palatable brew, attracting customers from all around the area. That all came to an end in 1919 however, when Prohibition was enacted and it became illegal to sell, consume or manufacture alcohol. Reitmayer never let that stop him though. He simply moved his beer-making apparatus to a cellar that was hidden behind the chicken coop. The elaborate copper tubing system that he devised to carry the beer from the cellar to the restaurant still exists today. The accidental uncovering of the tubing and the old stills occurred during renovations in the 1970's.

As beer and alcohol distribution became big business with organized crime, Reitmayer was forced to start buying beer from the mob. Competition among the various crime factions was fierce and according to James' wife, Gladys Reitmayer Meyers, Capone's men would be in the restaurant pushing their product one week and Dion O'Bannion's men would be in the next. Reitmayer just wanted to mind his own business but he eventually stopped making his own beer and bought only from Capone. Years later, when recalling the "good old days", Gladys laughed about the fact that Capone's cronies were always in sampling free food and booze. She and her husband complained to the State's Attorney and he "wished them luck."

As the restaurant and speakeasy began attracting customers who weren't afraid to travel outside of the law for a drink, rowdy brawlers became the norm. Reitmayer's soon gained a reputation for gangsters and rough railroad men and on Sundays, when crowds were the largest, many traveled from the city to sample the wares.

However, the brawls and the raids by federal agents don't happen anymore. In December 1973, the restaurant was renovated and remodeled by Bill and Claudia Brooks. The place had been called the Hideaway Lounge when they bought it but they expanded the name and added Al Capone's moniker to it in the middle 1990's, when interest in Capone and the gangster era peaked once again. Much has changed since the early days of the place but the rustic feel of the restaurant is not the only thing that has remained behind -- the ghosts of the past are still here as well.

There have been many odd happenings in the building over the years and the Brooks family, and the staff, has witnessed much of it. Claudia Brooks' mother, Annamae Mosher, worked in the kitchen and as a hostess for the restaurant for years. She had not heard any rumors of the place being haunted prior to her daughter and son-in-law buying the restaurant but soon after she started helping out, she became convinced that it was. She was never frightened by it though, although it was often annoying to her.

She first realized that something mysterious was occurring in the building when she started to notice the odd behavior of a swinging door that led into the bar area from the kitchen. For several weeks, Annamae noted that it would suddenly swing open as if someone was walking through it. She checked to see if there might be a draft coming from somewhere that could be responsible but could find nothing. Then, she started to notice a connection between the movement of the door and something that she herself was doing. For some reason, she realized that whenever she called out "everybody upstairs", a signal for the servers to check their stations, the door would move. She tried experimenting with this and called out at various times to see what might happen. Each time, the doors would swing open, as if an unseen server had just pushed through them. Still not convinced that it wasn't her imagination though, she told the others about her unusual discovery. Before long, the staff and Annamae's family members were all convinced the restaurant was haunted too.

The second floor of the building also began to be regarded as an active area. Several of the staff members and a number of customers pointed out that they felt very strange on this floor, as if someone were nearby or standing over their shoulder as they worked or dined. A couple of the servers noticed something more definite though, mostly in regards to one particular table. No matter how many times they replaced it, they would find a certain napkin setting had been unfolded and the napkin itself, tossed on the floor. It would be fixed over and over again, but to no avail. Someone would always find it thrown away, under a chair and beneath a neighboring table.

But who are the ghosts of Al Capone's Hideaway and Steak House? No one can really say for sure although many would point to the criminal past of the place for answers. The violence of the Prohibition era would surely have left a lasting mark on the place and perhaps the strange activity can be blamed on a customer from the past who simply never left. Perhaps another answer might be found with a past employee who still works his or her shift, repeating actions from the past over and over again? This might explain Annamae's swinging door, as a server from days gone by still responds to the call to check their work station. Who knows?

Or perhaps the ghostly activity in the restaurant is nothing more than a distant memory, recorded to play again and again in an endless loop. Maybe the past is doomed to repeat itself, whether we learn from it or not!

THAT STEAK JOYNT

Of all of the haunted drinking and dining spots in Chicago, there was none so haunted as That Steak Joynt, which was formerly located on North Wells Street. Before the restaurant was closed down, customers and staff members reported bizarre, supernatural experiences here for years. Owner Billy Siegel, who allowed dozens of séances and paranormal investigations to be held in the place, always believed that the haunting was the result of two unsolved murders that took place around the turn of the last century. Both of the victims were found in what was called Piper's Alley, an open corridor that passed just outside of the restaurant. Siegel speculated that the ghosts of these past crimes had somehow found their way into his establishment.

And perhaps he was right, for the history of the building, and the surrounding neighborhood, certainly lends itself to hauntings. Regardless of the identities of the ghosts though, there was little question that while it was in operation, That Steak Joynt enjoyed a reputation for being one of the most haunted places in Chicago!

In the late 1860's, the future location of That Steak Joynt, at 1610 North Wells, was Piper's Bakery. This large factory employed over 500 workers and even housed a school for their children to attend. It was one of the busiest bakeries in the region and shipped out bread and baked goods all over the country. The Great Chicago Fire of 1871 should have brought all of that to an end but Henry Piper refused to give up. He rebuilt on the same site, making the new bakery even bigger and more magnificent than the original. He continued baking for 60 years before finally retiring and closing Piper's for good.

The building was never shuttered though and was constantly in operation with a variety of businesses from a laundry to a hardware store and in 1962, became That Steak Joynt. Like the other businesses before it, the restaurant enjoyed the exquisite architecture and design of Piper's restored bakery. The interior of the place was amazing and was filled with hand-carved art and woodwork, including an original bakery case that was used as a back bar in the new establishment. The remodeling and renovations that were done by owner Billy Siegel and Raudell Perez, the driving force behind the business, only added to the remaining designs from Piper's Bakery.

For instance, the bakery case that had been turned into a bar had been hand-carved from black walnut by artisans who were booked passage from Europe specifically for the project. The shelving had a leaded glass window installed and in the center section was fixed a marble bust of a grinning peasant with a wine flask grasped in his hands. The bust was a relic from the defunct Matson Steamship Line and over the years, it gained an unusual reputation of its own. According to the stories, if you looked at it long enough, the expression on the peasant's face would change -- and that wasn't all. Some even claimed that the bust had unique powers. A stockbroker boasted that the statue fed him stock tips and others claimed that it could cure a variety of ailments. Interestingly, during a later paranormal investigation of the building, a photograph was taken of the bust (using special infrared film) and two white fingers of energy appeared, seemingly being generated by the marble peasant! The photograph remains unexplained.

Other remnants from the Piper Bakery could be found throughout the building. The sculptured baroque ceiling in the lounge was from the old bakery, as was the grandfather clock that stood outside the door to the main dining room. Along the rear of a nearby alcove was another Piper bakery case, also hand carved from black walnut, that had been converted into a sideboard.

Other oddities and antique pieces were scattered throughout the restaurant and had been salvaged from various homes, businesses, structures and mansions in Chicago and beyond. Suspended above the bar was a massive candle and gas fixture that once hung over the billiards table at Peale Castle in Scotland. The Wrigley Mansion in Lake Geneva provided a number of items for the lounge, including a set of leather banquettes, window shutters and a number of stained glass window valances. The foyer of the restaurant also held a number of wonderful pieces, including a mahogany stair railing that had been salvaged from Chicago's L'Aiglon Restaurant; a bronze statue with a light fixture that was fixed atop a newel post and was a signed piece from the French artist Moreau; a chandelier that was once a gas fixture from the McCormick estate; and a Second Empire mirror that was a refugee from the Thorne Mansion. Another piece from the Thorne estate was a teak and gold pedestal that stood at the top of the stairs. It supported a marble figure from the Armour Mansion's rose garden that represented "summer". The pedestal had been used as a base for the Thorne family's main dining room table.

The entryway to what was called the Edwardian Room had pockets that housed French doors in which had been fitted Lalique glass from a mansion in Lombard, Illinois. Inset in the ceiling overhead was another relic from L'Aiglon, a stained glass skylight. The Wine Room featured hand carved wine racks from China that were designed to hold 287 bottles of wine. Nearby was the original Piper Bakery safe, still in place and still bearing un-retouched paintings of a clipper ship and other decorative scrolls and designs.

Along the walls of the staircase leading to the upper dining room were hung portraits of William and Catharine Devine. Devine was a milk merchant who came to Chicago from Ireland in 1864 to work for his brother. He started his own operation two years later and quickly made his fortune. The two portraits were purchased from Al Morlock of Victorian House Antiques in Chicago. They had come from the contents of the Devine house on East Huron Street but Morlock said that the portrait of Catharine Devine began to make him quite uneasy a short time after he purchased it to re-sell in his business. It became so bad that he even considered destroying the portrait but instead, sold it to Warren Black, the interior designer for That Steak Joynt. Black bought the portrait but confessed that he too felt uncomfortable around it. Soon after it was hung next to that of William Devine on the staircase, restaurant customers began to complain of feeling a cold area on the stairs between the paintings. Some also reported that they had seen the woman smile slightly when the painting was reflected in the mirror at the bottom of the steps. When looked at directly though, the smile would vanish. Many others said that were unnerved by Catharine's eyes as her portrait watched them on the staircase. Like an old spooky movie, they stated that her eyes would follow them no matter where they walked.

During the 1980's, séances were regularly held in the restaurant by prominent local medium Robert Dubeil. During one widely reported session, Dubeil and his circle made contact with what they claimed were three spirits haunting the place. One of them was said to be the architect who designed the building, the second was a female customer from the original bakery and the third would not reveal his identity. It could only be discovered that he had some connection with the building in the 1800's. Could this have been one of the murder victims that Billy Siegel believed was haunting the restaurant? The séance was attended that night by a reporter from the *Chicago Sun-Times*, Celeste Busk, and strangely, she became violently ill during the session.

The attempts to discover the identity of the ghosts did not reveal much information unfortunately and did even less to explain the amount of activity that was plaguing the place. The late Raudell Perez reported on many occasions that he had a difficult time getting employees to work at night in the restaurant, especially janitors and cleaning crews. No one wanted to be in the building after hours, thanks to reports of singing sounds and the numerous claims of apparitions that had been seen. One night, a janitor became so frightened by what he saw that he ran out of the restaurant, leaving the door unlocked and his paycheck uncollected. He never returned.

Perez was not really surprised by this, or the other incidents, because he had experienced plenty of them for himself over the years. He and some of the waiters had spotted shadowy figures on numerous occasions. One evening, he was sitting in the bar and looked up to see two people walking up the staircase to the second floor. The restaurant had long been closed and he couldn't imagine who would still be there. He climbed off his stool and hurried up to the second floor, close enough behind that he saw the figures just disappearing around a corner. Raudell dashed up to the upper story and did a quick search of the premises -- only to find that no one was there! There was no other exit to the restaurant and yet he could find no one else on the floor. Concerned that they may have slipped past him, he returned downstairs and looked around. He questioned a couple of the night workers and they had not seen anyone out of place. Whoever the figures had been, Raudell realized, they had been from beyond this world!

But not all of the encounters in the place were so benevolent. A few of them were very frightening and even bordered on violent at times. In May 1991, a staff member was locking the front door at the end of the day when he felt a hand grip his shoulder and pull him backwards. When he spun around to see who was there, the foyer was empty and there was no one else around. One of the bartenders had a similar experience as he was going upstairs one day. He started up the staircase and felt a hand grip the back of his shirt and pull him back down the steps. As he stumbled, he nearly pitched over backward. Regaining his balance, he searched for the culprit but there was no one around. On several occasions, women who used the restroom would also have close encounters. Not only did they often hear the sound of someone entering the room when no one was visible (the sound of hard-sold shoes would be unmistakable, as well as the rustle of clothing) but sometimes the doors to the stalls would jam shut and would refuse to open -- as if someone were forcing them closed on the other side!

Undoubtedly, the most frightening occurrence in the restaurant's history took place one night when a female server was clearing tables in the upstairs lounge. She had just stacked several dishes and had placed them in a wash tub when she felt a rough hand savagely grab her around the wrist! Startled, she turned to see who was holding her and realized that no one was there. The pressure on her wrist was intense and she could even see her own skin starting to redden from the hold the hand had on her and yet the hand itself remained unseen. Then, the invisible assailant began dragging her away from the table and towards the staircase. She struggled but the force was so powerful that she only managed to try and fight back as she was tugged along against her will. Finally, she began to scream as loudly as she could and her shrill cries brought Raudell Perez and one of the waiters upstairs to see what was going on.

When they arrived, they found the server lying on the floor. One of the heels on her shoes had snapped off as she was dragged across floor and she had painful-looking red welts on her arm -- welts that looked strangely like human fingers! Immediately thinking that the server had been attacked by an intruder, Perez snatched a large steak knife from the tub of dirty dishes and searched the second floor. However, the place was empty. The server then explained to him that it had not been an intruder but rather she had been assaulted by an invisible being of some kind. She was visibly shaken and upset and Perez had no reason not to believe her story. He sent her home for the night but she did not return the next day and later quit working for the restaurant.

Even though the séances that had been held in the restaurant never really produced any clues or solid answers as to reasons behind the haunting, Billy Siegel granted permission to author Dale Kaczmarek and members of the *Ghost Research Society* to spend the night inside of That Steak Joynt on two occasions in 1991 and 1994. On both occasions, they remained in the building from closing time until dawn. In 1991, they were joined by reporter Celeste Busk and for the second investigation, by Janet Davies of WLS Television.

The restaurant was divided into several sections that were manned by investigators using cameras, tape recorders and other electronic devices. Although paranormal investigations involve hours of drudgery and waiting around for anything to happen, occasionally they can pay off, especially in very active locations like That Steak Joynt. The 1991 investigation resulted in some exciting and often chilling happenings, including a glowing red light that was seen by several witnesses; the detection of some magnetic disturbances in the building that shouldn't have existed; and a glowing, candle-light image that was seen by several witnesses.

Some of the photos obtained that night were nothing short of amazing. The first, mentioned earlier in connection with the marble bust of the grinning peasant, was actually an energy that was sensed by a psychic who accompanied the investigation team. The strange fingers of light that she divined were verified by a 35mm camera, adding stock to the psychic's additional observations. Other photographs revealed a white, crescent-shaped light near the women's restroom but most unusual were the almost identical photos that were taken with two different cameras in a dining room. In each of the photographs, a monk-like figure in what appears to be a robe is superimposed over a table. His upper torso and lower extremities can be plainly seen but the middle of the man's body is missing, as if he is inserted into the table itself!

The later 1994 investigation was just as eventful, at least in terms of strange experiences and reports. While filming with a video camera on the first floor, one of the *Ghost Research Society* members managed to capture a door that led into the kitchen actually opening under its own power. Moments after this occurred, the team conducted airflow tests of the doorway and discovered that there was indeed a draft that blew through the area -- however, the door actually opened against the draft! This could only mean that the door had to be physically pushed open. What could not be explained is how this could happen when there was no one present who could have pushed it.

The investigators also documented flickering lights, cold spots, phantom footsteps, the sound of something being dragged across the floor in an empty room and a dim figure that was seen sitting at a downstairs dining room table. When the team members tried to approach the figure for a closer look, it vanished. There was no one else around the area and the researchers were convinced that it had not been a trick of the light. Who it might have been remains a mystery.

After That Steak Joynt closed down, the building on North Wells remained empty for a number of years, although it is currently open again as the Adobo Grill, serving upscale Mexican food. If there have been any strange happenings in the old bakery since it has re-opened, I have not heard about them. If there are any new happenings, are they being kept secret? Or did the years of silence serve to quiet the haunting for good? No one knows, or at least no one is talking, so only the future will reveal if the spirits are still restless here. The mysteries of the place certainly still have yet to be revealed...

COUNTRY HOUSE RESTAURANT

Located west of Chicago in Clarendon Hills is a popular establishment called the Country House Restaurant. For many years, the place has been the home to not only fine food and spirits, but to a ghost or two as well. Like many haunted spots, the Country House has its share of rattling dishes, lights that turn on and off, moving objects that go bump in the night, strong smells of flowers in otherwise empty rooms, shutters that open and close and other sorts of strange happenings. In addition to all of that, there are the apparitions too.

One afternoon a customer came into the place and asked owner David Regnery about the woman he saw looking out the attic window. The man joked with him and asked Regnery if he was running a bordello or something? When he was asked what he meant, the customer replied that a young woman had been beckoning to him from a window overlooking the parking lot. Strangely, that part of the attic was a locked storeroom and no one was upstairs at that time.

Regnery was not surprised by the report as he had already had his own experiences in the place. They started nineteen years before when he and another man witnessed some shutters open by themselves. Other experiences occurred while doing paperwork in an upstairs office, after the restaurant had been closed for the night. On several occasions, he heard the door downstairs open, people come in and then walk up to the bar. He went down the stairs, still listening to their muffled conversations, but when he reached the bar it was dark and empty.

There are a couple of different stories to explain the identities of the resident ghosts here. A story claims that one of the lingering spirits is that of a man from the 1800's. Apparently, he was a worker at a grist mill that was located on the property long before the restaurant existed. But there was another ghost as well and one whose story the owners were later able to confirm!

David and Patrick Regnery bought the restaurant in the spring of 1974. They spent a large part of the next year gutting and remodeling the place. Shortly after re-opening in the winter of 1975, they began to realize that strange occurrences were apparently going to be frequent in the place. Concerned that the restaurant might be haunted, they contacted a number of psychics about the building. There was one story that all of the psychics seemed to agree on and they believed this ghost was the most dominant one haunting the restaurant.

According to several independent sources, the spirit was that of a young, blond woman who had been killed in an auto accident in the late 1950's. She had been angry when she left the place, the psychics said, because of a fight with one of the bartenders. She was killed a short time later when her car collided with a telephone pole about a half mile away.

When David Regnery heard this story, he decided to check it out with the former owner of the restaurant, Richard Montanelli. He confirmed the account and told Regnery of a regular customer who was involved with one of the bartenders back in 1958. Apparently, their relationship was on the rocks and they were often seen fighting. One afternoon, she showed up in the tavern visibly distraught and asked if she could leave her baby there and return for him later in the day. When the owner refused her request, she left the bar very upset. A short time later, news reached the tavern that she had driven her car into a pole on 55th Street. It was thought that she had killed herself, along with the baby.

The phenomena has continued over the years. Many of the strange noises that have been heard in the place, including the disembodied voice of an infant crying, have been heard around table 13. This seems to be an especially active corner of the restaurant. Even so, there is no pattern to when strange things might occur, as weeks or even months sometimes pass before anything unusual happens.

The ghost does seem to have a liking for electronics though. Lights often turn on and off. The old jukebox, since replaced with a modern CD player, used to stop and re-start itself for no reason. A few employees also say they have seen an adding machine operating by itself. The public address system also malfunctions with no explanation. On busy nights, customers waiting for tables often come to the hostess after hearing their names being called. Staff members swear that they are nowhere near the top of the list and have not been called!

While managers only remember one person quitting because of the ghost several years ago, most employees say they would not spend the night in the building. However, one person did spend the night there about a decade ago, despite the stories of a haunting. A friend of Regnery's, who was a police officer, was going through a divorce and needed a place to stay. Regnery let him live temporarily in one of the attic rooms. "He used to get up in the middle of the night with his pistol and flashlight because he'd hear someone coming up the stairs," Regnery said. "He said he did it three or times and there was never anyone there, so he began just sleeping through it."

Psychics, ghost hunters, photographers and students are among the curiosity-seekers that have spent hours and nights in the restaurant, trying to experience the unexplained. Some have succeeded in getting something strange on film or tape, but there has been nothing definite so far that constitutes proof. Regardless, most staff members are convinced that there is something here. They have no desire to get rid of it though. They believe the ghost is merely playful, not dangerous.

If you are looking for a place where good food and ghostly chills go hand in hand, consider dropping in at the Country House Restaurant some evening. Whether you are a believer or not, it's unlikely that you'll go away disappointed!

CHAPTER FIVE
HOLY SPIRITS
HAUNTED CHURCHES, MIRACULOUS VISITATIONS & BLESSED APPARITIONS

Visitations from angels and the Virgin Mary are nothing new in the history of the world, although most probably believe that such miracles ended long ago. This may not be the case though, especially in Chicago, where the Virgin Mary makes regular appearances, and where shrines, paintings, and relics bleed, ooze and mystify the faithful!

Visitors from the heavens have reportedly been around since the beginning of recorded time, from the "burning bush" of Moses to Ezekiel's wheel and the numerous stories of angels in earthly form that graced the biblical writings. In fact, some of the lustier angels even mated with the "daughters of men" and created a race of giants and demi-gods that led to God wiping out the earth in a flood. Perhaps the most famous of the heavenly visitors (at least in more modern times) is Mary, the mother of Jesus. After the death of her son, she became the core of the early Christian church and since the third century, Mary has made countless visitations, especially to those of the Catholic faith, who hold Mary in higher esteem than other churches.

Several of these visitations have been more famous than others. The first was in December 1531, when Mary was said to have appeared to a Mexican peasant named Juan Diego and left an impression of herself on his cloak. This visitation, and the cloth, can be seen today at the Shrine of Guadalupe in Mexico. I visited this location a number of years ago and while I found the "image" to be questionable at best, there is no doubt that it holds a special meaning for the literally thousands of people who were visiting the location that day.

Another famous visitation came at Lourdes, France in February 1858. A young girl named Bernadette Soubrious was gathering firewood near a stream when she heard a terrific noise from a nearby cave. A shimmering cloud appeared and from it, came a beautiful woman who claimed to be Mary. She asked Bernadette to have a chapel built on the spot and this grotto has come to be known as one of the most famous religious shrines in the world. Thousands and thousands of people have come here for the healing powers of the water and many have reported further apparitions of the Virgin Mary.

In May 1917 came the mysterious visitations in Fatima, Portugal, which began as a powerful wind and a blinding light for three children, Lucia dos Santos, Francisco Marto and Jacinto Marto. Mary's appearances at Fatima were witnessed by thousands of people and at one point, a massive crowd claimed to witness impossible movements of the sun in the sky. Divine Intervention or mass hallucination? No one knows for sure, but the faithful will tell you that Mary did appear at Fatima and that she did pass along cryptic messages to the children. Her final message was said to be so earth-shattering that it was kept secret by the Vatican for many years. When revealed, the Church stated that the prediction had accurately foretold the assassination attempt on Pope John Paul II. Some are not convinced that this was the final message however and believe that darker things are still ahead for humanity.

In 1983, Mary began an annual appearance at the farm of Nancy Fowler near Conyers, Georgia. The crowds were so massive that they peaked at more than 80,000 people and a resulting traffic jam prevented emergency workers from reaching a woman with heart problems. However, by 1998, attendance had dropped off so much that Mary announced this would be her last visit. Fowler was the only person able to see or hear Mary, but witnesses did report that the sun changed color during communions and that the scent of roses was often (inexplicably) in the air. Even though Mary no longer appears at the farm, there is a water well here that, along with having alleged curative powers, was personally blessed by Jesus Christ (who apparently traveled to Georgia with his mother). Visitors to the site will find that the well is marked with a sign that warns drinkers of potential health risks for in 1991, it tested positive for unsafe levels of bacteria.

The Lady of the Snows Shrine in Belleville, Illinois has also been the setting for visits from the Virgin Mary. She was first encountered by Ray Doiron here in 1993 and appeared for a number of years afterward. Doiron had been through three near-death experiences and was deaf in his right ear before being visited by Mary. He had been sleeping one afternoon when he heard a soft voice that instructed him to go to the nearby Lady of Snows Shrine, which is a duplicate of the shrine at Lourdes. He was told to first go on February 11 and then on the 13th each successive month.

At first, the visitations were kept secret, but were always the same. There would be a strong wind, that would suddenly stop, and then a statue at the shrine would turn blue, just before a bright light would appear. From the light would appear the form of Mary. She would speak and impart lessons on Doiron, which he would write down to keep from making mistakes. Later, he was allowed to bring a small number of friends to the shrine and then was told to make the visitations public. Since then, hundreds have visited the site (and still come here), although Mary's final alleged appearance was on May 13, 1999.

In recent times, Mary has also reportedly appeared to six children in war-torn Bosnia, an event that has attracted more than 11 million people from around the globe. One such man was Joseph Reinholtz, a retired railroad worker from Hillside, Illinois. He had been suffering from blurred vision and periods of blindness and journeyed to Bosnia to pray and meet with one of the children who had reported seeing Mary. She prayed over Reinholtz in 1987 and upon his return to Illinois, his sight slowly returned.

Reinholtz returned to Bosnia in 1989 and the young woman then instructed him that he was to look for a large crucifix, next to a three-branched tree. Here, he was to pray, she explained to him. He later discovered this location at Queen of Heaven Cemetery in Hillside and began to make frequent trips to the spot to pray. On August 15, 1990, Reinholtz had his first visitation from Mary and it was repeated on November 1, when she returned, he claimed, with St. Michael and three other angels. Soon, word of the visitations leaked out and thousands of people began flocking to the cross. It wasn't long before complaints about the number of spectators caused the cemetery officials to move the cross to another location in 1992. It is very accessible now, having a paved parking lot next to it.

The visitations have reportedly continued and occur every day but Tuesday, which is coincidentally the day that the Archdiocese of Chicago placed a "restriction of obedience" on Reinholtz and asked that he not visit the cemetery. But the late Hillside man is not the only person to report miracles at the site of the Queen of Heaven cross. There have been dozens of photographs taken here that purport to show angels and various types of light phenomena. Others claim to have seen blood coming from the cross and have reported the scent of roses in the air.

I visited the site a couple of years ago and found it surrounded by the faithful, praying and passing out religious literature. I was also shown a number of the "miraculous" photos taken here and confess that it looked like bad photography and a lot of sun glare to me -- but cannot argue about the importance of the photos in the lives of the believers.

Sadly, Joseph Reinholtz suffered a stroke in February 1995 and was hospitalized, where Mary continued to visit him. He passed away in December 1996, but his legacy remains in Queen of Heaven Cemetery, where a crucifix stands and where those who believe still experience miraculous visitations.

In addition to sightings of the Virgin Mary, Chicago has also played host to religious apparitions and a few "miraculously" weeping statues and relics as well. Over the past three decades, there have been more than a dozen reported religious apparitions and unexplained happenings in the Chicago area, each of them drawing dozens, or even hundreds, of believers. They include statues, paintings and icons that appear to weep and more and images, shapes and shadows that appear on windows, walls and even tree trunks.

One such relic was a painting of the Virgin Mary that was hanging in the St. Nicholas Albanian Orthodox Church in 1986. One day, the painting suddenly began to weep, a phenomenon that continued for the next seven months, during which time water also dripped from her fingers. Hundreds of people came to witness the event but the icon abruptly ceased crying in July 1987. A year later, the weeping started up again, but didn't last long. At that time, the tears that she produced were used to anoint 19 other icons in Pennsylvania and they all began weeping too.

A barely remembered strange event took place at St. Adrian's Church on Chicago's south side in May 1970. According to witnesses, the 1700-year old remains of St. Maximina, a first-class relic, began oozing watery blood.

In June 1984, a wooden statue of the Virgin Mary appeared to shed tears at the St. John of God Catholic Church on the southwest side. The Archdiocese of Chicago investigated the phenomenon for more than a year before announcing that it could not positively rule out natural causes for liquid oozing from the wood, despite the wood's age and composition.

Another painting, this one an inexpensive rendition of Mary and Jesus, reportedly began to weep in April 1987. This one was not located in a church however, but in the apartment of a retired tailor on West Devon.

Several icons at Apanacio and St. John on the north side of the city reportedly began weeping in the early 1990's. The icons were stolen by an unknown thief, but later were later returned. Once they came back, the tears no longer appeared on them. The church has since been disbanded.

A icon panel of the Virgin Mary began weeping oil at the beginning of Holy Week in Cicero during April 1994. The icon was located at St. George's Antiochan Orthodox Church. Eight orthodox bishops examined the tears and declared them to be genuine. Mary has continued to cry and the relic has since been renamed Our Lady of Cicero.

In November 1994, the owner of a religious gift store in St. Charles, Illinois claimed that six plastic statues of Mary bowed their heads after being unpacked from a shipping box and having rosaries placed around their necks.

An Orthodox bishop declared that an event was "an extension of the miracle of Our Lady of Cicero" in Schiller Park in May 1997. The event he referred to was when a tiny paper copy of the St. George Antiochian icon began to ooze oily tears. Moments later, the faithful who were gathered claimed to see a life-sized image of the icon appear on a picture window behind the makeshift shrine that housed it.

The Virgin of Guadalupe was said to have visited Hanover Park in July 1997, appearing on the wall of an apartment complex located at 2420 Glendale Terrace. The image appeared from shadows created by a security light that was angled at the building. When the light was turned off, the image vanished, but the faithful remained, convinced that a holy miracle had taken place. Today, at the southwest end of the parking, a tent is standing next to the building where it happened. Inside are hundreds of votive candles and a statue of the Virgin Mary.

In July 1999, another shadowy image of Mary appeared in Joliet. This time, she was seen in the second-story window of a vacant house. Hundreds of people came to see the image, blocking traffic and trampling the lawns of those who lived nearby.

In July 2001, Mary dropped in again, this time in Rogers Park. This sighting was unique (at least in Chicago) as the Virgin reportedly appeared in an oval-shaped scar in the trunk of a tree. Despite the fact that skeptics insisted that the faithful were merely seeing "whatever they wanted to see", scores of people flocked to an area in the park near the corner of Honore and Rogers Avenue and surrounded the tree with candles, rosaries and prayer offerings.

"It's very hard to describe it," said one man who came to visit the site," but I can feel it's in there."

He and hundreds of others visited the sight after it was first seen by a neighborhood woman on July 9. The alleged apparition appeared about 10 feet from the ground, inside of the scar on the trunk. The scar looked like a medallion on a chain and the folds in the scar tissue created the image of cloaked person. As the story spread of the sighting, so many onlookers came to the park that Chicago police had to close the street to be able to handle the crowd.

Church officials were cautious about commenting on this most recent apparition. "People want to know 'is it authentic?' The scientific authenticity is not as important as does it cause an authentic response in faith by the people?" said the Rev. Patrick Lagges, vicar for canonical services of the Roman Catholic Archdiocese of Chicago. "We tend to put too much stock in the scientific proof of these things. If we're talking about a miracle, we're talking about something that is not measurable by science but is on the level of faith."

With that said, he sidestepped the suggestion that someone might want to look into the reality of the Virgin Mary in a tree a little more closely. Rev. Lagges added that in most cases where people report seeing the shape of the Virgin Mary in a tree trunk, window or wall, or see tears flow from a statue or picture, "the Archdiocese doesn't start any formal process to investigate them." (This proved to be accurate in the Rogers Park case as well for the church did not investigate the reports) He also said that no apparition of the Virgin Mary or an incident where an icon or relic appeared to weep has been verified by the Vatican as an "official" miracle. He pointed out the fact that even though the case of Bernadette Soubrious in Lourdes, France occurred in 1858, she was not declared a saint until 1933. This was even after thousands from all over the world came to seek out the curative waters of the grotto where the girl reportedly encountered Mary. Such events are only declared to be "miracles" after intense investigations and studies have been performed.

Which was something that was not going to happen with a tree in Rogers Park...

The miraculous visions and visitations of Chicago are among the greatest oddities of the city and many are torn between belief and disbelief. What do you, the reader, make of these strange (and perhaps wonderful) sightings and experiences? If you are not a believer, you are apt to dismiss them as the fevered imaginings of a religious mind. Perhaps -- or perhaps not -- regardless, I'd prefer to leave that up to you to decide.

CHURCH MYSTERIES & HAUNTINGS

Located along Roosevelt Road on the south side of Chicago, the magnificent spires of Holy Family Church lift point toward the sky -- or toward heaven, if you prefer. The gothic structure stands as the centerpiece of one of Chicago's oldest Catholic parishes and is a wonderful example of local and architectural history, as well as legend and lore.

According to church history, the parish that Holy Family Church serves was founded by Father Arnold Damen, a Jesuit missionary for whom Chicago's Damen Avenue is named. In 1857, the church was built over the running water of Red Creek, an ancient practice in Europe, and the building's main altar is said to be positioned directly over the water. As an aside, tradition has it that the river received the name of "Red Creek" after an Indian battle that was fought here centuries ago caused the water to run red with blood. The site came to be considered sacred by the Native Americans, making it the a perfect candidate for another holy site in years to come.

The church saw what was considered to be its first miracle just a few years after it was constructed. On the east side of the main altar is a large, badly proportioned statue of Our Lady of Perpetual Help that was created by a local man sometime in the 1860's. It came to be considered the protective guardian of the church after a crack was discovered one day that threatened the very structure of the building. The crack had made its way down one wall of the church, from the ceiling to the floor. If it enlarged further, church officials were warned, a wall, or several of the walls, could collapse. Father Damen decided to place the church under the protection of Our Lady of Perpetual Help and he moved the large wooden statue so that it stood under the crack. Somehow, it held for many decades and was never repaired until a major renovation in the 1980's. For more than a century, despite years of water damage and decay from rain seeping through the fissure, parishioners were confident in the fact that the building was never in any real danger, thanks to the watchfulness of the church's protector.

Other miracles and strange happenings followed. Perhaps the greatest was the salvation of the church during the Great Chicago Fire of 1871. Although Mrs. O'Leary's cow never really kicked over a lantern, the fire did start near DeKoven and Jefferson Streets, just a few blocks away from Holy Family. When the fire broke out, Father Damen was in New York but he received a telegraph from Chicago that alerted him to the fact that the city was in flames and the church and the parish were in danger. There was little that he could do from so far away, other than to pray and to trust in God and Our Lady of Perpetual Help. Mysteriously, the fire somehow shifted away from the church and burned a path to the north instead, destroying the downtown business district, but sparing Holy Family. The parish was saved and the event was acknowledged as a miracle. When Father Damen returned home to Chicago, he ordered seven candles to be kept burning on a side altar to commemorate the event. After a few years, the candles were replaced by gas jets and then light bulbs, but have burned brightly ever since.

Father Arnold Damen

Without a doubt though, the most famous story of Holy Family also involves Father Damen and supernatural assistance of another sort. The legend has been referred to in parish histories of the church and it involves what many believe to be the curious additions to the décor of Holy Family. These additions are two wooden statues that depict altar boys who are dressed in old fashioned cassocks. The two young boys were said to be brothers who drowned together while on a parish picnic in 1874. No one had any idea at the time that they would return to play a very mysterious part in the history of this spiritual community.

According to the story, Father Damen was awakened one night around in the late 1880's, during a terrible snow storm, by the insistent ringing of the bell at the rectory. When the porter opened the door, he found two young boys on the doorstep, shivering in the cold, anxiously asking for a priest to come and call on a sick woman who was not expected to last through the night.

Father Damen overheard their pleas and he told the boys that he would come with them immediately. Bundling up into his warmest coat and scarf, he followed the boys out into the night. They trudged for blocks through the nearly blinding snow to a dilapidated cottage on the far edge of the parish. As they reached the door, the boys told the priest that the sick woman had taken to her bed at the top floor of the house, the garret. He quickly opened the door and went inside and began climbing the rickety steps to the upper floor. As Father Damen turned to speak to the two boys, he realized that they were gone.

At the top of the steps, he entered a small room and found an old woman lying on a bed in the corner.

She turned to look at him weakly but managed to smile when she saw that her caller was a priest. She thanked him for coming and he heard her confession and gave her the last rites of the church. The elderly woman was comforted and yet confused by his presence. She asked him how he knew to come to her, admitting that she was very ill and needed a priest, but that she had know no one to send for one.

Father Damen explained that two boys had awakened him and asked him to come. He assumed that they were neighbors, perhaps sent by their parents to fetch him. But the woman insisted that she had spoken with no one. She did not know her neighbors anymore and no one knew she had been ill. There had been simply no one for her to send to summon spiritual help.

"Have you no boys of your own?" Father Damen asked her.

"I had two sons many years ago, altar boys at the church," she replied. "But they have long since died."

Father Damen had the stunning revelation that the two vanished boys had been the woman's sons, returning to help her in her hour of need. He explained his feelings to the woman as she lay dying and when she passed away near morning, she did so with a smile on her face. She had found peace and believed that she would soon be reunited with her lost children. Father Damen was so moved by what had occurred that he commissioned two wooden statues of altar boys and had them placed high above the main altar of the church. They have been watching over the parish ever since.

Throughout modern times, reported hauntings at Holy Family seem to suggest that Father Damen still makes occasional appearances here as well, watching over his beloved parish. If this is true, then he may not linger here alone. According to accounts from Father David McCarthy, who has researched much of the history and lore of the church, a shadowy figure is sometimes seen in the old choir loft, which is not open to the public. Some of these sightings he has personally witnessed himself. On occasional mornings when saying mass, Father McCarthy has turned to the congregation and has noticed the figure in the loft. He knows that no one can actually be there because the loft has been considered unsafe and off limits for quite some time. The first time a sighting occurred though, Father McCarthy investigated but found that the door to the loft was locked. Regardless, he went into the loft and checked the spot where the figure had been standing. He found that the dust of the years had been undisturbed and that the only footprints left here were his own. Apparently, there is a old Catholic tradition that says that those who miss Sunday mass during their lifetime will have to make up for the services they missed after death. Could this explain the baffling figure?

Likely the most welcome ghost at Holy Family though would be that of Father Damen himself. During the latter part of the 1900's, clergy members and staff here have reported a figure, wearing clerical dress, who passes through the church or patrols the hallways of St. Ignatius College Preparatory High School next door. These sightings were especially prevalent during the 1990's, when the church and school were being renovated. Just a few years before, the Jesuits had considered destroying the aging landmark and selling off the empty lot but donations and fund raising had garnered the necessary funds to restore the place. Many believe that perhaps Father Damen returned because of the all of the activity that was occurring in the building.

Or perhaps he was already here, worried about the original plans to tear down the church in the early 1980's. Late one evening in 1985, a St. Ignatius student was working in the library with several others on some of the fund raising programs and decided to take a break. He walked out into the hallway and saw a figure, dressed in clerical garments, turn and enter a classroom further down the corridor. Thinking that it was odd that someone else was working so late, he mentioned to the other students what he had seen. They laughed as he tried to explain it to them for they already knew who the priest was -- Father Damen, still making his rounds.

THE APPARITIONS AT ST. RITA'S

By far, the most mysterious and controversial event to ever occur in a church in Chicago was the strange happening that is said to have taken place at the St. Rita of Cascia Church on All Souls Day, November 2, of 1960. To this day, church officials deny that it ever happened and yet first-hand accounts and neighborhood gossip insists that it did. It has sparked debate among the faithful in Chicago for more than 40 years now and has remained an incident of great interest for supernatural enthusiasts for nearly as long. Did an unexplained event really take place or is the whole thing, as one priest stated, merely "an old wife's tale". Once again, I'll have to let the reader decide for himself!

St. Rita's Church was established in 1905 by the Augustinian Fathers of Pennsylvania, who were invited to construct a church in Chicago by Archbishop James E. Quigley. They broke ground on the church and a college (now a high school) later that same year at 63rd and Oakley Avenue. As the parish grew, a new church was constructed north of 63rd Street, between Fairfield and Washtenaw Avenue. The first mass was celebrated in this church in 1923. In 1948, the cornerstone of the present St. Rita's was laid, building over the old site at 63rd and Fairfield. But it was in late 1960 that the church's most mysterious event allegedly occurred.

The last days of October and the first days of November are important dates on the calendar of the Catholic Church. Halloween is considered the eve of a holy day, All Saints Day, when the faithful are to honor all of the saints of the church. All Souls Day, November 2, follows and this is the day when remembrance and prayers are offered for those who have died. It was on this day that a group of 15 to 17 parishioners gathered in the sanctuary of St. Rita's to offer prayers and devotions for their deceased loved ones. In the midst of this, a series of inexplicable events began and while they did not last for long, they left an indelible mark on those who were present.

It began with the church organ, which was located in a loft over the main doors. The instrument suddenly began to emit shrill tones, even though no fingers had been placed on the keys. The hands of the clock started to spin wildly in opposite directions. The commotion from the organ attracted the attention of those gathered in the church and when they turned in its direction, they were stunned to see six monk-like figures standing on either side of it. Three of the figures wore black robes and three wore white. For some reason that remains unknown to those of us who were not present that day, the parishioners were filled terror. They scrambled from their seats and began to run toward the doors on the east and west sides of the church. However, when they reached the doors, they were unable to open them. They struggled to get out but the doors refused to open, as if some invisible force was holding them closed!

Now, paralyzed with fear, they could only watch as the robed figures began to glide through the air from the organ loft. They settled just above the main floor, passing directly through pews and other solid objects as they traveled toward the front of the building. The organ blared once more and then a strange voice was heard, croaking in a rough whisper. "Pray for me!" it cried and immediately, a strong wind blew through the sanctuary and the once sealed doors burst open. The trapped congregation ran outside, fleeing in fear from the horrific scene.

What happened next remains as much a mystery as the event itself. According to some accounts, the church's pastor, Rev. Clement McHale, met privately with those who shared the bizarre experience and insisted that they not speak about it to anyone -- for the good of the church. Several of the unnerved parishioners were too frightened to even return to the church though and the story did not remain a secret for long. In fact, it spread through the close-knit community like wildfire. For months after, few could refrain from talking about the terrifying afternoon at St. Rita's.

But what really happened that day? Supporters have long been split over what occurred, torn between a supernatural manifestation and a prank gone awry. There has been talk of devious altar boys, mass hallucinations brought on by fervent prayer and even the suggestion that the figures were real. Some believe that the day of the event was no coincidence in that some doomed spirit returned to the church to implore the parishioners to pray for his soul. Church officials weren't buying any of it though and later pastors blamed their predecessors for allowing the story to continue for as long as it has. The late Rev. Francis Fenton grew so tired of the story that he actually denounced it from the pulpit.

But if the event never happened, then how did such a strange story get started in the first place? Was it merely a parable of good and evil (black and white) that became horribly misconstrued, or something else? No one knows, although St. Rita's has remained quiet ever since. There have been no return visits by the puzzling figures and each All Souls Day has passed without incident since 1960 -- making this Chicago mystery all the more mysterious.

THE GHOST OF ST. TURIBIUS

St. Turibius Church is located in a quiet neighborhood on the southwest side of the city, not far from Midway Airport. The largely Polish population of the area is middle class and conservative and still holds closely to the values and traditions of those who came before them. The church was established by Cardinal Mundelein in 1927, although they met at that time in the assembly hall of Peck School at 59th and Hamlin Avenue. In the early years of the Great Depression, construction was somehow financed for a small church to be built that would accommodate about 300 people. By 1930 though, the church already had nearly 500 parishioners.

In March 1950, under the guidance of Rev. Joseph Lechert, ground was broken for a new church at the corner of 57th Street and Karlov Avenue. Mass was celebrated for the first time here at Christmas 1951 and most consider Father Lechert to be the man responsible for not only the new church but the school and hall that joined it. He was a great influence on the people of the parish and many current residents believe that his lasting impression has created the good reputation that their neighborhood still enjoys. For many years, he guided those in the parish with a firm, but gentle, hand, keeping watch over everything. In those days, the local pastor made all of the decisions on how church money was spent, what jobs had priority and how all of the local parish business was conducted.

All of that changed though when John Cardinal Cody came to the Archdiocese of Chicago. He strongly disagreed with the old ways of strong local pastors and was determined to change the financial dealings of the archdiocese. Money soon began to be controlled by a central board and pastors were forced to completely change how they had been doing things for years. This was a hard thing for men who had independently operated for years and many of them saw this as a betrayal of the people who lived and worshipped in their parishes. Many of the priests simply refused to change and these holdouts found themselves forced into a form of early retirement. Anyone who resisted change found himself with the status of "pastor emeritus" and were stripped of all of their duties. Father Lechert was just one of the many Chicago priests who was treated in this manner. He was made pastor emeritus of St. Turibius in November 1967 and a new pastor was brought in.

Father Lechert died on May 21, 1968 and although a heart attack was listed as his official cause of death, many of his friends maintained that he died from a broken heart.

Not surprisingly, this stubborn priest, who watched over and cared for the people in his parish for more than two decades, was not interested in just moving on after death. He simply refused to give up his position as pastor, both in life and in death. Not long after he passed away, people in the community began to maintain that Father Lechert had returned and was still watching over the church. In fact, he remains a strong presence there today -- just as his good works do.

Over the years, pastors, parishioners and altar boys reported seeing a spectral priest in a black cassock walking around inside of the church building and hall. Some of the encounters have been nearly indisputable, putting skeptics on edge with no method to debunk the stories. One such report came from a priest named Father Marc Pasciak, who served at St. Turibius in the 1970's. He told long-time Chicago ghost hunter Richard Crowe that some of the altar boys told him of a figure they had seen in the darkened church. They said that he was a priest but that he wore a strange hat and walked funny. Father Pasciak realized that the "funny hat" was a biretta, a square hat with a tassel that, while out of style for many years at the time of the sighting, was once popular with monsignors in the church. Father Lechert often wore one. In addition, the strange walk they described also matched with that of Father Lechert. Several years before he had died, he had suffered a minor stroke and he always walked with an odd gait during the final years of his life.

The story is so convincing in light of the fact that debunkers would have us believe that anyone who claims to see a ghost is likely lying or imagining things. But how could several young men, who had never met Father Lechert, describe him in such an unusual that he became identifiable to a priest who actually had to research the man to know that the ghost had been his? This seems to defy logic and there were those who were not so sure about the possibility of Father Lechert's continuing presence who became believers after that!

THE IRISH CASTLE

In the south side neighborhood of Beverly stands one of the most unique of the reportedly haunted houses in Chicagoland. It has been known by several names over the years, from the Givens Mansion to the Irish Castle, although its present incarnation is as the Beverly Unitarian Church. After the destruction of Palmer Potter's castle on Lakeshore Drive, this structure became designated as the only actual castle in the Chicago area. It is located on a slight hill at the corner of 103rd and Longwood Drive and has a strangeness about it that contrasts with the elegant homes nearby. If legends and lore about it are any indication, it certainly lives up to its odd appearance!

The man who erected the Irish Castle was Robert C. Givens, a Chicago real estate dealer of the 1880's. After working for some time with the realty firm of E.A. Cummings & Co., he decided to tour Ireland and Europe for a time and then returned to Chicago to establish his own real estate company. The firm prospered and soon Givens decided to construct his own home. The story goes that during his tour of Ireland, he became enamored of an ancient, ivy-covered castle on the banks of the River Dee. Possessing some amount of artistic ability, he sketched the castle and had plans drawn up for a home to be built on a bluff above Tracy Avenue (now Longwood). The neighborhood at that time was called Washington Heights. The castle was completed in 1886 and legend has it that Givens actually built the place for his wife. However, she died before she could ever live there.

Heartbroken, he moved into the house anyway and attempted to enjoy the structure that he had labored so long to be able to afford. He moved in a variety of Irish antiques and hung collected tapestries on the walls. Givens was never able to realize the quiet, retired life that he had hoped for in the castle though and he sold the house to John B. Burdett in 1908.

As time passed, it went through a variety of owners. It was used by a manufacturer, a doctor and a girl's school before becoming the church. The house was sold to the Unitarian Church in 1942 and in the late 1950's, new additions were constructed for classrooms. Later, they planned to tear down the castle altogether for a new building, but these plans were discarded in 1972 and the church remains in the old castle today.

There have been a wide variety of strange happenings in the building. The source of the hauntings is said to be a previous occupant from the time when the castle was the Chicago Female College. According to the story, a young girl became ill with a serious case of influenza and died in the early 1930's. The legends say that her name is "Clara" and that she had never left this place.

The ghost was first encountered in the 1960's by a church custodian, who came upon a young girl in a long dress standing in one of the rooms. The two of them chatted for a few minutes and the young girl remarked that the place had changed much since she had lived there. The custodian left the room and then suddenly recalled that the church had been in the building for more than 20 years. Such a young girl couldn't possibly have lived there before that. She ran back to the room, but the girl had vanished! She then searched the entire building, only to find the doors and windows all locked. She even looked outside and discovered that a fresh layer of snow now blanketed the ground. There were no footprints leading in or out of the church.

Many believe that the young girl's fatal illness, and her confused state because of it, led to her spirit lingering behind. This is something that can be testified to by the church's pastor, Reverend Leonetta

Bugleisi. She told author Ursula Bielski that in 1994, shortly after she was installed at the church, she saw two small arms embrace her husband's waist. While the pastor clearly saw this occur, her husband claimed to feel nothing.

Members of the congregation and visitors to the castle have also reported strange phenomena. Several attendees at a wedding reception here discovered that a number of utensils mysteriously vanished, only to show up again later. Others have noted half-full wine glasses that have emptied when no one is around. There have also been a number of strange noises. Occupants of the building have described a "jingling" sound, like the tinkling of glasses and silverware at a dinner party. A former pastor, Reverend Roger Brewin, stated that he often tried to track down the source of these mysterious sounds but he never could. He said that they seemed to come from everywhere, and yet nowhere, all at the same time! Reverend Bugleisi also mentioned muffled voices that are sometimes heard from empty floors of the castle. A quick search reveals no one else is present.

A photo of the Irish Castle that was taken shortly after it was constructed. (Michelle Bonadurer)

Even the neighbors have seen odd things. They report what appears to be candles drifting past the windows of the castle at night, even when no one is here. One woman also said that she saw a female figure walking across the grounds in the snow. The figure appeared to be solid and yet left no footprints behind. Some believe this spirit might be that of Eleanor Veil, who lived in the castle and maintained it through the Great Depressions. It has been suggested that perhaps she loved the place so much, she simply decided not to leave.

Who these ghosts are, or why they have remained here, remains a mystery but it seems certain that they are at peace in this place. There are no terrifying encounters that take place within the walls of this sanctuary and for this reason, officials at the church (who are more open-minded than most) are content to let the ghosts remain. The Beverly Unitarian Church, or the Irish Castle if you prefer, continues to appeal to not only the spirits of the past -- but the spiritual side of those who come here as well. The restless spirits do not seem so restless here and perhaps they have finally found comfort at last.

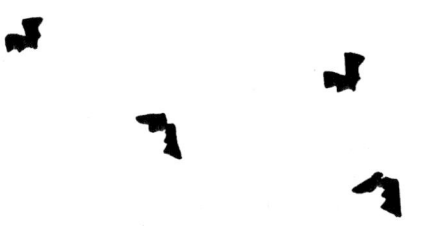

CHAPTER SIX
NO REST FOR THE WICKED

HISTORY & HAUNTINGS OF CHICAGO CRIME

Chicago was born in blood -- from the murder of early settler Jean Lalime to the massacre of soldiers and civilians at Fort Dearborn -- but actual crime in Chicago grew slowly. This is in spite of the fact that the first white man to build a shelter on the site of the city was a criminal. His name was a Pierre Moreau and he was a French bootlegger who sold whiskey and illegal goods to the Indians before vanishing from history and from Chicago. He is little more than a phantom today but he was the one who set the stage for the gangsters, killers and thieves who would follow him in the years to come.

The settlers who followed him were a rough lot but there was no record of criminal activity in Chicago until the first real population booms of the early 1830's. Thousands swarmed into the region from the east and among these was Chicago's first thief -- or at least the first one to be caught at it. In addition, the mob also brought with it the first man to be housed in the city jail. This drifter, known only as Harper, was apparently arrested in the early fall of 1833 as a vagrant. Thanks to Illinois law at the time, vagrants could be offered for sale into slavery. Public sentiment was opposed to the sale of a white man and even though a large crowd attended the auction, the only bid came from George White, a black man who was employed as the town crier. Harper was sold to him for a quarter and White led him away at the end of a chain. What became of him after that is unknown but it's thought that he escaped that night and was never seen again.

The name of Chicago's first thief has never been recorded but he reportedly stole $34 from a fellow boarder at the Wolf Tavern. He was arrested by Constable Reed and the missing funds were discovered when the man was taken to Reed's carpenter shop and ordered to strip. The money was found wadded up in the toe of one of the man's socks. The defendant was held over for trial, which took place at the tavern, and after much argument and speech making, was found guilty. He was released on a nominal bail, pending a motion for a new trial by his boisterous attorney, Giles Spring, and he promptly disappeared.

By 1840, Chicago newspapers were publishing an increasing number of accounts detailing thefts, hold ups, drunken disturbances, street brawls and small riots. Other cities jumped on the bandwagon and in the summer of 1839, a newspaper in Jackson, Michigan commented that the "population of Chicago is principally composed of dogs and loafers".

One of these "loafers" was a young Irishman named John Stone who went to the gallows and became the first legal execution in Chicago history. Stone arrived in America at the age of 13 and came to Chicago in 1838, after having served prison time for robbery and murder in Canada. He worked off and on as a woodcutter but spent most of his time in saloons and in the city's first billiard hall. In the spring of 1840,

Stone was arrested for the rape and murder of Mrs. Lucretia Thompson, the wife of a Cook County farmer and in May was tried and convicted for it. On Friday July 10, Stone was taken in chains and handcuffs by wagon to a spot on the lake shore about three miles south of the court house. He was escorted by about 200 mounted citizens and 60 armed militiamen under the command of Colonel Seth Johnson. He was hanged in front of a large crowd of interested spectators and after his death; his body was taken by doctors Boone and Dyer and dissected for medical study.

Even from these early days, Chicago thrived on its reputation for being a "wide-open town". As far back as the 1850's, the city gained notoriety for its promotion of vice in every shape and form. It embraced the arrival of prostitutes, gamblers, grifters and an outright criminal element. A commercialized form of vice flourished during the Civil War era and according to author Richard Lindberg, an estimated 1,300 prostitutes roamed the dark evening streets of Chicago. Randolph Street, he wrote, "was awash in bordellos, wine rooms and cheap dance halls in plain view of the courthouse". The area became known as "Gambler's Row", mostly because a man gambled with his very life when braving the streets of this seedy and dangerous district.

The Great Fire in 1871 would sweep away the worst of the city's vice areas, destroying both gin rooms and disease-ridden prostitution cribs, but a desire for illicit activities caused it to rebound quickly. By the 1880's, Chicago had gained its place as a mature city and also as a rail center for the nation. Waves of foreigners and immigrants poured into the city and with the arrival of the World's Fair in 1893, thousands of new citizens followed.

During the latter part of the 1800's, street crime came into its own. It became a good general rule for citizens to avoid all but the busiest thoroughfares at night. Many places were considered unsafe after dark and the lack of well-lighted streets in many areas added to the danger. It was suggested to travelers coming to the city that they might always consider walking in the center of the street if possible. That way, they would be out of reach of any hold-up man who might step out of an alley. Weapons among the criminal element could mean anything, from a club to a knife, a canvas bag filled with sand or a pistol. As there were no laws in those days against concealed weapons, any drifter or drunk who got hold of a pistol could become a deadly menace. The thief may have only been looking for a little cash or some jewelry but his "harmless" crime could easily become murder with a gun involved.

CHICAGO COPS & ROBBERS

As crime began to wreak havoc on the city, it came to the realization of many that the police officers who had been hired to offer protection for the citizens were hardly better than the criminals themselves. The Chicago Police Department has been plagued for many years by allegations of corruption and graft -- allegations that were well deserved during the turbulent years of Prohibition -- but in the early years of the city, the complaints about the police force were mostly due to a lack of confidence in their abilities. The job requirements for law enforcement positions were rudimentary at best and it was necessary for the policemen on the beat to be tough and for this reason, other problems were often overlooked in favor of brutality. The behavior of many  officers, which ranged from graft taking to covert alliances with criminals, generated public mistrust of policemen at large. Undoubtedly, there were many brave, upstanding and conscientious men in the ranks but a bad reputation was earned for the force by the men who were inclined toward violence or eager for a handout. The good men on the police force often faced an uphill battle from the late 1800's through the early decades of the Twentieth Century.

Chicago had no police officer of any kind until the fall of 1825, when Archibald Clybourne, a native of Virginia and one of the founders of Chicago's meat-packing industry, was appointed the constable of Peoria County, a huge wilderness tract that included all of northeastern Illinois. There is no way that any one person could have possibly have patrolled this entire region, even though the white population of the area amounted to less than 100 people at the time. The records say that Clybourne never made an arrest and his official duties consisted of little more that attending the frontier courts and serving documents that were required by the courts.

There is no mention of a police official in the roster of town officials at the time of the first municipal election in 1833 and nothing to indicate that there was a police force of any kind for another two years. The peace in the settlement was kept by Constable Reed and a mysterious figure referred to in historical records as only "Officer Beach", who carried the keys to the jail. Crime was discouraged by the placement of signs and placards that were posted at prominent street corners, which notified the residents that violations of law were punishable by fines and that one-half of the fine would be paid to those who informed on the lawbreakers. Those unable to pay their fines were fitted with a ball and chain and were forced to work on the streets for various lengths of time.

The city's first policeman was O. Morrison, about whom nothing is known, save for the fact that he was elected to the position in 1835 and again in 1836. In 1837, John Shrigley was elected High Constable, an office that had been created when Chicago became a city. Samuel J. Low took over the position (also called Chief of the City Watch) in 1839 and three assistants were appointed, although the city charter allowed for as many as six. This same type of organization was maintained over the next 15 years, when Chicago's police force never numbered more than nine men. Needless to say, the officers were greatly outnumbered by the population of the city, which ranged from 4,500 to nearly 80,000 during that same time period. Is it any wonder that Chicago gained its "wide open town" reputation?

Needless to say, it was impossible for such a small body of men to control the crime of the entire city and yet Chicago had nothing better than the constable and watchmen system until 1855, when the city council adopted ordinances that created an actual police department. Cyrus P. Bradley, a prominent volunteer fireman and later a famous private detective and member of the Secret Service, was appointed as the first Chief of Police. Three precincts were formed, stations were established and about 80 officers were hired. These officers had no insignia to designate their position until 1857, when Mayor John Wentworth issued leather stars and allowed the cops to carry heavy canes in daytime and batons at night. Each man was also equipped with a "creaker", a sort of loud rattle that was later replaced by a whistle. In 1858, Mayor John Haines changed the leather star to brass and introduced the first uniform, which was a blue frock coat and a blue hat with a gold band. He also hired another 20 or so men.

Chicago's new police force received its baptism of fire during the infamous Lager Beer Riot in 1855, the city's first serious disturbance. The riots were the result of German beer hall owners refusing to pay unfair taxes that were being forced on them by the city's separatist mayor of the time, Levi Boone. Their protests erupted into violence and a mob of over 400 Germans marched on the court house and then stopped traffic on Randolph and Clark Streets. A large number of police officers charged the mob with clubs and they retreated back to the north side.

The Germans returned again to face not only all of the police officers on the force, but also 150 special deputies who had been pressed into service. Later in the afternoon, a mob of about 1,000 men, armed with shotguns, knives, clubs and sticks marched down Clark Street in two groups. The first group swarmed onto the Clark Street Bridge and under orders from the mayor, the bridge-tender swung the draw and prevented the second portion of the mob from following. The rioters threatened the bridge-tender, pleaded with him and even offered bribes. Eventually, the mayor ordered the bridge to be opened again and the protestors swarmed across to be met by a solid line of 200 police officers and deputies. With cries of "Shoot the Police!" the mob attacked. To the credit of the officers, they stood firm and despite the injuries that followed, only one man was known to be killed. For several days after, the public square was guarded by two companies of militia with artillery, but no further disturbances occurred.

It wasn't long before Chicago's police department became an extension of the local political machine and the men hired for law enforcement jobs depended on the success of their party at election time to retain their jobs. Before the first civil service laws were enacted in Chicago in 1895, an incoming mayor could simply fire everyone on the police force and replace them with men sympathetic to his new administration. The biggest problem was that the Chicago political machine was composed of liquor men, gamblers and tavern owners who saw politicians, and the police force, as a necessary evil. They controlled the politicians and politics, in turn, controlled the police.

This made law enforcement in Chicago haphazard as best and a policeman's lot was never a happy one. The hours were long, pay was minimal and the prospects of an early death were many. In addition, he had to be resourceful because his livelihood depended on not only how well he did his job, but how well he pleased his masters too. In many cases, the policeman's choices were not guided by any moral obligation to the badge but by a desire to survive the complexities of local politics. An officer who was singled out for an appointment by the ward boss, who had a connection with the chief or some higher up in the department, would be beholden to the party and would pay for it in a variety of ways. He would likely be called on to offer protection to some crony of an alderman, to perform political work or to sell tickets to a fund-raising event that would line the pockets of the politician. The rare honest policeman in those days quickly realized the peril of his convictions when he attempted to arrest gamblers or brothel owners who were protected. One wrong step could mean a transfer to what was called the "woods", which meant working midnight shift in a precinct far from home. The officers who protected these establishments though could expect job longevity and the gratitude of his sponsor's political party -- as long as they continued to be successful on the next election day.

As mentioned already, many of the police officers in these days were hired more for their brutality and willingness to work for the party than for their knowledge or skills. Because of this, most officers were the product of poor neighborhoods or drawn from the blue-collar trades. The Irish, because of their familiarity with political strife in their homeland, gravitated toward public sector occupations in America. Such jobs were considered to be low status but for the Irish, were a step up from poverty and they began filling the open political positions in increasing numbers after 1860. By 1865, one-third of the Chicago Police Department was Irish and for many of these immigrant families, police work was multigenerational and one of good social standing in their parish neighborhoods. Even today, fourth and fifth generation Chicago police officers, with little or no connection to green hills of Ireland, faithfully gather to partake in Irish-American traditions that are sponsored by the Emerald Society.

By the late 1800's and early 1900's, Chicago's veteran street officers had become cynical and case hardened after years of patrolling the crime-ridden streets and vice districts of the city. They soon gained a reputation for being the toughest police officers in the nation, especially during labor problems and periods of civil unrest. Their aggressive approach to the Haymarket bombings and their dealings with strikers sent a clear message that Chicago cops were not men to be trifled with. Reputations of individual men were built on the streets and Chicago newspaper columnists and crime reporters glorified the exploits of the city's most intimidating officers. By the middle 1900's, Sylvester "Two-Gun-Pete" Washington and Captain Frank Pape were said to have gunned down more felons in the line of duty than the "Wyatt Earp, Wild Bill Hickok and Bat Masterson combined."

Captain Pape served the Chicago police force for 39 years and during his career was credited with killing nine armed criminals and for solving the notorious murder case of Susan Degnan in 1946. The young girl had been snatched right out of her bedroom window and killed. The public applied intense pressure to the police force and the case was finally broken and pinned on a University of Chicago student who always maintained that he was forced to confess by ruthless police tactics. Regardless, Pape and his major crime squad served as the inspiration for the 1950's television series *M-Squad*, starring Lee Marvin as the tough as nails captain.

Perhaps the hardest things for police officers of the era to deal with, outside of the internal politics of the department, were the moral ambiguities of the age. In the fashionable residential and commercial districts, the police were expected to close down the gambling parlors and to make sure that the prostitutes stayed off the streets. However in what was called the "tenderloin" district, vice was allowed to flourish and existed in such a way that police graft was tolerated, if not expected. Everyone seemed to be "on the take" and various services required various forms of payment. Desk sergeants in the various districts maintained index files that contained pertinent information about the prostitutes who worked in their area. A young woman who joined the life was required to come in and register, and pay the required fee, before she could start making her living in one of the local dives. Police inspectors and captains became rich and powerful in their respective neighborhoods, thanks to the nature of the city politics that allowed vice to exist. Corrupt arrangements between the police and the criminal element were inevitable given the contradictions and the lack of definite rules against them.

Over a period of nearly 100 years after the formation of the police department, any improvements in the training, equipment or deployment of the men came following the detection of some scandal in the department. The resulting changes were almost always in reply to a cry for reform from the public, the press or the clergy. Many wondered why the improvements had to be forced in such a way but there seemed to be no other way to accomplish anything, as the department and the local political machine refused to police themselves. Even the employment of a civilian review board was judged a failure and disbanded. In 1890, five commissioners were appointed to keep an eye on several district captains who were involved in dealings with gamblers and underworld figures. The scandal was exposed in the newspapers a year later, but it did little to change anything. In 1911, these same commissioners were exposed for accepting their own bribes and the Civil Service Commission recommended that the board of five commissioners be replaced with three deputy inspectors, including one civilian, who would be responsible for upholding public morals. More scandal followed when the civilian deputy became involved in the accidental shooting death of a uniformed officer in 1914. The department was again thrown into an uproar and the city council buckled to pressure from the mayor and disbanded the commission in 1919.

The city continued looking for answers but major reorganizations in 1920 and 1931 failed to halt the citywide corruption that took place during Prohibition, a period in which over half the city police department was estimated to have received payoffs. In the long run, the unwelcome intrusion of civilian boards into the department could not succeed and neither could the attempts to recruit "spies" from within the ranks to report on illegal activities. For more than 100 years, graft, bribery and political back dealings continued at the highest levels of the police department. Promotions and appointments were given to those who did favors or who possessed the ability to pay. Captains continued to become wealthy and ordinary patrolmen, not to miss out on the possibility of graft, began shaking down ordinary motorists during routine traffic stops.

A 1961 *Chicago Tribune* article has been extensively quoted from over the years concerning this problem and it included an interview with a Chicago driver who recalled his own encounter with some less than honest cops. "I remember some years ago, driving to work before dawn and being stopped by a police officer who told me I'd been speeding. I hadn't, by they said that would have to take me in. I told them to go ahead but instead they asked me how much money I had. I told them that I had exactly one buck for lunch. They said 'Okay, we'll settle for that, we have to eat too!' And by golly, they took it."

Modern corruption in the department reached its highest point (or rather, its lowest!) in 1960, when a gang of eight officers in the Summerdale Police District organized a burglary gang that looted north side businesses that they were supposed to be protecting. The resulting scandal not only embarrassed Mayor Richard J. Daley but exposed the Chicago Police Department to ridicule that it is still enduring today. Summerdale became a black eye for the department but it did set into motion another reform movement, although this one would finally separate the force from the image of the past.

Orlando Winfield Wilson was chosen by a panel as the man to restore order and competence to the department. Wilson was a member of the faculty of the California School of Criminology and had attained international prominence in police administration. He now turned his much-needed attentions to the Chicago Police Department and began implementing many changes. Younger, college-educated men were recruited and promoted and officers were encouraged to complete their degree work and pursue graduate studies without fear of ridicule from the old-timers, many of whom were forced into retirement as the Summerdale scandal continued to unfold. The cops who ran their districts under the old methods of political favors and graft were finally being forced out. He also consolidated 38 police districts into 21, diminishing the power of the local aldermen when it came to influence hiring. He also closed down six dilapidated station houses from the 1800's and changed Chicago policing forever by placing the beat cop in a squad car, instead of walking the streets.

Perhaps the main thrust of Wilson's reforms though was the creation of the Internal Investigations Division (IID), which was meant to "police the police" and to root out corruption in the force. The unit (later re-named Internal Affairs Division -- IAD) was a daring move for Chicago, a police force that had always imposed stiff sanctions on "rats" and lived by a rather dubious "code of honor" that allowed no one to inform on brother officers, no matter how heinous the grievance. The success of the IAD unit is plainly visible in the decline of major scandals since the time of its inception -- but it by no means stopped corruption completely.

In 1973, Captain Clarence E. Braasch, and 18 men in his command, at the East Chicago Avenue District were indicted for collecting payoffs gained from shaking down tavern owners along Rush and Wells Street. No one had seen this coming either. Braasch was a family man and father and had been a shining light in the Wilson administration with a number of commendations and honors.

That same year, Captain Mark Thanasouras, and 18 men who served under him, in the Austin District were indicted on charges of extorting thousands of dollars from tavern owners who wanted to operate in the neighborhood. Thanasouras was another rising star under Wilson but had been exposed for collecting graft in 1968 by newspaper columnist Bob Wiedrich. It took the department five years to make the charges stick and in 1973, he was relieved of his command. Thanasouras pled guilty and received a three and a half year prison sentence. He was sent to the Terminal Island Prison and into a living hell. Prison turned out to be a nightmare for the former cop and he offered to provide information about police and mob corruption in return for a shorter sentence. After 18 months, he was back out on the street, working as a bartender at the L & L Club in north suburban Lake Bluff and providing testimony that resulted in the indictments of four Austin District watch commanders. He was planning to tell more but was shotgunned to death at his girlfriend's home in the early morning hours of July 21, 1977.

Another scandal hit the department in 1982, when 10 officers from the west side Marquette District were caught allowing a multi-million dollar drug ring to operate in their area. In 1996, the Austin District once again made the news when it was revealed that seven police officers in the district had been robbing and extorting independent drug dealers who threatened the large scale narcotics operation protected by the cops. These scandals revealed the changes that had come to corruption in the Chicago police department. It was no longer about segregated vice districts, gambling, bootlegging and prostitution but about the immense power of the drug trade. Police corruption now comes from the willingness of dirty cops to provide protection to the drug dealers in return for staggering amounts of bribe money -- sums that most officers would never see in a lifetime. This makes the work of the Internal Affairs Division and the honest police officers more difficult, but certainly not impossible.

It's true that the Chicago Police Department still has a long way to go before it can remove the tarnished image that it gained in years gone by but great strides have been made over the last few decades. The department today is better managed and a far superior force than at any point in its history. Unfortunately, so many people only think of the corruption and the graft of the past when they think of the Chicago Police Department and they forget about the brave and honorable men and women who have been the majority of the force, even from the beginning. Perhaps in the future, we'll see that image begin to change.

BLOODY MAXWELL

The neighborhood of the old Maxwell Street police district has never been short on either dark history or hauntings. This notorious district earned the nickname of "Bloody Maxwell" in the early 1900's, thanks to the escalating murder rate. All matter of vice could be found here and one of the most famous spots in the district was "Deadman's Corner" -- a moniker whose meaning should be obvious to the reader. The community was a thriving one though, consisting of row after row of tenement houses that were filled with Greeks, Jews and Italians. All of these are gone now, having been consumed by the University of Illinois at Chicago, but their memories remain -- as do the legends.

Chicago's old Maxwell Street

By the time that the Maxwell Street police station became known to people all over America, it had already garnered a nearly century old reputation in Chicago. In the early 1980's, television watchers saw the station house appear as the fictional *Hill Street Blues* precinct house on NBC, however people in Chicago had long been privy to the rumors, stories and lore of the old building.

It had been constructed in 1889 to replace the old Second Precinct station, which had been located in the heart of the "Terror District" and abandoned that same year. This new building cost more than $50,000 to build from red and gray stone and it was meant to be a refuge in the "wickedest police district to be found within the confines of civilization."

Captain William Ward, who commanded the column of police officers who were blown up by the Haymarket Square bomb in 1886, was placed in command of Maxwell Street that first year. It had been because of the unrest at Haymarket Square that the police force had greatly expanded its numbers and had built two new stations, including the one at Maxwell Street. The station was meant to serve as a threat to worker unrest and also as a buffer between the central business district and the heavily populated immigrant areas that encroached on the business district from the south and west.

At that time, thousands of Jews, Italians, Greeks, Poles, Irish, Germans and other refugees from Europe came to the frenzied neighborhoods along Roosevelt Road, Taylor Street and Halsted. This was during the great wave of immigration that occurred between 1880 and 1920 and with the new arrivals came poverty, violence and crime. The *Chicago Tribune* said that the all around the neighborhood "are corners, saloons and houses that have seen the rise, the operations, and even the deaths of some of the worst criminals the land has ever known."

At the southern end of the area was the Walsh School, a public institution and the scene of one of the bloodiest feuds in American history -- a war between rival gangs of schoolboys that started in 1881 and continued for almost 30 years. During this time, several were killed and numerous others were shot, stabbed and beaten. The gangs called themselves the "Irishers" and the "Bohemians". The allegiance was not determined, as one might think, by nationality but rather by place of residence. The Irishers lived east of Johnson Street and those who lived west of Johnson were the Bohemians. For years, the boys carried knives and revolvers to school and occasionally slashed one another, or shot it out, in the classrooms, the streets and the playground. The last of the gun battles was fought in December 1905, when some 25 Irishers, led by Mike and George McGinnis, marched against an almost equal number of Bohemians, commanded by Joe Fischer. Between 40 and 50 shots were fired before the police arrived, but no one was hit. The ages of the gangsters ranged between 10 and 15 years-old and many of them were so small that they had to use both hands to raise their revolvers to fire them. For many years after this last climatic battle, every boy who attended Walsh School had to be searched before he was allowed to enter.

Just north of the Maxwell Street Station was the liquor warehouse of the six "Terrible" Genna brothers, Angelo, Pete, Tony, Jim, Sam and Mike. On the eve of Prohibition, they had been granted a special dispensation from the government to sell industrial alcohol from this location on Taylor Street. The formula for the brew had been invented by their brother-in-law Harry Spignola and the Genna's paid neighborhood residents $15 a week to cook up a home brew, which contained rotgut whiskey with caramel or coal tar added for color. The result was so vile that it actually killed the warehouse rats that were curious enough to sample it. From the filthy warehouse, the Genna's paid off the cops of the neighboring districts to leave them alone after it became apparent that the alcohol was not for "industrial" purposes. The Genna's sold the mixture for $3 a barrel, which was half the going rate that was being charged by Irish bootlegger, Dion O'Bannion, who hated the Genna's. However, the brothers managed to maintain a neutrality with not only O'Bannion but with Al Capone as well. That ended when they began selling their brew to north side barkeeps however. The Genna's had stumbled too far into O'Banion's territory and war erupted. The Genna's were all but wiped out in a few short years and the warehouse was closed down in 1926.

Around 1905, the term "Bloody Maxwell" was actually coined. Thanks to the horrific murder rate and the threats of the Black Hand, who terrorized the Italian immigrants in the neighborhood (see later in the chapter), the west side was starting to gain an even more fearsome reputation. Things were especially frightening for the immigrants here, who feared not only the criminals but the police as well. Thanks to the rumors that were circulating about the station, the immigrants were terrified of being arrested on some pretense and tossed into the rat-infested dungeon of the Maxwell Street station.

Prisoners who lacked the resources to buy their way out of this "hole" were often savagely beaten and this brutal treatment spawned many other shocking stories. For years, the prisoners in the dungeon urinated and bled into troughs that had been dug into the floors and which flowed beneath the cells of the other convicts. There were also stories of prisoners who "accidentally" fell down the two flights of stairs to the front desk, were beaten with telephone books (so as not to leave marks) and who suddenly turned up dead in their cells, even though nothing

Maxwell Street Police Station

had been wrong with them when arrested. In 1921, Health Commissioner Herman Bundsen declared the

Maxwell Street dungeon to be unfit for human habitation and a few years later, the basement was closed down. However, rumors that the dungeon continued to be used as a punishment for the worst offenders went on into the 1970's. The city of Chicago and station officials denied the charges.

The Maxwell Street Station closed down in December 1997, marking the end of an era on the west side. By this time, there was no longer a neighborhood to protect as it had long been reduced to empty lots and tennis courts by the university. The station house was saved though and is now being used by the UICC campus police as their headquarters.

Although the cops and robbers of yesterday are now gone, the legendary stories of the Maxwell Street dungeon still linger -- in more ways than one. Accounts persist in saying that the prisoners who were beaten and so hideously abused in the station's basement still linger here. As the years have gone by, police officers and passersby claim to have heard the sound of bloodcurdling screams coming from this part of the building. Moaning and crying sounds are commonplace, although when anyone checks to see who might be wandering about this darkened space, the rooms are always found to be abandoned.

Whether or not they are actually empty though is another matter entirely!

The old police station is not the only haunting that has been reported nearby. Another legend haunts this neighborhood, that of a mysterious lady in black who has been encountered walking the streets nearby. She is always seen wearing black, period clothing from the early 1900's and has been known to be a protector of local residents. Several years ago, the lady in black was featured on the television show *Unsolved Mysteries*, which documented a man who had been injured in a motorcycle accident near Maxwell Street and who was assisted by the black-clad stranger. She vanished into thin air, leaving the motorcyclist and the emergency workers who responded to the call as baffled witnesses to the event.

This was not the only time the woman has been seen and earlier residents of the neighborhood reported her for quite some time, speaking of her as a "good Samaritan" spirit, although there seems to be no real record of anything that she has done, outside of the incident with the motorcyclist and what occurred with a young Chicago police recruit in the spring of 1969.

At that time, Frank Ayers was enrolled in the Chicago Police Academy, which was located near Maxwell Street and the Dan Ryan Expressway. At that time, he had been attending the academy for several months and had gone to lunch on this spring afternoon with two other academy students. As they entered a small local restaurant, Ayers remembered seeing a white lady who was dressed in all black clothing that looked strangely old fashioned. She stood out to him because the neighborhood was predominantly African-American at the time and she was one of the few white people that he had seen on the streets.

As he stood there in doorway to the restaurant, the woman came and stood disconcertingly close to him and looked into his eyes. "Without a word or hand gesture or even a facial expression, she somehow communicated to me to hand her the pen and small note pad that I had in my upper left pocket," Ayers later recalled. He said that he did this, without really knowing why, and she took the pen and wrote something down on the notepad. Then, she looked at Ayers and began shaking her head over and over again, repeating the gesture for "no". She then thrust the pen and paper against his chest and quickly walked out of the restaurant.

Now even more confused, he looked at the note pad to see what the woman had written. Unbelievably, she had scrawled his own name and birth date on the top sheet of paper. Stranger still, Ayers swore that the scribbling was in his own handwriting -- even though he had seen the woman write it there. He quickly turned to his friends, sure that they would be as puzzled by the incident as he had been.

"Did you see what that lady just did?" he asked them.

But even though the two of them had been standing just inches away, they were oblivious to the entire thing. "What lady?" one of them replied and other looked just as bewildered by the question. They had never seen the woman at all.

Still wondering what it all meant, Ayers went into the restaurant with his friends to have lunch. He expected to forget all about the encounter but for some reason, it stayed with him and he always wondered if it meant that he should leave the police department. He began to fear that the woman had been telling him that if he did not choose a different career, police work would end his life. He eventually left the department and gradually, the incident with the woman faded from his memory. In fact, it was not until he saw the episode of *Unsolved Mysteries* about the motorcyclist who was saved by the Maxwell Street Lady in Black that he thought about her again. More than 30 years later, he became convinced that the woman that he had come into contact with outside the restaurant had been the same Lady in Black -- and that her cryptic message likely saved his own life as well.

CHICAGO'S FAMOUS CRIME & VICE DISTRICTS

By the late 1850's, Chicago was able to boast almost 1,500 businesses within its borders, dozens of banks, railroad lines, millions of dollars worth of imports and exports, 40 newspapers and periodicals, a half-dozen theaters, eighty ballrooms "where bands played from morning to night" and a still-growing population of more than 93,000 people. But not all of Chicago's accomplishments were ones to be proud of. Crime of every description had increased dramatically in just two decades and a national bank panic was spreading throughout the country, causing businesses to fail and widespread unemployment in the Windy City. This led to burglaries, shootings and holdups by bands of young men who had once been respectable laborers. They were driven, according to one lurid newspaper account "from sheer want and by the sufferings of their families to try their fortunes as garroters, highwaymen, burglars and thieves."

The newspapers published accounts of these and other criminals with almost hysterical warnings of worse to come. People became panic-stricken and the *Chicago Tribune* advocated a mass meeting of citizens to hire Alan Pinkerton and his detectives to clean up the city. This was never done but a group of businessmen did hire Pinkerton to stop gangs of vandals who were raiding the old City Cemetery on the north side, desecrating the graves and digging up the corpses to sell to medical students.

But such incidents of thievery and murder were not the real scourge of Chicago crime -- and certainly not where the questionable fortunes were being made. The real problems came from the vice and red-light districts. There has been some mention made of these districts already, like "Whiskey Row" and the "Sands", but there were many others, including some that have become legendary in Chicago history.

The Sands was called the "vilest and most dangerous place in Chicago" by the *Tribune* and by 1857 consisted of a few dozen ramshackle buildings, each housing gambling parlors, saloons and brothels, in which a charge for services ranged between 25 and 50 cents. Originally, the area, which was located on a stretch of lake shore just north of the Chicago River, catered mostly to sailors and canal men but expanded into a resort area and a hiding place for all manner of criminals. The leaders of this unsavory community were Dutch Frank, who operated a dog fights; Freddy Webster; Mike O'Brien; a burglar and former fighter; his son Mike, a pickpocket and a pimp for his four sisters; and John Hill and his wife, Mary.

The Hill's were said to be the first operators in Chicago to work the "badger game", an old-time sex swindle in which a woman picks up a man, brings him home, her husband "accidentally" comes in and catches them in the act and then demands satisfaction from the man, which comes in the form of the sucker's money. Unfortunately, John Hill had a wide jealous streak and after every con, he always tried to kill his wife for encouraging the victim in the racket to get into bed with her!

Freddy Webster, another operator mentioned, owned a brothel that was incredibly vicious, even for the Sands. One of his girls, Margaret McGinness, was said to have been neither sober nor out of the house for five years, and not to have had to have had her clothes on for three. She customarily entertained between 10 and 40 men each night. She died in March 1857 from drunkenness and hers had been the seventh unnatural death in the Sands that week.

The Sands came to an end during a period of violence that marked the tenure of Mayor "Long John" Wentworth. Long before Wentworth was elected mayor, there had already been talk of demolishing the haphazard shacks of the Sands but the land on which they stood was tied up in litigation with the courts. As the *Tribune* explained it "in view of the uncertainty of the law, the litigants were disinclined to take violent measures to eject the occupants". In other words, the land owners were too scared, or were being too well paid, to run the brothel and saloon keepers off the property. Finally though, in April 1857, William B. Ogden bought out several of the land owners and notified the denizens of the Sands to vacate the buildings and also told those who owned their own buildings that he would gladly purchase their shacks as well. A few sold out but most of the squatters vowed that they would never leave. This was reported to the Mayor and he promised to take action as soon as he could without risking bloodshed.

The opportunity came during a dog fight between one of Dutch Frank's dogs and an animal owned by Bill Gallagher, a Market Street butcher. The event was to be held at the Brighton racetrack and on April 20, every able-bodied man in the Sands accompanied Dutch Frank to the scene. Chicago legend has it that Mayor Wentworth may have arranged this fight and caused it to be advertised, but no one really knows for sure. Regardless, he did take advantage of it. Dutch Frank and his cohorts had barely left the Sands before Wentworth led a procession of about 100 well-meaning citizens, a Deputy Sheriff bearing orders of eviction, 30 or so police officers and a team of horses drawing a wagon that was loaded with hooks and chains. They managed to tear nine buildings down with hooks and chains by evening and by the time that darkness was starting to fall, they burned the rest of the district to the ground. When the male inhabitants of the Sands returned from the dog fight later that night, all they found of the district was ashes.

Unfortunately, Wentworth's plan to clean up vice in Chicago backfired though. Once the Sands was destroyed, the gamblers, criminals and whores who called the place simply crossed the Chicago River and, instead of being mostly confined to one small area, spread out all through the city.

As already explored, it was largely due to the helpless of the Chicago police force during the 1860's that the city acquired a reputation for being "the wickedest city in the United States". Attracted by the easy money of a boomtown, by thousands of soldiers on the loose with Army payrolls and by the knowledge that there was little to fear from the police, human refuse from cities all over America swarmed into Chicago.

The newcomers took over and enlarged the resorts that had been formed by the refugees from the Sands and within a year after the start of the Civil War, there was hardly a downtown street that didn't have a row of brothels, saloons, gambling dens and cheap boarding houses. The south side below Madison Street, from the lake to the river, was almost wholly occupied by the criminal class until the Great Fire finally burned them out.

One journalist of the period stated that the "very core of this corruption" was Roger Plant's resort on the northeast corner of Wells and Monroe Streets. Originally, the dive was situated in a single, two-story house but after one adjoining establishment after another was added on, the resort was extended about halfway down the block on both streets by the middle 1860's. The police called the place "Roger's Barracks" but Plant referred to it as "Under the Willow", thanks to a lone willow tree that drooped at one corner of the main building and the name stuck. The appearance of the place was further enhanced by a bright blue shade at each of the windows that bore the words "Why Not?" in gold lettering. This became a catch-phrase all over the city.

Under the Willow was described by author Fredrick Francis Cook as "one of the most talked about if not actually one of the wickedest places on the continent." It was believed that a tunnel ran from the resort under Wells Street to a number of underground dens that were located along Wells and along the south branch of the river. There were at least 60 rooms in the sprawling place and it offered just about every vice imaginable, including a saloon; two or three brothels where customers were often stripped, robbed and dumped into alleys; rooms for the men to meet the ladies of the night; cubicles that were rented to streetwalkers; and hideaways that were used by various species of crooks.

The landlord of the place was Roger Plant, a diminutive Englishman who only stood an inch above five feet and never weighed more than 100 pounds. In spite of this, he came to be regarded as a deadly fighter, adept with all kinds of weapons, especially his teeth. Ordinarily, he carried a knife and a gun secreted on his person but when he got drunk, he would put aside his weapons and ceremonially drench the willow tree outside with a mixture of whiskey and water. He managed to keep his customers in line but he was in turn dominated by his wife, a huge woman who tipped the scales at nearly 300 pounds. She was said to frequently tuck her spouse under one arm and spank him with her free hand. Mrs. Plant organized the affairs of the prostitutes in the resort and when she was not busy with this, she was producing children. No one knows the exact number of children the Plant's raised, but it was generally believed to be about 15. Each of them learned to pick pockets not long after learning to walk!

Under the Willow operated for about ten years with no interference. In 1868, having made more money that he ever expected to, Plant closed the resort, bought a house in the country and began living a respectable life.

The Great Fire in 1871 destroyed the worst of the city's vice areas, burning the dangerous saloons and the disease-ridden brothels but within half a decade after the rebuilding of Chicago had begun, a dozen vice districts that were even more vicious had been established. To the inhabitants and to the police, they were known by colorful nicknames like the Black Hole, Little Cheyenne, the Bad Lands, Satan's Mile, Hell's Half Acre, the Levee and more. Most of these areas were on the west and south sides and became places of renown in the annals of Chicago's criminal history.

THE BLACK HOLE

The infamous Black Hole district was a group of saloons, cribs and bordellos that were reserved for black customers only. They were located near Washington and Halsted Streets in the heart of a vice district that was bounded by Sangamon, Halsted, Lake and Monroe Streets. The "pride" of the Black Hole in the 1870's and 1880's was a placed called Noah's Ark, on Washington near Halsted. The place was described as a "queer old three story mansion" that was owned by Chicago alderman Jacob Beidler, a wealthy lumber dealer from a rich and devoutly religious family. The place was said to be a seething hive of corruption with two saloons and a half dozen brothels. A former drawing room of the old mansion had been curtained off into cubicles that were just large enough to hold single cots. These cribs were rented out to streetwalkers, who charged from 25 to 35 cents to a customer for a tumble -- depending on whether he removed his shoes or not. Noah's Ark became quite famous for robberies during its time in operation, thanks to the methods devised by two of the denizens of the place. One of the girls, seizing on a moment when she knew the man was completely distracted, would hold him by the arms while her partner cracked him over the head. Once relieved of the contents of his pockets, he was hurriedly deposited in the alley outside.

The largest whorehouse in the Black Hole was Ham's Place, a second floor dive that was famous for its company of uniformed women who were always clad only in white tights and green blouses. No one knew who really owned the place but it was believed to be an establishment under the control of Diddie Biggs, who ran another brothel on Halsted, in which the most popular girl was a midget named Julie Johnson. A member of the staff at Ham's was a 300-pound piano player named Del Mason. Her husband, a thief known as both Joe Dehlmar and Bill Allen, became a central figure in what some have called one of the most memorable incidents in the history of the Chicago Police Department.

On November 20, 1882, Bill Allen became involved in a fight that resulted in the death of one black man and serious injuries for another. Later that same night, Allen also killed a police officer named Clarence E. Wright when Wright attempted to arrest him in a shack at Washington and Clinton Streets. Allen fled to the basement of Diddie Biggs' whorehouse on Halstead and hid out there until December 3. On that day, Allen gave Julie Johnson a nickel and told her to go out and buy a newspaper for him. Instead, she informed the police of where Allen was hiding and for $2 sold the nickel to the famous gambler Mike McDonald, who thereafter carried the coin as a lucky piece. The coin turned out to be anything but lucky for Bill Allen.

A patrolman named Patrick Mulvihill followed up on the information provided by Julie Johnson and went straight to the brothel basement. Before he could get inside though, Allen opened fire on him through a window and then fled down an alley. Help was summoned from the closest precinct station and within a half hour, about 200 policemen had shown up and were ripping apart the Black Hole in a search for the fugitive. Meanwhile, word spread that the man who killed a police officer had been flushed out and was loose and a mob began to form. According to reports, as many as 10,000 armed men soon joined the police in the hunt.

Late that same afternoon, Allen was discovered hiding in a feedbox in the back yard of a house on Kinzie Street. Shots were fired and before he could flee, the fugitive was gunned down by Signal Sergeant John Wheeler. Allen's body was then dumped into a patrol wagon and taken to the DesPlaines Street station. Conflicting reports started to circulate though, saying that Allen had been captured instead of killed and when the patrol wagon reached the station, it was met by an angry mob. Shouts and cries demanded that the dead man be taken from the wagon and lynched!

As the crowd worked itself into a frenzy, Captain John Bonfield and a half dozen officers frantically tried to fend off the mob with revolvers. At a break in the furor, the wagon darted into the alley next to the station and Allen's body was shunted out of the wagon and inside through a window. The mob outside grew even more heated, threatening to tear down the police station, and soon it looked as though a riot was going to break out. Chief Doyle mounted a wagon and tried to quiet the crowd. He insisted that Allen was dead but soon, hoots and yells from the crowd drowned out his pleas for calm. The enraged mob shouted that the police were concealing the killer and encouraged one another to break out the station windows and to force their way inside.

Doyle and the other officers retreated inside and it was the Chief who finally figured out the best way to calm the situation. Allen's body was stripped naked and placed on a mattress in front of the barred windows so that it could be seen from the alley. Then, he and his men forced the crowd outside into a line and spent the afternoon filing them down the alley and past the window so that each of them could get a glimpse of the dead man. An eerie silence fell over this grim procession as one person after another filed past the bloody and bullet-riddled body of the black man. Not surprisingly, the crowd grew larger instead of smaller as the word spread of the display. After dark, a gas jet was used to illuminate the scene and the procession lasted all through the night and into the next morning.

Allen's body remained on display for 48 hours and then, after an inquest was held, it was offered to his wife, Del Mason, for a funeral. She refused it. "I wouldn't give a dollar to help bury the stiff!" she reportedly said.

THE BAD LANDS & LITTLE CHEYENNE

There were few who could tell the difference between where the Bad Lands ended and Little Cheyenne began. They were both located on Clark Street between Van Buren and Twelfth but the police considered the section south of Taylor Street to be the worst, so they dubbed the area the Bad Lands. The whole stretch of Clark Street was described by police detectives as being "about as tough and vicious a place as there was on the face of the earth."

The area was filled with saloons, dance halls and brothels and one of the most famous characters of the Bad Lands was Black Susan Winslow, who ran a brothel in a broken down, two-story shack on Clark Street, under the approach to the Twelfth Street viaduct. The roof of the place was level with the sidewalk, so entrance had to be gained by way of a rickety staircase. Winslow paid $40 a month in rent for the place, except during the 1893 Columbian Exposition, when the price was raised to $125. She employed from two to five girls to live with her and they employed all manner of methods of attracting the attention of men passing along the sidewalk. For a long time, they would ring a sheep bell and then started setting off an alarm clock at regular intervals. Then (for some reason) began tapping on the windows and hissing like snakes. Finally, they rigged up an electric battery and attached it to the figure of a woman with a hinged arm. The figure would strike the window and then swing back again, making a motion to theoretically invite customers inside.

There were so many complaints made about robberies at Black Susan's that scores of arrest warrants were issued for her over the years. But every officer who attempted to actually arrest her returned to the station house with no idea as to how he was actually going to do so. The problem was that Winslow weighed over 450 pounds and was wider than any door or entrance of her brothel. Officers often wondered how she could have gotten inside in the first place! The problem was finally solved by Clifton R. Woolridge, the famous police detective of the 1890's who billed himself as the "Sherlock Holmes of Chicago". He made it a mission to take Winslow into custody and so he journeyed to her bordello in a patrol wagon, passing through an alley to the back door. After reading the arrest warrant to Winslow, who laughed at him the entire time, he removed the back door from its hinges and using a handsaw, cut out the frame and about two feet of the wall. Then he placed two oak planks, each about 16 feet long and a foot wide, on the door sill and on the rear end of the wagon. One of the horses was unhitched and a heavy rope was attached to the animal's collar and the other end was looped around Black Susan's waist. At Woolridge's command, the horse lurched forward and pulled the enormous woman from her chair. She was dragged about three feet up the planks before she began to scream. Woolridge had used rough timber and Black Susan was now pierced with splinters. Finally, she agreed to enter the wagon on her own and thundered gloomily up the planks. As they rode to the police station, Winslow lay prone on the floor of the police wagon while one of her girls carefully removed the splinters from her large behind.

"After this", Woolridge later wrote, "the police had no more trouble with Susan Winslow."

Little Cheyenne was named in honor Cheyenne, Wyoming, which was considered to be the toughest of the "railroad end towns" that sprang up during the building of the Union Pacific like. Just north of the Bad Lands, a gin mill owned by Larry Gavin and the Alhambra, next door, were typical of the establishments in this area. The Alhambra was a place which was then called a "goosing slum", meaning that it was a small room with a low ceiling and sawdust on the floor. The liquor was of the cheapest sort and was staffed by the lowest of the area's streetwalkers. They would sit at the tables and wait for someone to buy them a drink or to make a proposal for anything else. In the 1870's, the Alhambra was run by three old women, one of whom boasted that she was once the "belle" of Mother Herrick's Prairie Queen.

Gavin's place was just as bad and was called "about as tough a place as you would want to visit" by a contemporary newspaperman. He stated that the "rickety old chairs are occupied by females even more dilapidated.... It was one of the vilest of places." The reporter took samples of liquor from Gavin's and from the Alhambra and had them analyzed. He reported that Gavin's whiskey was full of "pepper and acids" and that the Alhambra's brandy actually contained rat poison!

As bad as these places were though, they were no worse than the other joints in the district, like the Pacific Garden Saloon, Concert Hall and Oyster Parlor at Van Buren Street. This place was not as classy as it sounded and was nothing more than a typical vice district dive. Later on, the place closed down and became of all things, a religious mission. It is worth noting too that it was in this mission that famous evangelist Billy Sunday was converted and decided to quit professional baseball and become a preacher. Others included the 50 cent brothels of Nellie St. Clair and Candy Molly Jones, which gave every customer a stick of candy as a souvenir.

HELL'S HALF ACRE

The fabled Hell's Half Acre was an entire block that was bounded by Polk, State and Taylor Streets and Plymouth Place. It was said that every building here was occupied by a saloon, a bordello, a gambling den and that the area was so dangerous that police officers never entered save in pairs -- and seldom even then. The center of Hell's Half Acre's social activity as the Apollo Theater and Dance Hall, on Plymouth Place, which was noted in the 1870's and 1880's for the masquerade balls that were sponsored by the brothel musicians, or "professors". The balls became so famous because at midnight the dancers would remove not only their masks, but their clothing as well. The Apollo was in existence as late as 1910 but by the late 1890's was frequented by mostly low-class prostitutes and their pimps.

In the middle of Hell's Half Acre was Dead Man's Alley, a narrow passage that ran from Polk to Taylor Street between State and Plymouth Place. The dark and forbidding passage was always filled with trash and scattered debris and on one side of it were a number of abandoned carriages that were used by prostitutes. The alley was also frequented by thieves and cut throats and a man who dared to walk through it, having no business there, was almost inevitably robbed. For more than a decade, the leader of the gang that operated in this area was a man named Henry Foster, who was better known as Black Bear. His usual method of robbery was to sneak up on a passerby from behind, wrap his massive arms around him, fling him to the ground and then rifle through his pockets. This type of strong arm work was done by Foster and male members of the gang but the "brains" behind the operation was a skinny woman named Minnie Shouse, who lured men to the mouth of the alley and then divided the loot of those foolish enough to follow her into the shadows. She was arrested more than 300 times in a half dozen years but usually escaped punishment by returning a portion of the stolen money or by paying a policemen to threaten her victim with arrest for consorting with a prostitute. She managed to elude capture until early 1895, when she was finally sent to prison for robbing a farmer. Black Bear got into serious trouble not long after Minnie was locked up. He was hanged on July 1, 1895 for the murder of a saloon-keeper.

CUSTOM HOUSE PLACE

Adjacent to Hell's Half Acre, and almost a part of it, was Custom House Place. During the Civil War, there had been perhaps eight or ten brothels in the northern part of this district but after the Great Fire, this portion of the area was mostly taken over by businesses and the vice moved south of Harrison Street. The Custom House vice district that became renowned as one of the most famous red-light districts in America, sprang from the ashes of the Great Fire. For nearly 30 years, the area would be regarded as a blight on the downtown area. Like most segregated vice areas, where gambling, liquor and prostitution are indulged, the Custom House thrived on not only its proximity to the railroads but to an alliance with the police as well. The closest station could be found at the nearby Armory station and they turned a blind eye to questionable activity in the district, for a price, of course.

The Dearborn Street Station was essential to vice operations on the Custom House Place district.
(Chicago Historical Society)

The Custom House district existed between Harrison Street on the north and Polk Street and the Dearborn train station to the south. It is an area more popularly known as "Printer's Row" today. The boundaries of the area tended to change and expand with the opening of each new saloon or house of ill repute. It also tended to shrink when any of the owners neglected to make their protection payments. Such absent-mindedness was usually followed by a police raid.

The Dearborn Station became essential to operations in the area as it made a perfect recruiting spot for prostitutes during the gaslight era. Naive young women who stepped off the train were often greeted by one of the army of "pimps" who waited in the station. From that point, they were introduced to immoral acts and lured into the "scarlet patch" of the Custom House district.

The most infamous bordello here was Carrie Watson's place on South Clark Street. Despite the seediness of the area, the beautiful Miss Watson's "house" enjoyed a wide reputation for being a charming place, with

Carrie having 60 women in her employ. Over the years, she has become a character of legend in the annals of Chicago vice and her beginnings in Chicago have long been the subject of fascination.

Caroline Victorian Watson was the daughter of an upper middle-class family in Buffalo, New York, where she was born in 1850. According to the lore, she grew up and saw her older sisters and their friends doing little more than eking out a living working in stores or as servants. Knowing that such a life was not for her, Carrie was said to have taken stock of her capabilities and decided that her greatest opportunity lay in the field of prostitution. So, in 1866, sixteen years-old and still a virgin, she came to Chicago and became an inmate of a brothel called the Mansion in order to learn the business and to prepare herself for her future career as a madame. She remained in the house for two years, hoarding away her money and learning the ways of the customers.

When madame Annie Stewart left Chicago in 1868 after the killing of a police officer, Carrie Watson took over the lease of her bordello on South Clark Street, between Polk and Taylor, and immediately installed new beds and furnishings and new girls as well. She later bought the building with the help of her security man, Al Smith, who ran a saloon and gambling house up the street. Annie Stewart had run her brothel as a wide-open operation, admitting any customer who came calling, but from the beginning, Carrie catered exclusively to the carriage trade and was just beginning to build up a wealthy clientele when the Great Fire disrupted businesses of every type and description. According to legend, the house was destroyed by the fire but in fact, it was almost two blocks south of the burned area and was not damaged.

Early in 1873, Carrie made extensive alterations to the property and when they were completed, re-opened what must have been the finest resort of its kind in America. The three-story brownstone mansion had five parlors, more than 20 bedrooms, a billiard room and reportedly, a bowling alley in the basement. The furniture was expensively upholstered, imported rugs covered the floors, the walls were hung with rare artwork and European tapestries, a three-piece orchestra played music, wine was brought into the parlors in silver buckets and served in gold goblets for $10 per bottle. The girls, which numbered 10 to 20 ordinarily but twice that during the World's Fair, received callers in silk gowns and performed on linen sheets. The business of the house was conducted with great subtlety and there was no red light over the door, no red curtains and no hawkers hustling men in off the street.

Carrie's brothel operated on South Clark Street for nearly 25 years and enjoyed worldwide fame thanks to its high prices, the loveliness of the ladies who worked there and the luxurious surroundings of the building. Carrie Watson herself, who was extremely rich by the time she retired, was renowned for her silks and diamonds, her two white carriages with bright yellow wheels, her charities and the fact that she paid a larger personal property tax than most Chicago millionaires. Shang Andrews' *Sporting Life* stated with enthusiasm that "In all the world, there is not another Carrie Watson!"

There were other resorts in Custom House Place that were not so elegant or refined though. Of all of the brothels in the red-light districts, the ones that gave the police the most trouble were the "panel houses", which were more robbing dens than brothels. Often an unsophisticated visitor would stumble into one of these places, where he might be drugged and tied up while an accomplice slipped through a hidden panel in the wall and liberated him of his valuables. More often, the secret panels hid thieves with long hooks who could lift a customer's wallet from pants hanging on the bed post while he was "in the act". Few of these victims would report the robbery to the police, lest they suffer the humiliation of having their names printed in the newspaper.

This system of robbery was said to have been devised by a notorious New York thief and brothel-keeper known as Moll Hodges, who operated several panel houses in New York and later in Philadelphia. The first such resort in Chicago was opened at Clark and Adams Streets around 1865 by Lizzie Clifford, who worked for Hodges in New York. Clifford's house was destroyed during the Great Fire and Chicago seemed to be free of them until the middle 1880's, when they began to appear again in large numbers. By 1890, there were almost 200 of them, most on Custom House Place and in Hell's Half Acre. As much as $10,000 was often reported being taken from panel houses at the Harrison Street police station in a single night as the officers logged from 50 to 100 complaints. One can only wonder how many robberies were never reported at all. In 1896, the police managed to shut down 52 panel houses and they closed about 45 more in 1898. During that same year, the keepers of about 28 of these places were arrested and while there is no record to say that any of them were ever punished, by centering the attack on such establishments, the police soon put an end to the business.

By the time of the Columbian Exposition in 1893, Chicago had become known as the "Paris of America" for its many illicit attractions. Reformist W.T. Stead, in his book *If Christ Came to Chicago*, counted 37 bordellos, 46 saloons, 11 pawnbrokers, an opium den and numerous gambling parlors in the Custom House district while writing his expose on Chicago vice.

The official stance on such districts was to leave them alone, as long as the operators, thieves and undesirables stayed in the district and kept to themselves. However, this was rarely the case. Granted a wide berth by city officers, the dealers in vice exploited the situation with prostitutes being arrested in the theater district and posing as sales girls in reputable stores. By 1903, conditions had become intolerable and reformers would no longer stand for it. A wave of criminal indictments, pushed through by church groups and the mayor himself, sent the vice operators reeling. Most of them moved to the South Side Levee District (which was discussed in an earlier section about Chicago politicians), where they were welcomed with open arms. The Custom House Place Levee had vanished completely by 1910.

After that, the deserted area was slowly taken over by commercial printing houses and bookbinderies, creating the name the district bears today, "Printer's Row". Eventually, the printing houses joined the bordellos and they too faded away. The area finally gained its dignity around 1979 when it converted into the condominium and rental community that exists today. The railroad freight yards have also disappeared, although Dearborn station remains. It has been converted into a small shopping mall, serving the residents of this quiet street. The Custom House Levee is now only a memory.

THE MURDER CASTLE
H.H. Holmes -- The Monster of 63rd Street

H. H. Holmes - Regarded as America's First Real Serial Killer

Today, the neighborhood of Englewood is a part of Chicago but in the late 1800's, it was a quiet, independent community on the southern outskirts of the Windy City. It was a tranquil place and the abode of housewives and shopkeepers. Among these decent folk was a "Mrs. Dr. Holden", as the newspapers mysteriously referred to her, who ran a drugstore at 63rd and Wallace. There was almost too much trade for the woman to handle, as Englewood was rapidly growing, as so many of Chicago's suburbs were in those days. She was delighted, therefore, to find a capable assistant who said that his name was Dr. Henry H. Holmes. He turned out to be a remarkable addition to the place.

In 1887, a druggist was a chemist and most drugstores were rather crowded places that were stocked with all manner of elixirs and potions. When Dr. Holmes compounded even the simplest prescription, he did so with a flourish, as if he were an alchemist in the midst of some arcane ritual. His long, pale fingers moved with a surgeon's skill, his handsome face grew intense and his blue eyes grew bright. But he was no means a socially inept scientist, he was a gentleman of fashion and charming of manner. His politeness and humorous remarks brought many new customers into the drug store, especially the ladies in the neighborhood. In addition, he kept a sharp eye on the account books as well and was concerned with the profit the store was making. He was, in short, the perfect assistant to the proprietress.

It was not long before Holmes seemed to be more the manager of the store and less the prescription clerk. He began to spend more and more time working with the ledgers and chatting pleasantly with the ladies who came into the place, some of whom took a very long time to make a very small purchase. Dr. Holmes became a familiar figure as he strolled with his stick down 63rd Street, the main thoroughfare of Englewood. He appeared to be heading for a leading position in the local business community.

Trade at the drug store continued to improve, making Mrs. Dr. Holden exceedingly happy. But as for Holmes, he was still not satisfied with his lot and he had many plans and visions that drove him onward. Strangely, in 1887, Mrs. Dr. Holden vanished without a trace. A short time after, Holmes announced that he had purchased the store from the widow, just prior to her "moving out west". The unfortunate lady had (not surprisingly) left no forwarding address.

Two years later, he acquired a large lot across the street from the drug store and began construction on an enormous edifice that he planned to operate as a hotel for the upcoming Columbian Exposition in 1893. There are no records to say what Holmes decided to call this building but for generations of police officers, crime enthusiasts and unnerved residents of Englewood, it was known simply by one name -- "The Murder Castle".

Henry H. Holmes, whose real name was Herman W. Mudgett, was born in 1860 in Gilmanton, New Hampshire, where his father was a wealthy and respected citizen and had been the local postmaster for nearly 25 years. Early in life, Mudgett dropped his given name and became known as H.H. Holmes, a name under which he attended medical school and began his career in crime. He was constantly in trouble as a boy and young man and in later years was remembered for his cruelty to animals and smaller children. His only redeeming trait was that he was always an excellent student and did well in school. In 1878, Holmes married Clara Lovering, the daughter of a prosperous farmer in Loudon, New Hampshire and that same year, began studying medicine at a small college in Burlington, Vermont. He paid his tuition with a tidy legacy that had been inherited by his wife. Even as a student though, Holmes began to dabble in debauchery. In 1879, he transferred to the medical school of the University of Michigan in Ann Arbor while there, devised a method of stealing cadavers from the laboratory. He would then disfigure the corpses and plant them in places where it would look as though they had been killed in accidents. Conveniently, Holmes had already taken out insurance policies on these "family members" and he would collect on them as soon as the bodies were discovered.

A few months after he completed his most daring swindle, insuring a corpse for $12,500 and carrying out the plan with an accomplice who would later become a prominent doctor in New York, he left Ann Arbor and abandoned his wife and infant son. Clara returned to New Hampshire and never saw her husband again.

After that, Holmes dropped out of sight for six years. What became of him during most of this period is unknown and later on, even Pinkerton detectives were unable to learn much about his activities in these years, although they did come across traces of his trail in several cities and states. For a year or so, he was engaged in a legitimate business in St. Paul and so gained the respect of the community that he was appointed the receiver of a bankrupt store. He immediately stocked the place with goods, sold them at low prices and then vanished with the proceeds. From St. Paul, he went to New York and taught school for a time in Clinton County, boarding at the home of a farmer near the village of Moore's Forks. He seduced the farmer's wife and then disappeared one night, leaving an unpaid bill and a pregnant landlady.

In 1885, Holmes turned up in Chicago and opened an office (he was posing as an inventor) in the North Shore suburb of Wilmette. Upon his re-appearance, Holmes filed for divorce from Clara, Lovering but the proceedings were unsuccessful and the case dragged on until 1891. This did not stop him from marrying another woman however, Myrtle Z. Belknap, who father, John Belknap, was a wealthy businessman in Wilmette. Although the marriage did produce a daughter, it was nevertheless a strange one. Myrtle remained living in Wilmette while Holmes began living in Chicago. John Belknap would later discover that Holmes had tried to cheat him out of property by forging his name on deeds. He would also claim that Holmes had tried to poison him when he was confronted about the fraudulent papers. Myrtle ended the marriage in 1889.

Stories claim that the house in Wilmette where Myrtle lived is haunted today. One has to wonder if the spirit who walks here is that of John Belknap or Myrtle herself. It's possible that her unhappy marriage, and horror as the later crimes of her husband were revealed, has caused her to linger behind.

Shortly after Holmes married Myrtle, he opened another office, this time in downtown Chicago, with the A.B.C. Copier, a machine for copying documents, which was about the only honest device that he was ever connected with. He operated from an office on South Dearborn but the copier was a failure and he again vanished, leaving his creditors with $9,000 in worthless notes.

A few months later, he began working in a drugstore in the Englewood section at the corner of 63rd and Wallace Street. The store was owned by a Mrs. Dr. Holden, an older lady, who was happy to have the young man take over most of the responsibilities of the store. Strangely, in 1887, Mrs. Holden vanished without a trace. Apparently, no one had any reason to doubt Holmes about his "purchase" of her store and she was never found when the police finally began to investigate his activities a few years later.

In 1889, Holmes began a new era in his criminal life. After a short trip to Indiana, he returned to Chicago and purchased an empty lot across the street from the drugstore. He had plans to build a huge house on the property and work was started in 1890. His trip to Indiana had been profitable and he had used the journey to pull off an insurance scheme with the help of an accomplice named Benjamin Pietzel. The confederate later went to jail as a result of the swindle, but Holmes came away unscathed.

Holmes continued to operate the drug store, to which he also added a jewelry counter. In 1890, he hired Ned Connor of Davenport, Iowa as a watchmaker and jeweler. The young man arrived in the city in the company of his wife, Julia, and their daughter, Pearl. The family moved into a small apartment above the store and soon, Julia managed to capture the interest of Holmes. He soon fired his bookkeeper and hired Julia to take the man's place. Not long after, Connor began to suspect that Holmes was carrying on with his wife, and he was right. Luckily for him, he decided to cut his losses, abandoned his family and went to work for another shop downtown.

Now that Holmes had Julia to himself, he took out large insurance polices on the woman and her daughter, naming himself as a beneficiary. Years later, it came to be suspected that Julia became a willing participant in many of Holmes' schemes and swindles. When he incorporated the jewelry business in August 1890, he listed Julia, along with her friend Kate Durkee, as directors.

By this time, much of Holmes' interest was going into the construction of the building across the street. The building was an imposing structure of three stories and a basement, with false battlements and wooden bay windows that were covered with sheet iron. There were over 60 rooms in the structure and 51 doors that were cut oddly into various walls. Holmes acted as his own architect for the place and he personally supervised the numerous construction crews, all of whom were quickly hired and fired, discharging them with great fury and refusing to pay their wages. As far as the police were able to learn, he never paid a cent for any of the materials that went into the building. In addition to the eccentric general design, the house was also fitted with trap doors, hidden staircases, secret passages, rooms without windows, chutes that led into the basement and a staircase that opened out over a steep drop to the alley behind the house.

The first floor of the building contained stores and shops, while the upper floors could be used for spacious living quarters. Holmes also had an office on the second floor, but most of the rooms were to be used for guests -- guests that would never be seen again. Evidence would later be found to show that Holmes used some of the rooms as "asphyxiation chambers", where his victims were suffocated with gas. Other chambers were lined with iron plates and had blowtorch-like devices fitted into the walls. In the basement, Holmes installed a dissecting table and maintained his own crematory. There was also an acid vat and pits filled with quicklime, where bodies could be conveniently disposed of. All of his "prison rooms" were fitted with alarms that buzzed in Holmes' quarters if a victim attempted to escape. It has come to be believed that many of his victims were held captive for months before their deaths.

The castle was completed in 1892 and soon after, Holmes announced that he planned to rent out some of the rooms to tourists who would be arriving in mass for the upcoming Columbian Exposition. It is surmised that many of these tourists never returned home after the fair, but no one knows for sure. The list of the "missing" when the Fair closed was a long one and for most, foul play was suspected. How many of them fell prey to Holmes is a mystery but no fewer than 50 people who were reported to the police as missing were traced to the place. Here, their trails ended...

A rare photograph of Holmes' "Murder Castle" in Englewood. (Chicago Historical Society)

An advertisement for lodging during the fair was not the only method that Holmes used for procuring victims. A large number of his female victims came through false classified ads that he placed in small town newspapers, offering jobs to young ladies. When the ads were answered, he would describe several jobs in detail and explained that the woman would have her choice of positions at the time of the interview. When accepted, she would then be instructed to pack her things and withdraw all of her money from the bank because she would need funds to get started. The applicants were also instructed to keep the location and the name of his company a closely guarded secret. He told them that he had devious competitors who would use any information possible to steal his clients. When the applicant arrived, and Holmes was convinced that she had told no one of her destination, she would become his prisoner.

Holmes also placed newspaper ads for marriage as well, describing himself as a wealthy businessman who was searching for a suitable wife. Those who answered this ad would get a similar story to the job offer. He would then torture the women to learn the whereabouts of any valuables they might have. The young ladies would then remain his prisoners until he decided to dispose of them.

Amazingly, Holmes was able to keep his murder operation a secret for four years. He slaughtered an unknown number of people, mostly women, in the castle. He would later confess to 28 murders, although the actual number of victims is believed to be much higher. To examine the details of the story, the reader cannot help but be horrified by the amount of planning and devious detail that went into the murders. There is no question that Holmes was one of the most prolific and depraved killers in American history.

In 1893, Homes met a young woman named Minnie Williams. He told her that his name was Harry Gordon and that he was a wealthy inventor. Holmes' interest in her had been piqued when he learned that she was the heir to a Texas real estate fortune. She was in Chicago working as an instructor for a private school. It wasn't long before she and Holmes were engaged to be married. This was a turn of events that did not make Julia Connor happy. She was still involved with Holmes and still working at the store. Not long after his engagement became official, both Julia and Pearl disappeared. When Ned Connor later inquired after them, Holmes explained that they had moved to Michigan. In his confession, he admitted that Julia had died during a bungled abortion that he had performed on her. He had poisoned Pearl. He later admitted that he murdered the woman and her child because of her jealous feelings toward Minnie Williams. "But I would have gotten rid of her anyway," he said. "I was tired of her."

Minnie Williams lived at the Castle for more than a year and knew more about Holmes' crimes than any other person. Police investigators would state there was no way that she could not have had guilty knowledge about many of the murders. Besides being ultimately responsible for the deaths of Julia and Pearl Connor, Minnie was also believed to have instigated the murder of Emily Van Tassel, a young lady who lived on Robey Street. She was only 17 and worked at a candy store in the first floor of the castle. There is no indication of what caused her to catch the eye of Holmes but she vanished just one month after his offer of employment.

Minnie also knew about the murder of Emmeline Cigrand, a beautiful young woman who worked as a stenographer at the Keely Institute in Dwight, Illinois. Ben Pietzel went there to take a drunkenness cure and told Holmes of the girl's beauty when he returned to Chicago. Holmes then contacted her and offered her a large salary to work for him in Chicago. She accepted the job and came to the Castle -- only to never leave it. Emmeline became homesick after a few weeks in Chicago. She had planned to marry an Indiana man named Robert E. Phelps and she was missing him and her family. Holmes later confessed that he locked the girl in one of his sound-proof rooms and raped her. He stated that he killed her because Minnie Williams objected to his lusting after the attractive young woman. Some time later, Robert Phelps made the mistake of dropping by to inquire after her at the Castle and that was the last time that he was ever reported alive. Holmes described a "stretching experiment" with which he used to kill Phelps. Always curious about the amount of punishment the human body could withstand (Holmes often used the dissecting table on live victims), he invented a "rack-like" device that would literally stretch a person to the breaking point.

In April 1893, Minnie's property in Texas was deeded to a man named Benton T. Lyman, who was in reality, Ben Pietzel, the already mentioned accomplice of Holmes. Later that same year, Minnie's brother was killed in a mining accident in Colorado, which is said to have been arranged by Holmes. A visit to Chicago by Minnie's sister, Nannie, may provide more evidence of Minnie's murderous ways and her willingness to go along with Holmes. In June 1893, Holmes seduced Nannie while she was staying at the Castle and had no trouble persuading her to sign over her share of some property in Fort Worth. She disappeared a month later, with an explanation that she had gone back to Texas, but according to Holmes, it had been Minnie who killed her. When Minnie found out that Nannie had been consorting with Holmes, the two of them got into a heated argument. Minnie hit her sister over the head with a chair and she died, then she and Holmes dropped the body into Lake Michigan.

A short time later, Holmes and Minnie traveled to Denver in the company of another young woman, Georgianna Yoke, who had come to Chicago from Indiana with a "tarnished reputation". She had applied for a job at the Castle and Holmes told her that his name was Henry Howard and that Minnie was his cousin. On January 17, 1894, Holmes and Georgianna were married at the Vendome Hotel in Denver with Minnie as their witness! After that, the wedding party (which apparently consisted of the three of them) traveled to Texas, where they claimed Minnie's property and arranged a horse swindle. Holmes purchased several railroad cars of horses with counterfeit banknotes and signed the papers as "O.C. Pratt". The horses were then shipped to St. Louis and sold. Holmes made off with a fortune, but it would be this swindle that would later come back and destroy him.

The threesome returned to Chicago and their return marked the last time that Minnie was ever seen alive. Holmes explained that he believed Minnie had killed her sister in a fit of passion and then had fled to Europe. The police believed him, as he was known for being an upstanding citizen and it was not until much later that he confessed to killing her too. Although her body was never found, it is believed to have joined other victims in the acid vat in the basement.

In July 1894, Holmes was arrested for the first time. It was not for murder but for one of his schemes, the earlier horse swindle that ended in St. Louis. Georgianna promptly bailed him out, but while in jail, he struck up a conversation with a convicted train robber named Marion Hedgepeth, who was serving a 25-year sentence. Holmes had concocted a plan to bilk an insurance company out of $20,000 by taking out a policy on himself and then faking his death. Holmes promised Hedgepeth a $500 commission in exchange for the name of a lawyer who could be trusted. He was directed to Colonel Jeptha Howe, the brother of a public defender, and Howe found Holmes' plan to be brilliant.

Holmes then took a cadaver to a seaside resort in Rhode Island and burned it, disfiguring the head and dumping it on the beach. He then shaved his beard and altered his appearance and returned to the hotel, registering under another name and inquiring about his friend, Holmes. When the body was discovered on the beach, he identified it as "H.H. Holmes" and presented an insurance policy for $20,000. The insurance company suspected fraud though and refused to pay. Holmes returned to Chicago without pressing the claim and began concocting a new version of the same scheme.

A month later, Holmes held a conference with Ben Pietzel and Jeptha Howe and his new plan was put into action. Pietzel went to Philadelphia with his wife, Carrie, and opened a shop for buying and selling patents under the name of B.F. Perry. Holmes then took out an insurance policy on his life. The plan was for Pietzel to drink a potion that would knock him unconscious. Then, Holmes would apply make-up to his face to make it look as though he had been severely burned. A witness would then summon an ambulance and while they were gone, Holmes would put a corpse in place of the "shopkeeper". The insurance company would be told that he had died. Pietzel would then receive a portion of the money in exchange for his role in the swindle but he would soon learn, as some many others already had, that Holmes could not be trusted!

The "accident" took place on the morning of September 4, when neighbors heard a loud explosion from the patent office. A carpenter named Eugene Smith came to the office a short time later and found the door locked and the building dark. For some reason, he became concerned and summoned a police officer to the scene. They broke open the door and found a badly burned man on the floor. The death was quickly ruled an accident and the body was taken to the morgue. After 11 days, no one showed up to claim it and so the corpse was buried in the local potter's field. Days later, the police learned that the dead man (Pietzel) had come to Philadelphia from St. Louis and the police of that city were asked to search for relatives. Within days, attorney Jeptha Howe filed a claim with the insurance company on behalf of Carrie Pietzel and collected the money. He kept $2,500 and Holmes took the remainder. He later gave $500 to Mrs. Pietzel but then took it back, explaining that he would invest it for her.

The claim was paid without hesitation and everyone got their share of the money, except for Ben Pietzel and Marion Hedgepeth. Holmes never bothered to contact the train robber again, a slight that Hedgepeth did not appreciate. He brooded over this awhile and then decided to turn Holmes in. He explained the scheme to a St. Louis policeman named Major Lawrence Harrigan, who in turn notified an insurance investigator, W.E. Gary. He then passed along the information to Frank P. Geyer, a Pinkerton agent, who immediately began an investigation.

Ben Pietzel never received his share of the money either, but even if he had, he would not have been able to spend it. What Holmes had not told anyone was that the body discovered in the patent office was not a cleverly disguised corpse, but Ben Pietzel himself! Rather than split the money again, Holmes had killed his accomplice then burned him so that he would be difficult to recognize. Holmes kept his part of the plan a secret as he and Georgianna were now traveling with Carrie Pietzel and her three children. She believed that her husband was hiding out in New York. The group was last seen in Cincinnati and then in Indianapolis on October 1. Carrie was then sent east and the children were left in the care of Holmes and Georgianna. Holmes made arrangements for Carrie to meet him in Detroit, where he assured her that her husband was now hiding. He arrived in Detroit several days before the appointed time and put the three children into a boarding house. Then, he went to Indiana and returned with Georgianna and installed her in a second boarding house. When Carrie arrived, she was lodged in yet another establishment. Then, he began moving about the country, apparently aware that the Pinkerton detective was on his trail. The journey lasted for almost two months but on November 17, 1894, Holmes turned up alone in Boston and was arrested and sent to Philadelphia.

As fate would have it though, he was not arrested for insurance fraud but for the horse swindle that he, Minnie and Georgianna had pulled off in Texas. He was given the choice of being returned to Texas and being hanged as a horse thief or he could confess to the insurance scheme that had led to the death of Ben Pietzel. He chose insurance fraud and was sent to Philadelphia. On the way there, Holmes offered his guard $500 if the man would allow himself to be hypnotized. Wisely, the guard refused.

The entire insurance scheme was now completely unraveling. A week later, Georgianna was located at her parent's home in Indiana and Carrie Pietzel was found in Burlington, Vermont, where Holmes had rented a small house for her to live in while she awaited the arrival of her family. Holmes had lived at the house with her for several days but had left angry when she questioned him about a hole that he was digging in the back yard. The police came to believe that he was digging her grave, but for some unknown reason, he chose not to kill her. Mrs. Pietzel was arrested and was taken to Philadelphia but was soon released. No charges were ever brought against her.

Detective Geyer was slowly starting to uncover the dark secrets of Henry Howard Holmes, he realized, but even the seasoned Pinkerton man was unprepared for what lay ahead. He was beginning to sift through the many lies and identities of Holmes, hoping to find clues as to the fates of the Pietzel children. At this point, he had no idea about all of the other victims. Holmes swore that Minnie Williams had taken the children with her to London, where she planned to open a massage parlor, but Geyer was sure that he was lying. In June 1895, Holmes entered a guilty plea for a single count of insurance fraud but Geyer expanded his investigation.

Throughout his questioning, Holmes refused to reveal any other explanation for what had become of Carrie Pietzel's three children, Howard, Nellie and Alice. Fearing the worst Detective Geyer set out to try and discover their fate -- and his fears soon came to realization. In Chicago, Geyer learned that all of Holmes' mail had been forwarded every day to Gilmanton, New York. From Gilmanton, it had been sent to Detroit, from Detroit to Toronto, from Toronto to Cincinnati, from Cincinnati to Indianapolis and then on from there. He followed Holmes' trail for eight months through the Midwest and Canada, stopping in each city to investigate the house that he had been renting while residing there. In Detroit, a house that Holmes had rented was still vacant and a large hole was found to have been dug in the cellar floor. Geyer was relieved to discover that it was empty.

In Toronto, the Pinkerton searched for eight days before he found the cottage at No. 16 Vincent Street that had been rented to a man fitting Holmes' description. The man had been traveling with two little girls. Holmes borrowed a shovel from a neighbor, which he claimed he wanted to use to dig a hole to store potatoes in. Geyer borrowed the same spade and when digging in the same location, found the bodies of Nellie and Alice Pietzel secreted several feet under the earth. In an upstairs bedroom, he found a large trunk that had a piece of rubber tubing leading into it from a gas pipe. He had told the girls that he wanted to play hide and seek with them, tricked them into climbing into the trunk and then had asphyxiated them.

This shocking discovery made Geyer work even harder to find what had become of Howard Pietzel. While questioning the neighbors, he learned that the Pietzel girls had told them that they had a brother who was living in Indianapolis. With this small clue, Geyer went to Indiana and painstakingly searched 900 houses for any clue of Holmes. Finally, in the suburb of Irvington, he found a house that Holmes had rented for a week. The place had been empty since Holmes' occupancy and in the kitchen stove, Geyer found the charred remains of Howard.

Now the door was open for Geyer and Chicago detectives to search Holmes' residence in the Windy City. Geyer was sure that the remaining answers that he was seeking could be found inside of the Castle. He entered the place with several police officers -- and neither Geyer nor the veteran investigators would ever forget what they found there!

Detectives devoted several weeks to searching and making a floor plan of the Castle. The bottom floor had been used by Holmes himself as a drug store, a candy store, a restaurant and a jewelry store. The third floor of the building had been divided into small apartments and guest rooms and apparently, had never been used.

The second floor however proved to be a labyrinth of narrow, winding passages with doors that opened to brick walls, hidden stairways, cleverly concealed doors, blind hallways, secret panels, hidden passages and a clandestine vault that was only a big enough for a person to stand in. The room was alleged to be a homemade "gas chamber", equipped with a chute that would carry a body directly into the basement. The investigators suddenly realized the implications of the iron-plated chamber when they found the single, scuffed mark of a footprint on the inside of the door. It was a small print that had been made by a woman who had attempted to escape the grim fate of the tiny room.

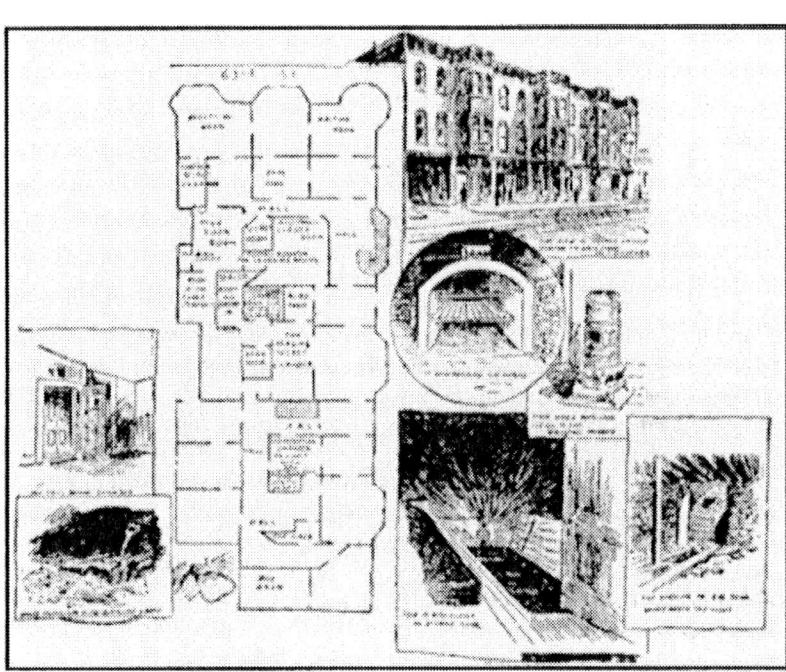

A diagram that appeared in the *Chicago Tribune* gave readers the chance to see (in lurid detail) the floor plan of Holmes' "Murder Castle", including illustrations of the secret passages, the crematory and quicklime pits.

In addition to all of the bizarre additions to the floor, the second level also held 35 guest rooms. Half of them were fitted as ordinary sleeping chambers, and there were indications that they had been occupied by the various women who worked for Holmes, by tenants during the Fair or by the luckless females Holmes had seduced while waiting for an opportunity to kill them. Several of the other rooms were without windows or could be made air tight by closing the doors. Others were lined with sheet iron and asbestos with scorch marks on the walls, fitted with trap doors that led to smaller rooms beneath, or were equipped with lethal gas jets that could be used to suffocate or burn the unsuspecting occupants.

This floor also contained Holmes' private apartment, consisting of a bedroom, a bath and two small chambers that were used as offices. The apartment was located at the front of the building, looking out over 63rd Street. In the floor of the bathroom, concealed under a heavy rug, the police found a trap door and a stairway that descended to a room about eight feet square. Two doors led off this chamber, one to a stairway that exited out onto the street and the other giving access to the chute that led down to the basement.

The "chamber of horrors" in the basement stunned the men even further. This subterranean chamber was located seven feet below the rest of the building and extended out under the sidewalk in front. Here, they found Holmes' blood-spattered dissecting table, his gleaming surgical instruments, his macabre "laboratory" of torture devices, various jars of poison and even a wooden box that contained a number of female skeletons. Built into one of the walls was a crematorium, with a heavy iron grate to hold the fire and another grate, fitted with rollers, by which a body could be slid into the flames. The crematoriums still contained ash and portions of bone that had not burned in the intense heat. A search of the ashes also revealed a watch that had belonged to Minnie Williams, some buttons from a dress and several charred tintype photographs. Under the staircase, Geyer also found a ball made from women's hair that had been carefully wrapped in cloth.

Buried in the floor, the police found a huge vat of corrosive acid and two quicklime pits, which were capable of devouring an entire body in a matter of hours. A loose pile of quicklime was also discovered in a small room that had been built into the corner. The naked footprint of woman was found embedded in the pile.

Dozens of human bones and several pieces of jewelry were found and could be traced to Holmes' mistresses. A wood burning stove in the center of the basement contained scraps of cloth and Ned Connor was summoned to the castle to identify a bloody dress that had belonged to Julia. In a hole in the middle of the floor, more bones were found. After being examined by a physician, they were believed to be the bones of a small child between the ages of six and eight. The fate of Pearl Connor was also no longer in question.

On July 20, some city workers began excavating the cellar and started a tunnel underneath 63rd Street. The hazy smell of gas hung in the air and as the men tore away one wall, they discovered a large tank or metal-lined chamber. As soon as they broke through, the basement was filled with the stench of death, driving the crew back. Noting the metal lining of the tank, they sent for a plumber and he struck a match to peer inside of it. Suddenly, the tank exploded, shaking the building and sending flames out into the basement. The men were buried in piles of debris but no one was seriously injured. The tank was lined with wood and metal and was 14 feet long, although thanks to the explosion, no one will ever know that it was used for. The only clue in the room was a small box that was found in its center. When it was opened by Fire Marshal James Kenyon, an "evil smelling" vapor rushed out. The gathered men ran, except for Kenyon, who was overpowered by the stench. According to the *New York World*, "he was dragged out and carried upstairs, and for two hours acted like one demented."

Following the excavation, and the discovery and cataloguing of Holmes' potential victims, the "Murder Castle" (as it came to be called) sat empty for several months. Not surprisingly, it drew onlookers and curiosity-seekers from all over the city. The newspapers were not yet filled with stories and illustrations about Holmes' devious crimes but rumors had quickly spread about what had been discovered there. The people of Chicago were stunned that such things could take place -- and in their glorious city! The people of the Englewood neighborhood watched the sightseers with a combination of fear and loathing, sickened over the terrible things that brought the crowds to their streets.

Then, on August 19, the Castle burned to the ground. Three explosions thundered through the neighborhood just after midnight and minutes later, a blaze erupted from the abandoned structure. In less than an hour, the roof had caved in and the walls began to collapse in onto themselves. A gas can was discovered among the smoldering ruins and rumors argued back and forth between an accomplice of Holmes' burning down the house to hide his role in the horror and the arson being committed by an outraged neighbor. The mystery was never solved, but regardless, the Castle was gone for good.

As time passed though, many would claim that the horrific memories here would linger.

The lot where the Castle was located remained empty for many years until finally, a U.S. Post Office was built on the site in 1938. There would be many in the area who had not forgotten the stories of Holmes' castle -- or the tales from people who claimed to hear moaning and crying sounds coming from the grounds. This had been a common tale in the community for years and there were those who stated that the ghosts of Holmes' victims did not rest in peace. The ground here was believed to be tainted by the death and bloodshed that had occurred on the spot and the overgrown lot was largely shunned and avoided. Most longtime residents would go out of their way to walk on the other side of the street from the area.

Even after the post office was constructed on the site where so much torture and murder took place, strange things were still reported. Passersby who walked their dogs past the new building claimed the animals would often pull away from it, barking and whining at something they could see or sense. It was something that remained invisible to their human masters, but which was terrifyingly real to the animals.

In addition, postal workers in the building had their own encounters in the place, often telling of strange sounds and feelings they could not easily explain. The location was certainly ripe for a haunting and if the stories can be believed, it was, and is, taking place!

The trial of Herman Mudgett, a.k.a. H.H. Holmes, began in Philadelphia just before Halloween 1895. It only lasted for six days but was one of the most sensational of the century. The newspapers reported it in a lurid and sensational manner and besides the mysteries of the Castle to report on, which were reported at length by several witnesses, Holmes created many exciting scenes in the courtroom. He broke down and wept when Georgianna took the stand as a witness for the state and eventually discharged his attorneys and attempted to conduct his own defense. It was said that Holmes' was actually outstanding, clever and shrewd as an attorney but it was to no avail. The jury deliberated for just two and half hours before returning a guilty verdict. Afterward, they reported that they had agreed on the verdict in just one minute but had remained out longer "for the sake of appearances".

On November 30, the judge passed a sentence of death. His case was appealed to the Pennsylvania Supreme Court, who affirmed the verdict, and the governor refused to intervene. Holmes was scheduled to die on May 7, 1896, just nine days before his 36th birthday.

By now, the details of the case had been made public and people were angry, horrified and fascinated, especially in Chicago, where most of the evil had occurred. Holmes had provided a lurid confession of torture and murder that appeared in newspapers and magazines, providing a litany of depravity that compares with the most insane killers of all time. Even if his story was embellished, the actual evidence of Holmes' crimes ranks him as one of the country's most active murderers.

He remained unrepentant though, even at the end. Just before his execution, he visited with two Catholic priests in his cell and even took communion with them, although refused to ask forgiveness for his crimes. He was led from his cell to the gallows and a black hood was placed over his head. The trap door opened beneath him and Holmes quickly dropped. His head snapped to the side, but his fingers clenched and his feet danced for several minutes afterward, causing many spectators to look away. Although the force of the fall had broken his neck, and the rope had pulled so tight that it had literally imbedded itself in his flesh, his heart continued to beat for nearly 15 minutes. He was finally declared dead at 10:25 a.m.

There were a couple of macabre legends associated with Holmes' execution. One story claimed that a lightning bolt had ripped through the sky at the precise moment the rope had snapped his neck -- but this was not the strangest one. The most enduring supernatural legend of H.H. Holmes is that of the "Holmes Curse". The story began shortly after his execution, leading to speculation that his spirit did not rest in peace. Some believed that he was still carrying on his gruesome work from beyond the grave. And, even to the skeptical, some of the events that took place after his death are a bit disconcerting.

A short time after Holmes' body was buried, under two tons of concrete, the first strange death occurred. The first to die was Dr. William K. Matten, a coroner's physician who had been a major witness in the trial. He suddenly dropped dead from blood poisoning.

More deaths followed in rapid order, including that of the head coroner, Dr. Ashbridge, and the trial judge who had sentenced Holmes to death. Both men were diagnosed with sudden, and previously unknown, deadly illnesses. Next, the superintendent of the prison where Holmes had been incarcerated committed suicide. The reason for his taking his own life was never discovered. Then, the father of one of Holmes' victims was horribly burned in a gas explosion and the remarkably healthy Pinkerton agent, Frank Geyer, suddenly became ill. Thankfully though, the diligent detective pulled through.

Not long after this however, the office of the claims manager for the insurance company that Holmes had cheated, caught fire and burned. Everything in the office was destroyed except for a framed copy of Holmes' arrest warrant and two portraits of the killer. Many of those who were already convinced of a curse saw this as an ominous warning.

Several weeks after the hanging, one of the priests who prayed with Holmes before his execution was found dead in the yard behind his church. The coroner ruled the death as uremic poisoning but according to reports, he had been badly beaten and robbed. A few days later, Linford Biles, who had been jury foreman in the Holmes trial, was electrocuted in a bizarre accident involving the electrical wires above his house.

In the years that followed, others involved with Holmes also met with violent deaths, including the train robber, Marion Hedgepeth. He remained in prison after his informing on Holmes, although he had expected a pardon that never came. On the very day of Holmes' execution, he was transferred to the Missouri State Prison to finish out his sentence. As time passed, Hedgepeth gained many supporters to his cause, including several newspapers who wrote of his role in getting Holmes prosecuted. In 1906, he finally got his pardon and was released.

Despite the claims that he had made about his rehabilitation, including that he spent each day in prison reading his bible, Hedgepeth was arrested in September 1907 for blowing up a safe in Omaha, Nebraska. He was tried, found guilty and sentenced to 10 more years in prison. He was released however when it was discovered that he was dying from tuberculosis. In spite of his medical condition, he assembled a new gang and at midnight on New Year's Eve 1910, he attempted to rob a saloon in (of all places) Chicago. As he was placing the money from the till into a burlap bag, a policeman wandered into the place for no reason, realized that a robbery was taking place and opened fire on the thief. Hedgepeth was dead before he hit the floor.

Perhaps Holmes got his revenge after all....

I was born with the devil in me. I could not help the fact that I was a murderer, no more than the poet can help the inspiration to sing -- I was born with the "Evil One" standing as my sponsor beside the bed where I was ushered into the world, and he has been with me since.
H.H. HOLMES

THE WIZARD OF CHICAGO

One of the most mysterious killers in Chicago history is one of the least remembered today. Although he did not claim as many victims as a monster like H.H. Holmes, he did arouse nearly as much public interest at the time of his crimes. Herman Billik was a stout, handsome Bohemian with piercing black eyes and like Holmes, a way with women. He was also a fortune teller who read the future for a small sum and carried on a lively trade in charms and potions. In addition, he was undoubtedly an accomplished hypnotist and claimed to possess strange occult powers that he said were inherited from his mother, who was allegedly a witch. However, when Billik carried out the murders of six people -- a father, mother and their four daughters -- he did so without supernatural forces and relied on poison instead.

Herman Billik, whose real name was Vajicek, came to Chicago in 1904 from Cleveland, where his mother had worked as a fortune teller (not as a witch) for many years. He established himself and his family, which consisted of his wife, two sons and a daughter, in a small house on West 19th Street. He immediately hung out a sign that announced that he was the "Great Billik, Card- Reader and Seer". Soon, he began to receive callers from the neighborhood and from the surrounding communities who wanted to avail themselves of his services. As his reputation spread, he began calling himself the "Wizard of Chicago" and people began to talk about the uncanny accuracy of his predictions and the worthiness of the love charms and spells that he peddled. There were also whispers of his skills as a lover as well for a number of women went away from his quarters satisfied by more than just a card reading. It's likely not a coincidence that Billik was an expert hypnotist as well as "seer".

Located three doors away from the Billik residence was the modest home of Martin Vzral, who lived there with his wife, Rose, and their seven children. Vzral was a milk dealer and one of the more prosperous inhabitants of the neighborhood in that he owned his own home, operated a successful business and had over $2,000 in the bank, a tidy sum in those days. Later, it was established that Billik had chosen the Vzral's for his victims before he moved into the neighborhood but he made no attempt to approach them for nearly a week after moving onto the street. Not surprisingly, the Vzral's knew who he was when he finally did make contact with them however, as he surrounded his movements with an air of mystery and had become the topic of gossip for blocks around. One day, he walked into the milk depot and ordered a can of milk. As Vzral filled the container, Billik started at him intensely, muttered a few words of gibberish and then said with great gravity: "You have an enemy. I see him. He is trying to destroy you."

Billik would tell him nothing else. He left the milk stand and let Vzral worry about his words for a few days. Then he called on him at his home and told him that Vzral's enemy was another milkman who lived across the street from him. Not to worry though -- Billik offered to use his supernatural powers in his new friend's defense and at the stroke of midnight, with the entire Vzral family looking on, Billik cooked a horrible smelling potion on the kitchen stove and then tossed the mixture onto the other milkman's front stoop. "Now you will prosper," he told them. "He cannot harm you."

And Vzral did prosper. Not because of any magic spells but because he was a hard-working and industrious man. He didn't see this though and credited Billik with his increase in business. He spread the word about the "wizard" even though Billik refused to accept payment for the "great service" that he had done for the milkman. The Vzral's were a strict Catholic family but were also very superstitious and saw no reason that Billik could not be everything that he claimed to be. They listened, night after night, to the litany of supernatural wonders he had allegedly performed and within a few weeks, his domination of the family was complete.

According to reports, he seduced Mrs. Vzral and her daughters and had sex with them in the same room where Martin Vzral stood watching. It was said that Mrs. Vzral's obsession with Billik was so intense that she refused to leave the house for days, fearing that he might come by while she was away. Billik also "borrowed" money from Vzral with every visit and by January 1905, had stripped him of his bank account and was siphoning off the profits from the milk business too. To provide more money to give to Billik, three of the Vzral girls went to work as domestic servants, turning over all of the money they earned to him.

Meanwhile, Billik bought new clothing, purchased a fashionable carriage and made frequent trips to New York and California, all of which the Vzral's paid for. At his suggestion, Mrs. Vzral insured the lives of her husband and four of her daughters and made Billik the beneficiary. The only members of the family who were not insured were the oldest daughter, Emma, the son, Jerry, and their infant daughter. It's no coincidence that they were the only ones to survive Billik's evil plans.

Early in March 1905, Martin Vzral began to show signs of realizing what was happening to himself and his family. He began to worry about money and the deplorable state of his business and even asked Billik for a loan -- of money that he had given to the charlatan in the first place! Billik wondered if perhaps he had pressed the milkman too hard but to cure the man's "unsettled feelings", he gave Mrs. Vzral a white powder (which he told her was a charm) and told her to put into her husband's food. A few days later, Vzral began to complain of sharp pains in his abdomen and Billik diagnosed his ailment as mere "stomach trouble". He treated him with his own concoction -- the same white powder, which was later revealed to be arsenic -- and Vzral slipped into a coma and died on March 27, 1905. Mrs. Vzral collected $2,000 in life insurance, which she immediately turned over to her depraved lover. Billik allowed her to keep $100 of it for burial expenses.

A few weeks passed and Emma and Mary Vzral, two of the late milkman's daughters, went to see Billik at Riverside, where he was telling fortunes in a tent. He showed Emma a strangely marked card and explained to her that it was a "death omen" and that "Mary will die soon". He was correct -- Mary died of "stomach trouble" on July 22, 1905. Her life had been insured for $800 and again, Billik took all but the money that was needed to pay for the poor girl's funeral.

By this time, Jerry Vzral had decided to speak up. He demanded that Billik be banned from their house and his anger provoked his mother to agree that she wouldn't see him anymore. Two days later, Jerry became very ill but his sister Emma insisted on calling a doctor and he soon recovered. The police later came to believe that Billik had not intended to kill the boy but had only administered a small dose of poison to frighten him.

In December of that same year, Billik struck again. Tillie Vzral was the next to die, succumbing again to "stomach trouble" and raising $620 in life insurance for Billik. For some reason, he stayed quiet until the following August, when 14 year-old Rose died of the same ailment. She was insured for $300. Three months later, Ella died. Her tender age of only 12 managed to garner Billik only a mere $105. As with all of the previous deaths, Mrs. Vzral turned over all of the money to the "wizard", save for the expenses for the funeral.

Now, with no more insurance money in sight, and with the milk business taken over by creditors, Billik persuaded Mrs. Vzral to put her home up for sale. She received $2,900 in cash and gave every bit of it to Billik. He took a leisurely trip to Niagara Falls with the windfall and told Mrs. Vzral that he planned to stop in Cleveland on his way back to "fix" his mother. That way, he could inherit what he claimed was a sizable fortune.

When Billik did return to Chicago, he found the befuddled remains of the Vzral family with no money, no food and waiting to be thrown out of a house that was no longer theirs to live in. On the night that Billik returned, he called on Mrs. Vzral during the early morning hours. By daybreak, she was dead.

During the two-year period that Billik preyed on the Vzral's, no one in the neighborhood realized that anything out of the ordinary was going. It seemed that the family was experiencing more than their share of misfortune but no one suspected foul play until a girl employed as a maid in a north side home was overheard by her employer remark to another servant that "someone ought to look into all of the deaths in that family". The chance remark led the woman to question the maid and she learned that the girl had known Mary Vzral and that although afraid of Billik, had been unable to resist him.

Inspector George M. Shippy first looked into the "Wizard" case. He would later go on to be the Chicago Chief of Police

The girl's mistress repeated the conversation to her husband and he was so troubled by it that he contacted a policeman that he knew who patrolled the neighborhood. The policeman included it in his daily report and eventually this report reached Inspector George M. Shippy of the Hyde Park station. He, in turn, assigned detectives to start an inquiry.

After a few days of investigation, the detectives were curious enough to obtain an order to have Mary Vzral's body exhumed. Chemists who examined the contents of her stomach discovered a number of grains of arsenic and Billik was immediately arrested. He was placed on trial in the early summer of 1907 and was found guilty of murder in the first degree. In July, he was sentenced to death but was reprieved by the governor. More appeals followed, even to the United States Supreme Court, and the case dragged out for another two years. During this time, Billik was held in the Cook County Jail, where he curiously became one of the most popular men, with prisoners and guards alike, to ever be incarcerated there.

While Billik's case was strange from the beginning, it became even more bizarre in the months to come. What was so unusual was the extraordinary fight that was waged to save the "wizard's" life. The battle was led by a Catholic priest, Father P.J. O'Callaghan of the Paulist Fathers, and a nun, Sister Rose of the Order of the Sacred Heart. They arranged mass meetings and prayer vigils and through private solicitation, raised considerable sums of money for Billik's legal expenses.

In June 1908, just before the appeal to the Supreme Court, a prayer service was held by Father O'Callaghan at the County Jail. It was reported that 400 of the prisoners attended, praying for God to save Billik from the gallows. Another service was held at the jail on June 9, at which prayers were offered by Father O'Callaghan, Billik, Billik's wife and daughter and unbelievably, Jerry Vzral! Many of the prisoners wept and moaned and Billik's cellmate, an infamous burglar, wrapped his arms around Billik, kissed him repeatedly and wept openly through the prayers. After the service was over, the prisoners presented flowers to Father O'Callaghan, Sister Rose and even the jailer.

On June 10, a petition that was signed by 20,000 people was presented to the State Board of Pardons and five rallies were held on Billik's behalf on the west side. Hundreds of women wept and screamed that he should not be hanged. They carried on to the point that many of them had to be treated for hysteria. Father O'Callaghan spoke at all of the meetings and was joined by Jerry Vzral, who tearfully claimed that he had committed perjury at Billik's trial.

Inspector Shippy was nonplussed by the rallies and weird performances. "Billik is a cold-blooded murderer of the worst type," he stated. "He is simply deceiving the people who are working in his behalf."

Guilty or not -- the mass meetings, which revolted the police officers in charge of the case -- had the desired result. Governor Charles S. Deneen commuted Billik's death sentence to life imprisonment in January 1909. He claimed to do so on the recommendation of the Board of Pardons but it's likely that the hysterical atmosphere of the rallies frightened the politicians into thinking that they would be losing votes if they failed to spare the influential "seer".

Billik was sent to the state prison at Joliet but eight years later, in 1917, the murderer of almost an entire family was pardoned by Governor Edward F. Dunne and set free. The Church, which had never let up on its crusade for him, headed a huge voting bloc in Chicago and the governor was never one to ignore any large group that threatened to vote against him or the party.

There is no record as to what became of Herman Billik after his release from prison. He vanished completely into the historical record -- leaving six victims in his wake. One has to wonder about this killer's appeal and how he managed to not only seduce and kill the greater part of one family but also how he ensnared the general public in the way that he did? How did he create a faithful following to do his bidding, beyond all reason and logic? Did he really possess some sort of strange, supernatural power or more likely, was he but one of the madmen who managed to create a "cult of personality" in modern history?

And most chilling of all -- what could Billik have accomplished if he had been of a later generation? Would he have been the leader of a "Heaven's Gate" cult? Another Charles Manson, Jim Jones or David Koresh? Or perhaps something even worse...

CHICAGO'S "THRILL KILLERS"

On an afternoon in May 1924, the sons of two of Chicago's wealthiest and most illustrious families drove to the Harvard School for boys in Kenwood and kidnapped a young boy named Bobby Franks. Their plan was to carry out the "perfect murder". It was a scheme so devious that only two men of superior intellect, such as their own, could accomplish. These two men were Richard Loeb and Nathan Leopold. They were the privileged heirs of well-known Chicago families who had embarked on a life of crime for fun and for the pure thrill of it. They were also a pair of sexual deviants who considered themselves to be brilliant, a claim that would later lead to their downfall.

Nathan Leopold had been born in 1906 and from an early age had a number of homosexual encounters, culminating in a relationship with Richard Loeb. He was an excellent student with a genius IQ and was only 18 when he graduated from the University of Chicago. Like many future killers, his family life was totally empty and devoid of control. His mother had died when he was young and his father gave him little attention.

Richard Loeb was the son of the Vice President of Sears and Roebuck and while he was as wealthy as his friend was, Loeb was merely a clever young man and far from brilliant. What he lacked in intelligence, he more than made up for in arrogance however. He fancied himself a master criminal detective but his dream was to commit the perfect crime. With his more docile companion in tow, Loeb began developing what he believed to be the perfect scheme. He also constantly searched for ways to control others. Not long after the two became friends, Leopold attempted to initiate a sexual relationship with Loeb. At first, he spurned the other's advances but then offered a compromise. He would engage in sex with Leopold, but only under the condition that the other boy begin a career in crime with him. Leopold agreed and they signed a formal pact to that affect.

Over the course of the next four years, they committed robbery, vandalism, arson and petty theft, but this was not enough for Loeb. He dreamed of something bigger. A murder, he convinced his friend, would be their greatest intellectual challenge.

They worked out a plan during the next seven months. For a victim, they chose a 14-year-old boy named Bobby Franks. He was the son of the millionaire Jacob Franks, and a distant cousin of Loeb. They were already acquainted with the boy and he went happily with them on that May afternoon. They drove him to within a few blocks of the Franks residence in Hyde Park then suddenly grabbed him, stuffed a gag in his mouth and smashed his skull four times with a chisel. He fell to the floor and bled to death in the car.

When the brief bit of excitement was over, Leopold and Loeb casually drove away, stopped for lunch and then ended up near a culvert along the Pennsylvania Railroad tracks. After dunking the boy's head underwater to make sure that he was dead, they poured acid on his face (so that he would be hard to identify) then stuffed his body into a drainpipe.

After this, they drove to Leopold's home, where they spent the afternoon and evening drinking and playing cards. Around midnight, they telephoned the Franks' home and told Mr. Franks that he could soon expect a ransom demand for the return of his son. They typed out a letter on a stolen typewriter and mailed it to Franks, intent on continuing their twisted "game". However, by the time the letter arrived, workmen had already stumbled upon the body of Bobby Franks.

Bobby Franks

Despite their "mental prowess" and "high intelligence", Leopold and Loeb were quickly caught. Leopold had dropped his eyeglasses near the spot where the body had been hidden and police had (cleverly) traced the prescription back to him. They also traced the ransom note to a typewriter that Leopold had "borrowed" from his fraternity house the year before.

After questioning, Loeb broke first. Leopold's confession came soon after. The people of Chicago, and the rest of the nation, were stunned and soon people were crying for the blood of the two killers. It was fully expected that the two would receive a death sentence for the callous and cold-blooded crime. Then, in stepped Clarence Darrow.

America's most famous defense attorney had been hired by the parent's of the two young killers. For $100,000 he had taken the case and agreed to seek the best possible verdict that he could, which in this case was life in prison. Darrow would have less trouble with the case than he would with his clients, who constantly clowned around and hammed it up in the courtroom. The newspaper photographers frequently snapped photos of them smirking and laughing in court and the public, already turned against them, became even more hostile toward the "poor little rich boys".

Police officers search the railroad culvert where Bobby Franks' body was found for clues. They found Leopold's eyeglasses in the water.

Darrow was fighting an uphill battle but he brought out every trick in the book and used shameless tactics in the case. He declared the boys to be insane. Leopold, he said, was a dangerous schizophrenic. They weren't criminals, he railed, they just couldn't help themselves! After this weighty proclamation, Darrow actually began to weep. The trial became a landmark (and some say a bad one) in criminal law. He then began to describe a detailed description of what would happen to the men as they were hanged, providing a graphic image of bodily functions and physical pain. Darrow even turned to the prosecutor and invited him to personally perform the execution.

Leopold and Loeb (center) as they left the courtroom during the trial

Darrow's horrifying description had a marked effect on the courtroom and especially on the defendants. Loeb was observed to shudder and Leopold got so hysterical that he had to be taken out of the courtroom. Darrow then wept for the defendants, wept for Bobby Franks -- and then wept for defendants and victims everywhere. The master manipulator won the case. The defendants were given life in prison for Bobby Frank's murder and an additional 99 years for his kidnapping. Ironically, after all of that, Darrow only managed to get $40,000 of his fee from the tight-fisted parents of his clients. He only managed to get that after threatening to sue them.

Leopold and Loeb were sent to the state prison in Joliet and officials there were ridiculed by the public and the press for the special treatment they received. Obviously, money was changing hands as each enjoyed a private cell, books, a desk, a filing cabinet and even pet birds. They also showered away from the other prisoners and took their meals, which were prepared to order, in the officer's lounge. They were also allowed any number of unsupervised visitors and were allowed to keep their own gardens.

Over time, Loeb became even more deranged and was feared as a brutal prison rapist. He terrified weaker prisoners and was avoided by the population at large. Even Leopold wanted nothing to do with him. In January 1936, he was killed by another inmate, who slashed him 56 times with a makeshift knife. He was found bleeding in the corridor by guards and he died a short time later.

Leopold lived on in prison for many years and was said to have made many adjustments to his character and some would even say rehabilitated completely. Even so, appeals for his parole were turned down three times. Finally, in 1958, his fourth appeal was pleaded by the poet Carl Sandburg, who even went as far as to offer Leopold a room in his own home. Finally, in March of that year, he was released. He went on to write a book about his experiences called *Life Plus 99 Years* and moved to Puerto Rico. There, he worked among the poor, married a widow and died in 1961.

Although ghosts of violent murder have often been believed to walk the earth, the spirit of Bobby Franks has always rested in peace, perhaps because his killers were brought to justice. There is one spirit believed to linger from this case however -- that of master lawyer Clarence Darrow.

In the books *Chicago Haunts* and *Windy City Ghosts*, authors Ursula Bielski and Dale Kaczmarek both tell of instances where the ghost of Darrow has been seen along the back steps of the Museum of Science and Industry in Chicago. The apparition is reported dressed in a suit, hat and overcoat and bears a striking resemblance to the attorney. The figure is reported to stand and stare out across the water before disappearing. Why his ghost walks is unknown, although perhaps the infamously agnostic attorney simply refuses to go on to the other side, a place that he didn't believe in anyway!

FAREWELL TO THE GRIMES SISTERS

Have you ever run across a place that just seems to be bad?

It might be a place that you really have no connection to or information about and yet it just seems to be a spot that you don't want to linger for very long. I have always been intrigued by the idea of what I think of as "haunted highways". These are stretches of roadway that perhaps cross through an area that has gained an unnerving reputation over the years or that simply manages to give the person traveling along them that always popular creeping sensation at the base of the spine. Often, we are bothered by these highways because of stories we have heard about them. Perhaps it was suggested that an unusually high number of accidents occur here or that people have seen things that they can't quite explain. Other roads are haunted by memories from the past -- death, murder and horrific events that can't quite seem to be forgotten by those who travel on the road. And even perhaps by the highway itself?

Have you ever had the misfortune to discover such a place? I have....

A few years ago, I had the opportunity to visit a roadway in Chicago called German Church Road. It was a place that just seemed "wrong" and that's the best description that I can give for it. Some say this roadway is haunted and frankly, I can believe it. It is a place where the shadows hang long and low and where a chill always seems to be in the air. But could my reaction to this "haunted highway" have been caused by my knowledge of what had occurred here in the past? Perhaps, for it was along this road that the victims of one of the most horrific crimes in Chicago history were found.

It was a heartbreaking event that has become one of the region's most puzzling unsolved crimes. It shattered the innocence of Chicago forever and according to those who have experienced it, left a chilling impression behind.

It was December 28, 1956 and Patricia Grimes, 13, and Barbara Grimes, 15, left their home at 3624 South Damon Avenue and headed for the Brighton Theater, only a mile away. The girls were both avid fans of Elvis Presley and had gone to see his film *Love Me Tender* for the eleventh and final time. The girls were recognized in the popcorn line at 9:30 PM and then seen on an eastbound Archer Avenue bus at 11:00 PM. After that, things are less certain but this may have been the last time they were ever seen alive. The two sisters were missing for the next twenty-five days, before their naked and frozen bodies were found along the banks of Devil's Creek in the southwest part of Cook County.

The girl's mother, Loretta Grimes, expected the girls to come home by 11:45 but was already growing uneasy when they had not arrived 15 minutes prior to that. At midnight, she sent her daughter Theresa, 17, and her son Joey, 14, to the bus stop at 35th and Hoyne to watch for them. After three buses had stopped and had failed to discharge their sisters, Theresa and Joey returned home without them. They never saw the girls again, but strangely, others claimed to.

The last reported sightings of the two girls came from classmates who spotted them at Angelo's Restaurant at 3551 South Archer Avenue, more than twenty-four hours after their reported disappearance. How accurate this sighting was is unknown, as a railroad conductor also reported them on a train near the Great Lakes Naval Training Center in north suburban Glenview. A security guard on the northwest side offered directions to two girls he believed were the Grimes sisters on the morning of the 29th, hours after they disappeared. On January 1, both girls were allegedly identified as passengers aboard a CTA bus on Damen Avenue. During the week that followed, they were reported in Englewood by George Pope, a night clerk at the Unity Hotel on West 61st Street, who refused them a room because of their ages. Three employees at Kresge believed they saw the girls listening to Elvis Presley songs at the record counter on January 3.

The police theorized that the girls had run away but Loretta Grimes refused to believe it. She was sure the girls were not missing voluntarily but the authorities were still not convinced. Regardless, it became the greatest missing persons hunt in Chicago police history. Even Elvis Presley, in a statement issued from Graceland, asked the girls to come home and ease their mother's worries. The plea went unanswered.

More strangeness would be reported before the bodies of the girls were found. A series of ransom letters, that were later discovered to have come from a mental patient, took Mrs. Grimes to Milwaukee on January 12. She was escorted by FBI agents and instructed to sit in a downtown Catholic church with $1,000 on the bench beside her. The letter promised that Barbara Grimes would walk in to retrieve the money and then leave to deliver it to the kidnapper. She and her sister would then be released. Needless to say, no one ever came and Mrs. Grimes was left sitting there for hours to contemplate her daughter's fate. By that time, it's likely that the bodies of the two girls were already lying along German Church Road, covered with snow.

But if that's true, then how can we explain the two telephone calls that were received by Wallace and Ann Tollstan on January 14? Their daughter, Sandra, was a classmate of Patricia Grimes at the St. Maurice School and they received the two calls around midnight. The first call jolted Mr. Tollstan out of his sleep but when he picked up the receiver, the person on the other end of the line did not speak. He waited a few moments and then hung up. About 15 minutes later, the phone rang again and this time, Ann Tollstan answered it. The voice on the other end of the line asked "Is that you, Sandra? Is Sandra there?" But before Mrs. Tollstan could bring her daughter to the phone, the caller had clicked off the line. Ann Tollstan was convinced that the frightened voice on the telephone had belonged to Patricia Grimes!

And that wasn't the only strange happening to mark the period when the girls were missing. On January 15, a police switchboard operator received a call from a man who refused to identify himself but who insisted that the girl's bodies would be found in a park at 81st and Wolf. He claimed that this revelation had come to him in a dream and he hung up. The call was then traced to Green's Liquor Market on South Halsted and the caller was discovered to be Walter Kranz, a 53 year-old steamfitter. According to a *Chicago Sun-Times* article, he was taken into custody after the bodies were found on January 22 -- less than a mile from the park that Kranz said he dreamed of! He became one of the numerous people who were questioned by the police and then released.

Finally, the vigil for the Grimes Sisters ended on January 22, 1957 when construction worker Leonard Prescott was driving south on German Church Road near Willow Springs. He spotted what appeared to be two discarded clothing store mannequins lying next to a guardrail, a short distance from the road. A few feet away, the ground dropped off to Devil's Creek below. Unsure of what he had seen, Prescott nervously brought his wife to the spot, and then they drove to the local police station. His wife, Marie Prescott, was so upset by the sight of the bodies that she had to be carried back to their car.

Once investigators realized the "mannequins" were actually bodies, they soon discovered they were the Grimes Sisters. Barbara Grimes lay on her left side with her legs slightly drawn up toward her body. Her head was covered by the body of her sister, who had been thrown onto her back with her head turned sharply to the right. It looked as if they had been discarded there by someone so cold and heartless that he saw the girls as nothing more than refuse to be tossed away on a lonely roadside.

The officials in charge, Cook County Sheriff Joseph D. Lohman and Harry Glos, an aggressive investigator for Coroner Walter E. McCarron, surmised that the bodies had been lying there for several days, perhaps as far back as January 9. This had been the date of the last heavy snowfall and the frigid temperatures that followed the storm had preserved the bodies to a state that resembled how they looked at the moment of death. As the newspapers broke the story on the morning of January 23, both the press and the investigators in the case began to draw connections between the murders of the Grimes sisters and the killings of three young boys who had been found under similar circumstances in October 1955.

One of the most shocking and terrifying events in the history of Chicago took place in that month, when the bodies of the three boys were discovered in a virtually crime-free community on the northwest side of the city. This was several years before the disappearance of the Grimes sisters and at the time of what was called the Schuessler-Peterson murders, the city would be stunned by the horror of violence against children.

The terrifying events began on a cool Sunday afternoon in the fall of 1955 when three boys from the northwest side of the city headed downtown to catch a matinee performance of a movie at a Loop Theater. The boys made the trip with their parent's consent because in those days, parents thought little of their responsible children going off on excursions by themselves. The boys had always proven dependable in the past and this time would have been no exception, if tragedy had not occurred.

With $4 between them, John and Anton Schuessler and Bobby Peterson ventured into the Chicago Loop to see a movie that Bobby's mother had chosen for them. Around 6:00 pm that night, long after the matinee had ended, the boys were reported in the lobby of the Garland Building at 111 North Wabash. There was no explanation for what they might have been doing there, other than that Peterson's eye doctor was located in the building. It seems unlikely that he would have been visiting the optometrist on a Sunday afternoon.

Around 7:45 pm, the three entered the Monte Cristo Bowling Alley on West Montrose. The parlor was a neighborhood eating place and the proprietor later recalled to the police that he recalled the boys and that a "fifty-ish" looking man was showing an "abnormal interest" in several younger boys who were bowling. He was unable to say if the man made contact with the trio. They left the bowling alley and walked down Montrose to another bowling alley, then thumbed a ride at the intersection of Lawrence and Milwaukee Avenue. They were out of money by this time, but not quite ready to go home. It was now 9:05 in the evening and their parents were beginning to get worried. They had reason to be, for the boys were never seen alive again.

Two days later, the boy's naked and bound bodies were discovered in a shallow ditch about 100 feet east of the Des Plaines River. A salesman, who had stopped to eat his lunch at the Robinson Wood's Indian Burial Grounds nearby, spotted them and called the police. Coroner Walter McCarron stated that the cause of death was "asphyxiation by suffocation". The three boys had been dead about 36 hours when they were discovered.

Bobby Peterson had been struck repeatedly and had been strangled with a rope or a necktie. The killer had used adhesive tape to cover the eyes of all three victims. They had then been thrown from a vehicle. Their clothing was never discovered.

The city of Chicago was thrown into a panic. Police officials reported that they had never seen such a horrible crime. The fears of parents all over the city were summed up by the grief-stricken Anton Schuessler Sr. who said, "When you get to the point that children cannot go to the movies in the afternoon and get home safely, something is wrong with this country."

Police officers combed the area, conducting door-to-door searches and neighborhood interrogations. Search teams combed Robinson's Woods, looking for clues or items of clothing. The killer (or killers) had gone to great length to get rid of any signs of fingerprints or traces of evidence. By this time, various city and suburban police departments had descended on the scene, running into each other and further hampering the search for clues. There was little or no cooperation between the separate agencies and if anything had been discovered, it would have most likely been lost in the confusion.

While investigators were coming up empty, an honor guard of Boy Scouts carried the coffins of the three boys from the St. Tarcissus Roman Catholic Church to a hearse that would take them to St. Joseph Cemetery. The church was filled to capacity with an estimated 1,200 mourners. This marked the end of innocence in Chicago. With the death of the Grimes sisters a few years later, it was apparent to all that America had changed for the worse.

The horror felt by parents in Chicagoland was only compounded by the disappearance of the Grimes sisters and the subsequent discovery of their bodies. Like the Schuessler's and Bobby Peterson, the girls had been found naked and dumped in a secluded, wooded area. And also like the murders a few years before (still unsolved at the time), the bodies had looked to be mannequins by those who discovered them.

The bodies along German Church Road sent the various police departments into action. A short time after the discovery, more than 162 officers from Chicago, Cook County, the Forest Preserves and five south suburban police departments began combing the woods -- and tramping all over whatever evidence may have been there. Between the officers, the reporters, the medical examiners and everyone else, the investigation was already botched. Despite the claims of Lt. Joseph Morris, the head of a special police unit investigating the Schuessler-Peterson murders, who said "We're not going to repeat some of the mistakes that we made the last time", things were already off to a bad start.

And the investigation became even more confusing in the days to come. The bodies were removed from the scene and were taken to the Cook County Morgue, where they would be stored until they thawed out and an autopsy became possible. Before they were removed though, both police investigators and reporters commented on the condition of the corpses, noting bruises and marks that have still not been adequately explained to this day. According to a newspaper article, there were three "ugly" wounds in Patricia's abdomen and the left side of her face had been battered, resulting in a possibly broken nose. Barbara's face and head had also been bruised and there were punctures from an ice pick in her chest. Once the bodies were moved, investigators stayed on the scene to search for clothing and clues but neither were found.

Once the autopsies were performed the following day, all hopes that the examinations would provide new evidence or leads were quickly dashed. Despite the efforts of three experienced pathologists, they could not reach agreement on a time or cause of death. They stated that the girls had died from shock and exposure but were only able to reach this conclusion by eliminating other causes. And by also concluding that the girls had died on December 28, the night they had disappeared, they created more puzzles than they had managed to solve. If the girls had died on the night they had gone missing, then how could the sightings that took place after that date be explained? And if the bodies had been exposed to the elements since that time, then why hadn't anyone else seen them?

Barbara and Patricia were buried on January 28, one month after they disappeared, although their mystery was no closer to being solved than it had been in December.

The residents of Chicagoland were stunned and the case of the murdered girls became an obsession. The local community organized searches for clues and passed out flyers looking for information. Money was raised to assist the destitute Grimes family and eventually the funds paid off their Damen Avenue home. The *Chicago Tribune* invited readers to send in theories about the case and paid $50 for any they published. The clergy and the parishioners from St. Maurice offered a $1,000 reward and sent out letters to area residents, hoping that someone might have seen the girls before they vanished. Even photographs were taken of friends of the girls that duplicated the clothing they wore on December 28 in hopes that it might jog the memory of someone who saw them. On the night they saw *Love Me Tender* for the last time, Patricia wore blue jeans, a yellow sweater, a black jacket with white sleeve stripes, a white scarf over her head and black shoes. Her sister reportedly wore a gray tweed skirt, yellow blouse, a three-quarter length coat, a gray scarf, white bobby sox and black, ballerina shoes. The clothing though, like the girl's killer, was never found.

The killer may have eluded the authorities but it was not because no one was trying to find him. Investigators questioned an unbelievable 300,000 persons, searching for information about the girls, and 2,000 of these people were seriously interrogated, which in those days could be brutal. A number of suspects were seriously considered and among the first was the "dreamer", Walter Kranz, who called police with his mysterious tip on January 15. He was held at the Englewood police station for some time and was repeatedly interrogated and given lie detector tests about his involvement in the murders. No solid evidence was ever found against him though.

The police also named a 17-year-old named Max Fleig as a suspect but the current law did not allow juveniles to be tested with a polygraph. Police Captain Ralph Petaque persuaded the boy to take the test anyway and in the midst of it, he confessed to kidnapping the girls. Because the test was illegal and inadmissible, the police were forced to let Fleig go free. Was he the killer? No one will ever know. Regardless, Fleig was sent to prison a few years later for the brutal murder of a young woman.

In the midst of all of this, the police still had to deal with nuts and cranks, more so-called psychic visions and a number of false confessions, making their work even harder. One confession that they investigated came from a transient who was believed to have been involved in some other murders around the same time period. His confession later unraveled and he admitted that he had lied.

Eager to crack the floundering case, Cook County Sheriff Joseph Lohman then arrested a Tennessee drifter named Edward L. "Benny" Bedwell. The drifter, who sported Elvis-style sideburns and a ducktail haircut, had reportedly been seen with the Grimes sisters in a restaurant where he sometimes washed dishes in exchange for food. When he was initially questioned, Bedwell admitted that he had been in the D&L Restaurant on West Madison with two girls and an unnamed friend but he insisted that the owners of the place were mistaken about the girls being the Grimes sisters.

According to the owners, John and Minnie Duros, the group had entered the diner around 5:30 on the morning of December 30. They described the taller girl (Patricia?) as being either so drunk or so sick that she was staggering as she walked. The couples sat in a booth for awhile and listened to Elvis songs on the jukebox and then went outside. According to Minnie Duros, "The taller girl returned to the booth and put her head on the table. They wanted her to get into the car, but she didn't want to. The other girl and the two men came back later and I told them to leave the girl alone -- she's sick. But they all left anyway and on their way out, Barbara said they were sisters."

Lohman found the story plausible, thanks to the unshakable identification of the girls by Minnie Duros, their respective heights, the fact that one of them said they were sisters and finally, Bedwell's resemblance to Elvis. Lohman believed this might have been enough to get the girls to go along with him. And then of course, there was Bedwell's confession, which related a lurid and sexually explicit tale of drunken debauchery with the two young women. He made and recanted three confessions and even re-enacted the crime for Lohman on January 27. Everyone doubted the story but Lohman. He booked Bedwell on murder charges, but the drifter's testimony was both vague and contradictory and (most likely) his confession had been beaten out of him. On January 31, he testified that he had confessed out of fear of Lohman's men, who had struck and threatened him while he was being questioned.

Another of the chief investigators in the case, Harry Glos, believed that Bedwell might have been implicated in the murders in some way but that he was a dubious suspect. State's Attorney Benjamin Adamowski agreed and ordered the drifter released. All charges against Bedwell were dismissed on March 4 and upon leaving the courtroom, he was re-arrested on a fugitive warrant from Florida for the rape of a 13 year-old girl. The crime he was charged with in Florida closely resembled the one that took the lives of the Grimes sisters but he managed to avoid conviction for it, thanks to the passage of time while he was a fugitive. According to reports, Bedwell's accuser had been held captive for three days before escaping and notifying the police of her abduction and rape. Bedwell later spend time in prison on a weapons charge and died at some point after he was released in 1986.

The dismissal of charges against Bedwell in the Grimes case set off another round of bickering between police departments and various jurisdictions and the case became even more mired in red tape and inactivity. It got even worse when coroner's investigator Glos publicly criticized the autopsy findings concerning the time and cause of death. He shocked the public by announcing that Barbara and Patricia could not have died on the night they disappeared. He said that an ice layer around the bodies proved that they were warm when they were left along German Church Road and that only after January 7 would there have been enough snow to create the ice and to hide the bodies.

Glos also raised the issues of the puncture wounds and bruises on the bodies, which had never been explained or explored. He was sure that they girls had been violently treated prior to death and also asserted that the older sister, Barbara, had been sexually molested before she was killed. The pathologists had denied this but the Chicago Police crime lab reluctantly confirmed it. However, they were angry with Glos for releasing the information because they wanted to keep it secret so that they could use it when questioning suspects.

The coroner, Walter McCarron, promptly had Glos fired and many of the other investigators in the case accused him of being reckless and of political grandstanding. Only Sheriff Lohman, who later deputized Glos to work on the case without pay, remained on his side. He agreed that the girls had likely been beaten and tortured by a sexual predator who lured them into the kidnap car under a seemingly innocent pretense. Lohman remained convinced until his death in 1969 that the predator who had killed the girls had been Benny Bedwell.

Other theories maintain that the girls may have indeed encountered Bedwell or another "older man" and rumors circulated that the image of the two girls had been polished to cover up some very questionable behavior on their parts. It was said that they sometimes hung around a bar on Archer Avenue where men would buy them drinks. One of the men may have been Benny Bedwell. Harry Glos, who died in 1994, had released information that one of the girls had been sexually active but later reports from those who have seen the autopsy slides say there is evidence that both of them may have been. It is believed that Coroner McCarron may not have released this because of religious reasons or to spare additional grief for the family.

Today, veteran detectives believe that there was much more to the story that met the eye. According to Richard Lindberg's book, *Return to the Scene of the Crime*, they are convinced that Barbara and Patricia were abducted by a front man for a "white slavery" ring and taken to a remote location in the woods surrounding Willow Springs. They are convinced that the girls were strangled after refusing to become prostitutes. It's also possible that the girls may have been lured into an involvement in the prostitution ring by someone they knew (perhaps one of the older men from the Archer Avenue bar?), not realizing what would be required of them, and they were killed to keep them silent.

Others refused to even consider this though and were angered by the negative gossip about the two girls. Some remain angry about this even today, maintaining that Barbara and Patricia were nice, ordinary, happy girls and were tragically killed on a cold night because they made the mistake of accepting a ride from a stranger. They didn't hang around in bars, these old friends maintain, they were simply innocent teenage girls, just like everyone else at that time.

As for myself, I'd like to think these old acquaintances are right. There are few stories as tragic as the demise of the Grimes sisters and perhaps it provides some cold comfort for us to believe that their deaths were simply a terrible mistake or the actions of deviant killer. It can provide us that comfort of knowing that the girls were simply in the wrong place at the wrong time and that such a thing could have happened to anyone. But does believing this make us feel better -- or worse?

Years passed. As there is no statute of limitations for murder, the case officially remained open but there was little chance that it would ever be solved. The Grimes family saw their hopes for closure in the case slowly fading away. Loretta Grimes passed away in December 1989 and by all accounts was a tragic and broken woman.

For the next several years, the investigation continued and more suspects were interviewed. A $100,000 reward was posted but the trail went cold. Then, decades later, hope was raised for the Grimes case when a solution was finally discovered to the Schuessler-Peterson murders from 1955. In a bizarre turn of events, a government informant named William Wemette accused one Kenneth Hansen of the murders during a police investigation into the 1977 disappearance of candy heiress Helen Vorhees Brach.

In 1955, Hansen, then 22 years old, worked as a stable hand for Silas Jayne, a millionaire from Kane County. Jayne himself was wild and reckless and had been suspected of many violent and devious dealings during his rise to power in the horse-breeding world. He went to prison in 1973 for the murder of his half brother, George. Hansen himself was no prize either and soon, investigators were able to build a case against him. The case resulted in the deviant's arrest in August 1994.

Cook County prosecutors showed jurors how Hansen had lured the Schuessler brothers and Bobby Peterson into his car under false pretenses. They retraced the path of the killer in what author Richard Lindberg called "chilling detail". His story was that he wanted to show the boys some prize horses belonging to Silas Jayne. According to the testimony of several men that Hansen had bragged to, he had molested and then killed the Schuessler's and Peterson one by one. When Jayne discovered his crime, the horse breeder burned the stables in order to obliterate any evidence that Hansen had left behind. Hansen's brother had then dumped the boy's bodies at Robinson's Woods and Jayne had filed a bogus insurance claim for the lost building.

This case came to trial in 1995 and breaking a 40 year silence, many of Hansen's other victims came forward, recalling promises of jobs made to young men in return for sexual favors. He forced their silence with threats that included warnings that they might end up "like the Peterson boy". Even without evidence and eyewitnesses to corroborate the prosecution's allegations against him, a Cook County jury convicted Kenneth Hansen of the murders in September 1995. They deliberated for less than two hours and Hansen was sentenced for 200-300 years in prison.

Bobby Peterson and the Schuessler brothers could finally rest in peace -- but the same could not be said for Barbara and Patricia Grimes. Despite the new public awareness and police interest in their deaths, the case became cold once again. Apparently, the investigator's theories about a connection between their murders and those of the Schuessler and Peterson boys were not correct after all.

Now, more than 40 years later, the mystery of who killed the Grimes sisters remains unsolved. Those who still have an interest in the case will sometimes travel down German Church Road, in the southern suburb of Willow Springs, and wind up at a low point in this "haunted highway" where the bodies of the two girls were discovered so many years ago. The impact of tragedy is still being felt today, as is the impression of what may have been a depraved killer's most desperate moments.

Today, the tree-lined roadway is heavily shadowed and quiet. There is almost a silence in the air that a traveler only seems to notice if he knows the reason why this is a haunted place. Away from the road, those who listen closely can hear the rippling of Devil's Creek below and one has to wonder if the whispering of the water could actually speak -- what dark secrets would it have to reveal?

The bodies of the Grimes sisters were tossed without ceremony at the edge of a ravine, just over a guardrail and only a few feet from the shoulder of the road. A short distance away from this site, its entrance now blocked with a chain, was a narrow drive that once led to a house that was nestled in the trees. Mysteriously, the house was abandoned by the young family who lived there soon after the girl's bodies were discovered. Many of the belongings were left behind in the house and toys and furniture lay scattered about the yard for years. Even a 1955 Buick sat rusting in the driveway but it was eventually taken away. At some point, vandals set fire to the house and the owner had to demolish what was left. And while the owner never lived there again, people would occasionally see a tall, gaunt man roaming about the property in the spring and fall, when the trees and brush were thin. It was assumed that he had once occupied the place, but those who saw him were afraid to ask.

Until just a few years ago, the foundation of the abandoned house was still visible and landscaped hedges and a few remaining artifacts served to bear witness that a family had once lived here. Below the concrete slab of the house, a basement remained intact with a water heater, window screens and an old workbench littering the crumbling floor.

Why the family abandoned the home remains almost as great a mystery as who killed Barbara and Patricia Grimes. If anyone knows, they aren't saying but like the murder case, those with an interest have their theories. Some believe the owner may have been questioned about the crime and simply felt too embarrassed to stay. It has also been suggested that the family may have seen something on the night the bodies were dumped near their house and became too frightened to remain behind.

Others claim that the house, located so close to the place where the bodies were found, became haunted. And perhaps this is not as far-fetched as you might first think...

Since the discovery of the bodies, the police have received reports from those who say they have heard a car pulling up to the location with its motor running. They also say they have heard the door open, followed by the sound of something being dumped alongside the road. The door slams shut and the car drives away. They have heard these things -- and yet there is no car in sight!

According to author Tamara Shaffer, there was a young woman who took a number of her friends on a tour of the old house and the murder site one evening. They walked up the path that branched off from the driveway and circled the ruins of the house and under the light of the moon overhead, they saw a car approaching up the gravel drive from the road. It was a dark vehicle with no lights and it sped past them and around the house, then disappeared. The woman and her friends decided to leave and as they did, they encountered the police, who had been called to chase off the "tour group". The chain that had been used to close off the driveway was still hanging in place and the police officers had seen no other car.

Another woman claimed that in addition to the sounds, she saw what appeared to be the naked bodies of two young girls lying on the edge of the roadway. When police investigated, there was no sign of the bodies.

Many researchers believe in "residual hauntings", which means that an event may cause an impression to be left behind on the atmosphere of a place. It seems possible that the traumatic final moments of the Grimes sisters may have left such an impression on this small stretch of German Church Road. It may have also been an impression caused by the anxiety and madness of the killer as he left the bodies of the young women behind.

But believe in hauntings or not, that choice is up to the reader - but should you ever travel along German Church Road, I defy you to stop along the roadway where the bodies of Barbara and Patricia were found and to say that you are not moved by the tragedy that came to an end here.

Without a doubt, I think you will agree, this is a dark and haunted place.

BORN TO RAISE HELL

The young woman beneath the bed shivered once more, quaking in fear as she saw the legs of the intruder enter the room where he had earlier tied up her and her eight roommates. Corazon Amurao, a nursing exchange student from the Philippines, saw the other young women disappear one by one as the man dragged them from the room. They did not return. She could only pray that the man had not counted the women as he tied them up in the second floor bedroom -- and that he did not realize one of them was now missing.

The blank-eyed intruder was a man named Richard Speck. Born in Kirkwood, Illinois in December 1941, Speck was the seventh of eight children. Over the years, dozens of speculated about the reason behind

Richard Speck (UPI Photo)

Speck's brutal crimes and whether he turned evil somewhere along the way or if he was simply born bad -- or as the tattoo scrawled on his arm stated, whether he was "born to raise hell." Many have also wondered if perhaps things might have turned out different in the lives of eight nursing students if Speck's father, whom he adored, had not died when Speck was only 6 years-old. Regardless, Speck was raised by his mother in a strict Baptist setting that forbade alcohol and worldly influences. She later married Carl Lindberg, a Texan with an arrest record though, and they moved to Dallas, Texas, where Lindberg began taking out his drunken rages on step-son. By this time, Speck was a slow-witted failure with school work and on the fast track to nowhere. He started running with some older boys, drinking, fighting and getting into trouble.

Speck married and allegedly fathered a child but the marriage didn't last long, thanks to his abuse of his wife, Shirley, and his mother-in-law. According to her later accounts, Speck often raped his wife at knifepoint, claiming that he needed sex four to five times each day. He ended up spending a good portion of their marriage in prison and in January 1966, Shirley filed for divorce. In the same year in Dallas, Speck was involved in a burglary and stabbing and was fined $10 for the lesser charge of stabbing. The burglary charge would have sent him back to prison -- and might have saved the life of the eight young women. Unfortunately though fate had other plans.

With the help of his sister Carolyn, Speck took the first bus out of Dallas and headed for his sister Martha's home in Chicago. He only stayed with her for a few days and then went to Monmouth, Illinois, a small town where he had lived as a boy. He stayed with family friends and worked as a carpenter for a month. He soon quit his job in order to spend his time hanging out in a local tavern, the Palace Tap. Speck only managed to stay out of trouble until April 2, when Mrs. Virgil Harris, 65, was attacked in her home. The man grabbed her from behind, cut her housecoat into strips, tied her up with them and raped her. Mrs. Harris told police that her assailant spoke with a southern drawl, as Speck did after his years in Texas.

On April 13, Mary Kay Pierce, a barmaid at Frank's Place, was found dead in a shed behind the tavern. Her liver had been ruptured from a blow to the abdomen. Speck was brought in for questioning but the interrogation was cut short when he got sick. He promised to return on April 19 for more questions, but he never did. Investigators traced him to the Christy Hotel and when they entered his room, found jewelry and a radio that had been stolen from Mrs. Harris' home, as well as items from other burglaries in town. They did not find Speck however. The hotel manager told police that he had seen Speck leaving a few hours before they arrived with two suitcases. He told the manager that he was going to the laundromat, but he caught a bus instead -- heading for Chicago.

Speck now returned to the home of his sister, Martha, and his brother-in-law, Gene Thornton. Their second floor apartment on the city's northwest side was crowded but Speck didn't plan to be there much. He announced his intentions to search for work as a merchant seaman but after several days of doing nothing, Thornton got frustrated with him and drove his unwanted houseguest to the National Maritime Union Hall, located at 2315 East One Hundredth Street. The building still stands today as a church and was then located just a few doors away from three residential townhouses, including number 2319, which had been rented by the South Chicago Community Hospital for 24 of its 155 student nurses.

Thornton brought Speck to the Maritime Union Hall in hopes that there was still an open berth on a ship that was bound for Vietnam. As it turned out though, fate intervened once more. The position went to a man with greater seniority, leaving Speck without a spot. Disappointed, but unwilling to take Speck back in, Thornton handed him $25 and wished him well. He then drove off and left his brother-in-law to fend for himself.

In May, Speck managed to get a position aboard and iron ore ship on the Great Lakes, where he was stricken with appendicitis and hospitalized in Hancock, Michigan. When he returned to Chicago in mid-June, he was fired for being drunk and disorderly. He had been warned repeatedly about his drinking and violent behavior but he disregarded the threats. After that, he spent the next three weeks in cheap hotels, sleeping in the park and financing his liquor and his visits to prostitutes with whatever odd jobs he could come up with. On July 13, a depressed and angry Speck was drinking heavily in the Shipyard Inn. After a volatile combination of pills and liquor, he suddenly got the urge to "raise some hell". He would later say that he remembered nothing after this point.

Speck left the bar with a hunting knife, a pocketknife and a borrowed .22 caliber pistol and walked over to one of the nearby student dormitories. For the past several weeks, the drifter had seen the women coming and going from the buildings, sunbathing in Luella Park and walking back and forth to their classes. He was familiar enough with their schedules to know that, at nearly 11:00 p.m., they would be home in bed.

A loud rapping came at the door of one of the townhouses and Corazon Amurao, who shared a second floor bedroom with two other young women, went to the door to answer it. She found a tall, lean stranger standing on the doorstep. He smelled of liquor and had a knife in one hand and a gun in the other. He slurred that he was not going to hurt her. "I'm only going to tie you up," he said. "I need money to go to New Orleans."

He shoved his way into the townhouse and ordered the three Filipino students, Valentina Paison, Merlita Garguilo and Corazon, into a bedroom at the back of the building, where Pamela Wilkening, Nina Schmale and Pat Matusek were getting ready for bed. Speck took the sheets from the beds and cut them into strips, which he used to bind the women by their wrists and ankles. At 11:30, a seventh nurse, Gloria Davy, returned home from a date and she was also imprisoned. Then, a half-hour later, Suzanne Farris and her friend, Mary Ann Jordan, came to the front door. Speck pulled them inside and led them into the back bedroom at gun point.

In the course of the hour, Speck had systematically tied and gagged each of the women. As author Richard Lindberg has stated: "How he accomplished this with minimal to no resistance is one of the enduring mysteries in the annals of Chicago crime." Why did none of the women try to escape? Why did they not try and overpower Speck as he was tying another victim? Why did none of the women in the other townhouses hear anything that was taking place? No one knows and as Lindberg has noted -- it remains a mystery.

By 3:30 a.m., Speck's lust was finally spent. One by one, he had taken the eight young women out of the bedroom and had killed them. Only one of them, Gloria Davy, had been raped but all were dead -- save for Cora Amurao, who had managed to roll under a bunk bed and cower there in fear and shock until Speck finally left. Apparently, in his frenzy, he had lost count of the women in the house. Amurao remained hidden, frozen in terror, until nearly 6:00. When she finally emerged from her hiding place, she climbed out of the apartment window and then perched on a ledge, began to scream. "My friends are all dead!" she cried. "I'm the only one alive! Oh God, I'm the only one alive!"

Her screams caught the attention of Judy Dykton, a student who lived across the street. She had gotten up early to study and was startled by the cries from outside. Snatching her robe, she ran over to find Cora shaking and crying on the window ledge. Judy entered the open door of the townhouse and stepped into the living room. She discovered the naked body of Gloria Davy, her hands tied behind her and a strip of cloth wrapped tightly around her throat. Her skin had turned cold and a dusty blue color. She was obviously dead. She turned and fled to the apartment of the housemother, Mrs. Bisone. "There's trouble in 19!" she screamed.

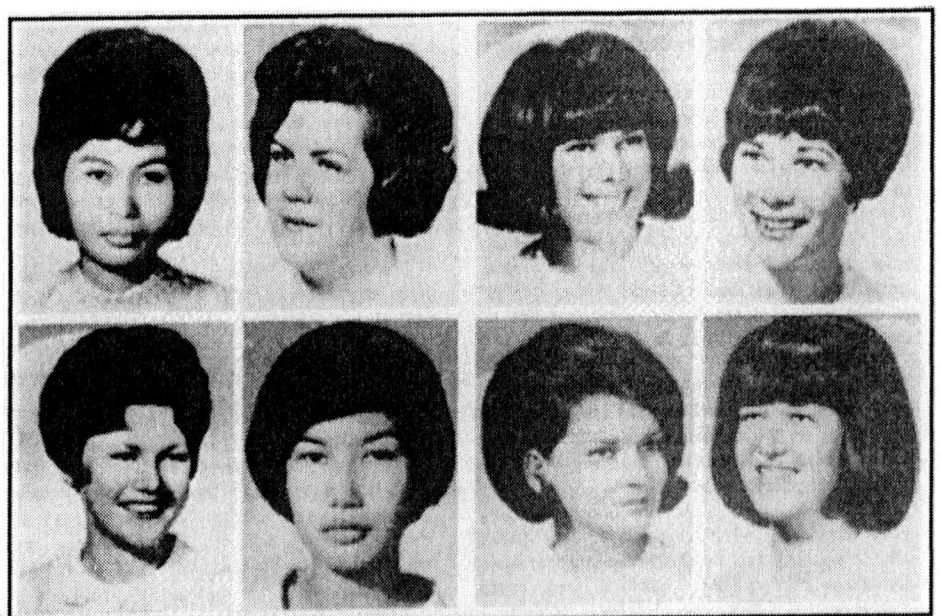

Speck's Eight Victims: (Top Row - Left to Right) Valentina Paison, Pamela Wilkening, Patricia Matusek, Suzanne Farris (Bottom Row) Mary Ann Jordan, Merlita Garguilo, Gloria Davy, Nina Schmale (UPI Photos)

The housemother woke up the other student nurses and ran from the house toward 2319. She brought Leona Bonczak with her, who entered the house. She first checked to see if Gloria showed any signs of life and then mounted the stairs and looked down the hall. In the bathroom, she found the body of Pat Matusek and then crept into the other bedrooms, where she discovered the rest of the students so drenched in blood that she was unable to recognize any of them, save for Nina Schmale. A pillow covered most of the girl's face but she lay on her back, hands tied behind her, a cloth around her neck, legs spread apart -- and a fatal knife wound to her heart.

Stunned, she went downstairs and numbly told Mrs. Bisone that everyone was dead. The housemother, shaking and sick, picked up the phone and called South Chicago Community Hospital and told them that all of her girls had been murdered. When the hospital asked her who had been killed, she was unable to tell them. The only words she uttered were "send help!"

Someone on the street managed to flag down police officer Daniel Kelly, a young patrolman who had only been on the job for 18 months. He radioed in that there was trouble and then entered the house. He was shocked to discover the body of Gloria Davy in the living room. Kelly had dated her sister some time back. Upset, he drew his gun, searched the house and found the other bodies. The townhouse looked like a charnel house and in places, the blood in the carpeting was so thick that it pooled over Kelly's shoes. He ran outside to his car radio and called it in. Soon, Kelly heard the comforting sounds of approaching sirens beginning to fill the air.

The street outside filled with cops and people ran from door to door alerting their neighbors of the horror found in 2319. The first detective on the scene was Jack Wallenda, a big powerful man with a soft voice who was shocked by the utter brutality of the killings. He entered the house and viewed the bodies one by one.

He found Gloria first. She was nude, belly down on the couch and tied with double-knotted bed sheets. He noticed what appeared to be semen between her buttocks and found buttons from her blouse strewn down the stairs. The killer had apparently torn them off her as he pulled her to the living room. Also tossed on the floor was a man's white t-shirt, size 38-40.

Wallenda then checked the upstairs bedroom and found the body of Pamela Wilkening. She had been gagged and stabbed through the heart. Suzanne Farris lay nearby in a pool of blood and a white nurse's stocking had been twisted around her neck. The detective counted 18 stab wounds to her chest and neck. He studied Mary Ann Jordan next. She had been stabbed three times in the chest and once in the neck.

In the northwest bedroom, he found Nina Schmale with her nightgown pulled up to her breasts and her legs pulled apart. She had also been tied and stabbed and it looked as though her neck might be broken. Valentina Paison was found under a blue cover, lying face down. Her throat had been cut. Tossed carelessly on top of her was the body of Merlita Garguilo, who had been stabbed and strangled.

Wallenda walked out the door and to the right and saw the legs of Patricia Matusek protruding from the bathroom. She was lying on her back with her hands bound behind her. She had been strangled with a piece of the bed sheet, double knotted, and her nightgown had been dragged up over her breasts. Her white panties had been pulled down to expose her pubic hair. Blood-soaked towels were strewn all over the bathroom floor.

Wallenda's hands were shaking as he left the townhouse. It was the worst crime scene that he had ever witnessed.

The police immediately went to work and within hours were on the trail of Richard Speck. Cora, although heavily sedated, had managed to give an excellent description of the killer and a gas station attendant who worked nearby remembered one of his managers talking about a guy of the same description who had been complaining about missing a ship and losing out on a job just a couple of days before. Police sketch artist Otis Rathel put together an uncanny likeness of Speck. Investigators took the sketch to the Maritime Union Hall and questioned the agent in charge. He remembered an irate seaman who lost out on a double booking -- two guys sent for one job -- and he fished the crumpled assignment sheet from the wastebasket. The sheet gave the name of Richard Speck.

State's Attorney Daniel P. Ward would later call the manhunt for Speck the "finest bit of police work" he had ever seen. The Chicago Police, Sheriff's deputies, the Coroner and a number of amateur investigators managed to neatly compile the case and detectives began tracking his movements.

After the murders, Speck moved from bar to bar, drinking himself into oblivion, not knowing that the police were on his trail. Detectives had convinced the agent at the Maritime Hall to call Speck's last known telephone number, his sister's, to tell him that he was needed to ship out. The agent connected with Gene Thornton, who agreed to try and track Speck down. He managed to find him at the Shipyard Inn and told him that the union hall had a job for him. Speck called the union hall and was told to come down for an assignment on a ship that Speck knew had shipped out several days before. Suspecting a trick, he told the agent that he was up north and it would take him at least an hour to get there. He never showed up.

Immediately, Speck went upstairs, packed his bags and called a cab. He waited in the tavern, playing pool, and three detectives came in looking for a tall blond man with a southern accent. The bartender was no help and Speck stayed quiet, listening and shooting pool just ten feet away from them. When the cab arrived, he refused to give the driver an address and told him to take him to his sister's house, which he said was in a poor and slummy section of town. The cabbie drove north and again asked Speck for an address. Clueless, he pointed to a building that turned out to be part of the Cabrini Green housing project. He got out of the cab and watched the cabbie drive away.

Speck started walking and ended up on Dearborn Street at the Raleigh Hotel, a flophouse that had once been a luxury apartment building. He registered under the name of "John Stayton", one of his friends in

Texas. A desk clerk later recalled a drunken Speck and his "cracker" accent coming in with a prostitute and giving him the wrong room number. He didn't want to wake his boss, so he let the couple go. Just before the elevator door closed, he heard the girl call him "Richard". A half hour later, the girl came back downstairs and told the clerk that her "date" had a gun. This prompted a call to the police and two officers from the 18th District police station showed up at the hotel at 8:30 a.m. Speck, still drunk, awoke to find two cops standing over him. He had the gun tucked into the waistband of his pants and when asked why it had it, told the officers that it belonged to the prostitute. When asked what his name was, he told them that it was Richard Speck. They checked his wallet and found his seaman's I.D. and passport but unfortunately, not all of the police had been notified of the identity of the student nurses' killer yet. He was questioned for 15 minutes and the officers confiscated the gun but never reported it. When they left the hotel, they told the desk clerk that he was "harmless."

Not realizing that Speck had narrowly escaped capture, the police searched the south side. They managed to track him from the Shipyard Inn to the cab company to Cabrini Green. But while they canvassed the housing project, Speck drank himself into another stupor. Later in the afternoon, he ran into some old friends who suggested that he hop a freight train with them and head out of town. Speck went back to the Raleigh and packed his bags and on his way out, told the manager that he was going to do some laundry. He never returned. Just 15 minutes after he walked out though, two detectives came in and flashed a photo of Speck in front of the manager. Her eyes widened. "It's him," she said. "It's Richard, he just left!"

Oblivious, Speck then headed for the Starr Hotel, a rundown dive on West Madison Street that offered temporary refuge to winos and bums. The "rooms" were nothing more than windowless cubicles with concrete floors where losers could sleep off a drunk amidst the sounds of coughing and moaning and the smells of sweat, booze and vomit. The place was the last rung on the ladder for the dregs of humanity and Speck fit right in. He tossed his bags on a bed and went out to sell some of his belongings to raise money for another night of drinking. He picked up some wine at a local liquor store and several newspapers with his name and photo on splashed across them. Speck stumbled back to the Starr Hotel and finished off the entire bottle of wine. He then walked down the hall to the bathroom, smashed the wine bottle and then used the broken glass to cut his wrist and inner elbow. Blood splashed the wall and onto the floor and Speck wobbled down the corridor to his cubicle. He collapsed onto the bed, still bleeding badly and then called out to his neighbors for water and for help. They ignored him.

An anonymous call was made to the police but no patrol car was sent. Eventually, Speck was taken to Cook County Hospital. The ambulance drivers ignored Speck's cries for water and missed the police bulletin on their dashboard that had the injured man's photo on it. In the emergency room, Nurse Kathy O'Connor prepped Speck and first year resident Leroy Smith checked his wounds. He noticed something familiar about the man. He checked his arm, looking for a tattoo and saw it there, as he suspected, "Born to Raise Hell". He compared a newspaper photo with the man and realized that he had the killer on his table.

Speck pleaded with the young man for water but Smith grabbed him by the back of the neck and squeezed it as hard as he could. "Did you give water to those nurses?" he demanded. He dropped Speck's head back onto the gurney and called in a policeman who was guarding another patient down the hall. He told him that Richard Speck, the suspect in the murders, was there on the table. The stunned officer started making telephone calls and all hell broke loose.

Speck was in police custody a few hours later and William J. Martin, a young and hard-working state's attorney was faced with putting together and trying the case. He based most of it on the sincere and compelling testimony of Corazon Amurao, who had to be persuaded to remain in the United States long enough to secure the conviction of the monster who had killed her friends. She was understandably unhinged from her ordeal and she wanted nothing more than to return to the Philippines to try and forget the horrific experience. Martin brought her mother and a cousin to Chicago for moral support and kept them in secret location away from the press. Her quiet testimony galvanized the courtroom and convinced a jury in Peoria (the defense had argued that Speck could not get a fair trial in Chicago) to convict him in just 49 minutes. Speck was given the death sentence for the murders.

He managed to avoid the death penalty though when the Supreme Court changed its ruling on capital punishment. He was re-sentenced to 50-100 years in prison but died on December 5, 1991 from a massive heart attack. His autopsy showed that he had an enlarged heart and occluded arteries, having blown up to 220 pounds at the time of his death. No one claimed his body and he was cremated. His ashes were disposed of in an undisclosed location.

But unfortunately, in 1996, Speck was back.

In May of that year, television journalist Bill Kurtis went behind the walls of Stateville prison and came back with a secret videotape that showed a bizarre Richard Speck with women's breasts -- apparently from hormone treatments -- wearing blue panties and having sex with another inmate. Segments of the video, which also showed sex and drug orgies, were shown on the program *American Justice* and plunged the Illinois Department of Corrections into a major scandal. The video had been shot in the middle 1980's and viewers were as repulsed to see what had become of Speck as they were by his bloody crimes.

Even after death, he was still raising hell.

THE CLOWN THAT KILLED

To everyone who met him, John Wayne Gacy seemed a likable and affable man. He was widely respected in the community, charming and easy to get along with. He was a good Catholic and sharp businessman who, when not running his construction company was active in the Jaycees and was also a Democratic Party precinct captain, when he had his photo taken with then First Lady, Rosalynn Carter. He also spent much of his free time hosting elaborate street parties for his friends and neighbors, serving in community groups and entertaining children as "Pogo the Clown". He was a generous, hard working, friendly, devoted family man, everyone knew that -- but that was the side of John Wayne Gacy that he allowed people to see.

Underneath the smiling mask of the clown was the face of depraved fiend.

John Wayne Gacy was a home-grown monster. Born on St. Patrick's Day 1942 at Edgewater Hospital in Chicago, little Johnny was the second of three children. His older sister Joanne had preceded him by two years and two years after his birth came that of sister Karen. The Gacy children were raised as Catholics and all three attended Catholic schools where they lived on the north side. Growing up, Gacy was a quiet boy who worked odd jobs for spending money, like newspaper routes and bagging groceries, and busied himself with Boy Scout activities. He was never a particularly popular boy but he was well-liked by his teachers, co-workers and friends from school and the Boy Scouts. He seemed to have a normal childhood, except for his relationship with his father and a series of health problems that he developed.

When Gacy was 11, he was playing on a swing set and was hit in the head with one of the swings. The accident caused a blood clot in his brain that was not discovered until he was 16. Between the time of the accident and the diagnosis, Gacy suffered from blackouts that were caused by the clot. They were finally treated with medication. At 17, he was also diagnosed with a heart ailment that he was hospitalized for several times during his life. He complained frequently about it over the years but no one could ever find a cause for the pain that he claimed to be suffering.

In his late teens, he began to experience problems with his father, although his relationship with his mother and sisters remained strong. His father was an alcoholic who physically abused his wife and berated his children. He was an unpleasant individual, but Gacy loved his father and constantly worked to gain his attention and approval. Gacy Sr. died before his son could ever get close to him.

His family problems extended out into his schoolwork and after attending four high schools during his senior year and never graduating, Gacy dropped out and left home for Las Vegas. He worked part time as a janitor in a funeral home and saved his money to buy a ticket back to Chicago. Lonely and depressed, he

John Wayne Gacy -- An outwardly normal man whose depravity spun out of control (UPI)

spent three months trying to get the money together. His mother and sisters were thrilled to see him when he returned.

After his return, Gacy enrolled in business college and eventually graduated. While in school, he gained a real talent for salesmanship and he put these talents to work in a job with the Nunn-Bush Shoe Company. He excelled as a management trainee and he was soon transferred to a men's clothing outlet in Springfield, Illinois. Soon after his move, Gacy's health took a turn for the worse. He gained a great deal of weight and began to suffer more from his mysterious heart ailment. He was hospitalized and soon after getting out, was back in the hospital again, this time with back problems. He continued to have problems with his weight, heart and back throughout his life. It's interesting to note that all three of these types of ailments can often be traced to psychosomatic illnesses and are sometimes assisted more with mental health treatment than by standard medicine. Unfortunately, Gacy never received any.

While living in Springfield, Gacy became involved in several organizations that served the community, including the Chi Rho Club (membership chairman); the Catholic Inter-Club Council (member of the board); the Federal Civil Defense for Illinois; the Chicago Civil Defense (commanding captain); the Holy Name Society (officer) and the Jaycees, to which Gacy devoted most of his efforts and was eventually a vice-president and named "Man of the Year". Many who knew Gacy considered him to be ambitious and working to make a name for himself in the community. He was an overachiever who worked so hard that he had to be hospitalized for nervous exhaustion on one occasion.

In September 1964, Gacy met and married a co-worker named Marlynn Myers, whose parents owned a number of Kentucky Fried Chicken restaurants in Iowa. Gacy's new father-in-law offered him a position with the company and soon the newlyweds were moving to Iowa. Life seemed to hold great promise for Gacy and there was no foreshadowing of the horrific events to come.

Gacy began learning the restaurant business from the ground up, working 12 to 14 hours each day. He was enthusiastic and eager to learn and hoped to take over the franchises one day. When not working, he was active with the Waterloo, Iowa Jaycees. He worked tirelessly performing volunteer work and he made many friends. Marlynn gave birth to a son shortly after they moved to Iowa and not long after, added a daughter to the happy family. They seemed to have the picture perfect life -- a loving and healthy family, a good job, a house in the suburbs -- and it seemed almost too good to be true. And it was...

Rumors were starting to spread around town, and among Jaycees members, about Gacy's sexual preferences. No one could help but notice that young boys always seemed to be in his presence. Stories spread that he had made passes at some of the young men who worked in the restaurants but those close to him refused to believe it -- until the rumors became truth. In May 1968, a grand jury in Black Hawk County indicted Gacy for committing an act of sodomy with a teenaged boy named Mark Miller. The boy told the courts that Gacy had tricked him into being tied up while visiting Gacy's home and he had violently raped him. Gacy denied the charges but did say that Miller willingly had sex with him in order to earn extra money.

Four months later, more charges were filed against Gacy. This time, he was charged with hiring an 18 year-old boy named Dwight Andersson to beat up Mark Miller. Andersson lured Miller to his car and then drove him to a wooded area, where he sprayed mace in his eyes and began to beat him. Miller fought back, breaking Andersson's nose, and managed to run away. He called the police and Andersson was picked up and taken into police custody. He informed the officer that Gacy had hired him to attack the other boy.

A judge ordered Gacy to undergo a psychiatric evaluation to see if he was mentally competent to stand trial. He was found to be competent but psychiatrists stated that he was an antisocial personality who would likely not benefit from any known medical treatment. Soon after the report was submitted, Gacy entered a guilty plea to the sodomy charge. He received ten years at the Iowa State Reformatory, the maximum time for the offence, and entered prison for the first time at the age of 26. Shortly after he went to prison, his wife divorced him on the grounds that he had violated their wedding vows.

Gacy adhered to all of the rules in prison and stayed out of trouble. Described as a model prisoner, he was paroled after only 18 months. On June 18, 1970, he left his cell and made his way back to Chicago. He moved in with his mother and obtained work as a chef in a city restaurant, settling into the position and trying to get his life back on track after serving time.

Gacy lived with his mother for four months and then decided to move out on his own. She helped him to obtain a new house at 8213 West Summerdale Avenue in the Norwood Park Township. Gacy owned one-half of the house and his mother and sisters owned the other. He was very happy with his new, two-bedroom ranch house. It was located in a clean, quiet neighborhood and he quickly went about making friends with his neighbors, Edward and Lilla Grexa, who had lived in the neighborhood since it had been built. Within seven months of moving in next door, Gacy was spending Christmas with the Grexa's. They became close friends and often gathered for drinks and card games. The Grexa's had no idea of Gacy's criminal past -- or his most recent run-in with the law.

Just a month before the Grexa's had invited Gacy over for Christmas dinner, he had been charged with disorderly conduct for forcing a young boy, whom he had picked up at the bus station, to perform sexual acts on him. It seems as though once Gacy stepped over the line with Mark Miller, there was no turning back for him. His slide into complete depravity had begun and these charges had done nothing to halt his descent. He managed to slip through the system when the charges against him were dropped, thanks to the fact that his accuser never showed up in court.

In June 1972, Gacy married Carole Hoff, a newly divorced mother of two daughters. Gacy romanced her when most vulnerable and she fell for his charm and generosity. She knew about his time in prison but believed that he had changed his life for the better. Carole and her daughters soon settled into Gacy's home and forged a close relationship with the Grexa's. The older couple was often invited over to the Gacy's house for elaborate parties and cook-outs. However, they were often bothered by the horrible stench that often wafted throughout the house. Lillie Grexa was convinced that an animal had died beneath the floorboards of the place and she urged Gacy to do something about it. He blamed the odor on a moisture buildup in the crawlspace under the house though -- refusing to reveal the true, and much more sinister, cause for the smell. He would keep this secret for years to come.

In 1974, Gacy started a contracting business called Painting, Decorating and Maintenance or PDM Contractors, Inc. He hired a number of teenaged boys to work for him, explaining to friends that hiring young men would keep his payroll costs low. This was not the real reason though for Gacy's deviant desires were started to get out of control. He could not longer hide what he was and while he believed that it was all still a secret; it was starting to become very apparent to those who were close to him, especially to his wife.

By 1975, Carole and Gacy had drifted apart. Their sex life had ended and Gacy's moods became more and more unpredictable, ranging from jovial to an uncontrollable rage that would have him throwing furniture. He had become an insomniac and his lack of sleep seemed to make his mood swings even worse. And if his personality changes were not enough, his choice of reading material worried her even more. Carole had started to find magazines with naked men and boys in them around the house and when confronted, Gacy casually admitted they were his. He even confessed that he preferred young men to women. Naturally, this was the last straw for Carole and she soon filed for divorce. It became final on March 2, 1976.

Gacy dismissed his marital problems and refused to let them hamper his need for recognition and success. To most people, Gacy was still the outgoing and hardworking man that he always had been. So many people had experienced divorces that no one thought a thing about it. Gacy made up for any lingering questions about him with his natural talent for persuading others to his ideas and thoughts and he always came up with creative ways to get himself noticed. It was not long before he gained the attention of Robert F. Matwick, the Democratic township committeeman for Norwood Park. As a free service to the committeeman, Gacy volunteered himself and his employees to clean up and repair Democratic Party headquarters. Unaware of the contractor's past and impressed by his sense of duty and dedication to the community, Matwick nominated Gacy to the street lighting commission. In 1975, Gacy became the secretary treasurer but his political career was short-lived -- no matter how he thought he was hiding it, rumors again began to circulate about Gacy's interest in young boys.

One of the rumors stemmed from an actual incident that took place during the time that Gacy was working on the Democratic headquarters. One of the teenagers who worked on the project was 16 year-old Tony Antonucci. According to the boy, Gacy made sexual advances toward him but backed off when Antonucci threatened to hit him with a chair. Gacy recovered his composure and made a joke out of it. He tried to convince Tony that he was only kidding and left him alone for the next month. Several weeks later, while visiting Gacy's home, Gacy again approached Antonucci. He tricked the young man into a pair of handcuffs and then tried to undress him. Antonucci had made sure that he was loosely cuffed though and when he slipped free, he wrestled Gacy to the ground and cuffed the older man instead. He eventually let him go when Gacy promised not to bother him again. That was the last time that Gacy ever made advances toward Antonucci and the boy remained working for the contracting company for almost a year after the incident.

Tony Antonucci would not realize how lucky he had been that day. Others would not fare as well.

Johnny Butkovich, 17, began doing remodeling work for Gacy's company in an effort to raise money for his racing car. He enjoyed the position, it paid well, and he maintained a good working relationship with Gacy until one pay period when Gacy refused to pay Johnny for two weeks of work. This was something that Gacy often did in order to save money. Angered that Gacy had withheld his pay, Johnny went over to his employer's house with two friends to collect what was rightfully his. When he confronted him, Gacy refused to pay and a loud argument erupted. Finally, he realized there was little that he could do and Johnny and his friends left. Butkovich dropped off his friends at home and drove off -- never to be seen again.

Michael Bonnin, 17, enjoyed working with his hands, especially carpentry and woodworking, and often had several different projects going at the same time. In June 1976, he had almost completed restoring an antique jukebox -- but the job was never finished. When on his way to catch a train to meet his stepfather's brother, he vanished.

Billy Carroll, 16, was a long time troublemaker who had first been in trouble with the authorities at the age of 9. Two years later, he was caught with a gun and he spent most of his life on the streets of Chicago, making money by arranging meetings between teenaged boys and adult men for a commission. Although he came from a very different background that Michael Bonnin and Johnny Butkovich, they all three had one thing in common -- John Wayne Gacy. Like the others Carroll also disappeared suddenly. He left home on June 13, 1976 and was never seen alive again.

Gregory Godzik, 17, started working for PDM Contractors in order to finance parts for his 1966 Pontiac.

He considered it an eyesore but it was a consuming hobby for him. The work that he did for Gacy paid well and he liked it a lot. On December 12, 1976, Gregory dropped his date, a girl he had had a crush on for awhile, at her house and drove off towards home. The following day, the police found Gregory's Pontiac but the boy was missing.

On January 20, 1977, John Szyc, 19, also vanished. He had driven off in his 1971 Plymouth Satellite and was never seen alive again. Interestingly, a short time after Szyc disappeared, another teenager was picked up by police in a 1971 Plymouth Satellite while trying to leave a gas station without paying. The boy said that the man he lived with could explain the situation -- John Wayne Gacy. He told the officers that John Szyc had sold him the car some time earlier. The police never checked the title, which had been signed 18 days after John's disappearance. Szyc had not worked for PDM Contractors but he was acquainted with Gregory Godzik, Johnny Butkovich and fatally, John Wayne Gacy.

On September 15, 1977, Robert Gilroy, 18, also disappeared. Gilroy was an avid outdoorsman and on that date, was supposed to catch a bus to meet friends for horseback riding. When he never showed up, his father, a Chicago police sergeant, immediately began searching for the boy. A full scale investigation was launched but Robert was nowhere to be found.

More than a year later, another young man named Robert Piest would vanish as well. The investigation into his disappearance would lead not only to the discovery of his body but the bodies of Butkovich, Bonnin, Carroll, Szyc, Gilroy and 27 other young men who suffered similar fates. These discoveries would horrify not only Chicago, but all of America.

Before Robert disappeared though, a weird event would occur that would later turn out to be a chilling prediction of events to come -- or rather a stunning revelation of events that had already occurred. At a pre-Christmas party that was held on December 2, 1978, a well-known local psychic known as Florece (Florence Branson) had been hired to provide cards readings for the guests. The party was held at the home of a contractor associate of Gacy's and Gacy was one of the many in attendance.

The evening was almost over when it came time for Gacy to have his fortune told. Up until this point, the party and the readings had been going well and everyone was having a great time, including the psychic, and then Gacy approached her for his reading. As soon as he spoke to her, Florece later reported that she sensed something was very wrong with the man. She also said that she became physically ill when she laid out his cards. She was unable to discern any details but knew there was an evil hiding below the surface of this man. She bluffed her way through the reading, much too frightened to say anything to Gacy.

At the end of the evening, she felt compelled to speak to the hostess about her horrific impressions of Gacy. She told what she had sensed and added that she was afraid of him and that Gacy was "perverted and violent."

The hostess refused to hear such things as "John" had been a family friend for several years. Florece didn't argue with her but was not surprised several weeks later when the story of Gacy and his murderous crime spree made the papers.

Gacy's web of secrets began to unravel with the vanishing of a young boy named Robert Piest. Robert, 15, disappeared mysteriously just outside the doors of the pharmacy where he worked. His mother, who had come to pick him up after his shift, was waiting outside for him when he vanished. He had told her that he would be back in just a minute because he was going to talk to a contractor who had offered him a job -- but he never returned. She began to get worried but as more time passed, her worry turned to terror. She searched the pharmacy and looked outside but Robert was nowhere to be seen. Finally, three hours after his disappearance, the Des Plaines police were notified. Lieutenant Joseph Kozenczak led the investigation.

The first lead to follow was the most obvious one and officers quickly obtained the name of the contractor who had offered Robert the job. Kozenczak went straight to Gacy's home and when the Gacy came to the door, he told him about the missing boy. He also asked him to accompany him to the police station for some questions. Gacy refused. He explained that there had been a recent death in his family and that he had to attend to some telephone calls but he agreed to come down later. Several hours later, Gacy arrived and gave a statement to the police. He said that he knew nothing about the disappearance and was allowed to leave with no further questioning.

Something about Gacy did not sit right with Kozenczak though and he decided to do a background check on him. He was stunned when he discovered that Gacy had earlier done time for sodomy with a teenaged boy. He quickly obtained a search warrant for Gacy's house and on December 13, 1978, a legion of police officers entered the house on Summerdale Avenue. Gacy was not at home at the time.

From the items that were recovered from the house, it is obvious that Gacy's lusts had consumed him by this time. He was still trying to maintain outward appearances but a number of damning items were discovered in the residence that would lead to the discovery of his dark side. Some of them items included a box containing two drivers licenses and several rings, including one that was engraved with Maine West High School class of 1975 and the initials J.A.S.; a box containing marijuana and pills like amyl nitrate; a stained section of rug; a number of books with homosexual and child pornography themes; a pair of handcuffs; police badges; sexual devices; a hypodermic needle and small brown bottle; clothing that was too small for Gacy; nylon rope; and other items. The police also confiscated three automobiles that belonged to Gacy, including a 1978 Chevrolet truck with a snow plow attached and the name "PDM Contractors" on the side, a van with "PDM Contractors" also painted on the side and a 1979 Oldsmobile Delta 88. In the trunk of the car were pieces of hair that were later matched to Robert Piest.

As the investigation continued, the police entered the crawl space under Gacy's home. They were discouraged by the rancid odor but believed it to be sewage. The earth in the crawl space had been sprinkled with lime but appeared to be untouched. They left the narrow space and returned to police headquarters to run tests on the evidence they had obtained.

Gacy was again called to headquarters and was told about the evidence that had been removed from his house. Enraged, he immediately contacted his attorney, who also told him not to sign the Miranda waiver that was presented to him by detectives. The police had nothing to arrest him on and eventually had to release him after more questioning about the Piest disappearance. They placed him under 24-hour surveillance but this was the best they could do.

In the days that followed, friends were called into the station and were also questioned. The detectives were unable to get any information from Gacy's friends that connected him to Robert Piest and all of them insisted that Gacy simply was not capable of murder. Gacy had told his friends earlier that the police were trying to charge him with murder but that he had nothing to do with it.

In the midst of the investigation, one of these same friends was asked by Gacy to stop by his house and to check on his dog, making sure that the animal had enough food and water. Gacy said that he didn't want to go there because the police were harassing him and trying to pin the crime on him. The friend agreed, borrowed a house key from Gacy and went over to 8213 West Summerdale. Nervous about being seen going to Gacy's house, even though at this point, he was sure that his friend had nothing to do with any criminal activities, he decided to go around to the back door instead.

He put the key into the door lock and just as he began to turn it, he heard what sounded like a group of people moaning and crying inside of the house. The groans were so chilling that he immediately closed the door, re-locked it and left. He hurried away from the house and when he returned to the site where Gacy was working, he lied to him and told him that everything in the house was fine, including his dog.

There is no way to know if the sounds the man heard in the house were natural or supernatural. It's possible that one of Gacy's victims was still alive and that his eerie cries sounded like a chorus of moans to the already unnerved friend, but this seems unlikely as by this time, Gacy had begun disposing of the bodies of his victims in locations outside of his home. It seems more likely that, if this account is true, that the friend may have actually heard the voices of victims whose deaths were yet to be avenged. Could the spirits of some of Gacy's victims have lingered behind in the house -- or at least could some sort of supernatural energy have been pressed on the atmosphere of a place where such horrid things had occurred?

The investigation continued and the police became increasingly discouraged by their attempts to gather information from Gacy's friends and acquaintances. Finally, frustrated by the lack of evidence connecting Gacy to the Piest disappearance, the police decided to book him on possession of marijuana.

While Gacy was being charged with possession, the police lab and investigators were coming up with critical evidence against Gacy from the items taken from his home. One of the rings found in Gacy's house belonged to another teenager who had disappeared about a year earlier -- John Szyc. They also discovered that three former employees of Gacy's had also disappeared. Furthermore, a receipt for a roll of film that was found in Gacy's home had belonged to a co-worked of Robert Piest and he had given it to Robert on the day of the boy's disappearance. With this new information, the investigators suddenly began to realize the enormity of the case that was starting to unfold.

Detectives and crime lab technicians returned to Gacy's house again. With everything starting to crumble around him, Gacy finally confessed to the police that he had killed someone but that it had been in self defense. He said that he was frightened and had buried the body under his garage. He told the police where they could find the body and investigators marked the gravesite in the garage but did not immediately begin digging. They decided to search the crawl space first -- and minutes after starting to dig, they found the remains of the first corpse.

That evening, Dr. Robert Stein, the Cook County Medical Examiner, was called into help with the investigation. He began to organize the search by marking off areas of earth in sections, as would be done with an archaeological site. The excavation of a decomposing body has to be carried out in a meticulous manner in order to preserve the integrity of the evidence and so throughout the night and into the days that followed, the digging progressed under the medical examiner's watchful eye.

On Friday, December 22, 1978, detectives confronted Gacy with the news that digging was being done under his house. With this, the monster finally broke down. He admitted to the police that he had killed at least 30 people and that most of their remains were buried beneath the house. The first murder took placed in January 1972 and the second in Jaunary 1974, about a year and a half after he was married. He explained that his lured his victims into being handcuffed and then he would sexually assault them. To muffle their screams, Gacy stuffed a sock or their underwear into their mouths and would often kill them by placing a rope or board against their throats as he raped them. He also admitted to sometimes keeping the corpses under his bed or in his attic for hours or days before burying them in the crawl space.

Meanwhile, the police discovered two bodies during the first day of digging. One of these was John Butkovich, who was found under the garage, and the other was in the crawl space. As the days passed, the body count grew higher. Some of the victims were found with their underwear still lodged in their throats and others were buried so close together that investigators believed they had been killed, or at least buried, at the same time.

By December 28, the police had removed a total of 27 bodies from Gacy's house. Another body had also been found weeks earlier, not in the crawl space but in the Des Plaines River. The naked corpse of Frank Wayne "Dale" Landingin had been found in the water but at the time, the police were not yet aware of Gacy and his crimes. It would not be until his drivers license was found in Gacy's house that he could be connected to the young man's murder. And he would not be the only victim to be found in the river…

Also on December 28, the body of James Mazzara was removed from the Des Plaines River. His underwear was found stuffed down his throat, linking him to the other victims. Gacy told the police that he had started disposing of bodies in the river because he was running out of room in his crawl space and because all of the digging was bothering his chronic back problem. Mazzara was the 29th victim to be found -- but was still not the last.

Much to the horror of the neighbors, the police were still excavating Gacy's property at the end of

February. They had gutted the house but had found no more bodies in the crawl space. Bad winter weather had kept them from resuming the search but they believed there were still bodies to be found. While workmen began breaking up the concrete of Gacy's patio, another horrific discovery was made. They found the body of a man, still in good condition, preserved in the concrete. The following week, another body was found.

The 31st victim to be linked to Gacy was found in the Illinois River. Investigators were able to learn his identity thanks to a tattoo on his arm, which friends of the victim's father recognized while reading a newspaper article about the grim discovery. The victim's name was Timothy O'Rourke and he was believed to have been acquainted with Gacy.

Around the time that O'Rourke was discovered and pulled from the river, another body was found on Gacy's property, this time beneath his recreation room. It was the last body to be found on the property and soon after, the house was destroyed and reduced to rubble.

Although the death toll had now risen to 32, the body of Robert Piest was still missing. Tragically, his remains were discovered in the Illinois River in April 1979. The body had been lodged somewhere in the river but strong winds had worked it loose and carried it to the locks at Dresden Dam, where it was finally discovered. An autopsy report showed that Robert had been strangled by paper towels being shoved down his throat.

Police investigators worked hard to identify Gacy's victims, using dental records and other clues, and eventually, all but nine of the young men were identified. A mass burial was held for these unknown victims on June 8, 1981. And while the investigation had ended, Gacy's trial was just beginning.

John Wayne Gacy's murder trial began on February 6, 1980 at the Cook County Criminal Courts Building in downtown Chicago. Jury members, five women and seven men, listened closely as prosecutor Bob Egan outlined the case for them, detailing the short years of Robert Piest's life, his gruesome death and how Gacy was also responsible for the murders of at least 32 other young men. He told them about the investigation that led to the horrible discoveries under Gacy's house and also noted that Gacy's actions had been carefully planned and were rational and premeditated. He knew that the defense would work to make Gacy appear insane and Egan needed to counter this as much as possible. When he finished, it was obvious that Egan's statement had a chilling effect on the jury and on the courtroom spectators.

Egan's opening statement was followed by one of Gacy's defense lawyers, Robert Motta, who opposed Egan's statement and insisted that Gacy's actions had been completely irrational and impulsive. He had been insane and no longer in control of his actions. And while most would agree that only a madman would commit the acts that Gacy was being tried for, the legal definition of insanity is much harder to prove. Besides that, prosecutors wanted to make sure that Gacy was kept off the streets -- permanently if possible -- and only a "guilty" verdict would accomplish this. If Gacy was found to be insane, he would become a ward of the state mental health system with no time limits on the how long he might be incarcerated. In many cases, killers were freed when they were deemed mentally stable to re-enter to society, only to kill again. Prosecutors did not believe that this type of commitment was just punishment in Gacy's case.

After the opening statements, the prosecution bought their first witness to the stand, Marko Butkovich, the father of Gacy's victim, Johnny Butkovich. He was the first witness on a list that included the family and friends of many of the other victims. Many of them broke down on the stand, recalling their loved ones or recounting their last goodbyes. This testimony was followed by those who worked for Gacy and who survived sexual or violent encounters with him. They spoke of his mood swings and how he tried to trick them into handcuffs, using magic tricks that he perfected as "Pogo the Clown". The testimony continued for several weeks and included friends and neighbors of Gacy (legitimately shocked at the various clues to his behavior they had missed over the years), police officers involved in the investigation and psychologists who examined Gacy and found him to be sane. Before the state rested, prosecutors had called some 60 witnesses to the stand.

The defense then took over, never trying to refute the evidence that established their client as a killer but rather to paint him as insane and unable to controls his actions. They called friends and family members of Gacy to the stand, including his mother, who testified that her husband would often beat Gacy with a leather strap. His sister told of how she saw Gacy being verbally assaulted by their father on many occasions. Others who testified for the defense told of how Gacy was a good and generous man, who helped those in need and who always had a smile and kind word for everyone. Lillie Grexa even took the stand and spoke of what a wonderful neighbor he was. However, she also said something that turned out to be damaging to the case. She refused to say that he was crazy and instead told the court that she believed him to be a "very brilliant man". One has to wonder if she knew that her statement would conflict with the defense theory that Gacy was insane and out of control.

The defense then called Thomas Eliseo, a psychologist who had conducted interviews with Gacy before the trial. He said that he found Gacy to be extremely intelligent but believed that he suffered from borderline schizophrenia. Other medical experts who testified gave similar testimony, reciting a litany of schizophrenia, multiple personality disorder and antisocial behavior. They also reported that Gacy's mental disorder prevented him from understanding the magnitude of his crimes. In conclusion, each of the experts found him to be insane at the time of the murders and with the testimony of the medical experts, the defense rested its case.

In their closing statements, both sides emotionally argued their side to the jury but it only took them two hours of deliberation to come back with a verdict -- "guilty". Gacy had been convicted of the deaths of 33 young men and had the notoriety of being convicted of more murders than anyone else in American history. Gacy received the death penalty and was sent to the Menard Correctional Center to await execution. After years of appeals, he was put to death by lethal injection on May 9, 1994.

Finally, Gacy's terrifying string of crimes could be relegated to memory -- or could it?

By the spring of 1979, Gacy's home at 8213 West Summerdale had been reduced to ruin. Once the remains of the house were cleared away, it became a muddy, vacant lot and a continuing reminder to the neighborhood of the monster who had once been in their midst. All vestiges of the house, even the driveway and barbecue pit, were hauled away but still the onlookers came, macabre curiosity-seeking tourists who flocked to the once peaceful residential area. Neighbors hoped that with all traces of the house removed that the line of cars would finally stopped. The quiet would return, they believed, once the notoriety of the spot began to fade, warmer weather came and the grass began to grow back over the open scar where the house of John Wayne Gacy had once stood.

Perhaps the most chilling image of Gacy of all....
(Chicago Tribune)

Unfortunately though, the grass did not return. Even more than 18 months after the house was destroyed, the land remained strangely barren. Some weeds had started to grow near the front sidewalk but the back of the lot, where the house had stood and where the bodies had been buried, remained completely empty of plant life, despite the fact that there was no logical reason for the soil to be bare.

Those searching for an explanation suggested that perhaps the lime that Gacy had dusted the bodies of his victims with had contaminated the soil in some way but police officers who were involved in the actual recovery of the bodies disputed this. They insisted that Gacy had never used enough lime to cause any damage to the lot. The shallow graves where the bodies lay had been carefully unearthed and then later, a backhoe had been brought in to dig down 8 to 10 feet to be sure that nothing was missed. The small amount of lime that had been used would not have survived this and even so, no lime had been used under the garage or in the backyard -- and yet no grass would grow there either.

It was as though the evil deeds that had occurred on the spot had left a supernatural mark on the site, not allowing the grass to grow or for the events to be forgotten.

The mystery of the barren soil lasted for a few more years and then the lot was sold and a new house was built on the site. The new owners even went to the trouble of changing the physical address of the location so that the stigma would be removed. Fortunately for them, their efforts worked and once the construction was completed, the grass began to grow once again. The nightmare, it seemed, was finally over.

A VOICE FROM THE GRAVE

Thick smoke rolled from the fifteenth-floor windows of the apartment building at 2740 North Pine Grove in Chicago. Against the darkened evening sky, the dance of flames could be seen behind the glass as the firefighters arrived and ran into the building. They made their way upstairs to be greeted at the stairway by a heavy wall of noxious smoke. The smoke could be seen coming from under the door of an apartment that belonged to Teresita Basa, an employee of Edgewater Hospital. None of her neighbors knew if she was home or not.

The door was forced open and the firefighters entered the hazy room on hands and knees. Windows were opened to try and let some of the smoke escape, while other rescuers looked for the source of the fire. They found it in the bedroom. Flames had completely engulfed a mattress that was lying on the floor. They worked quickly to extinguish the blaze and then removed the soggy blankets and pillows. At that point, the unmistakable stench of seared human flesh filled the room.

The firefighters turned the mattress over and beneath it, found the slightly charred remains of a naked woman. Her legs had been spread apart and a butcher knife had been rammed into her chest so hard that half of the wooden handle had slipped between her ribs. The question of whether or not Teresita Basa was at home had just been answered.

Police detectives were dispatched from the 23rd district to investigate. From all indications, Teresita had been the victim of a random rape and robbery. Unfortunately, this sort of crime was not uncommon in the neighborhood where she lived. Once the officers began to investigate though, they discovered that things were not as they first appeared. They found no evidence at the scene of the crime and there was no sign of a forced entry. It appeared that Teresita had known her killer and had let him into the apartment. They considered looking for a friend or a boyfriend who may have raped and killed her. Then, the coroner came back with another odd piece of information. Teresita had not been raped at all and in fact, was still a virgin. A motive for the bizarre crime had just vanished.

Detectives doggedly pursued the case, making lists of suspects and speaking with co-workers and friends of the dead woman. Every one of the suspects managed to come up with an unbreakable alibi and the investigation was stopped dead in its tracks. Days turned into weeks and then weeks into months. The detectives had stopped hoping for new leads in the case and soon, it was placed on the proverbial back-burner as new investigations demanded attention. They never thought to count on a new lead that would come from Teresita herself. And one that come from beyond the grave!

Teresita Basa was a 48-year-old respiratory therapist who worked at Chicago's Edgewater hospital. She had been born and raised on Negros Island in the Philippines and had come to the United States, where she studied classical music. She was considered a gifted musician and had also studied in Europe at the Royal Conservatory of Music in London. She was pursuing a career in music and worked at the hospital to make ends meet. She spent much of her free time working on a children's book about classical music and on her nights off, filled in as a pianist in a local jazz club. Although she was quiet and was slow to make close friends, she lived a full and active life. Although this life did not include men. She rarely dated, leaving her co-workers to ponder whether she simply hadn't found the right man or if she had a fear of them. Her lack of interaction with the opposite sex made the investigation into her death all the more perplexing.

As time passed and the inquiries into the murder faded away, Teresita became less and less a topic of conversation among her former co-workers at the hospital. She would never be forgotten, but after many months was rarely mentioned anymore. This is what made an event that took place in the spring of 1977 even more astonishing!

Remy Chua was another respiratory therapist who worked at Edgewater Hospital. Like Teresita, she had been born and raised in the Philippines and had moved to the United States. Her husband, Joe, was a doctor who worked at another local hospital. Although Remy and Teresita had never been close, they had always maintained a friendly relationship. Remy had been shocked and saddened when Teresita had been killed but the other woman was far from her thoughts that spring afternoon.

Remy was on her break that day, nearing the middle of her shift, and she went into the employee's lounge to relax for a few minutes. She sat down on the couch and leaned her head back. With her eyes closed, she could see nothing around her but she soon got the distinct feeling that someone else was in the room, watching her. She tried to ignore the feeling.

It's foolish, she told herself, if someone else had come into the lounge, I would have heard the door open and close.

Despite assuring herself that there simply couldn't be anyone else there, the sensation became stronger and she finally opened her eyes. She found that she was not alone! There was a woman standing several feet away from her, staring at her. The woman wore hospital scrubs and looked very familiar. Then Remy realized why she seemed familiar to her -- the woman was Teresita Basa! It was impossible and yet, there she was. She did not appear to be ghost-like at all but completely solid. Her face was just as Remy remembered it, but filled with sadness and pain. Without thinking, she lifted her hand to touch Teresita and then suddenly changed her mind. The sudden realization came to her again that the other woman was dead!

Remy sprang up from the couch and crashed through the door of the lounge. She tried breathlessly to scream, but no words came out. As she spun into the hallway, she collided with a male technician in the corridor. The hospital charts that he was carrying clattered the floor. He started to protest and then saw the look on Remy's face. She appeared to be terrified. He grabbed her arm and quickly asked her what was wrong. To his surprise, Remy explained that she had just seen Teresita Basa in the lounge.

"But, that's impossible!" the technician sputtered. He replied that she had been dead for months, but Remy swore that was whom she had seen. Together, the two of them opened the door of the employee lounge and peered inside. The room was empty.

In the weeks following the strange encounter, Remy's husband and friends began to notice a change in her personality. She began to act very moody and sad and one of her co-workers quietly suggested to another one that she was starting to act just like Teresita had. A nurse on staff would also later recall that Remy would sometimes stand transfixed in front of Teresita's old locker. In the cafeteria, Remy moved away from the table where she normally sat with her friends and began sitting alone in the same spot that Teresita used to occupy. Her friends also noticed that Remy would often seem to slip into a daze and would hum little snatches of songs. Co-workers remembered them as being tunes that Teresita often sang. When they mentioned this to Remy, she claimed that she had no idea what they were talking about.

Soon, Remy's personality changes began to cause her to have nightmares that she would vividly recall later. It seemed that whenever she closed her eyes to sleep, Teresita would appear. Before long, she began to show up when Remy was wide awake as well. One morning while she was waiting for a stoplight to change, she saw Teresita standing near her car. In moments, her image was replaced by that of an orderly that Remy worked with at the hospital. His name was Allan Showery and while Remy didn't know him very well, she found it strange that he would appear in her vision. She had never really thought about him before, but lately she had started to feel an intense hatred for the man. She couldn't understand it because he was virtually a stranger and yet she felt her stomach clench whenever he passed her in the hallways.

Remy realized that she had to discuss the situation with her husband. She told him that she had not been sleeping well and that she was having terrible dreams. He had also noticed her personality change and guessed that it had something to do with stress. She was obviously upset about something having to do with Teresita Basa, but what? He couldn't imagine that a ghost was haunting her dreams, but his wife was obviously disturbed. She explained to him that she continually saw the face of Teresita and also that of Allan Showery, an orderly that she barely knew. Joe Chua tried to reassure her. He was convinced that the nightmares would go away.

But they didn't go away and in fact, they became worse. The two faces would appear in her dreams, jolting her awake, and as she became conscious, she would experience the lingering smell of smoke in her bedroom. On a few nights, the smell was so strong that she actually got out of bed to be sure that the house was not on fire.

One afternoon while Remy was in bed trying to rest, Joe called his attorney on the phone. Just as the other man answered, both of them heard a deafening scream from the bedroom. Stunned, Joe dropped the phone and ran into the other room. He found his wife still in a deep sleep on the bed. Remy's parents, who were staying with them at the time, reached the bedroom just moments after Joe did. When they entered, they found the temperature in the room was a good 10 or 15 degrees colder than in the rest of the house. Remy's mother said later that her scalp began to tingle and she could feel the hair on her arms standing on end. It was as if someone had charged the room with static electricity. But it was soon to get much stranger!

Remy, still asleep, began to rise from the bed with her arms outstretched in front of her. She walked toward her husband and parents and then suddenly fell backwards, collapsing back onto the bed. Joe, assuming that she was sleepwalking, tried to relax her arms into a more comfortable position but they would not budge. They remained stiff and upright, no matter what he did. Thanks to his medical training, it reminded Joe of a corpse that he entered a state of rigor mortis.

Then, Remy began to speak. Her breath hissed out from between her lips. "I.... I am Teresita Basa", she said. Joe was surprised. He had never heard the voice before and he knew that it was not his wife's. The odd voice continued. "Nothing has been done about the man who killed me. You must help me! Go to the police! You are a doctor. They will listen to you."

"What do you want me to tell them?" Joe asked her. His voice quavered with fear.

"Tell them a man came into my apartment and choked and stabbed me!"

"What man?"

The voice from within Remy pleaded with him once more to go to the police and then warmth seemed to settle over the room. Remy's arms dropped and relaxed and her eyes flickered open. "What.. what happened?" she asked.

Joe and Remy's parents looked at one another. They were unsure of exactly how to answer her question. Joe had never seen anything like it before. He was a man of science, he didn't believe in the supernatural, but he was unable to explain what had just happened to his wife. Finally, Remy's father spoke up. He believed that his daughter had been possessed by the spirit of a dead woman named Teresita Basa.

Several days later, it happened again. Once more, Joe and Remy's parents were present. This time, the voice that came from Remy was even more upset. It demanded to know why Joe had not gone to the police with the information that he had been given. The voice never referred to him as Joe either, as his wife would have done, but instead as Dr. Chua, as if he was a stranger. Of course, to Teresita, he would be.

"I can't go to them unless you tell me who killed you," he answered.

"Allan killed me. I let him into my apartment and he killed me. You must go to the police." The voice explained that Allan was a friend from the hospital and then once again demanded that Joe go to the police. After that, Remy seemed to come out of the trance once more.

She opened her eyes and looked around the room at the faces that were staring at her. She asked for a glass of water but had no idea what Joe was talking about when he told her that if he went to the police with his story they would think he was crazy. He just didn't know what to believe, or what to think about the strange affliction that had come over his wife.

A few days passed and a priest and relatives visited with Remy. Some of them believed that she needed psychiatric treatment, while others, like her father, believed that she was possessed. In the middle of one of her eerie trances, her father had tried to convince the spirit to leave his daughter alone. Teresita (as they had started to believe the voice was) told him that she would not be driven away until her killer was brought to justice.

One evening, Remy once again slipped into a trance. She fell down and began to scream that she was burning. She wrapped her arms around her body and cried out. Joe quickly came to her aid. As he leaned over her, a hand clutched him by the shirt front. "You have not done what I asked you to, Dr. Chua," said the chilling voice.

"If I told the police about you, they'd never believe me," Joe insisted. He was scared of what was happening to his wife, but angry too. He snapped at Teresita. "Leave my wife and family alone! I want you to get the hell out of our lives!" he snapped at the entity.

Remy fell silent and her body stiffened. A chill seemed to pervade the room but the spirit did not speak for nearly a minute. Finally, the voice spoke once more, emerging loudly from Remy's throat. "They will believe you," it said. "Allan Showery, the orderly, stole my jewelry and gave it all to his girlfriend."

Joe asked how it could be proved that the jewelry was Teresita's and the ghost replied that her cousins would recognize the pieces as family heirlooms. She also went to on give Joe the telephone numbers of her cousins. If he had any doubts remaining about the reality of the supernatural, it vanished with these last words. There was no possible way that his wife could have known the names and telephone number of Teresita's family.

Then the voice continued. "Tell the police that Allan came to fix my television, and he killed me and burned me". After that, the voice was gone.

On August 8, Joe finally gathered up enough nerve to go to the police with his story about his wife being possessed by the spirit of Teresita Basa. One can only imagine what it must have taken for the respected physician to go to the authorities with a tale that he knew they would find ridiculous. At the precinct house, he was introduced to a detective named Joe Stachula, who had been assigned to the original case. The veteran investigator listened politely to Joe's story, but confessed that he had little faith in its authenticity. However, having nothing else to go on and no other leads to follow, Stachula agreed to at least check out the orderly for a past criminal record.

The detective set to work and put Allan Showery's name into the system. He soon discovered that Showery did have a record. In fact, he had been arrested several times in New York, twice for rape. Further investigation also revealed that complaints had been filed against Showery by relatives whose loved ones had passed away at Edgewater Hospital. It was alleged that Showery had removed and had stolen jewelry from the deceased. After discovering this information, Detective Stachula and his partner, Lee Epplen, brought Allan Showery in for questioning.

During the interrogation, Showery admitted to knowing Teresita and working with her at the hospital. Stachula told him that they had information that Showery was supposed to go to her apartment and fix her television on the night she was killed. Showery admitted that he was but said that he had stopped off in a neighborhood bar on the way. He lost track of time and then, since it was too late to go to Teresita's, went home instead.

Despite the suspect's quick answers, Stachula had a feeling that something was not quite right with the alibi. He pressed a little harder. "That doesn't fit with the information that we've heard," he told Showery. "It doesn't sound right."

But Showery insisted that he had never been to Teresita's apartment, even when Stachula told him that a number of people had seen him at the building. He replied that he had carried groceries for her into the lobby, but he had never been up to the apartment itself.

Finally, Stachula relented, or at least he appeared to. "All right," he said with a sigh. "We'll just take your fingerprints and compare them with the ones that we found at the scene. If they don't match up, you're free to go."

Showery balked at the prospect of having his fingerprints taken and his story changed once again. "Okay, I was in her apartment that night, but just for a minute or two. I didn't have the right tools to fix her TV, so I left. I went home and did some work around the apartment. Ask my wife, she'll tell you!"

Stachula and Epplen left Showery in lock-up and went to his apartment to talk to his wife. He advised Showery to think about his dates and times while they were gone and to see if he could get his story straight. All the while, Stachula had a funny feeling about Showery's version of the events -- and about the weird story told to them by Joe Chua. He and Epplen recalled that the "spirit" had said that Showery had given the jewelry to his girlfriend, not his wife. One of the first things that he asked the woman who answered the door at Showery's apartment was about whether or not she and Showery were married.

"We're only living together now," she answered, "but we're planning to get married soon."

The detectives were happy with the answer and they quickly asked her if Showery had given her any jewelry between January and June. She replied that he had given her an antique ring around the end of February or the beginning of March. It had been a belated Christmas gift, she said. She went to the bedroom and returned with a box containing several other pieces of jewelry. Stachula and Epplen looked at one another and they asked the woman to accompany them back to the police station.

Before leaving the apartment, Stachula asked to use the telephone. He opened his notebook and looked at the list of names and telephone numbers that Joe Chua had given him. Any remaining doubts that he had about the story evaporated as one by one the people on the list answered his calls and said that they were relatives of Teresita Basa. He asked each of them to meet he and his partner at the station house.

As Showery's girlfriend waited with Epplen, Stachula met with Teresita's family. Each of them identified the jewelry that had been taken from Showery's apartment as having been Teresita's. Many of the pieces had been in her family for years.

The detective then took the jewelry into the interrogation room and showed it to Allan Showery. Even when confronted with this evidence, Showery protested his innocence. He had bought the jewelry in a pawn shop, he swore.

Stachula frowned and he tossed the suspect a notebook and a pencil. "Okay, you write down the name of the shop and when you bought the stuff," he told him. "Then, we're going to need a receipt that proves you bought it there."

Needless to say, Showery had no receipt and claimed that he was unable to remember where he bought the merchandise. His story was interrupted by a knock on the door. Detective Epplen was outside and he led Showery's girlfriend into the room. By this time, Epplen had apprised her of the situation and the look on her face when she saw Showery must have shocked the suspect in a way that the detective's interrogations had been unable to do. As soon as he saw the girl walk in, Showery confessed to having killed Teresita.

On February 21, 1977, Allan Showery had gone to the apartment of Teresita Basa at approximately 5:00 in the evening. Shortly after he arrived there, he inspected her television set and told her that he did not have the necessary tools to fix it. He left and then returned at around 7:30. As soon as he was admitted to the apartment, he struck Teresita until she was unconscious and left her lying on the floor. He then proceeded to ransack the apartment, finding only $30 in cash but finding her collection of jewelry. After that, he drug Teresita into the bedroom, where he removed all of her clothing and spread her legs apart to make it appear that she had been raped. He was totally unaware that Teresita was a virgin. Showery then went into the kitchen and took a butcher's knife from a drawer. He plunged the knife into Teresita's chest, narrowly missing a rib. He then covered the body with a mattress and set it on fire. Showery fled the scene just before the firefighters arrived.

The orderly had confessed to the brutal and gruesome crime, but that was not the end of the story. After engaging a lawyer, Showery recanted the confession and a trial that was held two years later ended in a hung jury. He was returned to a holding cell to wait for his new trial date but before it got under way, Showery pleaded guilty to the murder. The plea came as a complete surprise to both his attorney and the prosecutor, especially in light of the fact that Showery had been claiming that he was innocent of the crime for months. He was later sentenced to fourteen years in prison.

Some have wondered if perhaps Showery didn't have a visitor in his cell one night -- a visitor who was not of this world. Who knows?

As for Teresita Basa herself, her spirit was never heard from again. She did not return to the Chua family and they were able to live out their lives in peace. They must have wondered why Teresita had chosen them to seek justice on her behalf, but that question remains unanswered. Regardless, the dead woman did find a voice and murder was finally avenged.

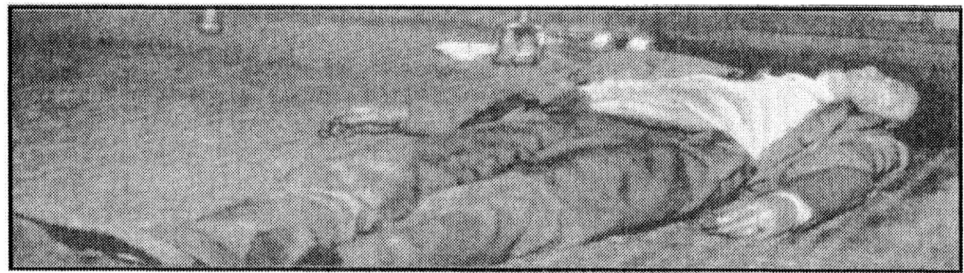

GANGLAND GHOSTS

When I sell liquor, they call it bootlegging. When my patrons serve it on silver trays on Lake Shore Drive, they call it hospitality.

I'm a businessman, I've made my money supplying a popular demand. If I break the law, my customers are as guilty as I am.

Whatever they may say, my booze has been good and my games have been on the square. Public service has been my motto... I've been spending the best years of my life as a public benefactor. I've given people the light pleasures, shown them a good time. All I get is abuse.
AL CAPONE

Nobody shot me.
FRANK GUSENBERG...
mortally wounded in the St. Valentines Day Massacre

Never trust a woman or an automatic pistol.
JOHN DILLINGER

There are few periods of American history as fascinating as that of the "gangster era" of the 1920's and 1930's. During this period, organized crime gained a foothold in America, especially in the larger cities, where gangsters became celebrities and "graft" being paid to cops and politicians was an everyday happening. During the years of Prohibition, the mob came into its own, "giving the people what they wanted" and then diversifying into other criminal pursuits once the liquor began to legally flow again.

But organized crime had come to America long before the years of Prohibition. Its American roots were born in the city of New Orleans but the "Mafia" was created in Sicily around 1282. At that time, it was a secret brotherhood that was dedicated to freeing the country from the French. For years, the Mafia was a champion of the people, waging guerilla warfare against the French and other invaders. The country's chief city, Palermo, became the hub of Mafia activity and the "dons" of the organization sent recruiters out across the land in search of young and ardent patriots who were skilled in the art of killing.

By the early 1800's, the Mafia had evolved from a benevolent society that fed the hungry and sheltered the homeless to an organization that extorted money and power from landowners and peasants alike. Its leaders, known as "capos", directed the group to infiltrate and threaten business, government and even the military.

By 1889, the Mafia had come to America and it has been said that it came first to New Orleans. At that time, New Orleans was probably the most anti-Italian city in America. The city had recently been flooded with thousands of Italian immigrants and statements from the Mayor's office didn't help matters any. In one letter, Mayor Joseph A. Shakespeare called Southern Italians and Sicilians ".... the most idle, vicious and worthless people among us." Of course, not all of the blame could be laid at city government's door either. In addition to dirty politicians and cops on the take, late 1800's New Orleans was also filled with Italian criminals. There was no denying that the French Quarter ghetto was turning out productive Italian citizens, but it was also turning out lawbreakers as well. Undoubtedly, many of these criminals were not "Mafia", but it has long been conceded that New Orleans represented one of the main ports of entry for the Mafia into the United States. Between 1888 and 1890, the New Orleans Mafia, made up of several Sicilian groups, committed an estimated 40 murders without opposition. From New Orleans, organized crime and the Mafia spread across America, gaining footholds in Kansas City, New York, St. Louis and of course, Chicago.

THE BLACK HAND

The Black Hand first became associated with Chicago crime around 1900. The area where this menace has been most associated was a tenement area that was known as "Smoky Hollow" in the early 1890's. At that time, this was a quiet and hard-working community that was mostly free of serious crime, save for family squabbles and the occasional clash between rival Irish gangs. By the end of the decade, most of the Irish had left the area though and it had mostly been taken over by poor, working-class Italians. It would be during this period, when the Italian immigrants began to be terrorized by the Black Hand, that the neighborhood became better known as "Little Hell".

During a period that last from roughly 1900 to 1920, there were an alleged 400 murders ascribed to a shadowy world known as the Black Hand. The gangs preyed on the Italian and Sicilian immigrants who lived along Oak and West Taylor Streets and along Grand and Wentworth Avenue and so many murders were committed near the intersection of Milton and Oak Streets that the locality became popularly known as "Death Corner". This was the favorite killing field of a vicious and mysterious killer called the "Shotgun Man" and he was believed to be responsible for at least one-third of the 38 unsolved Italian and Sicilian murders that occurred between January 1910 and March 1911. Four of the victims were killed in a single, 72 hour period of that final month.

There were probably as many as 60 or 80 Black Hand gangs at work in Chicago during the first two decades of the Twentieth Century but all of them appeared to be independent units and the police were never able to connect one with another. And despite the magnitude of their operations, none of the extensive investigations conducted by the police ever revealed a Black Hand organization that reached national or even citywide proportions. The "Black Hand" was not an actual group, it was realized, but a method of crime. It was used by individuals, by small groups and by large and organized gangs and in Italy and Sicily was employed by the Mafia. It was called the Black Hand because as a general rule, extortion letters, which formed the initial phase of the terrorism, bore the imprint of a hand in black ink, as well as crude drawings of a skull and crossbones or sometimes crosses and daggers.

The way the Black Hand operated was both simple and direct. First, a victim would be chosen from among the Italian immigrant population that showed signs of prosperity. For instance, if a man purchased any property and that fact became public knowledge, he could almost count on the attention on the Black Hand. A letter, bearing a signature of the Black Hand was then sent to the victim demanding money. If the letter was ignored, or the victim refused to pay, his home, office or business would be bombed. If he still refused to pay, then he would be murdered. Most of the letters were blunt instructions about sums of money and where they were to be delivered. Others were more clever and worded with politeness and Italian courtesy. No matter how they were phrased though, each brought the promise of death if the instructions were not carried out to the letter.

Dozens of bombs were exploded in the Italian quarter in retaliation for non-payment of extortion. In 1910, the *Chicago Tribune* reported that there had been 25 unsolved murders connected to the Black Hand; 43 murders in 1911; 33 in 1912; 31 in 1913 and 42 in 1914. During the first six months of 1915, six men were killed and 12 bombs were detonated.

As the police attempted to combat the Black Hand gangs though, they were faced with impossible obstacles. Hundreds of arrests were made but suspects were usually released within hours because no evidence connecting them with specific crimes could be secured. Many cases of murder and extortion were brought into the courts but convictions were nearly impossible to obtain and those few who were sent to prison, were usually quickly paroled thanks to payoffs to corrupt politicians. The reason that it was so hard to prosecute the Black Hand gang leaders was for the same reason they were so terrifying in the first place. As soon as a Black Hand suspect was arrested, witnesses and members of the victim's family were threatened with death if they gave information to the police. Judges, jurors, members of the prosecutor's staff and even their families received threats. In one case, a witness was about to give the details of a Black Hand extortion plot when a man entered the courtroom and waved a red handkerchief at him. The witness froze and refused to speak anymore. The state was then forced to abandon the case.

According to the *Tribune*, "the police, hampered at every turn by the silence of the Italian colony, are compelled to resign themselves... at present the police acknowledge the futility of further investigation."

By the latter part of the 1910's, the police officials were forced to try and downplay the Black Hand. They simply had no way of controlling the situation and no way to combat the threats or apprehend the killers when the extortion went one step too far. Most Chicago cops paid them a grudging respect as an elusive and resourceful prey, while others denied their existence altogether, as the Federal Bureau of Investigation would do a few years later when forced to confront the reality of the Mafia. The prejudices of those in the city government who sought to dismiss the Black Hand failed to take into account the helplessness and despair of the Italian immigrants as they tried to cope with the hardships of life in a new and unpredictable country -- only to be faced with being terrorized on top of it.

Because of this, some of the Italian business and professional men decided to try and take matters into their own hands. They formed what was called the White Hand Society, an organization that was sponsored by wealthy businessmen, the Italian Chamber of Commerce, Italian newspapers and several fraternal orders of Italians and Sicilians. It was formed to work with the police and to try and exterminate the Black Hand. Although virtually every member of the society was threatened with death at one time or another, it was active for several years. Private detectives were employed to help the police investigate Black Hand cases and agents were even sent to Italy and Sicily to look into past histories of the most notorious gangsters. They also arranged for protection for witnesses and their family members. Several murderers and extortionists were sent to prison through the efforts of the White Hand, but they were soon paroled and resumed their activities. For this reason, this society of neighborhood vigilantes was more of a symbolic gesture than anything else. Their intentions were good but they were up against a much too difficult adversary. The

White Hand was no longer heard from by around 1912.

The Black Hand gangs endured for about another eight years and it was finally a federal law that forced them out of existence. Once the federal government began prosecuting extortion as misuse of the United States mail, dozens of Black Hand gangsters began to be convicted, fined and sent to Federal prisons. The Chicago politicians were unable to help them and most of the convicted men served their full sentences. Thanks to government intervention, the bombings, murders and extortion that still took place were carried out by other methods than the mail and soon the Black Hand began to disappear. By 1920, and the coming of Prohibition, most of the extortionist gangs found that bootlegging and rum-running was a greater field for their talents and the Black Hand was a thing of the past.

CURSE OF THE "GREEN CHAIR"

Organized crime in Chicago became involved in gambling, prostitution and extortion but it would be an American law that would actually bring the underworld its greatest power.

When the 18th Amendment to the Constitution, which abolished the sale and distribution of alcohol, took effect on January 16, 1920, many believed that it would cure the social ills of America. Little did they know at the time, but it would actually do just the opposite. America's great thirst for the forbidden liquor bred corruption in every corner. Law enforcement officials became open to bribes because the majority of the men just did not believe in the law, but worse yet, Prohibition gave birth to the great days of organized crime. The gangsters of America had previously concerned themselves with acts of violence, racketeering and prostitution but the huge profits that came to be made with the sale of illegal liquor built criminal empires.

Across the country, over 200,000 "speakeasys" opened. These drinking establishments were so named because many of them were located behind, above or below legitimate businesses and patrons often drank in silence. Huge bootlegging operations sprang into being to supply the speakeasys and those who chose to ignore the new law. In addition, ordinary people began brewing their own beer and distilling their own liquor. Some of them even sold the stuff from home, and the product called "bathtub gin" came into existence. Disrespect for the law became the fashion as people who would have never dreamed of doing anything illegal before now found themselves serving illicit liquor in their homes or drinking in the neighborhood speakeasy.

Prohibition was widely considered to be doomed by 1928, but it hung on for another five years before being repealed in 1933. By then, it had taken its toll, leaving law enforcement in disarray and leaving the mobster organizations so powerful they were able to move onto other pursuits, like legalized gambling, with wide public approval.

In Chicago, names like Al Capone and Dion O'Bannion were no longer spoken in merely the poor neighborhoods, but among the rich of Lake Shore Drive as well. Newspapers carried accounts of gangland slayings and bootleg wars across the country. Author Herbert Asbury wrote that "the average tourist felt that his trip to Chicago was a failure unless it included a view of Capone out for a spin. The mere whisper: 'Here comes Al', was sufficient to stop traffic and to set thousands of curious citizens craning their necks along the curbing."

Crime ran rampant during this period and even inspired phrases that are still in use today among law enforcement officials. The term "Chicago Amnesia" is still used to describe the reticence of witnesses to testify against organized crime. In Chicago of the 1920's, law enforcement officials found it almost impossible to prosecute gangsters because of the fear they instilled in possible witnesses. Even eyewitnesses who eagerly came forward after seeing a crime take place suddenly developed a memory loss when they learned the identities of the culprits. And it seemed that the disease was contagious, often contracted through bribes, but usually through threats and even murder attempts.

The Prohibition era also spawned a number of curious legends among Chicago underworld figures. Perhaps one of the strangest was that of the "Green Chair Curse", also referred to as the "Undertaker's

Friend." The curse was named after a green leather chair found in the office of William "Shoes" Shoemaker, who became the Chicago chief of detectives in 1924. Several of the city's top gangsters were hauled into Shoemaker's office for questioning and ordered to sit in the green chair. Several of them died violent deaths a short time later.

This could hardly be that surprising, given the death rate during the gang wars in Chicago, but the newspapers quickly seized on the story and a belief in the "curse" of the chair began to grow. Shoemaker, probably delighted with the attention, stated that he was now keeping track of the criminals who sat in the chair and later died violently. When the inevitable later occurred, he would put an X by the gangster's name. These men included the Genna brothers (Angelo, Tony and Mike), Porky Lavenuto, Mop Head Russo, Samoots Amatuna, Antonio "The Scourge" Lombardo, John Scalise, Albert Anselmi, Antonio "the Cavalier" Spano and others. Legend had it that other well-known gangsters, even Al Capone, absolutely refused to sit down in the chair.

Chief of Detectives William Shoemaker (Left) in 1928

When Shoemaker retired in 1934, there were 35 names in his notebook and 34 of them had an X after their name. Only one criminal, Red Holden, was still among the living and he was doing time in Alcatraz for train robbery. "My prediction still stands", Shoes told reporters upon his retirement. "He'll die a violent death. Maybe it'll happen in prison. Maybe he'll have to wait until he gets out. But, mark my words, it'll happen."

But Holden managed to outlive Shoes. The detective died four years later and the green chair was passed on to Captain John Warren, who had been Shoemaker's aide. He continued to seat an occasional hoodlum in it, perhaps hoping to "scare them straight" with the eerie legend. By the time that Warren died in September 1953, the chair's death rate stood at 56 out of 57 men. Only Red Holden was still alive!

Holden had been released from Alcatraz in 1948 and afterwards was involved in several shoot-outs, all of which he survived. Then, he was convicted on murder charges and was sent to prison for a 25-year sentence. He died in the infirmary of Illinois' Statesville Prison on December 18, 1953. According to the newspapers, he was smiling when he passed -- because he had beaten the green chair!

Holden's death set off a search for the mysterious green chair. No one knew what had happened to it after Captain Warren had died. Finally, it discovered that the chair had been destroyed. It was traced to the Chicago Avenue police station, where it had been confined to the cellar after the death of Captain Warren. When it was found to be infested with cockroaches, it had been broken apart and burned in the station's furnace. This had happened shortly before Red Holden had died in his hospital bed.

Otherwise, some claimed, he would have never escaped the curse!

THE ST. VALENTINE'S DAY MASSACRE

For a city that is so filled with the history of crime, there has been little preservation of the landmarks that were once so important to the legend of the mob in Chicago. The most tragically destroyed of these landmarks was the warehouse that was located at 2122 North Clark Street. It was here, on Valentine's Day 1929, that the most spectacular mob hit in gangland history took place -- the St. Valentine's Day Massacre. The building was called the S-M-C Cartage Company and was a red, brick structure on Clark Street. The events that led to the massacre did not begin on the morning of February 14 as many who have you believe however, they began years before with the complex creation of several criminal empires in the Windy City.

And although the events of February 14, 1929 did not end the machinations of organized crime in Chicago, they certainly led to the destruction of the many of those involved in the events. Their demise also led to the so-called "glory days" of the Chicago mob and ended an era forever. To understand what happened on St. Valentine's Day, and after, we have to go back several years to the time of a man named Johnny Torrio, who brought Al Capone to Chicago.

One of the most important criminals in pre-Prohibition Chicago was Big Jim Colosimo, who ran a restaurant in the South Side Levee District for many years. Colosimo was an influential brothel-keeper and was tied closely to important city officials, thus insuring both political clout and his ability to operate his criminal endeavors without interference. While operating his string of

The S-M-C Cartage Company in the 1930's

whorehouses, Colosimo brought a young man named Johnny Torrio from New York to be his bodyguard and right-hand man. By 1915, he was the acknowledged overlord of prostitution on the south side and thanks to his political powers, was important in other sections of the city as well.

Ironically, Colosimo's downfall came at the same time that he developed a romantic interest in one of the few respectable women that he had ever known. Her name was Dale Winter, a young musical-comedy actress who had been stranded in Chicago after an unsuccessful theatrical tour. She accepted an invitation to perform in one of Colosimo's establishments and the two fell in love. In 1920, he divorced his wife and married Winter three weeks later. They took a two-week honeymoon in Crown Point, Indiana and returned to Chicago.

On the afternoon of May 11, 1920, Colosimo left for his restaurant with plans to meet his new wife later that night for dinner. When he arrived, he went to his office and spoke with his secretary, Frank Camilla, who had been meeting with the chef about that evening's dinner. Colosimo spoke with them for a few minutes and then, about 4:30, allegedly took a telephone call from Johnny Torrio that explained that a shipment of whiskey was being delivered to the restaurant that Colosimo had to sign for personally. Colosimo left the office and walked out in the lobby, likely preparing to step outside. A moment later, two shots were fired and Frank Camilla went to investigate the sounds. He found Colosimo's dead body lying on the floor of the lobby with a bullet wound to the back of his head. The second bullet was lodged in the plaster wall. From the angle of the shots, the killer, the police concluded, must have been hiding in the cloak room.

The funeral of Big Jim Colosimo was held on May 15 and was the first of the gaudy burial displays that were the fashion in Chicago's underworld throughout the 1920's. Thousands attended, including both gangsters and politicians, further underscoring the alliances between the two.

The murder of Colosimo remained a mystery, at least as far as legal evidence was concerned. Most everyone believed though that the murder had been carried out by Johnny Torrio in an effort to take over Colosimo's operation. And who was the trigger man? According to all accounts, it was a young man who had worked for Torrio in New York named Alphonse Capone. He had been working for Colosimo since coming to Chicago and a waiter saw him fleeing the scene after Colosimo's murder but he identified him to the police only as a "stranger".

Capone was born in Brooklyn in 1899 and made a name for himself as a slugger and a gunman with the famous Five Points gang in New York, of which several of his cousins were members. Capone was only 23 when he came to Chicago but Torrio soon promoted him to the post of manager in one of his toughest dives, the Four Deuces on South Wabash Avenue, a brick building with a saloon on the first floor, Torrio's offices on the second, a gambling den on the third and a brothel on the fourth. During his time at the Four Deuces, Capone became Torrio's first lieutenant and the chief of his gunmen. As far as the general public was concerned though, he remained an obscure member of Torrio's organization for the first two years he was in Chicago. As late as August 1922, he was still so little known that when he became involved in an automobile accident, the newspaper account referred to him as "Alfred Caponi". In those days, he was rough and brutal and there was little to indicate that he was destined for criminal greatness in the years to come. In the underworld, he was generally known as Scarface Al Brown, a nickname that was due to the two parallel scars on his left cheek that had been left behind during a knife fight. Soon though, all of Chicago would be familiar with his name.

Torrio and Capone moved up quickly after Colosimo's death. The gangs on the south side, where Torrio had his greatest influence and Capone had the most muscle, quickly fell in line with their plans. Torrio's beer began to flow to the local gangs at $45 a barrel (each costing about $5 to produce) and were distributed by Ragen's Colts and Ralph Sheldon's gang on the south and by the Circus Gang, led by Claude Maddox, Marty Guilfoyle's gang and the Druggan-Lake mob on the west side.

Up until 1922, the Chicago gangland remained at peace. Then, the south side O'Donnells, then led by Spike O'Donnell, decided to rise up against Torrio. They were massacred back into their place over a period of about two years, between 1923 and 1925. Not long after, the Genna Brothers, who supplied Torrio with poorly made liquor that was manufactured in neighborhood stills, began to get greedy and demanded a larger piece of the action. Wars began to erupt but most of the trouble seemed to come from the north side mob, an eccentric legion of mostly Irish gunmen led by Dion O'Bannion. The high quality Canadian liquor that was sent to Torrio by the Purple Gang in Detroit was constantly being hijacked by the North Siders. O'Bannion also moved his bootlegging operation into Cicero, which Torrio and Capone had already staked out as their exclusive territory.

Dion O'Bannion

Torrio constantly tried to negotiate with O'Bannion, rather than use the violence that Capone urged. Dozens of meetings were held between Torrio, Capone and the North Siders and each ended with the same results. O'Bannion always promised to recognize the territory of the South Siders and then turned right around and began encroaching upon it again. O'Bannion insulted the Genna's and they came to Torrio, seeking retribution but Torrio insisted that they wait. O'Bannion killed several of Capone's gunmen but when Capone urged Torrio to hit O'Bannion, his boss again asked him to wait.

Torrio's hesitation backfired on him in May 1924 when O'Bannion came to him and told him that he planned to retire and wanted to sell Torrio his largest gambling den and his brewery, Sieben's. Torrio agreed to buy up O'Bannion's concerns and reportedly paid him half a million dollars in cash two days later. The gang leaders agreed to meet at Sieben's on May 19, as Torrio wanted to inspect his new property. But he had not been there for more than ten minutes before Police Chief Collins, leading 20 officers, raided the place and arrested O'Bannion, Earl "Hymie" Weiss and Torrio. This was Torrio's second arrest for violating prohibition.

He had been arrested once and fined in June 1923 but a second arrest could mean jail time -- a fact that O'Bannion had been very much aware of. Torrio also realized that O'Bannion had no intention of retiring. He had conned Torrio into buying a brewery that he knew the police were about to shut down. It was time, Torrio finally decided, to get rid of O'Bannion.

He waited for five months. On the pretext of buying flowers (O'Bannion ran a floral shop on North State Street), three of Torrio's gunmen approached the unsuspecting Irishman and shot him to death at close range while one man held his hand in the infamous method of the "handshake murder". The other two blasted him, leaving six bullets in his body.

O'Bannion's death ignited an all-out war in Chicago and Torrio was the first to feel the wrath of the North Side mob. On November 10, 1924, Torrio and his wife got out of a chauffer-driven limousine in front of their house at 7011 Clyde Avenue (Torrio lived here under the name Frank Langley) and Anna Torrio began to walk inside. As Torrio reached in to pick up some packages from their shopping trip, a black Cadillac screeched to a stop across the street. Inside, four men with pistols and shotguns watched for a moment and then two of them, George "Bugs" Moran and Hymie Weiss, jumped from the car and ran towards Torrio with their guns blazing! Torrio fell immediately with a bullet in his chest and one in his neck. The other two men in the Cadillac, Schemer Drucci and Frank Gusenberg, opened fire on the limousine with their shotguns. Meanwhile, Moran and Weiss ran to the fallen Torrio and, standing above him, fired bullets into his right arm and another into his groin. Moran leaned over to put the next one into Torrio's head but his gun was empty. As he reached for another clip, Drucci began honking the horn of the Cadillac, signaling frantically that they needed to leave. Moran and Weiss ran to the car and they sped away.

Newspaper photographers captured Johnny Torrio wearing a scarf to hide the bandages on this throat when he appeared in federal court.

Somehow, Torrio managed to start crawling to the house and his wife, who was screaming, came out and pulled him inside. A neighbor, who witnessed the shooting, called an ambulance and Torrio was raced to the hospital. Unbelievably, he survived with a permanent scar to his neck. Reporters soon surrounded his hospital bed, demanding more information. Torrio stated that he knew all four of the assailants involved but "I'll never tell their names," he said.

In February, Torrio (still bandaged) was sent to federal court for the Sieben's brewery fiasco and he received a nine-month jail sentence to be served in the Waukegan County jail, which had medical services for the still ailing mobster. Earl Weiss, who had taken over the leadership of the North Side gang was fined for his first offense on violation of Prohibition charges and when the clerk called the name of Dion O'Bannion and the prosecutor announced that he was "deceased", Weiss shot Torrio an evil look. Torrio got the hint -- the North Siders may have botched their first attempt to kill him but they wouldn't miss the second time. He left for Waukegan filled with fear.

The treatment that Torrio received in prison though was equal to the status of the gangland boss. The windows of his cell were covered with bulletproof glass and he was guarded day and night by extra deputies. Easy chairs, throw rugs, books and other luxuries were added as well and Torrio received the special privilege of taking his evening meals in the sheriff's home and being allowed to relax on the sheriff's front porch for awhile each night, visiting with his wife and associates like Al Capone.

As he finished serving his time, Torrio had a lot of time to think. When he got out, he announced that he was tired of the rackets and that he was turning his entire operation over to Capone. All that he needed, he told his younger friend, was to get out of Chicago alive. Capone promised that he would and made good on his assurances. Torrio and Anna left the city in an armor-plated limousine and were escorted by two roadsters filled with gunmen. When they reached a train station, just over the Indiana state line, Capone's men patrolled the station with shotguns and machine guns until the train departed and took the Torrio's first to Florida and then they went on to Italy, living in Naples for three years.

Torrio got bored in Italy but knowing that he couldn't return to Chicago, he went to New York instead, where he went into the real estate business with the blessing of Meyer Lansky and Charles "Lucky" Luciano. He also helped to establish a liquor cartel along the Atlantic Seaboard and established himself as an elder statesman of the underworld. He lived a sedate and quiet life after Prohibition was repealed but in 1936, was arrested for income tax evasion. After a series of trials and appeals, he served two years in Leavenworth and was paroled in 1941. He died in a barber's chair (of natural causes) in 1957.

Torrio's departure from Chicago shoved Al Capone into the violent spotlight of the Chicago underworld and it also made him the top man in the city at only 25 years of age. He now had an annual income that would actually land him a place in *the Guinness Book of World Records*. And he also had a bloody gang war on his hands. Hymie Weiss offered to stem further violence by having Capone hand over John Scalise and Albert Anselmi over to him. They had reportedly been in the flower shop when O'Bannion had been murdered. Capone refused and made plans to knock off Hymie Weiss instead. He was too slow though for Weiss and Bugs Moran had already planned their next move.

Capone was sitting with his bodyguard, Frank Rio, in the restaurant of the Hawthorne Hotel in Cicero on September 20, 1926. The street outside was filled with shoppers and automobiles and no one noticed at first as the nine cars filled with north side gangsters slowly cruised down Twenty-Second Street. One of the cars accelerated away from the others and as it passed the windows of the restaurant, black barrels of machine guns appeared from the windows and opened fire. Glass shattered and wood splintered as bullets riddled the

"Scarface" Alphonse Capone

restaurant! The car sped off and Frank Rio jumped to his feet, gun in hand. But as Capone started to get up from the floor, his bodyguard pushed him back down again, for he spotted the other cars in the procession.

The other eight touring cars were filled with men and machine guns. They opened fire on Capone's Cicero stronghold, emptying clip after clip into the hotel, spraying everything in sight. Hymie Weiss boldly climbed from his car with Moran close behind him. Capone had over 100 men inside of the heavily armed fortress and yet none of them faced the withering fire from outside. Weiss ran up to the door of the hotel and opened fire with his machine gun, waving the weapon back and forth across the width of the passageway beyond the doors. When he finished firing, he walked coolly back to the car and with honking and shouts, the North Siders drove away. Over 1,000 rounds had been fired into the building and every window in the place was shattered. Amazingly, no one had been killed.

That violent incident was Hymie's one moment of glory and revenge for O'Bannion's murder. And while he continued to live a fearless life (to the point of stupidity) and to goad Capone at every opportunity, his days were numbered. On October 11, Weiss was attending the murder trial of "Polack Joe" Saltis and his driver Frank "Lefty" Koncil and decided to take a break and return to his office above O'Bannion's flower shop. Waiting for Weiss and gunman Patrick Murray in a rented room at 740 North State Street were four machine gunners believed to be John Scalise, Albert Anselmi, Frank Diamond and Frank Nitti. Weiss was a marked man as soon as he left his car on Superior Street, just south of the Holy Name Cathedral. He approached the flower shop with Murray at his side and with the deafening sound of Tommy guns, the pedestrians on the street scattered.

Murray died instantly but Weiss took ten bullets and survived long enough to be pronounced dead without regaining consciousness at Henrotin Hospital. The bullets that killed Weiss tore away portions of the inscription on the church's cornerstone and left bullet holes as a graphic reminder of the event until the church obliterated them years later.

Meanwhile, the assassins fled their third-floor lair, exited the rear of the building and disappeared into the crowds along Dearborn Street. A discarded machine gun was found in an alley off Dearborn but it couldn't be traced back to the killers.

And one has to wonder how hard the police looked for them. Chief Morgan Collins issued a gruff statement. "I don't want to encourage the business, but if somebody has to be killed," he said, "it's a good thing the gangsters are murdering themselves off. It saves trouble for the police."

The other partners in the North Side gang were wiped out, or fled Chicago, one by one, leaving only Bugs Moran.

George "Bugs" Moran

George "Bugs" Moran was born in Minnesota in 1893 but moved to Chicago with his parents around the turn-of-the-century. Here, he joined up with one of the North Side Irish gangs and was befriended by young tough named Dion O'Bannion. The two began working together, robbing warehouses, but after one fouled-up job, Moran was captured. He kept his silence and served two years in Joliet prison without implicating O'Banion in the crime. He was released at age nineteen and went back to work with his friend. He was soon captured again and once more, kept silent about who he worked with. He stayed in jail this time until 1923.

When Moran, known as "Bugs" because of his quick temper, got out of prison, he joined up with O'Bannion's now formidable North Side mob. They had become a powerful organization, supplying liquor to Chicago's wealthy Gold Coast. Moran became a valuable asset, hijacking Capone's liquor trucks at will. He became known as O'Bannion's right hand man, always impeccably dressed, right down to the two guns that he always wore. When O'Bannion was killed in his flower shop in 1924, Moran swore revenge. The war that followed claimed many lives and almost got Moran killed in 1925 when he was wounded on Congress Street in an ambush.

By 1927, Moran stood alone against the Capone mob, most of his allies having succumbed in the fighting. He continued to taunt his powerful enemy, always looking for ways to destroy him. In early 1929, Moran sided with Joe Aiello in another war against Capone. He and Aiello reportedly gunned down Pasquillano Lolordo, one of Capone's men, and Capone vowed that he would have him wiped out on February 14. He was living on his estate outside of Miami at the time and put in a call to Chicago. Capone had a very special "valentine" that we wanted delivered to Moran.

Through a contact in Detroit, reportedly Abe Bernstein, the leader of the Purple Gang, Capone arranged for someone to call Moran and tell him that a special shipment of hijacked whiskey was going to be delivered to one of Moran's garages on the north side. Adam Heyer, a Moran stooge, owned the garage. A sign out front read "S-M-C Cartage Co. Shipping - Packing - Long Distance - Hauling".

Moran received a call at the garage on the morning of February 13, probably from Bernstein, or at least from someone that he knew and trusted. Bernstein, who had always been Capone's supplier, likely would have been sending Moran quality liquor for a month or two before St. Valentine's Day to gain his confidence. Whoever made the call, Moran went along with it and planned the delivery for the next day.

On the morning of February 14, a group of Moran's men gathered at the Clark Street garage. One of the men was Johnny May, an ex-safecracker who had been hired by Moran as an auto mechanic. He was working on a truck that morning, with his dog, a German Shepherd named Highball, tied to the bumper. In addition, six other men waited for the truck of hijacked whiskey to arrive. The men were Frank and Pete Gusenberg, who were supposed to meet Moran and pick up two empty trucks to drive to Detroit and pick up smuggled Canadian whiskey; James Clark, Moran's brother-in-law; Adam Heyer; Al Weinshank; and Reinhardt Schwimmer, a young optometrist who had befriended Moran and hung around the liquor warehouse just for the thrill of rubbing shoulders with gangsters.

Bugs Moran was already late for the morning meeting. He was due to arrive at 10:30 but didn't even leave for the rendezvous, in the company of Willie Marks and Ted Newberry, until several minutes after that.

While the seven men waited inside of the warehouse, they had no idea that a police car had pulled up outside, or that Moran had stopped for coffee or that he had spotted the car and had quickly taken cover (whichever you would like to believe). Five men got out of the police car, three of them in uniforms and two in civilian clothing. They entered the building and a few moments later, the clatter of machine gun fire broke the stillness of the snowy morning. Soon after, five figures emerged and they drove away. May's dog, inside of the warehouse, began barking and howling.

The landlady in the next building, Mrs. Jeanette Landesman, was bothered by the sound of the dog and she sent one of her boarders, C.L. McAllister, to the garage to see what was going on. He came outside two minutes later, his face a pale white color. He ran frantically up the stairs to beg Mrs. Landesman to call the police. He cried that the garage was full of dead men!

The police were quickly summoned and on entering the garage, were stunned by the carnage. Moran's men had been lined up against the rear wall of the garage and had been sprayed with machine-guns. Pete Gusenberg had died kneeling, slumped over a chair. James Clark had fallen on his face with half of his head blown away and Heyer, Schwimmer, Weinshank and May were thrown lifeless onto their backs. Only one of the men survived the slaughter and only for a few hours. Frank Gusenberg had crawled from the blood-sprayed wall where he had fallen and ended up out in the middle of the dirty floor. He was rushed to the Alexian Brothers Hospital, barely hanging on. Police sergeant Clarence Sweeney leaned down close to him and asked who had shot him.

"No one --- nobody shot me," he groaned and he died later that night.

The death toll of the massacre now stood at seven but the killers had missed Moran. Most figured that he had spotted the police car outside the garage and figuring it for another random shakedown by the cops, headed back home. When the police contacted him later and asked who had sent the men to the garage, he "raved like a madman". To the newspapers, Moran targeted Capone as ordering the hit. The authorities claimed to be baffled though, since Capone was in Florida at the time of the massacre. When he was asked to comment on the news, Capone stated "the only man who kills like that is Bugs Moran". At the same time, Moran was proclaiming that "only Capone kills guys like that".

And Moran was undoubtedly right. The murders broke the power of the North Side gang and while there have been many claims as to who the actual shooters were that day, most likely they included Scalise, Anselmi and "Machine Gun" Jack McGurn, all of whom were some of Capone's most trusted men. All three men, along with Joseph Guinta, were arrested but McGurn had an alibi and Scalise and Guinta were killed before they could be tried.

The St. Valentine's Day Massacre marked the end of any significant gang opposition to Capone but it was also the act that finally began the decline of Capone's criminal empire. He had just gone too far and the authorities, and even Capone's adoring public, were ready to put an end to the bootleg wars. The massacre started a wave of reform that would send Capone out of power for good.

Perhaps the strangest bit of history in regards to the massacre involves the fact that Capone had not seen the last of the men who were killed on that fateful day. In May 1929, Capone slipped out of town to avoid the heat that was still coming down from the massacre and to avoid being suspected in the deaths of several of the men believed responsible for the killing of the Moran gang. While in Philadelphia, he and Frankie Rio were picked up on charges of carrying concealed weapons and were sentenced to a year in prison. They eventually ended up in the Eastern Pentitentiary.

The Lexington Hotel at Michigan Avenue & 22nd Street

Capone continued to conduct business from prison. He was given a private cell and allowed to make long-distance telephone calls from the warden's office and to meet with his lawyers and with Frank Nitti, Jack Guzik and his brother, Ralph, all of whom made frequent trips to Philadelphia. He was released two months early on good behavior and when he returned to Chicago, he found himself branded Public Enemy Number One.

It was while he was incarcerated in Pennsylvania that Capone first began to be haunted by the ghost of James Clark, one of the massacre victims and the brother-in-law of Bugs Moran. While in prison, other inmates reported that they could hear Capone screaming in his cell begging "Jimmy" to go away and leave him alone. After his release, while living at the Lexington Hotel, there were many times when his men would hear from begging for the ghost to leave him in peace. On several occasions, bodyguards broke into his rooms, fearing that someone had gotten to their boss. Capone would then tell them of Clark's ghost. Did Capone imagine the whole thing, or was he already showing signs of the psychosis that would haunt him after his release from Alcatraz prison?

Whether the ghost was real or not, Capone certainly believed that he was. The crime boss even went so far as to contact a psychic named Alice Britt to get rid of Clark's angry spirit. Not long after a séance was conducted to try and rid Capone of the vengeful spirit, Hymie Cornish, Capone's personal valet also believed that he saw the ghost. He entered the lounge of Capone's apartment and spotted a tall man standing near the window. Whoever the man was, he simply vanished.

Years later, Capone would state that Clark followed him to the grave.

On May 8, 1929, just a little more than a week before Capone was arrested on gun charges in Philadelphia, the bodies of Joseph Guinta, John Scalise and Albert Anselmi were found on the floor of an automobile that was parked near Gray's Lake in Douglas Park. Each of the men had been shot several times and had been badly beaten. The crime was never solved but it was thought that either Moran and his men had gotten their revenge for the killings in the Clark Street garage; that Capone had killed the men in order to keep the peace with the remnants of the North Side mob; or most likely, that Capone had killed the men for his own reasons. It is believed that Capone wanted to silence the men because they were becoming too powerful on their own, especially Scalise. He had become a bodyguard for Capone after the collapse of the Genna gang and had amassed a fortune of his own. He had also been recently appointed as the assistant to Guinta as the president of the Unione Siciliana and had moved Guinta into the background in his own quest for power. It's believed that Capone feared the three men were plotting to move against him and that the three were bludgeoned to death and then shot at a gangland banquet given to celebrate the victory over the North Side gang.

When Capone returned to Chicago in March 1930, he found the climate of the city had changed considerably during the time he had been away. His popularity had waned and the police were adamant about putting his operations out of business. Police Captain John Stege even posted a guard of 25 policemen in front of the Capone home on Prairie Avenue with orders to arrest him as soon as he arrived from Pennsylvania. Capone slipped quietly into the city though and took up residence at the Hawthorne Inn in Cicero, when he spent four days answering mail and getting caught up on the state of operations. Then, he and his attorneys blatantly called on Captain Stege and the United States District Attorney and found that neither of them had an actual warrant for his arrest. With that settled, he returned to Chicago.

Police Captain John Stege

While no charges had actually been filed against Capone, there was nothing to prevent the police from keeping him under surveillance. Two unformed policemen were then assigned to follow Capone everywhere he went, day and night. Capone's empire was staring to crumble and even his hangers-on were getting out of control. Eccentric newspaperman Jake Lingle of the *Chicago Tribune* bragged that he was the man who actually fixed the price of beer in town -- and he was on Capone's payroll.

Lingle was found in a subway underpass on Michigan Avenue with his brains blown out. Capone lamented that "Jake was a dear friend of mine" but his sentiments fell on deaf ears as it was widely known that Capone had given Lingle $50,000 to use his influence to clear a dog track operation in the city. Lingle, who referred to himself as the "unofficial chief of police" never delivered. After Lingle's death, it was found that the reporter, who earned $65 a week, actually had an income of more than $65,000 per year. He drove a new car, owned an expensive summer home, bet heavily at the races and maintained suites at one of the city's most expensive hotels. Leo Brothers, a St. Louis gunman, was convicted of Lingle's murder and sentenced to prison for 14 years but served just 10.

He also began losing some of his men as well. Fred "Killer" Burke was one of the most deadly of Capone's gunmen and was allegedly one of the machine gunners at the St. Valentine's Day Massacre. He was a known murderer and he and his partner, James Ray, had robbed several banks in Ohio dressed as policemen -- the same m.o. used by the St. Valentine's Day killers. After the Clark Street slaughter, Burke was spotted in December 1929 by policeman Charles Skelly in St. Joseph, Michigan, fleeing the scene of an auto accident. Skelly curbed Burke's car and jumped on the running board. Burke shot him three times in the stomach and drove away. Skelly died three hours later. The gunman was badly unnerved and he crashed his car into a telephone pole, where police found it and traced it to his address. In the house, they found a machine gun that was later traced to the guns used during the St. Valentine's Day massacre. Burke was captured in April 1930 but was never convicted for the massacre. He was convicted of Officer Skelly's murder instead and was sent to the Michigan State Penitentiary for life.

Michael "Mike de Pike" Heitler was another Capone henchman, although Heitler turned on Capone after he was ignored and demoted in 1931. Angry, he wrote a letter to State's Attorney John A. Swanson and disclosed all that he knew about Capone's prostitution organization. A few days later, Capone had Heitler brought to his headquarters at the Lexington Hotel and threw the unsigned letter in the gunman's face. He told Heitler that he knew that only he could have sent the letter but Capone never explained how he had gotten his hands on it. On April 29, 1931, Heitler's corpse was found in a burned-out house in Barrington. Investigators reported that Heitler had been burned alive.

Capone bodyguard Frank Rio

Frank Rio had been Capone's must trusted bodyguard, having saved his boss' life during the attack on the Hawthorne Hotel. It was also Rio who learned about the plot being hatched by Guinta, Scalise and Anselmi and informed Capone about it. According to the story, Rio heard Scalise bragging about being a "big shot" and he managed to convince Capone of a possible plot after a fake argument in which Capone slapped Rio in front of Scalise and Anselmi. Scalise later approached Rio and told him that the Aiello brothers had a $50,000 reward for anyone who would kill Capone. They wanted to know if Rio would join them in collecting the reward. Three days later, the bodies of the would-be assassins were found dumped in a car in a Chicago park. Rio's loyalty apparently faded through when Capone went on trial for tax evasion in 1931. One report has it that he smarted off to Capone as the mobster was being fitted for some new suits, remarking that he wouldn't need them in prison. Capone was enraged and Rio vanished shortly after.

By 1930, the United States government had gotten involved in Chicago's dilemma over how to get rid of Al Capone. Washington dispatched a group of treasury agents (Eliot Ness and his "Untouchables") to harass Capone and try to find a way to bring down his operation. In the end though, it would not be murder or illegal liquor that would get Capone, it would be income tax evasion. He was arrested on October 6, 1931 and indicted. On October 17, he was convicted on five counts, three of evading taxes from 1925 to 1928 and two of failing to file tax returns in 1928 and 1929. He was sentenced to spend 11 years in a federal prison and was first sent to Leavenworth and in 1934 was transferred to the brutal, "escape proof" prison known as Alcatraz.

The prison was a place of total punishment and few privileges. One of most terrible methods of punishment was the "hole", a dungeon where prisoners were housed naked on stone floors with no blankets, toilets and only bread and water for nourishment. The slightest infraction could earn a beating. Capone spent three stretches in the "hole", twice for speaking and once for trying to bribe a guard. He returned from the "hole" just a little worse for wear each time. Eventually, it would break him.

Many of the prisoners at Alcatraz went insane from the harsh conditions and Capone was probably one of them. The beatings, attempts on his life and the prison routine took a terrible toll on Capone's mind. After he was nearly stabbed to death in the yard, he was excused from outdoor exercise and usually stayed inside and played a banjo that was given to him by his wife. He later joined the four-man prison band. After five years though, Capone's mind snapped. He would often refuse to leave his cell and would sometimes crouch down in the corner and talk to himself. Another inmate recalled that on some days Capone would simply make and re-make his bunk all day long. He spent the last portion of his stay in the prison hospital ward, being treated for an advanced case of syphilis. He left Alcatraz in 1939.

Jake 'Greasy Thumb' Guzik, who helped run the South Side mob in Capone's absence, was asked by a reporter if Capone would take control again when he was released. "Al," said Guzik, "is nuttier than a fruitcake."

The massacre also began the decline of Bugs Moran as well. With the remnants of his gang, he attempted to take back control of the Gold Coast, but Capone's men were too powerful. His lot did improve somewhat after Capone went to prison in 1931 but it didn't last long. Although Moran did drift into oblivion after Capone was sent to prison, he did have one small piece of revenge for the events on Clark Street. According to reports, Bugs and two others caught up to "Machine Gun" Jack McGurn in a bowling alley on February 14, 1936. McGurn was machine-gunned to death with his sleeves rolled up and a bowling ball in his hand. A small paper valentine was found on his bloody corpse.

The once powerful gangster was reduced to petty burglaries by the end of World War II. He first moved to downstate Illinois and then Ohio before a failed robbery got him arrested by the FBI. He was sentenced to serve ten years in 1946 and his release found him quickly re-arrested for another robbery. This time, he was sent to Leavenworth, where he died from lung cancer in February 1957.

Chicago, in its own way, memorialized the warehouse on Clark Street where the massacre took place. It became a tourist attraction and the newspapers even printed the photos of the corpses upside-down so that readers would not have to turn their papers around to identify the bodies.

In 1949, the front portion of the S-M-C Garage was turned into an antique furniture storage business by a couple who had no idea of the building's bloody past. They soon found that the place was visited much more by tourists, curiosity-seekers and crime buffs than by customers and they eventually closed the business.

In 1967, the building was demolished. However, the bricks from the bullet-marked rear wall were purchased and saved by a Canadian businessman. In 1972, he opened a nightclub with a Roaring 20's theme and rebuilt the wall, for some strange reason, in the men's restroom. Three nights each week, women were allowed to peek inside at this macabre attraction.

The club continued to operate for a few years and when it closed the owner placed the 417 bricks into storage. He then offered them for sale with a written account of the massacre. He sold the bricks for $1,000 each, but soon found that he was getting back as many as he sold. It seemed that anyone who bought one of the bricks was suddenly stricken with bad luck in the form of illness, financial ruin, divorce and even death. According to the stories, the bricks themselves had somehow been infested with the powerful negative energy of the massacre! Whatever became of the rest of the bricks from the building is unknown. Or that's what the legend says....

According to a Canadian man named Guy Whitford, things may not be just as the legend has them. In fact, he writes "you were correct when you wrote about the bricks being offered for sale in the 1970's, but the fact is, although he had many offers, George never sold a single brick". You see, Whitford claims to be a friend of the Canadian businessman, George Patey, who originally bought the back wall of the warehouse many years ago and later began trying to track down a buyer for the authenticated wall of 417 bullet-marked bricks. "He always had a problem with breaking up the wall," Whitford continued. "The last substantial offer for the entire wall was made by a Las Vegas casino about a decade ago, but George quaffed at the offer -- so that "bad luck to those who bought one" concept must be a rumor or a journalistic embellishment".

The two men tried to sell the wall for some time. The original lot came with a diagram that explained how to restore the wall to its original form. The bricks were even numbered for reassembly. They remained on the market for nearly three decades, but there were no buyers. Eventually, he broke up the set and began selling them one brick at a time for $1,000 each. But were these all of the surviving bricks from the warehouse?

In recent years, other bricks have emerged that claim to have come from the wall and from the building itself. These were not bricks purchased from Patey but were smuggled out of the lot by construction workers and curiosity-seekers. It was said that from these bricks come the legends of misfortune and bad luck. Are these bricks authentic? The owners say they are, but you'll have to judge for yourself!

Whatever the legend of the bricks themselves and whether or not they have somehow been "haunted" by what happened, there is little doubt about the site on Clark Street itself. Even today, people walking along the street at night have reported the sounds of screams and machine guns as they pass the site. The building is long gone now, demolished in some misguided attempt by city officials to erase all vestiges of Chicago's gangster past. A portion of the block was taken over by the Chicago Housing Authority and now the area where the garage once stood is marked by a fenced-in lawn that belongs to a senior citizen's development. Five trees are scattered about the area and the one in the center actually marks the point where the rear wall once stood -- where Moran's men were lined up and gunned down.

Passersby and the curious have sometimes reported strange sounds, like weeping and moaning, and the indescribable feeling of fear as they walk past. Skeptics have tried to laugh this off, saying that the sounds are nothing more than the overactive imaginations of those who know what once occurred on this site but based on the reports of those who had no idea of the history of the place, something strange was apparently occurring. And those who were accompanied by their dogs also reported their share of weirdness too. The animals seemed to be especially bothered by this piece of lawn, sometimes barking and howling, sometimes whining in fear. Their sense of what happened here many years ago seems to be much greater than our own.

According to reports, residents of the senior housing complex had strange encounters of their own, especially those who lived on the side of the building that faced the former massacre site. A television report from Canada interviewed a woman who once lived in an apartment that overlooked the small park area and she often complained that at night, she would hear strange voices, sounds and knocking on her door and her window. She complained to the management, who dismissed her claims as imagination but assigned her another apartment. A new tenant moved into the rooms and she too complained of odd happenings, including knocking sounds that would come at her door at night. When she opened the door to see who was there, she never found anyone nearby. One night, the new tenant even stated that she saw a dark figure who was wearing an old style hat. He remained in place for a few moments and then faded away. Most of the strange phenomena experienced by the new tenant also faded away and soon eerie events either stopped completely -- or she got so used to them that they no longer bothered her anymore.

The inexplicable sounds and the odd behavior of the animals continue along the street though. Even after all of these years, the violent events of the city's gangster era still reverberate over time. Men like Al Capone, whether city officials want to admit it or not, left an indelible mark on Chicago. It appears that the events of St. Valentine's Day 1929 have left one too!

LAST WALK OF CAPONE'S ENFORCER

On the evening of March 19, 1943, a lone figure left his home in Riverside and began strolling along the streets of his quiet neighborhood. It was a cool, almost spring night and the man seemed to have no cares in the world as he walked along, his hands tucked into his pockets and a soft whistle on his lips. His casual manner gave no hint to the turmoil that he felt inside though. Or that he had a loaded handgun weighting down the pocket of his coat.

The man left the street and began walking along the Illinois Central Railroad tracks that ran west of Harlem Avenue and around Cermak Avenue. He picked his way carefully over the railroad ties and walked along until the shadows seemed to envelope him. Darkness was just beginning to fall and this seemed as good a time as any for one last look at the world. The man took the gun from his pocket and he raised it to his head. His hand began to tremble as he squeezed the trigger and then a deafening roar filled his ears and echoed in the stillness of the city around him.

When the first shot was fired, railroad workers who were standing just a little further along the line, doing routine maintenance, looked up to see the walking man. His hands shook as he held the pistol and a thin ribbon of smoke curled from the barrel of it. The gun had been aimed at his head but the first shot had somehow missed. One of the railroad men started to call out to the man as he saw him calmly lift the gun again. Before the words could leave the railroader's lips, the man pulled the trigger again and this time when the gun went off, the bullet did not miss. It blew apart the top of the man's head and he stumbled once, and then collapsed onto the railroad tracks. The man's blood began to spread over the wooden ties and the iron rails, looking black in the fading light.

Frank Nitti, once thought of as being one of the most powerful men in Chicago and enforcer to Al Capone, lay dead on the ground, slain by his own hand.

Frank Nitti (or Nitto, which was the preferred family spelling) was a many of mystery. Intensely private and quiet, he is only scarcely remembered today as being part of the legendary Capone gang. If not for the television series based on the exploits of Eliot Ness and his *Untouchables*, it's possible that he would only be known to the most dedicated gangster buffs and researchers and not to the general public at all. Nitti was a small man but one with incredible will. He maintained discipline in the ranks and acted as Capone's enforcer and troubleshooter. He was also one of the only gangsters in the organization who never used an assumed name, which got him into trouble when investigators discovered a check that he was endorsed. This put him into prison for 18 months in the early 1930's, an experience which had a lasting effect on him.

Nitti was born in 1888 and started out in crime as a barber who also fenced stolen goods. His methods of peddling stolen whiskey put him in touch with Capone and Johnny Torrio at the start of Prohibition and he was a high-ranking member of Capone's organization by the middle 1920's. After Capone went to prison, the newspapers looked for a new leader for the mob and Nitti was hailed as that man. It's possible that he may have even believed this himself but insiders knew that the remaining men in Capone's gang would not take orders from Nitti. While an efficient organizer under Capone, it had been his job to make sure that Capone's orders had been carried out, not to give them himself. Other mobsters, including Lucky Luciano and Meyer Lansky, when establishing a national crime network in the 1930's, dealt with Paul "the Waiter" Ricca as the leader of the Chicago mob and not with Nitti.

However, Ricca and the others did use Nitti's high profile with the press to keep the heat off the real inner workings of the mob and also as a valuable man to take the heat. Even Chicago mayor Anton

Capone Enforcer Frank Nitti

Cermak would dispatch his own police "hit men" to try and take out Nitti so that he could replace him with other gangsters that kept him on the payroll. On December 19, 1932, two police officers invaded Nitti's headquarters, allegedly under orders from new mayor Cermak, who was determined to assist Ted Newberry (who had taken over the O'Bannion and Moran mob) redistribute the territories of the Capone gang. Shots were fired and Nitti was badly wounded. He lingered near death for a time but recovered only to end up standing trial for the shooting of one of the cops during the gun battle. However, the jury was convinced that the officer had actually shot himself in the finger in order to look like a hero and the trial ended in a hung jury. Nitti walked away a free man and the officer lost his job.

Strangely though, rumors lingered for a time that Al Capone himself reached out from the walls of the penitentiary to get revenge on Cermak a few months later.

Anton Cermak was a dynamic, albeit somewhat typical, Chicago mayor of days gone by. He was the city's first foreign-born mayor, emigrating from Prague to work in the Illinois coal mines. He started a real estate company and for years spoke out against banning alcohol. He also organized the "wet vote", which would help to defeat Prohibition and that won him the appreciation of Franklin Delano Roosevelt, with whom Cermak was accompanying when the mayor was assassinated.

On February 15, 1933, Cermak was shot by a fanatic named Guiseppe Zangara at Bayfront Park in Miami, Florida. He was there with President Roosevelt, who had asked Cermak to join him on the reviewing stand. Shots rang out and Cermak was hit instead of the president. He was rushed to the hospital but died a short time later. As he was taken from the reviewing stand, Cermak was supposed to have said to the president "I am glad that it was me instead of you" and they became the most famous words that Cermak ever uttered -- or they would have been if he had ever really said them. A reporter who was there that day, Ed Gilbreth, stated that the phrase was created by the *Chicago Herald-American* to make a good headline and sell some papers. Cermak never said anything before he died.

Although some words uttered by another reporter who was standing nearby might have provided more of a clue in the shooting than officials would admit. Just as the shots rang out, a reporter who was nearby allegedly joked to Cermak: "Just like Chicago, eh Mayor?" And perhaps the event was more like Chicago than anyone knew, for the death of Cermak achieved subtle vengeance for the near murder of Frank Nitti. Ted Newberry had been killed just a few weeks earlier. He had been shot to death along Lake Shore Drive and his body had been dumped in a ditch in Porter County, Indiana.

Nitti served prison time for an income tax charge, related to the check that was discovered bearing his name, and stayed out the newspapers until November 1940, when he was indicted for influencing the Chicago Bartenders and Beverage Dispensers Union of the AFL. Nitti was accused of putting mob members into positions of power in the union and then forcing the sale of beer from mob-owned breweries. The trial rested on the testimony of one man, George McLane, the president of the union. He allegedly was forced to follow Nitti's orders but the pressure got to him and he went to the authorities and explained what the mob was doing. McLane was all set to testify until two mob soldiers showed up at his door and told him that if he talked in court, his wife would be mailed to him in small pieces. When the day came, McLane pleaded for his rights under the Fifth Amendment and the case was dropped.

The heat was on Nitti again in 1943 during what came to be called the "Hollywood Extortion case". Nitti's name was used as a terror tactic during a shakedown of movie moguls in Hollywood. Nitti and several other mobsters managed to get control of the International Alliance of Theatrical Stage Employees and began forcing the movie studios to pay huge sums of money to keep the union at work. A prolonged strike could have ruined any of them, a fact that the studios were well aware of. At that time, the movie studios controlled most of the theaters that exhibited their films and if the union went on strike, there would be no place to show the films that had cost thousands to make. In a short time, Warner Brothers, MGM, RKO, Fox and a number of smaller studios forked over the money and the racket turned out to be a big money maker for the mob. Things began to fall apart when a Chicago reporter, a nationally syndicated writer named Westbrook Pegler, started asking questions after spotting Willie Bioff and George Browne at a big Hollywood party. He recognized Bioff as a former Chicago pimp and couldn't figure out what he was being doing at such a party. He started asking around and discovered that Bioff had moved up the criminal chain and soon he also began to hear about the extortion racket. He took his information to the federal authorities and the whole enterprise began to unravel.

The investigators were soon able to get evidence against the Chicago gangsters and faced with hard prison time, Bioff and Browne decided to talk. As a result, indictments were brought against Nitti, Paul Ricca and a number of others. A meeting was called at Nitti's home in Riverside and Ricca decided that now was the perfect time to take advantage of Nitti's perceived top position in the mob. He ordered Nitti to plead guilty in the extortion case and to take the rap for everyone. He would be taken care of when he got out -- as long as he kept his mouth shut while he was inside.

But there was no "inside" for Nitti. He refused to go back to prison. His earlier jail time had so traumatized the gangster that he now had a terrible fear of small, confined spaces. He urged Ricca to come up with another plan or to allow some of the others to share the responsibility with him. Ricca was enraged and demanded that Nitti be a "stand up guy". When Nitti still refused, Ricca told him that "he was asking for it." Nitti took these words to mean his death sentence but he simply couldn't face another stretch in prison. He made a last-ditch effort to try and bribe the prosecutor in the case, M.F. Correa, but his attempt was coldly rebuffed.

So, on March 19, the day after the meeting, Frank Nitti placed a gun in his pocket and went for one last walk through his neighborhood. When he made it as far as the Illinois Central Railroad tracks, his journey came to an end -- or did it?

After his death, Nitti was laid to rest in Mount Carmel Cemetery, not far from where the body of Al Capone also lies. His simple stone is marked with his family name of Nitto and bears a direct and ominous inscription: "There is no life except by death". But it has never been believed that Nitti rests here in peace.

For many years it has been a local legend in the North Riverside and Forest Park areas that the ghost of Frank Nitti still walks along the railroad tracks where he committed suicide in 1943. There are many who claim to have not only sensed the last anguished moments of Nitti but also state that they have seen the eerie figure of a man here as well. The figure often appears along the railroad tracks at Cermak Avenue and begins walking west (eventually towards Mount Carmel Cemetery), plainly visible under the harsh lights of a shopping center that is located nearby. The tracks, which are seldom used these days, can be found next to a toy store, a restaurant and a large shopping mall. The area that marks Nitti's suicide is almost remote and isolated from the activity of the retail area, despite the fact that it's so close by.

I spoke to a man who became curious about this area after reading about it in a Chicago crime book and he decided to go out there one night and have a look for himself. Although a believer in ghosts, this had nothing to do with his survey of the railroad tracks. He was more interested in Nitti himself and never expected to see anything out of the unusual during his outing. The man parked his car at the nearby toy store and walked over to the tracks. As he stood there and looked down them, he explained to me that he could imagine what Nitti must have felt like during his last journey. Rumor had it that in addition to facing prison time, Nitti was also suffering from stomach cancer and this may have also led to his decision to end his life.

As the man walked slowly along the tracks, he froze for a moment at what he saw ahead of him. Keeping pace with his own walk, he claimed to see a dark silhouette about 15 yards ahead of him. He saw the figure step high to avoid the rails and even stumble once or twice as it moved along. He was unable to describe the figure for me and only said that "it gave the impression of a man who was wearing a thigh-length coat". The witness followed the figure for a short distance and then he described to me that it seemed to "spin" around and fall towards the ground. Moments later, it was gone.

The startled observer blinked once or twice, unable to believe what he had seen. Could he have just witnessed a re-enactment of the last moments of Frank Nitti? "I never went there expecting to see anything," he wrote to me a few months after the encounter took place. "And while I believed that some places and people might be haunted, I never thought that I would ever see anything like that. I am sure that it must have been Frank Nitti's ghost that I saw that night. It's up to you whether you want to believe me or not but I am sure about what I saw. I think he's [Nitti] haunting those railroad tracks."

DEPRESSION DESPERADOES

Shortly after the end of Prohibition, America was plunged into the Great Depression. This era of national poverty gave birth to another breed of criminal, the bank robber. John Dillinger, Baby Face Nelson, Machine Gun Kelly, Ma Barker and Bonnie and Clyde were just a few of the bank robbers who made headlines and history during the Depression and they became the last figures of the outlaw tradition that had been a part of American legend since the end of the Civil War.

Bank robberies had been taking place almost since the time that the first Americans entrusted an establishment with their hard-earned money, but the robbers of the 1930's were different. They were no longer the outlaws of the "Wild West" for these bank robbers had the new and novel advantage of motorized transportation. Never before in American crime had outlaws possessed the means to escape so easily from law enforcement officials. Now, they went on the rampage through various states using motor cars.

Most of them got their start because of the police preoccupation with bootleggers, allowing the better equipped bank robbers to work with little harassment. Many of the jobs made huge headlines because of the amount of loot that was stolen but as author William Helmer has noted, identification methods were so primitive that newspapers could only report that some unknown strangers had pulled off a "daring daylight robbery" and had disappeared without a trace. Because of this, some criminals were able to plunder the Midwest with an anonymity that leaves them unknown today while lesser outlaws became Depression-era celebrities once Al Capone went to prison and the new federal laws unleashed the FBI.

This new era gave birth to what are considered legendary criminals today. Many of them not only gained a place on the FBI's new "Most Wanted" list, but they became folk heroes too. There were few Americans who didn't feel a twinge of jealousy as they saw these free-wheeling bank robbers get their revenge on the banks, the wealthy and the government itself. Stories were told that some of these outlaws actually stole from the rich and then gave back part of the money to those who really needed it. And in the 1930's, there were a lot of folks who needed it.

Many of these images were created by the newspapers, which thanks to the competitiveness of the market in cities like Chicago were always looking for a headline, and to the crime magazines and pulps, many of which abandoned fiction for "fact" at a time when gangsters were making daily news. This resulted in making the criminals more recognizable in some cases to the general public than to the police. This only made them all the more popular to the people of the day.

Without a doubt, these folk heroes, bank robbers and stone-cold killers left their mark on the American landscape and many of them died just as they lived, fast and hard. It's not surprisingly that many of their stories still linger with us today -- or that some of their ghosts do too!

DILLINGER... DEAD OR ALIVE?
Who is the Ghost that Haunts the Alley Next to the Biograph Theater?

On the evening of July 22, 1934 a dapper-looking man wearing a straw hat and a pin-striped suit stepped out of the Biograph Theater where he and two girlfriends had gone to see a film called *Manhattan Melodrama* starring Clark Gable. No sooner had they reached the sidewalk than a man appeared and identified himself as Melvin Purvis of the FBI. He ordered the man in the straw hat to surrender but the dapper-looking man decided to run instead. Several shots rang out and the fleeing man in the straw hat fell dead to the pavement, his left eye shredded by one of the shots fired by the other agents who lay in wait.

And so ended the life of John Herbert Dillinger, the most prolific bank robber in modern American history and the general public's favorite Public Enemy No. 1 -- or did it?

One of the most famous haunted theaters in the history of Chicago is the Biograph Theater, located on North Lincoln Avenue. It was here, in 1934, that John Dillinger supposedly met his end. The theater has gained a reputation for being haunted, but the story of the ghost seen here actually revolves around the alleyway outside. But the theater, and the surrounding businesses, has banked on the criminal's name for many years. On the day after the fatal shots were fired, the bar next door placed a sign in the window that read "Dillinger had his last drink here". Theater patrons can examine a window in the box office that describes the set-up of Dillinger by the FBI. They can sit in the same seat where Dillinger sat in 1934 and after the film, they can emerge into "Dillinger's Alley". It is here where the ghost is said to appear.

But what really happened in the final moments of Dillinger's life? To answer the strange and perplexing questions surrounding his possible death, we have to first look at his bloody and violent life.

On the evening that he was killed, Dillinger left the theater in the company of Anna Sage (the famed "Lady in Red") and with another girlfriend, Polly Hamilton. He had been hiding out in her North Halstead Street apartment but for months he had been pursued diligently by Melvin Purvis, the head of the Chicago branch of the FBI. Purvis had lived and breathed Dillinger (and would, after the robber's death, commit suicide) but had narrowly missed him several times at a State Street and Austin Cafe, at Dillinger's north woods hideout in Sault St. Marie, and at Wisconsin's Little Bohemia, where FBI agents recklessly killed a civilian and injured two others. It was finally at the Biograph where Purvis caught up with Dillinger and put an end to his career.

John Dillinger

John Herbert Dillinger was born in 1903 in Indianapolis. He came from humble rural beginnings and work dominated his early life. His mother died prematurely in 1907 and Dillinger was raised by his older sister Audrey and his father, John Wilson Dillinger, who ran a grocery store and maintained several houses that he rented out. Dillinger's father was strict but never had much trouble with his son, who was a quiet child with good grades and who was well-liked by friends and teachers. When he was quite young, he proved to be an excellent athlete, especially excelling at baseball.

Dillinger's first brush with the authorities took place when he was in sixth grade and was charged with stealing coal from the Pennsylvania Railroad yards and selling it to neighbors. He was released into the custody of his father and soon after, the elder Dillinger packed up his family and moved them to a modest farm outside of Mooresville, Indiana, about 20 miles south of Indianapolis. He reportedly wanted to get his son away from the corrupting influences of the city. It didn't seem to do much good though. Dillinger refused to help his father on the farm and to return to school. He instead took a job back in Indianapolis as an apprentice machinist, driving back and forth to the farm each day on his prized motorbike.

Eventually, he decided to go back to school, to please his father, but dropped out during his first semester at Mooresville High School. Dillinger did however join the Martinsville baseball team and became known as a remarkable second basemen. He also started dating a young woman named Frances Thornton, his Uncle Everett's stepdaughter. The two of them fell in love and Dillinger asked his uncle for her hand in marriage but he refused, telling John that they were both too young. In truth, he actually wanted the girl to marry a wealthy boy from Greencastle, Indiana.

Angry, Dillinger returned home and on the night of July 21, 1923 he impulsively stole a car from the parking lot of the Friends Church in Mooresville. Hours later, he abandoned it in Indianapolis but fearing arrest, he enlisted in the U.S. Navy. Unknown to Dillinger, the owner of the car, Oliver P. Macy, knew John and refused to press charges. Regardless, Dillinger enlisted under his real name but gave a false St. Louis address when he filled out his paperwork. After basic training at Great Lakes, he was assigned to the U.S.S. *Utah*. He went AWOL several times and was thrown in the brig and when the ship was anchored off Boston in December, Dillinger jumped ship permanently. The Navy listed him as a deserter and posted a reward for his capture but Dillinger went back to Indiana.

At home, Dillinger met and began courting Beryl Ethel Hovius,16, and the two of them married in the spring of 1924. They moved in with Beryl's parents but Dillinger spent more time playing baseball and shooting pool than paying attention to his wife and the marriage didn't amount to much.

On the night of September 6, 1924, Dillinger finally stepped completely over the line of the law. Cooking up a plan with a former convict and umpire for the Martinsville baseball team named Edgar Singleton, the two men decided to rob Frank Morgan, a Mooresville grocer who carried his week's receipts home on Saturday nights. They jumped him and hit him over the head but the 65 year-old man refused to go down. One of the would-be robbers brandished a gun but Morgan knocked it away and a shot was accidentally fired. Dillinger and Singleton, both frightened, took off running.

Morgan's head required 11 stitches but he told Deputy Sheriff John Hayworth that he couldn't identify his attackers. Hayworth looked into the case though and came to believe that Dillinger was involved. He took Morgan out the Dillinger farm with him and the grocer confronted John. He recalled how the boy had purchased candy from his store and insisted that he wouldn't have hurt him. Hayworth took him in for questioning anyway and when Dillinger's father came to collect him from the county jail, the tearful young man confessed the hold-up attempt. The prosecutor promised the elder Dillinger that his son would receive a lenient sentence if he threw himself on the mercy of the court. The farmer convinced his son to do so and Dillinger, just 20 years old, entered a guilty plea. To his surprise, he was fined $100 and sentenced to concurrent sentences of up to 10-20 years in prison. His accomplice, through his attorney, received a change of venue and a much lighter sentence that resulted in his parole in just two years.

Betrayed and angry, he was sent to the Indiana State Reformatory with no plans to cause trouble, he said, "except to escape." Over the course of the next several years, Dillinger tried over and over again to escape, always getting caught. One night he was found missing from his cell and was found under a pile of clothing in the laundry. Another time he made a saw and cut his way out of his cell. He was captured in the corridor. He tried again in 1925 and was again captured.

About this time, Dillinger met a man who would influence his future career, a bank robber named Harry Pierpont. The soft spoken ladies' man had been captured after single-handedly robbing a Kokomo, Indiana bank. He and Dillinger became close friends and were soon joined by another young bank robber, Homer Van Meter. The two earned Dillinger's respect by being the toughest criminals in the prison. They spent more time in solitary confinement than in their cells. Eventually, they were both shipped off to the state prison in Michigan City by officials who couldn't control them.

In 1929, the same year his wife filed for divorce, Dillinger came up before the parole board. He was turned down but luckily for him, Indiana governor Harry Leslie was sitting in on the hearing. Dillinger had once been playing baseball in the prison yard and had overheard the governor remark that he ought to be playing professional ball. When he knew that he would not be getting out of jail, he asked the board to send him to the state prison in Michigan City because it had a real baseball team. Governor Leslie convinced the board that a move was in order, as it might help Dillinger to find work when he did finally get out. Dillinger was sent to the state prison on July 15 and happily hooked up with Pierpont and Van Meter again.

His friends introduced him to another bank robber, John Hamilton, who began instructing Dillinger on the art of robbing banks. He also met Charles "Fat Charley" Makley and Russell Lee Clark. Both men had been arrested on robbery charges and Clark especially was known as a dangerous and brutal man. He had attempted escape several times and had even tried to kill guards on several occasions. He and the others would figure into Indiana's largest prison break (masterminded by Dillinger) four years later and would form a gang of bank robbers who would make headlines around the country.

Since Dillinger would be out of prison before any of the others, he was cultivated as the contact man on the outside. It would be his job to hit a number of small town banks, targeted by Pierpont and Hamilton, and use the funds to finance the prison break. During his last four years inside, Dillinger was a model prisoner, which was all part of the plan. In addition, Governor Paul McNutt also received a petition from Dillinger's Mooresville neighbors, asking that he be released to help his father on the farm. Even the judge who had sentenced him, perhaps regretting his harsh decision, signed the petition. Dillinger was set free on

May 22, 1933 and he immediately rushed to Mooresville, where his stepmother was seriously ill. She died just an hour before Dillinger arrived.

The following Sunday, Dillinger attended church with his father and sat weeping as he listened to the pastor give a pointed sermon on the return of the "prodigal son". When the service ended, he told the minister how much good it had done him -- and two weeks later began robbing small stores and companies!

Dillinger recruited a small-time hoodlum named William Shaw and using the list that his friends devised, robbed a bank at New Carlisle, Indiana, netting $10,600. Unfortunately, Dillinger would find that many of Pierpont's targets had gone under during the Depression and he was often met with empty buildings instead of banks that were ripe for the picking. Shaw was arrested a short time later (luckily, he only knew Dillinger as "Dan") and Dillinger recruited Harry Copeland, another bank robber and former convict from Michigan City.

They struck the Commercial Bank at Daleville, Indiana on July 17. Dillinger strolled into the bank wearing what became his trademark straw boater and walked up to cashier Margaret Good, who was the only person in the bank at the time. He pulled out a gun and reportedly said: "This is a stick-up, honey." He then jumped over the railing and entered the vault. Harry Copeland left the getaway car parked in front of the building and also came inside, lining customers up at gunpoint as they entered the bank. Dillinger packed up $3,500 and ordered everyone inside of the vault. Then, he and Copeland casually walked out and drove away. Margaret opened the door from the inside and a short time later, told police that Dillinger was "the most courteous of bank robbers." His identity as a polite but daring bank robber was verified by the other witnesses and now police throughout Indiana were looking for him.

But Dillinger was already in Ohio, seeing his new girlfriend, Mary Longnaker, who lived in Dayton. Dillinger took Mary to Chicago to the World's Fair and he chuckled as he photographed a policeman and then asked the cop to snap a picture of himself and Mary.

On August 4, Dillinger and Copeland robbed the National Bank of Montpelier, Indiana. He was thrilled to find $10,100 in the small bank's vault. His next haul would not go so well. A short time later, Dillinger, Copeland, Sam Goldstine and two other, unknown men hit the Citizens National Bank in Bluffton. Dillinger and Copeland entered the bank and announced that it was a robbery. After going through the teller drawers though, Dillinger demanded to know where the rest of the money was. Bookkeeper Oliver Locher pointed to the bank's vault at about the same time that the alarm went off. One of the look-outs came in and called out that the police were coming but Dillinger ignored him and began filling a sack with small bills. The men outside began firing wild shots into the air to discourage the curious when Dillinger and Copeland didn't come out. Finally, after collecting only $2,100, they joined the men out on the street. They piled into a sedan and quickly sped away.

Dillinger was discouraged by the small take, still needing much more to finance the Michigan City prison break. He and Copeland decided to try a larger city bank the next time, settling on the Massachusetts Avenue State Bank in downtown Indianapolis. Using Hilton Crouch, a professional racetrack driver as a wheel man, Dillinger and Copeland entered the bank and immediately began cleaning out the teller drawers. Dillinger stole everything in sight and netted $24,800.

With a major share of this, Dillinger moved to Chicago and bribed the foreman of a thread-making company to secretly place several guns inside of a thread barrel being sent to the shirt shop at the Michigan City prison. It was sealed and marked with a red "X" on the top. Dillinger had earlier attempted to free Pierpont and the others by tossing handguns wrapped in newspaper over the prison walls under the cover of darkness. The guns were supposed to be found in the athletic field by Pierpont but were found by other inmates instead and they turned them over to the guards.

While the barrel was being shipped, Dillinger went to Dayton to see Mary Longnaker. Unknown to him, the police had received a tip from the Pinkerton Detective Agency that Dillinger was seeing a Dayton woman and the authorities had tracked Mary down because she was the sister of one of Dillinger's friends in prison. Mary's rooming house was staked out and her landlady phoned in a tip to the police when Dillinger arrived.

Dillinger Mug Shots

Two detectives, carrying shotguns, quickly broke into Mary's apartment and Dillinger was arrested on the spot.

As things would turn out, Dillinger was in the Lima, Ohio jail four days later, waiting to be indicted for the Bluffton bank robbery, when his friends escaped from the Michigan City prison using the guns that Dillinger had smuggled in to them. Ten men in all went out the front gates of the penitentiary, driving cars that were stolen from in front of the administration building. The escapees included Harry Pierpont, Charles Makley, Russell Clark, John Hamilton, Edward Shouse, Joseph Fox, Joseph Burns, Jim "Oklahoma Jack" Clark, Mary Longnaker's brother James Jenkins and Walter Dietrich. Pierpont, Makley, Clark, Hamilton, Shouse and Jenkins took one auto and headed for Leipsic, Ohio, where Pierpont's family lived. Somewhere near Bean Blossom, Indiana, a bizarre accident took place. Rounding a corner, the door of the car flew open and Jenkins fell out. Since the police were everywhere, searching for the convicts, Jenkins was left to fend for himself. He walked up the road about a mile and ran into three farmers who were part of a posse searching for the escapees. When Jenkins pulled out a pistol, the farmers blasted him with their shotguns and he was killed.

Before Dillinger had been captured, he left money with Mary Kinder, a contact for the gang. Pierpont used this money to equip his men with new clothes, a new automobile and an arsenal of weapons. He also decided to put together some traveling money by robbing the First National Bank in St. Mary's, Ohio, the hometown of Charles Makley. Inside of the bank, Makley ran into an old friend, W.O. Smith, who was the bank president. He chatted with his friend while Pierpont cleaned out the till. The gang left the bank with $14,000 without ever firing a shot.

On October 12, Pierpont, Makley, Clark, Hamilton and Shouse went looking for Dillinger. They arrived at the jail around 6:20 p.m. that evening, armed with pistols, and walked into the jail office. Sheriff Jess Sarber, his wife Lucy and Deputy Wilbur Sharp were reading newspapers after a dinner of pork chops and mashed potatoes. Sarber looked up when the men came in and asked if he could help them. Pierpont replied that they were officials from Michigan City and needed to speak with prisoner Dillinger. Sarber agreed but asked for the credentials. Pierpont pulled out a pistol instead and pointed it at the sheriff's face. "Here's our credentials", he said. Sarber gasped and put out a hand to wave away the gun. Pierpont fired two shots and hit the sheriff, once in the stomach and once in the hip. He fell to the floor, leaving his wife and deputy to gape in astonishment. Pierpont demanded the keys as Sarber tried to raise himself up. Makley smacked him on the head and he fell back to the floor.

"I'll get the keys," Lucy Sarber screamed. "Don't hurt him anymore!"

At the sound of the first shots, Dillinger knew that his gang had arrived. Pierpont, grinning, unlocked his door and the two men hurried out. As they reached the office, Dillinger knelt down to inspect the damage that had been done to Sheriff Sarber, who had been kind to Dillinger while he had been housed in the man's jail. Regretfully, he left the man behind on the floor. Sarber called out to him and asked why he had to do this, but the bank robber was gone. According to the story, he then looked over to his wife and said "Mother, I believe I'm going to have to leave you." Sheriff Sarber died moments later.

"The Terror Gang", as the press dubbed them, headed for Indianapolis, where Mary Kinder, who had taken up with Pierpont, and Evelyn "Billie" Frechette, who Dillinger had met in Chicago, waited for them. The gang made plans for a string of new bank robberies but first they had to arm themselves. The raided the police arsenal in Peru, Indiana and walked away with machine guns, bullet-proof vests, shotguns, handguns, rifles and bags filled with ammunition. To pull off such a daring robbery, Dillinger and Pierpont devised a new approach. Posing as tourists, they approached a policeman and asked him what preparations the local lawmen had taken in the event the Dillinger gang came to town. The officer and a desk sergeant proudly gave the men a tour of the arsenal, only to be restrained as the two men began carrying armloads of weapons out to their car.

Chicago became the base of operations for the gang, which Dillinger and Pierpont shared the leadership of. Pierpont was the more experienced of the two but he encouraged his friend to take the role of leader. Most of the decisions made by the group were made by these two, or by Hamilton, who was the "old pro" among them. The idea that there was an actual "Dillinger gang" was a product of the newspapers of the day. It was really more of a criminal community that included several robbers that Dillinger worked with when possible and when the law and luck allowed. The group lived in two and threes in several apartments on Chicago's north side. None of them drank hard liquor, sticking only with an occasional beer, so as not to draw attention to themselves.

On October 23, 1933, the gang traveled to the Central National Bank in Greencastle, Indiana. Clark stayed behind the wheel of a Studebaker touring car while Pierpont, Dillinger and Makley went inside. Hamilton stayed near the door to watch for suspicious activity on the street. Dillinger and Pierpont had cased the bank several days in advance, pretending to be newsmen, and knew where all of the important areas of the bank were. Dillinger quickly jumped over the counter and began walking through the teller cages, scooping money into a sack while his confederates kept guns pointed at the employees. Makley watched everything with a stopwatch in his hand. At the five-minute mark, Makley called time and Dillinger abruptly stopped filling the sack. He turned, hopped back over the counter and started to walk out. He looked over and saw an old farmer standing at one of the teller's windows. In front of him on the counter was a small stack of bills. Dillinger asked him if the money belonged to him or to the bank.

"It's mine," the farmer nervously replied.

"Keep it," Dillinger said. "We only want the bank's".

The men walked out without firing a shot and drove away. They traveled along back roads, following pre-marked maps, and drove leisurely out of the county. They avoided every single road block put up by the state and local police. In the car, Dillinger opened the bag from the bank and found $75,346 -- Dillinger's biggest haul yet.

Almost a month later in Chicago, Dillinger was almost captured. He was suffering from barber's itch, a skin disorder, and went to see Dr. Charles Eye for treatment. Edward Shouse, who had been kicked out of the gang for drinking and for making advances toward some of the other men's girlfriends, informed the Chicago police that Dillinger was being treated by Dr. Eye. They were not quick enough for Dillinger though. On the night of November 15, Dillinger and Billie Frechette were on their way to Dr. Eye's office but became suspicious when he saw several cars next to the doctor's office on Irving Park Boulevard. The cops had been dumb enough to park them facing the wrong direction. Dillinger quickly shifted gears and raced off down the street with the police cars in pursuit. Flooring the accelerator of his favorite car, a Hudson Terraplane, Dillinger lost all but one of the police vehicles, driven by Sergeant John Artery. With his partner, Art Keller leaning out the window with a shotgun, Artery pulled up alongside Dillinger's car, traveling almost 80 miles an hour along Irving Park Boulevard. Keller opened fire on Dillinger but the bank robber did a high-speed turn onto a narrow side street, causing Artery to speed on past. By the time they had turned around, Dillinger had vanished.

The gang moved on to Milwaukee and made plans for another robbery. On November 20, Harry Pierpont walked into the American Bank and Trust Company just before closing time. Staff members watched in bewilderment as Pierpont unrolled a huge Red Cross poster in the lobby and pasted it over the middle of the bank's large picture window. Moments later, Makley, Dillinger and Hamilton walked in. Makley pulled out a gun and pointed it at head teller Harold Graham -- who proceeded to ask Makley to step to the next window!

Oblivious, Graham didn't realize what was going on until Makley told him to put up his hands, that they were robbing the bank. Graham moved suddenly and Makley shot him through the elbow. When he fell, he triggered the alarm button, which did not ring in the bank but in the Racine police department headquarters instead. Two local policemen were slowly dispatched to the bank but they were in no hurry to get there. The alarm had gone off accidentally several times before when careless tellers had accidentally set it off. When they finally did arrive, Pierpont disarmed them but one of them was slow to hand over his gun. Makley shot him too, attracting the attention of a large crowd outside.

Once the gang had gotten the money together, they needed to get out of the building. By this time though, more people had gathered, including the police. Dillinger and the others pushed several women out the front door, evidently as shields from the shots that were being thrown from across the street. The police fired high to avoid hitting them and the other bystanders.

While the cops were distracted with this, Dillinger and the rest of the gang ducked out the back entrance, where Clark was waiting for them with the car. They piled into the car, dragging along the bank president and the bookkeeper as hostages. They drove frantically along back roads for a time and then let out the hostages before continuing on. The haul from the bank was $27,789.

After that, the gang decided to avoid the harsh Chicago winter and winter in Florida. Packing up, they headed for Daytona Beach, where they rented cottages along the ocean. They played cards, fished and listened to the radio for awhile before becoming bored and heading out to Arizona. Between the time the gang left Dayton Beach and arrived in Tucson, the First National Bank of East Chicago, Indiana was robbed by two unknown men and a policeman named Patrick O'Malley was machine-gunned to death. Dillinger and Hamilton were accused of the crime and Dillinger was said to have been the policeman's killer -- but he always denied it. Billie Frechette, who was interviewed by legendary crime writer Jay Robert Nash before her death in 1968, always maintained that Dillinger never left the gang during this period to commit this robbery.

Regardless of that, Tucson turned out to be a disaster. Clark and Makley were arrested there after a fire broke out in their hotel. They paid a fireman hundreds of dollars to rescue their suitcases but he became suspicious when he noticed one of the suitcases was extremely heavy. He opened it to find a machine gun and several pistols. Pierpont, Dillinger, Billie and Mary Kinder were soon identified and arrested and then sent back East. Dillinger was extradited to Indiana to stand trial for the East Chicago robbery (the one robbery that he probably *didn't* commit), while Clark, Makley and Pierpont were sent to Ohio to stand trial for the killing of Sheriff Sarber.

Dillinger was jailed in Crown Point, Indiana, which was said to be "escape proof". The grounds of the jail were patrolled by armed citizens, ready and waiting in case any of Dillinger's friends decided to break him out. But all of Dillinger's friends were also in jail so he decided to break out on his own. A month after he was locked up, he escaped using a fake gun that he had carved from a bar of soap (or a piece of wood) that had been blackened with shoe polish. The "gun", which looks extremely crude in old photographs, looked real enough to Officer Sam Cahoon and Deputy Sheriff Ernest Blunk when Dillinger waved it at them on the morning of March 3, 1934. In minutes, he rounded up a dozen guards and made his way down a flight of stairs with a couple of the officers along as hostages. He drove along back roads until he made it into rural Illinois. He let the officers out along the side of the road and gave them $4 for food and carfare. Dillinger apologized and told them that he would have given them more if he could afford it.

Dillinger waved as he drove off -- never realizing that by driving across the state line with the stolen car that he had made his biggest mistake ever. Now, the FBI had joined the hunt.

Dillinger avoided Chicago and moved on to St. Paul, Minnesota. Billie Frechette, who had been freed with Mary Kinder after the Tucson arrests, joined him there. Dillinger started putting together a new gang, including Michigan City parolee Homer Van Meter, Eddie Green, Tommy Carroll and John Hamilton, who had gone to Chicago instead of Tucson after leaving Daytona Beach. One more was needed and so Dillinger recruited a former Capone gunman named Lester Gillis, who became better known as Baby Face Nelson, an unhinged killer who had robbed banks all over the Midwest. He was known to be quick on the trigger and killed without mercy and without conscience.

Homer Van Meter had become Dillinger's right-hand man and he and Nelson argued constantly. Dillinger often had to step between them to keep them from killing one another. Dillinger needed to raise a large amount of cash though and needed Nelson to do so, whether he liked the man or not. By this time, Dillinger was planning a permanent escape and he also wanted to help Pierpont, Clark and Makley, who were still in jail awaiting trial.

On March 6, the gang struck the Security National Bank in Sioux Falls, South Dakota and the

Lester Gillis - "Baby Face Nelson"

robbery went off without incident until Nelson spotted an off-duty policemen getting out of a car outside. He jumped onto a desk and fired several shots though the bank window, wounding the officer. According to accounts, he began to laugh manically and to shout that he "got one of them!" Meanwhile, Tommy Carroll was outside, standing in the middle of the street with a machine gun. Without firing a shot, he had lined up the city's entire police force, including the chief. Thousands of spectators watched the scene, chuckling and laughing and unbelievably, under the impression that a Hollywood movie was being shot in their town -- and that the bank robbery was just part of the action. Just the day before, a movie producer had been in town spreading the word that he would be filming in Sioux Falls the next day. The "movie producer" had been Homer Van Meter.

The bank robbers piled into a Packard with a sack that was stuffed with $49,000. They raced out of town and after traveling for several miles, Dillinger ordered the driver to stop the car. He and Hamilton got out and sprinkled roofing nails all over the road, which would slow down any pursuit.

Eddie Green was sent out next to search for a target. He found one at the First National Bank in Mason City, Iowa when he learned that the vault contained more than $240,000. The gang arrived at the bank on March 13. Nelson stayed with the getaway car but the gang inside ran into one problem after another. When the bank president, Willis Bagley, saw Van Meter walk in carrying a machine gun, he thought that a "crazy man was on the loose". He ran into his office and bolted the door. Van Meter, knowing that Bagley had the keys to the vault, fired a number of shots through the door but gave up and helped his associates to clear out the teller drawers.

Moments later, a guard in a special steel cage above the lobby fired a tear gas shell at Eddie Green. It managed to hit him the back and almost knocked him down. As he swung around, he fired off his machine gun and some of the bullets hit the guard.

At the same time, a female customer who was missing a shoe, ran out of the bank and down the alley where she ran directly into a short man wearing a cap. She begged him to call for help -- the bank was being robbed. The short man was Baby Face Nelson though and he sent her back into the bank.

Meanwhile, John Hamilton was having his own problems. Cashier Harry Fisher had barricaded himself on the other side of a locked door with the vault. Since Hamilton could not open the door, he ordered Fisher to start passing money to him through a slot in the door. Fisher began handing him stacks of one dollar bills.

Dillinger was outside, guarding prisoners on the street. An elderly policeman named John Shipley spotted him from his third-floor office and took a shot at him. He winged Dillinger on the arm and the bank robber whirled around and fired a burst from his machine gun. The bullets bounced off the front of the building though and Shipley ducked away unhurt. With that, Dillinger decided that it was time to leave. He sent Van Meter inside to get the others.

Hamilton was still having problems with Cashier Fisher. He could see the stacks of bills on the shelves inside of the vault where Fisher stood. He demanded that the man open the door but Fisher told him that he couldn't do it without the key. Hamilton continued to threaten him with his gun and Fisher continued to load stacks of one dollar bills into the bandit's bag. He was enraged when Van Meter came inside and told him that they were leaving as he had only about $20,000 in his bag and there was over $200,000 still sitting in the vault. Gritting his teeth in frustration, he turned and ran out of the bank, leaving the crafty Fisher to count his blessings. Hamilton later groaned that he should have shot the man -- just out of spite.

At the same moment that Hamilton ran out of the bank to join the others, Officer Shipley returned to the overhead window and started shooting again. He wounded Hamilton in the shoulder but the bank robber managed to get to where Dillinger and the others were waiting. They had forced 20 hostages to stand on the running boards, the fenders and hood of the getaway car as human shields. The bank robbers piled inside and drove slowly away, the car groaning and creaking under all of the extra weight. The police were unable to shoot and try and stop them with all of the hostages on the vehicle and so they were forced to follow at a distance. A short way out of town, Baby Face Nelson climbed out of the car and fired his machine gun in their direction and the police eventually turned back. After following back roads at slow speeds for more than two hours, Dillinger dropped off their reluctant passengers and headed for St. Paul. What should have been a prosperous raid had netted the outlaws a disappointing $52,000.

When the gang reached St. Paul, Dillinger and Hamilton sought medical treatment for their wounds and then decided to lay low for awhile. Trouble was brewing though for local FBI agents received information that a man named "Carl Hellman" was living in a rooming house somewhere in St. Paul with a woman that was believed to be Billie Frechette. Hellman fit the description the agents had of Dillinger and they began working to find the rooming house.

All of this was unknown to Dillinger as he tried to recuperate from his wound. He wrote letters to his sister in Indiana and bemoaned the fact that he was unable to visit. He was worried about his father and could do nothing more than send funds to the family through intermediaries. He also worried about his friends in Ohio -- Pierpont, Clark and Makley -- who were standing trial for the murder of Jess Sarber. Each was tried and Pierpont and Makley both received the death penalty, while Clark was sentenced to life in prison. Dillinger knew there was no way that he could get to them and this sent him into a depression.

The guards around the Lima, Ohio jail were made up of regular officers, armed citizens, local and state policemen and even national guardsmen who had been called up for duty. Heavy machine guns had been mounted on rooftops around the jail and gigantic search lights were used to illuminate all approaches to the building. The authorities insisted that Dillinger was coming to free his friends with an army of outlaws.

Dillinger though, was far from Ohio and in enough trouble of his own. On the night of March 31, 1934, FBI agents learned that Carl Hellman was living at the Lincoln Court Apartments in St. Paul. They arrived at the door and Billie answered the knock. She explained that her husband, Hellman, was asleep and that she was not dressed. If they could wait a moment, she would get him up. She then locked the door back and ran into the bedroom to tell Dillinger / Hellman that FBI agents were at the door. He got dressed and grabbed a machine gun.

Waiting on the other side of the door, the agents were surprised to see a young man coming walking up the stairs to the same door. When they asked who he was, Homer Van Meter stated that he was a soap salesman. The agents asked to see his samples and Van Meter said that he had them out in the car and asked the agents to come downstairs with him. One of them followed him down and when they reached the first floor, Van Meter produced a handgun and shoved it in the agent's face. "You asked for it, so I'll give it to you!" he allegedly said. With that, the FBI agent ran for the door but Van Meter was laughing so hard that he didn't even fire at him. Instead, he ran outside and jumped on a horse-drawn delivery wagon that was parked at the curb. He donned the driver's cap and whipped the horses down the street.

Wondering what had become of his partner, the second agent also went downstairs to investigate, leaving the door to Dillinger's apartment unguarded. Dillinger and Billie then escaped down a flight of back stairs, firing a burst of bullets down the stairwell just in case. As the pair ran out the back, the second agent hurried after him and opened fire from the back door. Just as Dillinger was getting into the car, a bullet clipped him in the back of the leg and he stumbled into the driver's seat. He slammed the Hudson into gear and backed out of the alley at high speed.

Eddie Green tracked down a doctor to treat Dillinger's leg wound but by this time, the gang had decided to leave St. Paul. Pat Reilly, a fringe member of the group, told Dillinger about a quiet resort that he knew of in Wisconsin called Little Bohemia. It was a remote fishing camp that was not due to open until May and would make the perfect place to lay low for a time. Over the next day or two, they drove into the Wisconsin woods and camped out at the Little Bohemia lodge to plan their next robbery.

Little Bohemia seemed to be just the answer for the gang, but somebody talked and soon, Melvin Purvis, the head of the FBI office in Chicago, received a tip from a resort owner in Rhinelander, Wisconsin that Dillinger was at Little Bohemia. Within hours, he moved dozens of agents from Chicago and St. Paul to the forests of Wisconsin. They planned a raid on the lodge for April 22, 1934.

On the night of the assault, Purvis moved his men into position at the front of the lodge just as three men were emerging and getting into a parked car. As the engine started, Purvis shouted for the men to stop but they never heard his warning. Seconds later, the FBI agents unleashed a hail of gunfire and ripped the car apart. Eugene Boiseneau, a Civilian Conservation Corps worker, was killed instantly and his two fishing buddies were both wounded.

Hearing the gunfire outside, Dillinger, Van Meter, Carroll and Hamilton ran out the back of the lodge and disappeared into the woods along the lake. Baby Face Nelson, who was staying in a nearby cabin with his wife, ran outside, fired some random shots at the agents and also vanished into the woods.

FBI G-man Melvin Purvis

Purvis, believing that Dillinger was still inside the lodge, ordered the assembled agents to continue firing. They pounded the lodge all night long, shattering windows and splintering the walls, floors and ceilings with bullets. When morning came, and there was no resistance, they entered the building to capture only the gang's girls, who had been hiding all night in the basement.

Dillinger, Hamilton and Van Meter had stolen a car and had driven to St. Paul. Nelson, after killing an FBI agent making his escape from another nearby resort, had also stolen a car and headed for Chicago. And Tommy Carroll had stolen yet another vehicle and had taken off for Michigan.

The Little Bohemia fiasco put Purvis and J. Edgar Hoover under the harsh glare of public criticism. They became even more determined to get Dillinger and Hoover placed a shoot-to-kill order out on the bandit's head, along with a $10,000 reward. Another $10,000 was offered by five states in which Dillinger had planned bank robberies. The newspapers screamed Dillinger every day and over the course of the next couple of months, a half dozen men who resembled the bank robber were arrested or almost shot. The FBI and local authorities in Chicago, Illinois, Wisconsin, Minnesota and Indiana were looking everywhere for the elusive outlaw.

But Dillinger was nowhere to be found.

In May, Dillinger appeared briefly at his father's farm for Sunday chicken dinner and reportedly told the elderly Dillinger that he was soon going to be leaving on a long trip and his Dad wouldn't have "to worry" about him anymore. Then, he disappeared again.

Dillinger was then reported in Chicago. In preparation for his trip, or perhaps because he knew that his luck would only hold out for so long, he allegedly contacted a washed-up doctor who had done time for drug charges named Loeser. Dillinger was said to have paid him $5,000 to perform some plastic surgery on his recognizable face, getting rid of three moles and a scar and getting rid of the cleft of his chin and changing the bridge of his nose. The doctor agreed to the surgery and left Dillinger in the care of his assistant to administer the general anesthetic. An ether-soaked towel was placed over Dillinger's face and the assistant told him to breathe deeply. Suddenly, Dillinger's face turned blue and he swallowed his tongue and died! Dr. Loeser immediately revived the gangster and proceeded to do the surgery. Dillinger supposedly had no idea how close he had come to death, at least according to the story and the later testimony of Dr. Loeser. Many believe this story to be pure fiction and while the FBI would later contend that Dillinger had received recent plastic surgery, the medical examiner would be unable to detect any signs of it on the body that was taken to the morgue -- which the FBI claimed was Dillinger!

On June 30, 1934, some believe that Dillinger came out of hiding again, this time in South Bend, Indiana. Once again though, this seems to be a case of Dillinger getting credit for someone else's bank robbery. The Merchants National Bank in South Bend was robbed and the local police claimed that Dillinger was the culprit. Not only that, but they also said that his companions were Baby Face Nelson and Pretty Boy Floyd. This seems impossible though as Nelson was on his way to California, unnerved by the Little Bohemia Raid, Floyd was in Ohio and Dillinger was in Minnesota at the time. A number of people and events were now shifting and conspiring, leading up to the last days of John Dillinger.

The Biograph Theater in 1934

In early July 1934, Chicago police Captain John Stege was approached by Detective Sergeant Martin Zarkovich of the notoriously corrupt East Chicago, Indiana police department with an interesting deal. Zarkovich claimed that he could, with assistance from a long-time friend and whorehouse madame, deliver Dillinger to the Chicago police. There was only one catch though -- Dillinger had to be killed, not taken alive. Stege kicked Zarkovich out of his office, refusing to go along with it. "I'd even give John Dillinger a chance to surrender", he told him.

Melvin Purvis had no such qualms however. When Zarkovich presented his plan to the FBI official, he quickly agreed. Zarkovich's friend, Anna Sage, would agree to set up Dillinger but the FBI had to agree to stop deportation proceedings against her. Purvis agreed, as long as she delivered Dillinger. Ultimately though, Sage would end up being shipped back to Europe as an "undesirable" in 1936.

When Dillinger walked into the Biograph Theater on the night of July 22, 1934, Anna Sage promised her FBI contacts that she would be wearing a red (actually bright orange) dress for identification purposes. She would be accompanying Dillinger, along with his newest girlfriend, Polly Hamilton Keele. At about 8:30 p.m. Dillinger appeared at the Biograph's box office in the company of two women. He was outfitted in a white summer shirt, gray trousers, white canvas shoes and his usual straw boater hat. He seemed to be completely at ease.

Sixteen FBI agents, cops from the Sheffield Avenue precinct and Detective Martin Zarkovich waited outside the theater with Purvis for more than two hours, watching for the unknowing Dillinger to exit. Purvis paced nervously and chain-smoked cigarettes and several times even entered the darkened theater to be sure that Dillinger was still in there. Just before 10:30 p.m., the lights came up, the doors opened and the crowd filed out the doors into the street. Finally, Dillinger left the theater and was spotted by Melvin Purvis, who was standing in front of the Goetz Country Club, a tavern just south of the theater. Purvis fumbled with his cigar, a signal for the FBI agents and the police to move in.

Dillinger walked on, stepped down from the curb, just passing the alley entrance, and whirled around, as though reaching inside of his coat for a gun. It was too late though and four shots rang out, almost as one, fired by Agents Charles B. Winstead, Herman Hollis, and Clarence Burt. One bullet hit Dillinger in the back of the neck and two others struck his left side. He took three wobbly steps and then fell down, dead when he hit the pavement.

Purvis ordered Dillinger rushed to nearby Alexian Brothers Hospital. He was turned away at the doors as he was already dead and Purvis and the police waited on the hospital lawn for the coroner to arrive. A mob scene greeted the coroner at the Cook County Morgue where curiosity-seekers filed in long lines past a glass window for a last look at Dillinger. Little did they know that the man they were looking at might not have been the famed gangster at all.

The scene at the Biograph Theater was also chaotic. Tradition tells that passersby ran to the scene and dipped their handkerchiefs in the blood of the fallen man, hoping for a macabre souvenir of this terrible event. Others pried bullet fragments from a wooden light pole in the alley until the pole became so unsteady that it had to be removed by city workers. The theater would go on to become both a famous and infamous location in the days, weeks and even years to come.

And it is at this theater where the final moments of John Dillinger have left a lasting impression. It would be many years after before people passing by the Biograph on North Lincoln Avenue would begin to spot a blue, hazy figure running down the alley next the theater, falling down and then vanishing. Along with the sighting of this strange apparition were reports of cold spots, icy chills, unexplainable cool breezes, and odd feelings of fear and uneasiness. Local business owners began to notice that people had stopped using the alley as a shortcut to Halsted Street.

The place certainly seemed haunted. But is the ghost of the man who has been seen here really that of John Dillinger?

Ever since the night of the shoot-out at the Biograph, eyewitness accounts and the official autopsy itself have given support to the theory that the dead man may not have been Dillinger. Rumors have persisted that the man killed by the FBI was actually a small-time hood from Wisconsin who had been set up by Martin Zarkovich and Anna Sage to take the hit. Many historians have called this theory "revisionist nonsense" but it's hard to ignore some of the strange facts that have come to light.

The infamous alley next to the Biograph
(Photo by Michelle Bonadurer)

To start with, even debunkers have admitted that Zarkovich was a corrupt cop and that he was tied into the mob through Sonny Sheetz, crime boss of Lake County, Indiana. Until Anna Sage had been run out of Lake County in 1927, Zarkovich had been protecting her operation for a percentage of the take and privileges with Sage or one of her girls. Many have pondered the question as to why he would have gone out of the way to set up Dillinger unless he had been asked to for some reason. And why had he insisted that the bank robber be killed instead of captured? Did he owe someone a favor so that he would make sure that "Dillinger" was murdered -- perhaps making it for the real bank robber to permanently escape?

Most interesting though are the many striking errors in the autopsy report. The dead man had brown eyes while Dillinger's were blue. The corpse had a rheumatic heart condition since childhood while Dillinger's naval service records said that his heart was in perfect condition. He could not have played baseball, joined the Navy or have carried out many of his athletic bank robberies with the sort of heart condition that his corpse allegedly had. It's also been said that the man who was killed was much shorter and heavier than Dillinger and had none of his distinguishing marks. Police agencies claimed that Dillinger had plastic surgery to get rid of his scars and moles, but also missing were at least two scars on Dillinger's body. The dead man had not received any plastic surgery, although the FBI started that Dillinger had undergone surgery to compensate for the obvious facial differences between the dead man and Dillinger. So, which version of the "plastic surgery story" was the truth?

Newspaper reports almost immediately stated that the body was matched to Dillinger by way of a fingerprint card but there are those who insist the card was planted in the Cook County Morgue days before the murder.

But if the FBI killed the wrong man, who was he? On the night of the shooting, a local man named Jimmy Lawrence disappeared. Lawrence was a small-time criminal who had moved to Chicago from Wisconsin in 1930. He had lived in the neighborhood during the same time that Dillinger had been in prison in Michigan City, Indiana and often came to the Biograph Theater. He also bore an uncanny resemblance to John Dillinger!

In addition, a photograph taken from the purse of Dillinger's girlfriend, Billie Frechette, after an arrest showed her in the company of a man who looked like the man killed at the Biograph. It is a photo that was taken before Dillinger ever allegedly had plastic surgery. Could Jimmy Lawrence gone on a date to the Biograph, not knowing (thanks to Anna Sage) that the FBI was waiting for him there?

Some writers have suggested this is exactly what happened. Respected crime writer, Jay Robert Nash, an expert on Dillinger, reported in his book *The Dillinger Dossier* that Dillinger's attorney, Louis Piquett, Martin Zarkovich and Anna Sage rigged the whole affair. According to Nash, Sage was a madame from England who was in danger of being deported. To prevent this, she went to the police and told them that she knew Dillinger. In exchange for not being deported, she would arrange to have Dillinger at the Biograph, where they could nab him. She agreed to wear a bright, red dress so she would be easily recognized. While FBI agents waited, "Dillinger" and his girlfriends watched the movie and enjoyed popcorn and soda. When the film ended, the FBI agents made their move. Nash believes however, that they shot Jimmy Lawrence instead of Dillinger. He also believes that when they learned of their mistake, the FBI covered it up, either because they feared the wrath of J. Edgar Hoover, who told them to "get Dillinger or else", or because Hoover himself was too embarrassed to admit the mistake.

So, what happened to the real John Dillinger? Nobody knows for sure, but some claim this American Robin Hood, who supposedly only robbed from banks and gave some of his spoils to the poor, married and moved to Oregon. He disappeared in the late 1940's and was never heard from again.

And this always ended the story for me. To be honest, I have long been fascinated with the story of Dillinger and always enjoying a good conspiracy, wanted to believe that perhaps he really did get away in the end. Despite the fact that I had been assured several times that this could never really happen, I always wondered about the conflicting autopsy evidence but never thought it a lot about it. Then, in 2001, I received a letter from the son of former police chief who once claimed to know John Dillinger and who got me thinking that maybe there was more to the story of his escape after all. Regardless, it was no longer just a story in a book for me but a real encounter with a very real person.

The letter that I received came from Norm Alder. His father, Norman John Alder (now deceased) had grown up in Loda, Illinois, a small town in Iroquois County, which is south of Chicago and along the Indiana state line. According to the elder Mr. Alder, he had met John Dillinger when he was a small boy in the early 1930's.

When he was eight or nine, Norman would hang around the local tavern in Loda with several friends. The tavern was owned by the Maddox family and the neighborhood kids often did odd jobs like emptying boxes, sweeping the porch and taking out the trash to earn a little spending money that could be spent on soda and candy. One day, a new customer showed up in town and claimed to be a farm hand, even though he certainly didn't dress like one. He became friendly with the local boys and when they got to know him, he introduced himself as "John". He often gave the kids money for candy and played cards with them. One day, he asked if they wanted to play blackjack and most of the boys were excited and agreed, although Norman was embarrassed because he didn't know how to play. Realizing the boy's awkwardness, John took him aside and taught him how the game was played. On many days that followed, John and the boy would sit by themselves and play blackjack.

Then one day, John suddenly disappeared. The kids were disappointed that their friend never told them goodbye, Norman especially. Not long after though, he was in the Loda post office and happened to see a picture of John on the wall -- it was a "wanted" poster, listing his friend as John Dillinger. Norman later told his son that he knew that it was his friend John without any doubt, even though the John in the picture was missing his mustache. "Dad soon learned that Dillinger was often in the area," Norm Alder wrote, "and that he even had a girlfriend outside of town. Dad's uncle, Earl Alder, ran a service station not far away and he claimed that Dillinger often stopped in for gas."

A few weeks passed and Norman heard the sudden, sad news that his friend John was shot to death by police in Chicago. Notorious bank robber or not, the stranger had been a good friend to the young boy and he was devastated by the news.

A few years later, when Norman was a teenager, he traveled with his parents to visit relatives in Mooresville, Indiana, outside of Indianapolis. His father and his uncle decided to stop in the local barbershop for a haircut so Norman waited outside for them on bench in front of the shop. An old man with white hair and a beard was also sitting on the bench and they struck up a conversation. Norman finally got around to asking the man, since this was John's hometown, if he knew John Dillinger.

"You bet I knew him," the old man replied. "I knew him when he was only this tall." He indicated the height of a small child.

"Then I guess you know that he was shot and killed in Chicago," Norman replied.

"No, he wasn't," the old man told him. "I was at the funeral. It looked a lot like him, but it wasn't him."

"Really? Then where is he?" Norman asked in astonishment.

The old man gave him a shrewd answer before getting up and walking away. "He's on a chicken farm in Wisconsin and that's where he's gonna stay!"

"Many years passed and Dad often wondered about this," Norm Alder finished his story. "He even went into law enforcement himself, serving as police chief for two cities, and he wondered if the Chicago police might really have goofed when they thought they had gotten Dillinger. I enjoyed your account on the Dillinger mystery and hope that now I have gotten a chance to help you tell the whole thing."

CHAPTER SEVEN

HAUNTED HISTORY

SOME OF CHICAGO'S MOST FAMOUS AND LITTLE KNOWN HAUNTED HOUSES

Haunted Houses are separated from other, more ordinary abodes in being effective containers of the past. They clutch tight at old events and refuse to forget; they carefully shelter the hopes and the obsessions and the miseries of the humans who died in their bedrooms or fatally fell down their stairs or expired, all forgotten, from lack of air in their hidden chambers.
GAHAN WILSON

Chicago is America's most haunted city.

This is a statement that I believe has been clearly demonstrated in the preceding pages of the book, along with the fact that many of the hauntings that plague the city are connected to old homes and buildings. However, there are so many haunted houses in this city that we could never begin to collect them all. Of course, with that said, we have to establish what makes a house truly haunted. Could it be a one-time strange happening that occurred to a single occupant on a cold winter's night -- or should it be a repeated phenomenon that is witnessed by a number of different people over a period of many years? Everyone seems to have their own opinion but have no doubt, haunted houses do exist -- as the unlucky occupants of so many of them can tell you.

And it seems they have been here with us for many years. Even old newspaper accounts of the city speak of haunted houses. A note from the *Chicago American* of 1936 makes mention of a house on Erie Street that was once the habitat of phantom occupants. The corner of Erie and Seneca, which had been turned into a parking lot by 1936, had once been the location of a large, double stone front house. The neighborhood had been a fashionable one in the late 1890's and many complained of the eyesore the house had become with its boarded-up windows and dilapidated appearance. Real estate agents tried in vain to rent the place but no tenants could be found, as the neighbors had spread the word that the place was haunted.

According to their tales, strange noises were heard coming from the place in the night and the sounds of a large carriage pulling up out front had caused many on the street to peer outside into the darkness. Even the police investigated the sounds in 1898, but found nothing. Many of the neighbors claimed to hear the carriage but none of them had seen it, and it left no tracks behind. If anyone attempted to go outside and investigate, the sounds ceased. If they did not disturb it though, they would hear the wheels of the wagon grind to a halt, followed by the sound of a large, wooden box being moved and then mysterious footsteps walking to the house and going inside.

And it was no wonder to those in the neighborhood that the house was haunted. The last occupant of the double house had been the old National Medical College and the medical students there were known for playing careless pranks with human bodies and propping cadavers up to the windows to peer outside. On nearly every night during the college year, a wagon would draw up to the house and leave a corpse behind, explaining the eerie sounds of the horse-drawn carriage, the shifting of the wooden box and the labored footsteps that marched up the walk. But how did this continue after the college moved out and re-located to Wells Street?

The neighbors believed that the ghostly re-enactment was evidence that the spirits of those whose bodies had been used to benefit science were returning in protest of the way that their bodies had been treated.

In a 1957 edition of the *Chicago Tribune*, writers searched for evidence of some of the city's lost haunted houses. One of these was the Fanning House, which had been started by a Chicago stone cutter in the 1870's at the corner of Taylor and Sholto Streets. Fanning had grand plans for the place and completed a massive stone wall around the property, which was connected by iron gates, and carvings of sea creatures were scattered about the yard. Fanning employed all of his skills as a stone cutter to embellish the work with gargoyles, masks, carved imps and grotesque statues. Within the monstrous stone foundation of the house was a vault for storing Fanning's significant fortune. Fanning and a few trusted workmen worked hard to encase an iron safe within the solid masonry and the vault itself was equipped with secret passages and hidden entrances. No one was allowed inside of the walls and when not working, Fanning spent most of his time closely guarding the gates. When he died suddenly though, his daughters abandoned their father's plans, leaving the stone work to deteriorate for several years. Not surprisingly, stories began to make the rounds that the property was haunted.

Soon after his death, neighbors began to tell of seeing Fanning's ghost roaming about the stone ruins on the property. A rumor got started that Fanning had deposited treasures within the hidden vault on the property and soon treasure hunting parties were organized to search for them. Each night, the ghost apparently haunted the ruins while neighbors searched them during the daylight hours. Although no treasure was ever found, scores of people claimed to see the ghost as he walked about on the property.

At last, Fanning's daughters, Mary and Anna, decided to finish the house their father planned and to move into it. Instead of following what their father wanted to do though, they topped the magnificent foundation with an inexpensive clapboard house.

According to the legends, Fanning's spirit was enraged. Years later, a commercial structure was located on the site and perhaps because Fanning loved his daughters too much to bother them, he took out his vengeance on the new building instead. Each business that occupied the space met with financial ruin and it came to be believed that Fanning had placed a curse on the property.

In 1898, the last tenant became a man named Frank Garrity, who opened a saloon on the site. He announced that he was not afraid of curses and ghosts and planned to stay. However, when the makings for his free lunch for the grand opening vanished from the locked kitchen without a trace, he too abandoned the building.

The two Fanning sisters simply moved out one night and were never seen again. A forlorn "For Rent" sign hung on the front door for several years afterward. Eventually, the building was razed and the site was abandoned.

Not far from the Fanning House, at Aberdeen and Adams, was the notoriously haunted Schuttler Mansion. Peter Schuttler was a wealthy Chicago pioneer who made his fortune as a carriage manufacturer and as a builder of cannon trucks and wagons for the Federal Army during the Civil War. The house cost a fortune to build and was started in 1863. It was going to be the "finest house west of New York city" and for a time, most believed it would be the most magnificent house in Chicago. Unfortunately though, Schuttler died before the house was completed. According to the legend, he was climbing the stairs to admire the house and stubbed his foot on a nail. He received a bad cut and blood poisoning set in. Schuttler allegedly cursed the house as he lay dying.

Even though the house was unfinished, Schuttler's widow and their children lived in the house until Mrs. Schuttler's death. During this time, many residents in the area claimed to see the builder's ghost peering out of the windows on upper floors of the house. After the widow Schuttler died, the house was abandoned for many years. During this time, local cab drivers made extra money bringing tourists past the house to look for the resident ghost (Chicago's first ghost tours!). It was believed that Schuttler haunted the mansion because his dreams for the place were never realized.

In the 1880's, another attempt was made to occupy the house but the strange sounds, rattling noises and of course, the neighborhood rumors, proved to be too much for the residents and they soon moved out. After that, the mansion was boarded up and closed for good. As late as 1910 though, witnesses claimed to see Schuttler, accompanied by his wife, looking out from one of the tower windows.

The place was torn down in 1913, after being used as a stable for a time, and even the demolition was not safe from ghostly happenings. According to contemporary reports, workmen claimed to see eerie shadows within the walls, ghostly moans and sighs and were plagued by tools and equipment that inexplicably vanished.

Another historic haunting concerned a once fine home for which the owner offered free rent to anyone who would live it. No tenant could be found though because the agreement had a small catch -- that one room in the mansion had to remain locked and could never be opened.

The mansion had once been one of the finest in the city and had been built by Elizabeth McCarthy in the early 1870's along Cottage Grove Avenue. By the turn of the last century though, the mansion was in ruins, inspiring eerie legends about the home's former occupant. Local legend had it that Mrs. McCarthy had suffered from rheumatism during the last years of her life and could always be seen sitting at her window, looking out over the street outside. It was this room that her three daughters, who inherited the house when she died, wanted kept just as their mother had left it. They insisted that the house could be rented and occupied, but only under this condition. It became the only room in the old house to remain furnished and thanks to this mysterious codicil to the rental contract, stories began to spread that the house was haunted.

People who passed by the house at night often spoke of seeing the pale face of Mrs. McCarthy staring out of the window of her room. In 1957, an old woman, who once lived in Hyde Park, told of how she and her brothers had once looked into the chamber as children. Standing on their tiptoes, they bravely looked in through a broken shutter.

She described the room as, although dusty, looking as though it was still being occupied by the dead woman. Her furniture remained in place and the bed was still covered by an old quilt. A stack of books piled on a table and a frail pair of crutches still rested next to the bed where she had left them. A rocking chair, in which the house's ghost was said to rest, had been placed next to the window. Ghost or not, it was obvious from the dust and cobwebs that the chair had not rocked in some time.

Until the time that it was demolished, a sign that warned of "private property" and "no trespassing" was placed along the edge of the lawn. The sign was never really necessary though for neighbors gave the place a wide berth for decades. The house was destroyed and Mrs. McCarthy was never bothered by restless tenants again.

Located north of Chicago is the fading industrial town of Waukegan. Nestled along the edge of Lake Michigan, visitors are apt to find a number of boarded-up stores and empty homes today but at one time, this one was one of the busiest ports on the Great Lakes. The merchants here relied on the lake to turn the town into a bustling commercial center and thousands came, not only for the lake but also for the mineral springs that flowed through the ravines around the city. Many of the springs were commercialized and bottled to be shipped out all over the country. One group of springs was located near the center of town and another, Glen Flora Springs, was just west of Sheridan Road. Eventually, interest in the springs dried up and time wore away the veneer of Waukegan. Soon, the mansions that were constructed along Sheridan Road began to fall into decline and like so many other houses that become dilapidated, at least one of them invited tales of ghosts and haunts.

A look down Sheridan Road near Waukegan in 1903

The house of Dr. Norman J. Roberts once stood at the corner of Washington and Sheridan Road and originally belonged to Roberts, a prominent and world-famous oral surgeon. The eccentric doctor was a popular resident of Waukegan until his death in 1939 and became known not only for his pioneer work in dental surgery but for his curious ways with patients as well. For instance, on one occasion, he kept famous author Pearl S. Buck waiting in his dental chair, jaw propped open, for 45 minutes while he chatted with a neighbor in the backyard. Another story told of how a patient sat in his chair from early morning until later in the afternoon while the doctor puttered around the office straightening and doing paper work, occasionally dropping in to do some work on the baffled patient.

There are no traumatic events to explain why the Roberts house became haunted, other than that the good doctor simply decided not to leave. It's likely though that after Dr. Roberts passed away, the house fell into disrepair and began to "look" haunted. The stories soon followed. According to caretaker Leonard Vukadin though, the rumors of stories of a ghost were not without substance.

During the 30 years that he cared for the house, Vukadin lived only on the first floor of the house and he said that he always left a radio or a television playing loudly to drown out the eerie sounds that came from the rest of the place, like that of the piano playing by itself. Ghostly figures were seen by not only the caretaker, but by visitors as well and eventually Vukadin claimed to never wander from the confines of the first floor at all. He firmly stated that he would not set foot in the attic and would never go onto the third floor after dark. He considered the ghosts to be dangerous -- and was convinced that given the chance, one of them would push him down the stairs.

Vukadin's most disturbing experience occurred one day when he and his son were putting up plastic sheeting over a window to weatherproof it and saw a woman in a nurse's uniform staring out at them from inside. Vukadin came to believe that the phantom had once been one of Dr. Roberts' staff members and she looked to be in her 20's, had dark hair and remained framed in the window for nearly 30 seconds before fading away. After that, Vukadin refused to go onto the third floor at all and could barely be convinced to go up to the second.

In 1973, the house was purchased from the Roberts estate by the Sheridan Road Investment Trust. Plans were made to move the house to a new site in order to preserve it but after an appraisal, it was thought to be almost worthless, thanks to a fire on the third floor in the 1960's. The Trust offered to sell the house for one dollar to anyone who would be willing to pay the $10,000 to move it but there were no takers. The house was torn down in 1978 and another piece of haunted history was destroyed.

THE HAUNTING OF HULL HOUSE

Hull House was constructed by Charles J. Hull at Halsted and Polk Streets in 1856 at a time when this was one of the most fashionable sections of the city. After the Chicago Fire of 1871, the "better classes" moved to other parts of the city and the Near West Side began to attract a large immigrant population of Italian, Greek and Jewish settlers. By the 1880's, Hull House was surrounded by factories and tenement houses and soon after, became one of the most famous places in Chicago. Although it was never intended to be known as a "haunted house", it would not emerge from its heyday unscathed by stories of ghosts and the supernatural.

Jane Addams of Hull House

Hull House has long been known as a pioneering effort in social equality. Jane Addams and Ellen Starr Gates opened the house in 1889 to educate and improve the lot of the newly arrived European immigrants.

At that time, the overcrowded tenement neighborhoods west of Halsted Street were a jungle of crime, vice, prostitution and drug addiction. Jane Addams became the "voice of humanity" on the West Side, enriching the lives of many unfortunate people at the house.

Jane Addams was born and raised in the village of Cedarville, the privileged daughter of a wealthy merchant. Jane was raised under pleasant surroundings and tragedy first came into her life with the death of her father, which occurred the same year that she graduated from the Rockford Female Seminary. She went into a deep depression and unsure what to do with her life, she spent a portion of her inheritance traveling in Europe. It would be in London, in the terrible slums of Whitechapel, that she would find her calling.

In the company of her college friend and traveling companion, Ellen Starr Gates, Jane would spend time at Toynbee Hall, a settlement house for the poor. Here, young and affluent students lived and worked beside the poorest dregs of London, pushing for social reform and better standards of living. Jane was intrigued by the idea of it and after her return to Chicago, began making plans for such a place in the city. She soon discovered the run-down Halsted Street mansion and worse, the terrifying conditions in the Levee district to the west.

In his book, *Return to the Scene of the Crime*, author Richard Lindberg refers to the dark neighborhood near Hull House as the "Darkest Corner of Chicago", and he was right. Crooked cops and politicians collected graft from every type of offensive character imaginable in this violent area. It was home to brothels, saloons, dope peddlers and all-night "druggists", plying their trade along Sangamon, Green, Peoria, Curtis, Carpenter and Morgan Streets. The district was awash in vice. Exiled criminals from other parts of the city sought refuge on the west side, attracting the "lowest of the lowly" hoodlums. Prostitutes beckoned openly from the open doorways of the string of whorehouses that operated between Monroe and Lake Streets. In addition, cocaine, laudanum and over-the-counter patent medicines spiked with opium were available to purchase in district drugstores. It was a horrible place, and amidst it all were the broken-down refugees and immigrants.

It was to these people that Jane Addams' Hull House appealed. Jane and Ellen took control of the property in September 1889 and opened the settlement house. Addams was granted a 25 year, rent-free lease by Hull's confidential secretary, Helen Culver, and by the heirs to the Hull fortune, who were enthusiastic about Jane's efforts on behalf of the poor. They soon began turning the place into a comfortable house, aimed mostly at women, but affording food and shelter to the homeless and hungry as well. The house also provided education and protection for many and the staff worked to better the lives of the local people for many years to come.

Eventually, as the settlement expanded, more space was needed than the house could give. The verandah and the cupola were removed and a third floor was added to the structure. Over time, 12 more buildings were added, although were later destroyed when the house was renovated as a historic site. The third floor was also removed and the verandah and cupola were restored.

Jane Addams died in 1935 but the Hull House Association continued her work at the settlement house until the 1960's. At that time, the property was purchased by the University of Illinois, bringing an end to one of Chicago's greatest achievements in social reform.

Hull House as it looked in the days of Jane Addams (Chicago Historical Society)

At the time when Jane Addams took over Hull House, several years had passed since the death of Mrs. Charles Hull, but this didn't prevent her from making her presence known. She had died of natural causes in a second-floor bedroom of the mansion and within a few months of her passing, her ghost was said to be haunting that particular room. Overnight guests began having their sleep disturbed by footsteps and what were described as "strange and unearthly noises".

Mrs. Hull's bedroom was first occupied by Jane Addams herself, who was awakened one night by loud footsteps in the otherwise empty room. After a few nights of this, she confided her story to Ellen, who also admitted to experiencing the same sounds. Jane later moved to another room.

But she would not be alone in noticing the unusual happenings. Helen Campbell, the author of the book *Prisoners of Poverty*, reported seeing an apparition standing next to her bed (she took Jane up on the offer of staying in the "haunted room"). When she lit the gas jet, the figure vanished. The same peculiar sounds and figures were also observed by Mrs. Louise Bowen, a lifelong friend of Jane's, Jane and Mary Smith, and even Canon Barnett of Toynbee Hall, who visited the settlement house during the Columbian Exposition in 1893.

According to Jane Addams' book, *Twenty Years at Hull House*, earlier tenants of the house, which included the Little Sisters of the Poor and a second-hand furniture store, believed the upstairs of the house was haunted as well. They had always kept a bucket of water on the stairs, believing that the ghost was unable to cross over it. Regardless, the ghost was always considered to be rather sad, but harmless, and residents and guests learned to live with its presence. Unfortunately, it was not the only "supernatural" legend connected to Hull House!

Hull House received its greatest notoriety when it was alleged to be the refuge of the Chicago "devil baby". This child was supposedly born to a devout Catholic woman and her atheist husband and was said to have pointed ears, horns, scale-covered skin and a tail. According to the story, the young woman had attempted to display a picture of the Virgin Mary in the house but her husband had torn it down. He stated that he would rather have the Devil himself in the house that the picture. When the woman had become pregnant, the Devil Baby had been their curse. After enduring numerous indignities because of the child, the father allegedly took it to Hull House.

After being taken in by Jane Addams, staff members of the house reportedly took the baby to be baptized. During the ceremony, the baby supposedly escaped from the priest and began dancing and laughing. Not knowing what else to do with the child, Jane kept it locked in the attic of the house, where it later died.

Rumors spread quickly about the baby and within a few weeks, hundreds of people came to the house to get a glimpse of it. How the story had gotten started, no one knew, but it spread throughout the west side neighborhood and was reported by famous Chicago reporter Ben Hecht. He claimed that every time he tried to run down the story, he was directed to find the child at Hull House. Many people came to the door and demanded to see the child, while others quietly offered to pay an admission. They believed the wild story to be absolutely true!

Each day, Jane turned people away and tried to convince them that the story was fabricated. She even devoted forty pages of her autobiography to dispelling the stories. Even though most of the poorly educated immigrants left the house still believing the tales of the Devil Baby, the stream of callers eventually died out and the story became a barely remembered side note in the history of Hull House. Or did it?

As the years have passed, some people still maintain the story of the Devil Baby is true -- or at least contains some elements of the truth. Some have speculated that perhaps the child was actually a badly deformed infant that had been brought to Hull House by a young immigrant woman that could not care for it. Perhaps the monstrous appearance of the child had started the rumors in the neighborhood and eventually led to Hull House.

Regardless, local legend insists that at some point, there was a disfigured boy that was hidden away on the upper floors of the house. The stories also go on to say that on certain nights, the image of a deformed face could be seen peering out of the attic window and that a ghostly version of that face is still seen by visitors today!

What remains of Hull House is located at 800 South Halsted Street in Chicago and is open to the public as a historic site. The University of Illinois at Chicago created their campus around the house in the 1960's, leaving no trace of the neighborhood that once existed here. The West Side Levee District no longer exists but was once bounded by Madison Street on the south and running north to Lake, east to Halsted and west to Center Street (now Racine Avenue). The bordellos and saloons have been replaced by loft apartments, parking lots, a few ethnic restaurants and Oprah Winfrey's "Harpo Studios" on Washington Boulevard.

The house is visited often today, not only by tourists and those with an interest in the history of the place, but by ghost enthusiasts as well. The stories told by Jane Addams and the occupants of Hull House are still recalled when weird happenings continue to take place in these modern times. It is common for the motion sensors of the alarm system to be triggered by themselves. When campus police respond, they find the house is empty and there is no sign of a break-in or any disturbance. Officers state that no building on campus has as many false calls as Hull House does. They have also answered reports about people inside of the house, or looking out the windows, but the police have never found anyone in the place.

Who still lurks here? The ghosts of long ago -- or the more recent specters of the people that Jane Addams so passionately tried to save?

THE HOUSE WITH NO SQUARE CORNERS

Near the tiny town of Bull Valley, Illinois is perhaps one of the strangest houses in the Chicago area. It was originally located far off the beaten path and remains secluded today along a quiet and mostly deserted country highway. George and Sylvia Stickney built this English country house in the middle 1800's. They chose such an isolated place for the peace and quiet and for their spiritualistic activities. Both of them were said to be accomplished mediums and they wanted to host parties and séances for their friends. The seclusion offered by the Illinois countryside made the perfect setting.

The house itself was very unusual in its design. It rose to a full two stories, although the second floor was reserved for a ballroom that ran the entire length of the building. During the Civil War, the house also served as quarters for Federal soldiers and was home to the first piano in McHenry County. But this was not why the house gained its fame, or rather its notoriety.

As devout practitioners of Spiritualism, the Stickney's insisted on adding distinctive features into the design of the house. These features, they assured the architect, would assist them when holding séances and gatherings at the property. Since the séances would be held quite often, they specified that the house should have no square corners in it. They explained that spirits have a tendency to get stuck in these corners, which could have dire results. It has also been suggested that the Stickney's believed that corners attracted the attention of evil spirits as well, a common belief in Spiritualist circles of the time.

Stickney Mansion (Michelle Bonadurer)

During the time that the couple resided in the house, Sylvia Stickney gained considerable fame as a spirit medium. The upstairs ballroom was converted into a large séance chamber and people came from far and wide to contact the ghosts of their deceased loved ones and relatives.

According to legend though, one corner of a room accidentally ended up with a 90-degree measurement. How this could have happened is unknown. Perhaps the architect either forgot or was unable to complete the room with anything but a right angle. Perhaps he thought that the Stickney's would never notice this one flaw. But they did notice! And here, the legend takes an even stranger turn.

The stories say that it was in this corner that George Stickney was discovered one day. He was slumped to the floor, dead from an apparent heart failure, although no visible signs suggested a cause of death. Was he right about the square corners? Could an angry ghost, summoned by a séance, have been trapped in the corner?

Apparently this was not actually the case though. This was a popular legend of the house but it's not really true. George Stickney did not die the mansion but passed away some time after moving out. However, it is thought that the house's single square corner did bring bad luck and misfortune to the Stickney's. They were plagued by tragedy and it's likely Sylvia's keen interest in Spiritualism was connected to the fact that seven of her children died over a short period of time. There are no records to say what the children died from but it must have come as quite a shock to them. As the couple grew older, they moved to a smaller home a short distance away, perhaps realizing that the one square corner had been their downfall after all.

Time passed and despite the séances and the legend of a mysterious death being suffered by George Stickney, the house never really gained a bad reputation until the 1970's. It had always been considered a strange and unusual place, connected to the spirit world, but it was never thought to be a bad one until a man named Rodrick Smith moved in. He lived in the house for several years and when he moved out, he began to claim that he had often heard strange noises in the place. He also added that his dogs were never comfortable there. This led him to believe that something was not right with the property. Smith's research led him to reveal that the house had become "tainted" by a group of "devil worshippers" who lived in it during the 1960's. He was convinced that their "black magic rituals" conjured up something unpleasant that now inhabited the house.

It later turned out that the so-called "devil worshippers" were actually a group of stoned-out hippies who painted the rooms in dark colors and built open fires on the floors of the house. When they departed, they left spray painted messages and drug paraphernalia in their wake. While it's unlikely that they worshipped the Devil, Smith was sure that they had changed the atmosphere of the Stickney Mansion.

He was certainly no help in getting the house sold but neither was one of the real estate listings that came after his departure. A local antique dealer would claim that he saw a real estate ad for the place in which a woman in a wedding gown could be seen pulling aside a curtain and peering out. The photographer who took the picture said that no one was in the house at the time. He also stated that he had seen no one at the window when he was snapping photos of the house. Was the woman a ghost?

Eventually, the house sold and the next owners claimed to experience nothing unusual in the place. They stayed on for several years but moved out when their plans to restore the mansion didn't pan out. Their occupancy leaves nothing to suggest that they were bothered by ghosts and apparently, neither are the owners today. The house is now the Bull Valley Village Hall and the local police department uses a portion of the restored house as their headquarters and claim nothing out of the ordinary. The official word is that, while the house was badly treated by vandals, it is not, nor was it ever, haunted.

So, who knows? Some area residents dispute the final word from the authorities. They say that ghostly things have been going on in the Stickney Mansion for many years, and continue to go on today, whether the local officials want to admit it or not. What is the truth? No one seems to be able to say and the ghosts, if there are any here, are certainly not talking!

GHOST OF THE GLESSNER HOUSE

Located about two miles south of Chicago's famous Loop, stand the remains of the once magnificent mansions of Prairie Avenue. In the period that followed the Great Chicago Fire in 1871, this was the most exclusive and fashionable neighborhood in the city. Here lived the Field's, Armour's, Pullman's, Hubbard's, Blackstone's and other great families of the late Victorian era. In those days, it was a quiet, elegant street that was shaded by trees, bordered by wonderful homes and admired by those visitors who were lucky enough to be invited to call here. As the years went by though, the millionaires fled the area to the North Side, fearing that the crime of the Levee was encroaching on their fabulous domain.

Commercial activity from the city also began to draw close to Prairie Avenue and in 1905, the Kodak Company built a factory on 18th and Indiana Streets and in 1915, the Hump Hair Pin Company erected a building on Prairie Avenue itself. By the 1920's, many of the grand homes here had become high-class rooming houses and only a few of Prairie Avenue's prominent residents remained in their Victorian neighborhood.

During the Great Depression and up until the 1960's, Prairie Avenue became a ghost of its former self. Most of the big, mansard-roofed and turreted mansions were deserted and only dust and cobwebs filled windows were lace curtains and draperies once hung. The once proud facades of the houses were now only pictures of decay and ruin. A few of the stone mansions were still in use, serving as offices and businesses but most of the houses fell vacant and most of them were town down.

It would be the salvation of one house though, the Glessner House, by a group of architects in 1966 that would provide the impetus for the creation of the Prairie Avenue Historic District ten years later. Today, Prairie Avenue is more of a historic site than a neighborhood, with only a small group of the original houses remaining but it does stand as a time capsule to the architecture of yesterday. In addition, new residents have come to the area and are giving the area a new vitality that it has not seen in years.

Perhaps we should not be surprised by the fact that the ghostly sounds of carriages have been heard traveling along the stone streets in the district in recent years. It seems that with the new awakening of Prairie Avenue that the spirits of the past have awakened as well.

However, if there is one house that remains here today that best captures the mystery of the past, it is the Glessner House, which stands at 1800 South Prairie Avenue. This stone mansion is not only a unique and unusual home but it is the last remaining of the district's haunted houses -- and one that is inhabited by the ghost of a man who never lived in this house at all.

Although it was regarded as something of an oddity when it was constructed on Prairie Avenue in 1886, the Glessner House has achieved worldwide fame for is strange design. The house was built in what was referred to as a Romanesque design, although this designation was later changed to "Richardson Romanesque" to reflect the special touches that the architect had achieved with this place. The architect who had been retained to design the home for John and France Glessner was Henry Hobson Richardson, of Boston, one of the America's foremost architects of the day. Glessner had likely been intrigued by the design that Richardson created for another Chicago building, the Marshall Field wholesale house

Glessner House (Chicago Historical Society)

(torn down many years ago), and hired him to create another magnificent design for this home along "Millionaire's Row". As it turned out, the Glessner House was Richardson's final design. He died, at the age of only 48, just three weeks after the house was completed.

Richardson took a look down Prairie Avenue, at the large Victorian style Greek and Gothic styles of the day and decided to break with tradition and to create something truly outstanding for the Glessner's. He wanted a building that was simple, direct, solid and tastefully designed. He believed that beauty could be found in strength and he achieved his goal in this house. Not surprisingly, Romanesque style buildings began to appear all over America soon after the Glessner mansion was completed.

As with other buildings of this style, the Glessner House is built of rough-hewn granite blocks, resembling a medieval fortress. This style pleased the Glessner's very much, according to their friends and family, as they wanted a place that would insulate them from the noise and confusion of the city. They were a quiet, conservative couple and the house reflects this as well. Richardson designed no bay windows or other unnecessary ornaments on the house but it was bright and comfortable on the inside and instead of looking out beyond the plain and solid walls, it opened to the interior and an open courtyard. And while it appears cold on the exterior, the interior of the house was meant to be warm with oak wainscoting, marble fireplaces, great wooden beams, a large kitchen and a glassed-in conservatory.

After the house was completed, the Glessner's lived here with their children and quietly entertained some of the leading members of Chicago society until the 1930's. They were important patrons of the arts in the city and principal contributors to the Chicago Symphony Orchestra. In 1932, France Glessner passed away and she was followed by her husband in death in 1936. John Glessner, one of the founders and for years a director of the International Harvester Company, deeded his home to the Chicago chapter of the American Institute of Architects with the stipulation that they take possession of it. The architects were to maintain the house as a museum, library, gallery and education institution, including a school of design. Unfortunately though, such an undertaking was beyond the means of the group at that time and they turned it back over to the Glessner heirs.

The house remained empty for some time and then the Human Engineering Laboratory was established in the house by the Illinois Institute of Technology. The company created vocational tests and through what they called "work samples" were able to determine what career an individual was best suited to follow. The residency by the Laboratory was short-lived but they did keep in accordance with one stipulation that had been contained in John Glessner's will -- they always kept a portrait of architect Henry Richardson hanging in their reception room. His presence was always to be retained in the house, Glessner had written, and he likely had no idea of how prophetic those words would turn out to be.

By 1965, the Glessner House, like the rest of the Prairie Avenue homes, had fallen into ruin and was scheduled for demolition. Realizing the historic importance of the building, a group of concerned architects and colleagues banded together and incorporated as the Chicago School of Architecture Foundation. In 1966, they purchased the Glessner mansion and saved it from the wrecking ball. Ten years later, the house was designated a National Historic Landmark and it became the centerpiece and catalyst for the restoration of the Prairie Avenue District. The foundation, which changed its name to the Chicago Architecture Foundation in 1977, began tours of the Glessner House and the Loop and also helped to development a four-acre park (which had been empty lots) and improvements for the streets along Prairie Avenue.

Eventually, the Foundation voted to spin off its historic property operations and the Prairie Avenue House Museums incorporated to own and operate the Glessner House on behalf of the City of Chicago. The house is open to the public today as a historic site -- and if the stories are to be believed, as a haunted site as well.

According to reports from a former caretaker of the house, he often spotted "something...in the shadows" of the house and in the courtyard area. He heard the sound of heavy footsteps walking through empty rooms and often those on tours of the house would complain of an "unsettling presence", especially in the chamber where the large portrait of Henry Richardson was hanging. There were also accounts of lights turning on and off by themselves in the house, even though no one was there at the time.

There also started to be consistent (and current) reports of the large shape of a man that was seen walking along the cobblestone path on the west side of the house and in the open area just south of the building. I have spoken to two different individuals who claim to have seen this shadowy figure. Neither of them knew the other but both gave nearly identical descriptions of a large, bulky man who walked slowly, as if admiring the line of the house. Each time, the man simply turned and then vanished. Both witnesses stated that they had no idea the man was not a real person until he disappeared.

At this point, the reader may have surmised that the resident ghost in the house is believed to be that of the architect, Henry Richardson, who never obviously lived in the house but he did love the place. He saw it as the pinnacle of his career -- a career that was cut short just three weeks after the house was completed. Richardson was very enthusiastic about the project and often stated that he wouldn't mind living in the place himself. Could his love of the house and his tragically severed life have been enough to cause his spirit to return to the place? Perhaps so, for it should be noted that Richardson was a large man, weighing in at around 350 pounds at the time of his death, which would certainly match the description of the ghostly figure who has been seen admiring the house from the walkway outside.

MYSTERIES OF THE SCHWEPPE MANSION

The north suburb of Lake Forest has become known over the years for its fabulous mansions and beautiful estates. This is a reputation that the area has gained over time, dating back to the early days of the last century when Chicago's millionaires began to leave the grime and bustle of the city in a search for more bucolic locales.

It was in Lake Forest that newlyweds Charles H. Schweppe and Laura Shedd were presented with a large Tudor Revival mansion as a wedding gift from the bride's father, John Graves Shedd, known in his day as the "dean of Chicago merchants". Shedd was a partner in the Marshall Field Co. and after the death of Field in 1906, he became president of the firm until his retirement in 1922, when he took over as chairman of the board. Before his death, Marshall Field called Shedd "the best merchant in the United States." After the marriage of his daughter Laura to Charles Schweppe, the Shedd's moved from their gothic mansion on Drexel Boulevard to Lake Forest, where he also purchased a home for his daughter and his son-in-law.

The Schweppe Mansion, as it came to be called, was the largest private residence in the region, boasting more than 20 acres of surrounding real estate, 20 bedrooms and 19 bathrooms. It had been constructed on a 90-foot bluff that overlooks Lake Michigan and was designed by prominent architects Frederick Wainwright Perkins and Edmund R. Krause, who had also created the Shedd Mansion in Chicago.

Thanks to the social standing of the family, Charles and Laura held lavish parties for Chicago friends and business contacts, as well as for important political and foreign visitors, including the Duke and Duchess of Windsor, Edward VII and Wallis Simpson, and even Sweden's Prince Gustavus Adolphus and Princess Louise stayed here as house guests for a time. They strolled through the luxurious house and gardens, admired the Italian statuary, the shimmering fountains and the fantastic view of Lake Michigan. But sadly, all good things must someday come to an end...

The Schweppe family fortune began to crumble after the stock market crash of 1929. Charles lost incredible amounts of money in the market and in the Depression that followed and then in 1937, Laura died at the age of only 58. Charles sunk into deep despair, which only worsened when he learned that his wife had left him little in her will. She had inherited half of her father's vast fortune and even had a personal estate that was valued at nearly $6 million. She left nearly all of her money to her children though, giving Charles a mere $200,000 with which to try and salvage the wreckage of his own career. He tried and failed and his financial future and physical health continued to decline. Schweppe began to suffer from chronic insomnia and he would wander through the vast house each night, pondering the loss of his fortune, stumbling about in his pajamas and robe. When friends insisted that he see a doctor, Charles began to be treated for a nervous condition, but it was too little, too late.

One dark night in 1941, the servants heard the crack of a single gunshot echo though the house. When they reached his bedroom, they found his body thrown back across the blood-spattered bed. A small .32 caliber pistol lay on the covers beside him, his lifeless fingers curled just inches away from its trigger. A red hole could be seen in the center of his forehead, leaving a ghastly wound to the back of his skull that had erupted in blood, bone and pieces of his brain. Charles had taken his own life and had left a tortured suicide note scrawled out on the dresser next to the bed. "I have been awake all night. It is terrible", he had written, never bothering to sign this last missive.

For reasons that remain a mystery, the heirs to the Schweppe estate decided not to live in the house, nor to do anything else with the property. The servants were given their leave and the house was simply closed up and abandoned. The furniture had been left behind, the table still set for the breakfast that Charles Schweppe would never eat and the dust of time was left to gather for 46 years. Although the house and grounds were maintained by a caretaker, it remained 1941 inside of the mansion for decades to come.

Not surprisingly, the period of decline spawned many ghost stories about the house. The dark history of the place and the feeling of decadent ruin about the estate were more than enough to attract the interest of ghost enthusiasts and the curious. Tales began to be told of phantom servants who still took care of the house, perhaps inspired by the legend of a pregnant maid who was found dead in the elevator years before. The story went on to say that the elevator always behaved erratically after that, coming to life on its own and moving up and down between floors.

Perhaps the most intriguing story though involved a mysterious window on the second floor. When the house had been constructed, beautiful leaded glass windows had been created for it but only one of them offered a clear view of the walk that led up to the front door of the mansion. Local lore had it that in the last days of Charles Schweppe, during the time when his mental health began to decline, that he would often peer out of a lower frame of the window, nervously looking out at the front of the house. In the years that followed his death, curiosity-seekers who visited the estate were chilled to see that this same pane of glass in the old window -- and only this pane of glass -- managed to always stay clean. The rest of the windows had become weathered and covered with dirt and grime over the years but somehow, this single pane always looked polished and clean. According to legend, it was kept that way by the ghost of Charles Schweppe, still looking outside as he had done in his final hours.

The Schweppe Mansion had become Lake Forest's local "haunted house", that proverbial creature that spawns dark tales and eerie visits on cool October nights. Only this time, the reputation just might have been deserved.

In 1987, the fate of the Schweppe Mansion took another turn. The house was purchased by a woman, who had also restored and renovated four other historic properties. She paid a large sum for the property and planned to live here with her family as they tried to undo the damage that had been done to the mansion by time and neglect. The mansion is now known as Mayflower Place and the dust and dirt of decades past is gone. The house is once again a North Shore architectural gem and has also been placed on the National Register of Historic Places.

And unlike most cases of renovations, when ghosts seemed to be disturbed by the activity in the house, the renovations of the Schweppe Mansion have had an opposite effect -- they have actually laid the ghost to rest. During the work, the old leaded glass windows were temporarily removed to also be restored. When it was no longer in place, the single pane that had looked out over the front walk became dirty just like all of the other glass did. The ghost had no reason to keep it clean anymore and Charles Schweppe, if that is who this spirit was, passed on to the other side. There have been no ghostly happenings here since the restoration has been completed.

THE MAPLE LAKE GHOST LIGHT

Maple Lake is a tranquil reservoir that is located at the swampy north end of the Sag Ridge. Just outside of Willow Springs, is a part of a line of forest preserves that follows the Des Plaines River. By day, it is a widely used recreational area but at night, long after the sun has gone down, it becomes home to one of the most famous "spook lights" in the Chicagoland region. This location was briefly mentioned in an earlier chapter about the oddities surrounding Archer Avenue but deserves a place in the book all its own.

But why should we find the Maple Lake Light in a chapter that was reserved for "haunted houses"? Because despite the popular legends, its likely that this mysterious light has less to do with beheadings and ghosts searching for missing body parts and more to do with a tragedy connected to a house that once stood nearby -- or most specifically, with the well that was to serve that house.

Maple Lake

The land where Maple Lake now rests was once owned by an Irish immigrant named James Molony. He was one of the early parishioners of the St. James-Sag Church and owned about 80 acres around 95th and Wolf Road. Members of the family owned this property from 1850 until it was taken over by the Forest Preserve District around 1920. At that time, the area from Archer Avenue southward was known as Maple Hill, thanks to the large number of sugar maple trees that were found on the land.

In 1924, the Forest Preserve contracted for the construction of a dam across a deep, narrow ravine that provided an outlet for a number of acres of swampland south of 95th Street and east of Wolf Road. The work was done in conjunction with the Cook County Highway Department, which was paving 95th from an intersection on Archer Avenue and up the hill to the east. The area that was submerged because of the dam came to be called Maple Lake.

Swimming became a popular past time along the south shore at the west end of Maple Lake. There was once located a bath house here, along with restrooms and a concession stand for the public. The biggest concern for some time was that the lake was overpopulated by fish, especially carp and bluegill. Eventually, a fish management program was started and rowboats were rented out to fishermen. In 1939 though, swimming was banned in the lake for reasons pertaining to public health, ending at era at Maple Lake.

In recent times, the lake has continued its appeal to picnickers, hikers, boaters and fishermen. The setting here is quiet and picturesque and offers much to outdoor enthusiasts during the daylight hours. At night though, things look much different at Maple Lake. The towering trees that are so awe-inspiring during the daytime become foreboding and ominous in the darkness. The vast expanse of the lake, so clear and crystal blue in the sunlight becomes a vast expanse of blackness after the sun sets.

And thanks to the Forest Preserve that surrounds the area, Maple Lake has also become home to both rumors and dark events. The region of woods that lie so close to the Chicago manage to entice not only families who want to get away from the rush of the city on weekends, but they also entice the darker element as well. For many years, the forest preserves have been plagued by stories of "black magic rituals" and "devil worshippers" and tragically have also been host to some very real tragedies as well. These wooded areas have often served as locations for dumping murder victims and Maple Lake is no exception. In April 1991, the body of a 17 year-old girl was found floating in the water near 95th and Wolf Road. Her killer was quickly apprehended by the Cook County Forest Preserve Police but the event cast a dark pall over the lake for some time afterward.

But it's not incidents like this one that has made Maple Lake so well known by those with an interest in the unknown. What attracts so many nocturnal visitors to the lake are the accounts of the ghost light that is said to appear here. This light appears out over the water between 95th and 107th Streets and can most often be seen along the northern edge of the water, across from the Maple Lake Overlook. It is from here that visitors have reported seeing a red light that moves slowly along the edge of the water on the far side of the lake. The light is always round and burns a brilliant red. It is often so bright that it casts a glare down onto the water before it.

No one knows for sure what this anomaly may be, but scientifically speaking, such lights appear all around the country in locations that are usually related to railroad tracks, power lines, long straight roadways or water. Maple Lake certainly fit's the criteria of water and long straight roads can also be found close by. There is also the mysterious nature of nearby Archer Avenue that should be factored into the puzzle.

Debunkers have tried many explanations to disregard this light (and others like it) including swamp gas, foxfire, ball lightning, car lights and even the reflection of street lights on the water. While swamp gas and foxfire could be possible in a marshy area like this, it seems improbable as the light appears to be red (which is unlike a naturally occurring glow given off by swamp gas) and it moves constantly, which these phenomenon never do. Ball lightning is even more difficult to believe as it is very rare and the chances of it occurring in the same spot over and over again during a lengthy period is next to impossible. Street lights reflecting on the water is another explanation that has been suggested, but once again, the light moves under its own power and gives off a reddish glow, which streetlights in the area do not. The most popular debunking of the phenomenon is the suggestion that the light is nothing more than red tail lights from an automobile. And while this seems plausible at first, it becomes less so when you realize that there are no through streets in the direction where the light is seen. The only other through street is 107th and it is on the other side of the ridge, which runs between it and the lake. No tail lights could be seen through this wall of dirt and stone.

Ruling out the simple natural and artificial explanations for the spook light, we are now faced with the dilemma of confronting the supernatural. In the case of the Maple Lake lights, familiar legends come into play. The most familiar of these stories claims that a Native American was beheaded near the lake and now is seen as the ghost light, searching for his missing head. Another variation of the same story claims that the headless ghost is that of an early settler who was attacked and killed by Indians. The strange light is now his lantern as he wanders the shoreline in a search for his head. Other explanations offered include the idea that the light is that of a man killed digging the nearby Illinois - Michigan Canal or the victim of gangland violence of the 1920's whose body was dumped nearby.

But in each case, no theory can point to a documented event that has taken place near Maple Lake that can explain the eerie light --- until now.

As mentioned earlier, the land where Maple Lake is now located was once owned by James Molony. He built a house on the property that is now Forest Preserve land surrounding Maple Lake. His home stood until about 1970 and was used by the Forest Preserve District until it burned down. The foundation of it is still visible today, just off the Bull Frog Lake parking lot, west of Maple Lake. However, this was not the first site where he planned to build his home. That location is now covered by the lake itself and Molony abandoned the site after a tragic event occurred here in 1858.

According to a 1923 edition of the *Palos in Autumn* magazine, Molony had just come from Ireland in the 1850's and had been given the management of a small store that supplied the woodcutters who were clearing the path for the canal. He met, fell in love with and became engaged to a young woman named Ellen Connelly and Molony soon began seeking out a site on which to build a home for himself and his bride. He soon found a pleasant location and purchased it with his savings. A spot was chosen where the house would be built and as the first improvement of the land, Molony began digging a well.

He and the workmen that he hired had gone down about 80 feet but laid off work on the morning of October 8, 1858 to attend the christening of a baby boy named Michael Scanlon who had been born in the neighborhood. Festivities and drinking followed the gathering and during the party, Molony invited several of his friends to go over and inspect his new well.

One of the men, named McGrade, climbed into the bucket that was being used by the workers and asked to be let down into the well. Before he had reached the bottom though, he fell out, to the uproarious laughter of his friends. Having had too much to drink himself, John Roach quickly pulled the bucket back up and climbed in to go down and rescue McGrade. He also fell out of the bucket and splashed down into the mud and trickle of water at the bottom of the shaft. The men above called down to them but there was no reply.

Now, Molony, still thinking that perhaps his friends had imbibed too much at the christening, pulled up the bucket and started to get inside. Before he could do however, his friend Jim Butler stepped forward and grabbed him by the arm. He warned his friend not to go down. "It might be the damps," he said, referring to an escape of gases that is sometimes experienced by miners working in swampy land. He offered to climb into the bucket and to call out if he noticed the gases, so the others could pull him back out. Butler stepped into the bucket, his eyes straining to see the men lost in the darkness below and his teeth clenched in case he had to cry out for assistance. He vanished into the shadows but was overcome by gases before he could call for help. Molony and the others pulled frantically on the rope but by the time Butler emerged into the sunlight again, he was dead.

Worried that their other friends might still be alive and were somehow down below the area of the shaft where the gas had escaped, the men found a stray dog that roamed the neighborhood and tied him into the bucket. As fast as they could, they lowered the dog to the bottom of the well and then quickly pulled him back out again. By the time he reached the top though, the dog too was dead.

Resigned to the fact that their friends were lost, the men tracked down a heavy rope and a grappling hook and managed to snag and retrieve the bodies of the dead men, one at a time. The women gathered as the men worked late into the night, illuminating the area with candles and oil lamps. At last, by the dim glow of the lights, the corpses were laid out on the ground and a priest came to serve the final rites. The men were then buried a few days at that at the cemetery on Sag Ridge.

After the horrific loss of his three friends, Molony had the well filled in and he built his house on one of the hills across the basin. He wanted nothing more to do with this cursed piece of ground.

If a paranormal explanation need be found as to the cause of the Maple Lake ghost light, this morbid incident from yesterday certainly provides us with a real and terrible event that occurred where the light is now seen. But is this light natural or supernatural? None can say with authority but one thing is certain, if history does create modern day hauntings, then Maple Lake certainly has the history to go along with its ghost.

TOM & MO'S HOUSE

I felt that it would be fitting to end this book with a story that I can actually vouch for myself. There are only a handful of locations within the bounds of Chicago that I can firmly state (without hesitation) are genuinely haunted. Many of the stories that I have collected about ghosts and things that go bump in the night are merely that, simply stories, legends and folklore. It's often hard for me to know where truth ends and imagination begins -- but this story is different. This is a place where things happen that cannot be explained by Chicago police officers, by ordinary people with no interest in ghosts and even by yours truly, who has had his own strange experiences here.

It is, quite plainly, a haunted house.

If there has even been a place that looks less like a haunted house though, it's the home of my friends Tom and Michelle Bonadurer. They have a nice, two story house in a quiet neighborhood on the southeast side of Chicago. It's an unassuming place and there is nothing out of the ordinary about it. It looks like a house that was built back in the 1940's by an older, conservative couple who liked to stay at home, tend the garden and occasionally go to the movies. And that's exactly what it is. Frank and Maxine were the home's original owners and they were average, middle class Chicagoans from a bygone era. They minded their own business and went about life with a feeling that it was important to be good neighbors and to care about what happened to other people. In turn, they would care about you.

Tom and Michelle bought the house in September 2000. It seemed to be the perfect location for the soon-to-be married couple, in the same neighborhood where both of them had grown up and just down the street from the church where they would be married. That same month, Michelle (or "Mo" as her friends call her) was in the house painting. She was there by herself and had all of the paint cans scattered around her on the floor. As she worked, she stood on a wobbly step ladder, never planning to spend enough time on it that she needed to look for something more secure. Just as she reached to get one last spot with the roller though, she lost her balance and started to topple over backwards. Knowing that she was beyond her balance, she braced herself for what was going to be a nasty fall on top of three paint cans. Just as she fell over however, she felt a solid hand connect with her back and push her forward to the ladder again. As she heaved a sigh of relief, she looked around to see who had come into the house but there was no one there! Shakily, she climbed down the ladder and looked around the house just to be sure, but the place was empty. No one could have pushed her back onto that ladder!

Mo didn't mention this strange happening to Tom until about two months after they moved in, when Tom would come to her with a weird incident of his own. He had been sitting on the couch in the living room, watching television at around 10:30 in the evening. The couch was positioned at that time so that Tom had the front window of the house to his back, the entertainment center was directly in front of him and a short hallway that led to the bathroom, two bedrooms and to the stairway to the second floor was just off to the left but still in his line of view. He was sitting quietly with the television on when he saw what he described as a "large shape of light" filling the hallway ahead of him. The light moved from the bathroom (the first door on the right) and then proceeded to cross the hallway and to go up the stairs on the left side of the corridor. He didn't think much of it at the time and dismissed it as a car light going by. A few nights passed and Tom was again watching television on the couch and the same event repeated itself. This time though, he got up to check and see if there really had been a car going past. He ducked outside and to his surprise, no car. Incidentally, Tom would experience this same thing several times in the coming year and to this day, nothing has been found to explain it away.

Puzzled, he told Mo about this weird happening the following day and she then told him about what had happened on that afternoon when she had been painting. At this point, they were both wondering if they could be sharing the house with previous residents who had not yet departed.

Mo decided that she would see what she could find out about the people who had owned the house before her and Tom. After talking to some of the neighbors, she was able to piece together some information about Frank and Maxine, the past owners of the place. They had been good people who had lived a quiet and comfortable life in the house, although both left this world a little earlier than they had planned. One winter's day, Frank was outside shoveling snow in the alley behind the house, trying to uncover Maxine's car so that she could do some grocery shopping. Unfortunately, his exertions proved to be too much for him and he had a heart attack. He crumpled to the snow covered lawn and he died there, never regaining consciousness so that he could tell his beloved wife goodbye. Maxine never recovered from her grief over Frank's passing. She died within a year of her husband, perhaps, as is often said, of a broken heart. The question then remained -- did Frank and Maxine ever really leave the house where they found such happiness in life?

It seemed that once Mo and Tom acknowledged the strange incidents in the house, they began to happen more and more often. Late at night, when Tom admitted that he should have been in bed asleep, he would often be working on the computer in one of the downstairs back bedrooms and would sometimes hear footsteps in the hallway outside. When he would look to see why Mo was up so late, he would find the corridor to be empty. At other times, he would have the uncomfortable sensation of someone watching him the doorway but when he looked, there would be no one there. On still other occasions, he told me that he would feel someone's fingers touching and caressing his hair. The experiences became so unnerving that he would stop what he was doing and go to bed. This seemed to satisfy the unseen presence.

One afternoon, Tom was working in the basement and heard Michelle call downstairs from the kitchen to him. He called upstairs to see what she wanted but there was no reply. He called again, this time louder, and when Mo finally replied, she had no idea what he was yelling at her about. Not only had she not called down to him but she had been in the back of the house at the time and nowhere near the kitchen. Tom explained that this experience was especially unsettling to him as he swore that he not only heard Mo call his name, but he had heard her walk about halfway down the basement stairs before she did so.

And the basement has continued to be a place where strange things happen. One evening, Tom, Michelle and their two Golden Retrievers, Kylie and Jaz, were all in the living room watching television. As they were sitting there, they heard a very loud noise from the basement. It was so sudden that it startled all of them, including the dogs. Tom went down to see what was going on and when he did, he found a box was sitting in the middle of the floor. He knew that it had not been there earlier and in fact, could look and see where the box had been sitting on a shelf -- about 20 feet away! There was no logical way that this box could have traveled such a distance without assistance. Tom was determined not to let the incident get to him though and he calmly bent down to pick up the box and to put it back where it belonged. As he bent over though, he felt a hand take hold of and tug on the tail of his shirt. There was no mistaking the sensation! He left the box where it was and hurried back upstairs.

Not all of the weird experiences that take place in the house occur to just Tom and Michelle either. One night, a few months after they moved in, they had some friends over. Neither Tom nor Mo had mentioned that they thought the house might have some odd additions to it but they soon had confirmation that they were not just imagining things. One of their friends was sitting on the end of the couch, which faced the hallway, and was in mid-conversation when she suddenly stopped and said that had seen someone come out of the bathroom and go up the staircase to the second floor.

And it would happen again and again -- friends would come over who had no idea that Tom and Mo were experiencing odd things in the house and they would have the same encounters. Most often, they would hear or see an object or a figure walking down the hallway, often disappearing up the stairs, or even peering around the corner into the living room as if checking to see who was there. Whoever this figure is (Frank or Maxine?) they never bother anyone, it's more like they are curious about who might be in their house.

I can vouch for the things that occur here because I have experienced them myself. When traveling to Chicago, I often stay with Mo and Tom and had spent nights in their house on a few different occasions before ever encountering anything odd. At the time that it happened, I had no idea that any of the incidents were occurring and it was not until I mentioned to Mo what had happened that she told me about the history of anomalies in the house.

About nine months after they moved into the house, I was in Chicago and spent the night in their guest room. I had to get up early the next morning and be on the road and after showering, I decided to wait around on the couch and watch television for a little while before waking up Michelle to tell her that I was leaving. We had been up very late the night before and if they felt anything like I did that morning, they needed their sleep! So, I sat down on the couch and turned on the TV. As I did, the dogs stirred and came in from the other room to sit with me. Believe me, I didn't mind. I love these two dogs -- I often joke that I don't stay at the house to see Tom and Michelle but Jaz and Kylie instead.

Jaz and Kylie -- my friends from Chicago

Anyway, the dogs sat down with me for a little bit and I was just contemplating calling upstairs to Tom and Mo and letting them know that I was leaving when I heard the unmistakable sound of someone walking down the stairs. The footsteps started on the upstairs landing and then descended the wooden staircase. I looked up and was not alone. Both of the dogs looked up as well and Kylie even got up and started to walk across the room, eager to greet whoever was joining us in the living room. The problem was, however, that no one came down. The footsteps came almost to the bottom of the steps and then stopped. After a few moments, I got up and went to see what was going on, but the staircase was empty. There was no one there!

That's weird, I thought, I wonder what Michelle was doing? Thinking that perhaps she had come down and then had gone back upstairs again for some reason, I sat back down on the couch again to wait. I stayed for another 20 minutes or so and then needing to leave, I finally went to the bottom of the steps and called out to Michelle that I was leaving. I heard her tell me to wait a moment and then heard the creak of the bed as she got up and came downstairs. The tread on the stairs was just the same as before and I asked her what she had been doing earlier.

She had no idea what I was talking about and had not been out of bed until I had called up to her.

Tom and Mo told me about the odd events that have occurred in the house after that and have kept me updated about them ever since. On subsequent visits, I have yet to experience anything like what I did that summer but the happenings do continue. In fact, in late November 2002, the most recent occurrence took place, involving not only Tom and Michelle but Michelle's mother and even two Chicago police officers!

It started one morning with a phone call. Tom was in a meeting and at about 8:30 a.m. and his cell phone rang. He didn't answer it at the time but when the meeting was over, he checked and saw that while there was no message, the call had come from home. Thinking that Michelle may have stayed home from work, he called the house but there was no answer. He decided to call her at work instead, just to check, and found that she was at her desk. If that was the case, then who had called Tom's phone from home?

In a panic and thinking that someone had broken into the house, Mo called her mother, who lives a short distance away. She immediately got into the car and drove over to Tom and Michelle's. When she got there, she went up to the front door and found that it was slightly open. Her worry for Jaz and Kylie outweighed any misgivings that she had about entering the house and so she went inside. Both dogs came hurrying over to see her, seemingly not worried about a thing. Michelle's mom decided to call the police though as Michelle was sure that the front door had been locked. Both Mo and Tom always left the house by the side door in the mornings and never had the front door open at all. She placed the call to the police and then took the dogs out front to wait for their arrival.

Two patrol officers arrived a short time later and after drawing their guns, proceeded to search the entire house, looking in closets, behind doors, under beds, everywhere. The house seemed to be empty though and all of their valuables, including electronics equipment and Christmas gifts that had already been purchased and wrapped, were just where they were supposed to be. Last, they decided to check the basement and Michelle's mom brought the dogs downstairs with them. They looked around and were getting ready to leave, again finding nothing, when they suddenly heard a booming noise from upstairs. The officers again drew their guns and ran up the staircase to find --- absolutely nothing. The house was just as empty as it had been before.

Looking for an explanation, one of the officers pounded his fist on the dining room table, making a loud, thudding noise. They all agreed that this sounded a lot like the noise they had heard while in the basement but had no explanation for what could have made the sound. They also had no explanation for how the phone call had gone out to Tom from the house, considering that no one was home. How did it happen and why? The police officers could shed no light on this.

Tom and Michelle believe (and I would lean in this direction myself) that either Frank or Maxine was trying to warn them that they had left the front door open -- or was trying to warn them that someone else had opened it! There had been a disturbing number of break-in's in the area lately and it's possible that someone had tried to get into their house. The could have also wanted to send a message that leaving the door open might make it too easy for the burglars to actually do so. Regardless, the police had no answers for them and they are willing to accept the incident as one more oddity to go along with the house.

As mentioned, the haunting here continues but Tom and Michelle are not concerned about it. "We all agree," Michelle told me, "that whatever is in this house is not out to harm or scare us but more to help us. Nothing really scares us; they just give us a few chills from time to time. No one ever really feels too uncomfortable here and often people who stay the night say that they get some of their best sleep here. The dogs never get jittery either and I think they would be the first to notice anything bad. We leave them alone but don't want them to leave because apparently, they keep a better watch over the house than the dogs do!"

BIBLIOGRAPHY & RECOMMENDED READING

Appelbaum, Stanley - The Chicago World's Fair of 1893 (1980)

Asbury, Herbert - Gem of the Prairie (1940)
There have been a lot of books written about Chicago crime but this one still rates as one of my favorites. Asbury writes a compelling account of the city's criminal history, from the early days, right up to the Capone era. It's a great read and one that's tough to put down!

Bernstein, Arnie - Hollywood on Lake Michigan (1998)
Bell, Rachael & Marilyn Bardsley - John Wayne Gacy Jr. (2001) (www.crimelibrary.com
Bergreen, Laurence - Capone: A Man and his Era (1994)
Bettenhausen, Brad - "Batchelor Grove Cemetery": Where the Trails Cross (1995)

Bielski, Ursula - Chicago Haunts (1998)
Bielski, Ursula - More Chicago Haunts (2000)
These two books were really the first titles, especially the original Chicago Haunts, to be written about Chicago's many ghosts. There had been a number of titles (including a couple of my own) that mentioned some of the city's more haunted locations, but none mentioned them so completely as Ursula's books did. Chicago Haunts remains one of my favorite ghost books of all time -- and it's author, one of my favorite people.

Bingham, Joan & Dolores Riccio - More Haunted Houses (1991)
Bingham, Joan & Dolores Riccio - Haunted Houses USA (1989)
Brown, John Gary - Soul in the Stone (1994)
An amazing collection of photographs from cemeteries all over the Midwest. One of the best books of this type that I have ever run across.

Brottman, Makita - Hollywood Hex (1999)
Brunvand, Jan Harold - The Vanishing Hitchhiker (1981)
Caren, Eric C. Collection - Crime Extra: 300 Years of American Crime (2001)
Chicago American Newspaper
Chicago Daily Herald Newspaper
Chicago Daily News Newspaper
Chicago Herald & Examiner
Chicago Sun
Chicago Sun-Times Newspaper
Chicago Times
Chicago Tribune Newspaper
Chicago Public Library
Chicago Historical Society

Cowan, David & John Kuenstler - To Sleep with the Angels (1996)
Cowan, David - Great Chicago Fires (2001)
These two books deal more in depth with Chicago's "other" fires that any that I have ever come across. To Sleep with the Angels presents a heartbreaking account of the Our Lady of Angels Fire, told in painstaking detail. David also put his knowledge as a firefighter to work in his more recent book and this is the first

time that some of these fires have ever been collected in a book. Both are a must-read!

Cowdery, Ray - Capone's Chicago (1931)
The first book to ever delve into the crime empire of Al Capone, written shortly after he was convicted and sent to prison. An amazing collection of articles and newspaper photos that presents a compelling accounting of recent events at the time. Find a copy of you can!

Cromie, Robert - The Great Chicago Fire (1958)

Crowe, Richard - Chicago's Street Guide to the Supernatural (2000)
While I don't know Mr. Crowe personally, I certainly have to give him his due as a pioneer in the field of Chicago ghosts. I have run across his name in a number of older publications that deal with Chicago hauntings and was glad to see him put out a book of his own on the subject a couple of years ago.

Davis, James E. - Frontier Illinois (1998)
Demaris, Ovid - Captive City (1969)
Drury, John - Old Chicago Houses (1951)
Drury, John - Old Illinois Houses (1948)
Fido, Martin - Chronicle of Crime (1993)
Fillippelli, Connie - Richard Speck (2001) (www.crime library.com)
Fraley, Oscar & Eliot Ness - The Untouchables (1957)
Guiley, Rosemary Ellen - Encyclopedia of Ghosts and Spirits (2000)
Halper, Albert - The Chicago Crime Book (1967)
Hauck, Dennis William - Haunted Places: The National Directory (1996)
Helmer, William - Public Enemies (1998)
Howard, Robert - Illinois: A History of the Prairie State (1972)
Hucke, Matt & Ursula Bielski - Graveyards of Chicago (1999)
Jarvis, Sharon - Dead Zones (1992)
Jarvis, Sharon - Dark Zones (1992)
Jarvis, Shaorn - True Tales of the Unknown: The Uninvited (1989)
Jarvis, Sharon - True Tales of the Unknown: Beyond Reality (1991)
Johnson, Curt - Wicked City (1994)

Kaczmarek, Dale - Ghost Trackers Newsletter (editor)
Kaczmarek, Dale - Windy City Ghosts (2000)
Kaczmarek, Windy City Ghosts II (2001)
Windy City Ghosts was a book that was 25 years in the making -- and well worth the wait! Dale managed to take years of research and his own paranormal investigations and put them all together into an intensely readable travel guide to Chicago ghosts and hauntings. His experiences as the president of the Ghost Research Society only helped to enhance the book and to establish him further as an authority on Chicago hauntings. Dale is also the host of the "Excursions into the Unknown" tours of the Chicago area, a bus ride that takes visitors to dozens of haunted sites. Reservations are available at (708) 425-5163

Kobler, John - The Life and World of Al Capone (1971)
This is the first book that I ever read about Al Capone. I found this book some time in the early 1980's and was hooked on the stories from the era and the gangsters of Chicago in general. There have been other books written on Capone, of course, but this one remains my favorite.

Kogan, Herman & Lloyd Wendt - Lords of the Levee (1944)
Lait, Jack & Lee Mortimer - Chicago Confidential (1950)

Lindberg, Richard - Chicago by Gaslight (1996)
Lindberg, Richard - To Serve and Collect (1991)
Lindberg, Richard - Return to the Scene of the Crime (1999)
Lindberg, Richard - Return Again to the Scene of the Crime (2001)
I have enjoyed all of the books that Richard has written but I can't tell you how excited I was when his first "Return to the Scene of the Crime" book came out. With the city of Chicago doing everything that it has been able to over the years to blot out the crime spots and the gangster era of the city, I have always delighted in the efforts of those who have tried to keep that history alive. Richard (in addition to being a nice guy) has done more than anyone else in my memory to re-create the events of the past in an unbelievably readable form. If you have not read these books -- go out and get them immediately!

Longstreet, Stephen - Chicago (1973)
Lowe, David - Great Chicago Fire (1979)
Lowe, David - Lost Chicago (1975)
Mark, Norman - Mayors, Madams & Madmen (1979)
McNulty, Elizabeth - Chicago: Then & Now (2000)
Miller, Donald - City of the Century (1996)
Myers, Arthur - Ghostly Register (1986)
Myers, Arthur - A Ghost Hunters Guide (1993)
Myers, Arthur - Ghostly Gazetteer (1990)

Nash, Jay Robert - Among the Missing (1978)
Nash, Jay Robert - Bloodletters and Bad Men (1995)
Nash, Jay Robert - The Dillinger Dossier (1970)
Nash, Jay Robert - Dillinger - Dead or Alive (1970)
Nash, Jay Robert - Murder, America (1980)
I have to admit it -- I am a Jay Robert Nash buff. I have long been an enthusiast of his work and while I am perhaps one of the only people with an interest in Dillinger who still lends credence to his theories about Dillinger surviving the shoot-out at the Biograph, I find the story fascinating. If you get a chance to pick up any of his books on the history of American crime, I highly recommend them.

Naud, Yves - Curse of the Pharaohs (1977)
Newton, Michael - Encyclopedia of Serial Killers (2000)
Nickel, Steven & William J. Helmer - Pretty Boy Floyd (2002)
Nickell, Joe - Looking for a Miracle (1993)
Norman, Michael & Beth Scott - Haunted America (1994)
Palos in Autumn Magazine (1923)
Parrish, Randall - Historic Illinois (1905)
Pohlen, Jerome - Oddball Illinois (2000)
Quaife, Milo - Chicago Highways Old and New (1923)
Rath, Jay - I-Files: True Reports of the Unexplained in Illinois (1999)
Sawislak, Karen - Smoldering City (1995)

Schechter, Harold - Depraved (1994)
Others have tried but none have succeeded in capturing the history and the depravity of H.H. Holmes like

Schechter has. This is the best current book on the subject, although if you can ever track a copy down, I would also recommend a novel that was done about Holmes in the 1980's by historical novelist Allan Eckert. It was called The Scarlet Mansion *and it's well worth the read. You can also try and find David Franke's* The Torture Doctor *(1975) and if you're really lucky Detective Frank Geyer's book on the case from 1896!*

Schechter, Harold - A to Z Encyclopedia of Serial Killers (1996)
Schoenberg, Robert - Mr. Capone (1992)
Scott, Beth & Michael Norman - Haunted Heartland (1985)
Scott, Gini Graham - Homicide: 100 Years of Murder in America
Sifakis, Carl - Encyclopedia of American Crime (1982)
Sifakis, Carl - The Mafia Encyclopedia (1987)
Smith, Henry Justin - Chicago: A Portrait (1931)
Speer, Lonnie - Portals to Hell (1997)
Stead, William T. - If Christ Came to Chicago (1894)
Sullivan, Terry & Peter Maiken - Killer Clown: The John Wayne Gacy Murders (1983)
Tally, Steve - Almost America (2000)
Taylor, Troy - Beyond the Grave (2001)
Taylor, Troy - Haunted Illinois (2001)
Taylor, Troy - No Rest for the Wicked (2001)
Taylor, Troy - Into the Shadows (2002)
Waskin, Mel - Mrs. O'Leary's Comet (1985)
Winer, Richard - Houses of Horror (1983)
Winer, Richard & Nancy Osborn - Haunted Houses (1979)
Winer, Richard & Nancy Osborn Ishmael - More Haunted Houses (1981)

Wright, Sewell Peaslee - Chicago Murders: True Crimes and Real Detectives (1947)
I had no idea how rare this out of print and obscure little book of Chicago crimes stories, penned by a variety of writers, was until someone gave me an autographed copy as a gift. It's a great treat if you ever happen to find a copy of it!

Personal Interviews and Correspondence

Note from the Publisher: Although Whitechapel Productions Press, Troy Taylor, and all affiliated with this book have carefully researched all sources to insure the accuracy of the information contained in this book, we assume no responsibility for errors, inaccuracies or omissions.

ABOUT THE AUTHOR

Troy Taylor is the author of 25 previous books about ghosts and hauntings in America, including HAUNTED ILLINOIS, SPIRITS OF THE CIVIL WAR, THE GHOST HUNTER'S GUIDEBOOK. He is also the editor of GHOSTS OF THE PRAIRIE Magazine, a travel guide to haunted places in America. A number of his articles have been published here and in other ghost-related publications.

Taylor is the president of the "American Ghost Society", a network of ghost hunters, which boasts more than 450 active members in the United States and Canada. The group collects stories of ghost sightings and haunted houses and uses investigative techniques to track down evidence of the supernatural. In addition, he also hosts a National Conference each year in conjunction with the group which usually attracts several hundred ghost enthusiasts from around the country.

Along with writing about ghosts, Taylor is also a public speaker on the subject and has spoken to well over 300 private and public groups on a variety of paranormal subjects. He has appeared in literally dozens of newspaper and magazine articles about ghosts and hauntings. He has also been fortunate enough to be interviewed over 300 times for radio and television broadcasts about the supernatural. He has also appeared in a number of documentary films like AMERICA'S MOST HAUNTED, BEYOND HUMAN SENSES, GHOST WATERS, NIGHT VISITORS and in one feature film, THE ST. FRANCISVILLE EXPERIMENT.

Born and raised in Illinois, Taylor has long had an affinity for "things that go bump in the night" and published his first book HAUNTED DECATUR in 1995. For six years, he was also the host of the popular, and award-winning, "Haunted Decatur" ghost tours of the city for which he sometimes still appears as a guest host. He also hosts the "History & Hauntings Tours" of Alton, Illinois and St. Charles, Missouri.

In 1996, Taylor married Amy Van Lear, the Managing Director of Whitechapel Press, and they currently reside in a restored 1850's bakery in Alton. In 2002, their daughter Margaret Opal was born and joined her siblings, Orrin and Anastasia.

ABOUT WHITECHAPEL PRODUCTIONS PRESS

Whitechapel Productions Press is a small press publisher, specializing in books about ghosts and hauntings. Since 1993, the company has been one of America's leading publishers of supernatural books. Located in Alton, Illinois, they also produce the "Ghosts of the Prairie" internet web page.

In addition to publishing books on history and hauntings, they also host and distribute the Haunted America Catalog, which features over 500 different books about ghosts and hauntings from authors all over the United States. A complete selection of these books can be browsed in person at the "History & Hauntings Book Co." Store in Alton.

Visit Whitechapel Productions Press on the internet and browse through our selection of over ghostly titles, plus information on ghosts and hauntings; haunted history; spirit photographs; information on ghost hunting and much more. Visit the internet web page at:

www.prairieghosts.com

Or visit the Haunted Book Co. in Person at:

515 East Third Street
Alton, Illinois 62002
(618)-456-1086

Printed in the United States
47730LVS00003B/133-172